Digital Phoenix

Digital Phoenix

Why the Information Economy Collapsed and
How It Will Rise Again

Bruce Abramson

The MIT Press
Cambridge, Massachusetts
London, England

MIT Press books may be purchased at special quantity discounts for business or sales promotional use. For information, please email <special_sales@mitpress. mit.edu> or write to Special Sales Department, The MIT Press, 5 Cambridge Center, Cambridge, MA 02142.

This book was set in Sabon by SNP Best-set Typesetter Ltd., Hong Kong and was printed and bound in the United States of America.

Library of Congress Cataloging-in-Publication Data

Abramson, Bruce.
 Digital phoenix : why the information economy collapsed and how it will rise again / Bruce Abramson.
    p. cm.
 Includes bibliographical references and index.
 ISBN 0-262-01217-0 (alk. paper)
 1. Information technology—Economic aspects. 2. Internet—Economic aspects.
I. Title.

HC79.I55A27 2005
303.48'33—dc22

2005042804

10 9 8 7 6 5 4 3 2 1

In loving memory of my grandparents.
Though they might not have grokked, they certainly would have kvelled.

Contents

Acknowledgments

If anyone you know has ever written a book, you know that authors require a certain amount of indulgence. They also require at least a few proofreaders to remind them that discretion is often the better part of valor. Though the list of those who have endured my brainstorming is too long to enumerate, I would like to thank the smaller list of friends and colleagues who read portions of earlier drafts and helped me get the final manuscript into place: Joe Bernstein, Jeff Itell, Cathy Johnston, and Miranda Xafa. Several anonymous reviewers also provided useful feedback.

I would also like to thank Charles River Associates Incorporated, where I was a consultant from 1998 to 2000, a Principal from 2000 to 2003, and which I recently rejoined as a consultant. CRA is a world-class economic consulting firm that respects academic-style analytic thinking while providing its clients with valuable expertise and advice. More to the point, my affiliation with CRA gave me the privilege of getting to know some of the world's best industrial organization economists and antitrust specialists.

That said though, every idea and opinion expressed in this book is mine and is not to be construed or deemed the opinion or position of CRA or any of its employees, officers, directors, or consultants. Nor, for that matter, should anyone attribute any of my ideas to any organization, any individual collaborator, or any client with whom I may have worked in the past or may work in the future.

The expressions of my ideas are also original. In some cases, I found previous authors who already said what I wanted to say in ways better than I could say it. In those cases, I quoted the previous authors—always with attribution. I also excerpted lyrics from several popular songs. I would have liked to have excerpted more lyrics, but most of the copyright owners attempted to impose unacceptable restrictions on me in exchange for allowing me to quote the words that they own. I would therefore like to thank the Grateful Dead's Ice Nine Publishing Company and Tori Amos's Sword and Stone Publishing Company, for allowing me to simply quote their lyrics. If you like *Digital Phoenix*, you'll love their music. If you don't like *Digital Phoenix*, you'll love their music anyway.

Finally, I couldn't have turned my manuscript into a book without the support of my agent, Susan Schulman, and a superb editorial team at The MIT Press: John Covell, Yan Ho, and Mel Goldsipe. Erin Hasley, also of The MIT Press, took the lead in preparing the truly funky design on the book jacket. Their contributions were both indispensable and greatly appreciated.

Prologue

Of Madness, War, and Untold Riches

In the beginning, the information sector was an idea. Not just any idea, a big idea. An idea so intoxicating that it drove a populace to the brink of madness. An idea so seductive that those caught in its grasp bet their savings, their homes, their careers, their futures, on its veracity. An idea so compelling that it riveted the attention of CEOs, captains of finance, and government leaders, along with the usual array of academics, analysts, and journalists. An idea so universal that it unified the cultures of Main Street and Wall Street. An idea so profound that it redefined popular culture, late night humor, fashion, design, taste, and style. Alas, it was also an idea so flawed that it died as spectacularly as it had lived, only to become mocked and scorned by its erstwhile adoring public. This exciting and creative idea that was once trumpeted from the rooftops was suddenly whispered only in hushed tones behind closed doors.

The fog of war obscured our early encounters with this idea. The crown engaged a leading citizen in mortal combat. Each claimed to represent the common weal. They pitched their battle in full view of the press, whose daily accounts fueled public debate. Was the crown out to expose this citizen's villainy, punish its transgressions, prevent their continuation, and deter their emulation? Or was it out to squelch the power and popularity amassed by a benevolent, hard working, ingenious, successful individual? The debate continues to this day.

But with the waning of public interest, the debate over ideas, riches, wars, and recovery returned to the primordial temples where the information sector dwelt during its pre-commercial evolution. There great, mysterious, priestly orders labor to comprehend the sector's past, diagnose its ills, divine the elixirs needed for its recovery, and restore it to a vigorous future. For these priests always understood what others may have forgotten. They knew that even in its debased state, the information sector remains very much alive, and that beneath its charred shell of an idea, more than a mere ember of truth continued to glow.

They saw those who labor in the sector's salt mines pioneer new ways to develop products. They saw those new ways threaten to upset the status quo, long beloved by entrenched interests. They saw those interests fight back to preserve their privilege and their profits. And they saw the confusion wrought among the public, now consumers, now investors, striving both to ignore the information sector and to comprehend the ways that it will alter their lives. And so these priests of the information sector continued to bide their time, increase their understanding, refine their ideas, and await the day when the information sector would rise again, like a phoenix, to soar back into public imagination and esteem.

This, then, is the all-too-familiar story of the information sector: raised in cloistered seclusion, schooled by priests, debuted as a superstar, beloved in its adolescence, scarred by war, exposed as fallible, abandoned by its courtiers, exiled from its place of glory, betrayed, despised, beaten, sullied, and finally forced to slink home to seek the ministrations of its creators while awaiting its ultimate and inevitable resurrection.

And then, slowly, with our attention focused elsewhere, the information sector began to stir, to emerge from its somnolence, and to test the waters gingerly while contemplating its return. And we began, once again, to take notice . . .

1

Net Assets

The Information Sector

Welcome to the information sector! We've entered a world devoted to buying, selling, managing, and manipulating digital information; a world that began with software, gave birth to the Internet, and stands poised to conquer entertainment. You've probably been here before. If you invested in a dotcom and watched your portfolio rise and fall, you were here. If you read about Microsoft and found yourself appalled at its monopolistic practices, or concluded that a vindictive government was out to punish corporate success, you were here. If you downloaded music using Napster, or smugly prided yourself on your refusal to do so, you were here. And if you ever wondered what all of these things had to do with the overall economy, you were here. So, welcome *back* to the information sector!

This time, we've arrived with a purpose. We're here to understand what happened and why. Now that we've had a chance to catch our breaths and to review some actual data, we've returned feeling that this time we can get it right—if only we could understand what went wrong the first time. How did the information sector suddenly descend upon us, seemingly from nowhere, in the middle of the 1990s? How did we integrate so many new technologies, toys, and productivity tools into our lives so quickly and so completely—and why did the flow of innovations suddenly seem to slow to a trickle? What was *really* going on with Microsoft, Napster, Linux, and all those other new products and companies? What role did the government have to play—and what role will it have in the future? How does any of this relate to the overall economic picture? What does it have to do with the apparent mismatch between job creation and productivity? And finally, how can we disentangle the threads of technology, economics, law, and public policy to understand why the information economy collapsed, how it will rise, and what it will look like when it does? These questions frame our inquiry and motivate our journey through the information sector.

The *information sector* is the part of the broader tech sector where people work entirely with information and products composed entirely of bit strings. Though we've had information *businesses* for at least as long as we've had a software industry, the information *sector* didn't exist until the commercial Internet exploded into public consciousness. But the sector's not done growing. Not by a long shot. As we move into the future, it will swallow increasing numbers of industries—often kicking and screaming. With each industry swallowed, we'll find ourselves facing new opportunities, new challenges, and above all, new wealth. Or at least, most of us will . . . And therein lies the key to understanding the future economy of the information age.

The first industries swallowed—software, the Internet, entertainment, publishing—all share an important feature. They never have to leave the digital realm. Most of the rest of the tech sector is very much in the physical world. Microchips, computers, switches, routers, cables, optics, and telecommunication systems are all physical devices that allow us to manipulate information. These industries define *information equipment sectors*, and many of their fortunes will move in lockstep with those of the information sector. But the information sector itself remains a uniquely interesting place, well worth our time and attention.

Prior to the mid-1990s, the information sector had been an exclusive club open only to the priests of academe and a few chosen followers. When it finally escaped from their temples to land on our desks, massive confusion ensued. Investors intoxicated with arcane buzzwords powered a huge investment boom. Daily reports about the government's antitrust suit against Microsoft added even more buzzwords to the mix, and a universal race to invest in "the next Microsoft" magnified our belief that *The Internet Will Make US All Rich!* We absorbed that belief with the zeal of new converts, and built a temple to Mammon atop our beloved NASDAQ. Our index bubbled ever higher until, seemingly without warning, the bubble burst. The Internet, it seemed, might not make us all so rich, after all.

The information sector's story flows from the source of our faith through a rough encounter with reality to the sea of legacies that we are still trying to comprehend today. Ideas born in the temples of academe not only drove the sector's development but also reveal the sector's key message: The Internet, in fact, *can* make us all rich, as consumers and as producers, if not as investors. The best evidence of this message lay not in the front-page stories of the trial and the bubble, but rather in the less told tales of the Linux operating system popular among hackers and the Napster file sharing system beloved of music fans. These systems exploited newly enabled business models to make information sharing cheap and easy. But both systems also met strong opposition from entrenched interests intent on preserving their own profits. The tension between information-sector business models that bring consumers and producers closer together and the entrenched expectations (and in many cases, legal rights) of traditional distributors, promises to play itself out time and again as the information sector swallows industry after industry.

The Internet is an innovative infrastructure improvement of immense public value. Like all such public assets, the Internet confers an immediate benefit upon anyone who uses it—it reduces the cost of exchanging information. The value of this benefit is already enormous. It will grow as we digitize more products, as more industries enter the information sector, and as more users join the network. All existing users will share in its increased value, but not necessarily evenly. Most users will emerge as small, incremental winners. But the big winners and the actual losers can both threaten our ability to enjoy those benefits. The biggest winners will be those who figure out how to collect tolls from a locked-in customer base, thereby privatizing our glorious savings. Powerful losers may bend laws and regulations to preserve the profitability of their own inefficient profit streams. These groups threaten the information sector's development. Toll collection and misregulation can slow technological development and reduce the Internet's value to us as consumers, to innovative producers, and to society as a whole.

The key to the entire information economy lies in the ways that we approach intellectual property and network economics. The centrality of these concepts is not surprising. Every society is shaped, in large part, by the way that it approaches property rights and the exchanges of those rights. Information products tend to define network industries. Network economics will necessarily govern the ways that we build and exchange products in the information sector. But we have some choice about the ways that we conceive of ownership and property rights inherent in those products. Our current approach to intellectual property has already caused a number of visible problems. It promises to create even more challenges as the information sector grows.

All told, a vibrant information sector must rest upon two pillars: public infrastructure and private entrepreneurship. The notion of an information infrastructure is expansive; it requires much more than wires, routers, and communication protocols. It includes a full range of government policies necessary to promote economic development in the information age. Education and employment policies that promote life-long learning, retraining, skill acquisition, and labor mobility are critical; an inability to move people fast enough to keep up with the flow of information and goods can strangle any society, including ours. Tax policies that maximize incentives, trade policies that eliminate barriers, and immigration policies that encourage people to locate where they can be most productive are equally critical. Security policies and social welfare systems that encourage calculated risk-taking enable entrepreneurship and small-business growth. And only foreign and defense policies that promote market expansion, freedom of choice, human dignity, individual responsibility, and the other values of liberalism can promote global integration and growth. Policy choices in each of these areas will guide American and global economic development as we continue our transition to the information age.

But the single most important infrastructure investment—and the one most directly relevant to the economy of the information age—lies in our conception of intellectual property and idea markets. Information products are, at heart, ideas. We need people to devise innovative ideas if we are to have any valuable information products at all. But ideas have a tendency to circulate freely. Once an inventor exposes an idea to public view, it tends to take on a life of its own. Numerous replicators share it broadly, often without the inventor's knowledge or consent. That characteristic of ideas complicates our goal of creating idea markets. Why pay an inventor for a freely available idea? Yet, without some hope of compensation, inventors are likely to innovate only to solve their own problems, and they will have no particular reason to share their solutions with others. Perhaps *the* critical infrastructure question of the information age is how to best motivate the creation and dissemination of ideas.

This policy environment, along with our ever-improving physical infrastructure, will define the platform atop which our private sector entrepreneurs will innovate, teach, and commercialize new information products. The first significant wave of their work powered the bubble. Though we lost many of their products in the ensuing undertow, we can expect further waves to follow. The lessons of both that first wave and first undertow are critical to shaping future products. And though we will spend some time exploring both those lessons and their implications to future entrepreneurs, our focus on this journey will be elsewhere.

Our primary goal is to understand the relationship among digital information products, intellectual property rights, and network markets—technology, law, and economics. We need to understand the infrastructure that our current system implies, to see how it has played itself out in the Microsoft trial, the Linux bazaar, and the Napster song, and to explore where it appears to be heading. We also need to consider whether or not we could do better. This focus will shape most of our journey, as we attempt to comprehend the public infrastructure that will make private entrepreneurship possible. In short, we have returned to the information sector to learn what happened and why—so that we can leverage that knowledge into a better, brighter, richer future.

Millennial Alchemy

Shortly before the turn of the millennium, public opinion came to be that the Internet represented a new economic order, unconstrained by the economic laws of the physical universe. The Internet would be easy to access and easy to use—but only by those who got there first. Late adapters would have to pay for access, at prices they could neither fight nor resist. The only key lay in securing a previously unclaimed Internet space. These beliefs set America on a quest for Internet gold.

A few brave souls applied lessons gleaned from economics, management science, and business experience to this daunting task. Most, however, relied on the time-honored principles of alchemy; they would turn base ideas into golden companies merely by placing them on the Internet. Citizen Microsoft felt itself threatened by the new alchemy. Its leadership and popularity began to slip away, as various upstarts nipped at its heels. Microsoft fought back to secure its hard-earned position as kingpin of computing. In its quest for continued supremacy, Microsoft destroyed its challengers, dominated its partners, harmed its captive consumers, tried to curb all innovation that it couldn't control, and earned the ire of the government—though hardly that of the public. Its own quest for Internet gold thus relied on a scheme at least as ancient as alchemy: a campaign of plunder.

The widespread Internet alchemy and Microsoft's unique form of plunder fed off each other, as revelations from the trial powered the bubble, and the bubble in turn affected Microsoft's perceptions and responses. Meanwhile, with the bubble in full bloom and the trial already underway, a young man from Finland marshaled the world's hackers into a software development bazaar, and an even younger man from Boston taught us how to share the music that we love. With that, Linux engaged Microsoft in a brewing battle over "open source" software, and Napster drew a reluctant entertainment industry into the center of an information-sector maelstrom. When investors bid up the value of Linux companies, the hackers settled into an information sector that long had been their home. But the opposite was true of the music business. Disoriented by their new surroundings in the information sector, the record companies accused the public of piracy most vile. Many of the accused were never sure why.

These tales marked the culmination of a decades-long revolution in our computing and communications infrastructure. But while the Internet investment bubble and the Microsoft trial may define the current terrain of the tech sector, the Linux bazaar, the Napster song, and the responses that they engender will frame the debate about the propriety of such unfettered innovation. Though that debate has already begun to unfold, neither its underlying causes nor its relationship to the trial and the bubble has received much attention.

Think back ten years: In early 1995, computer users were split among those who favored the flexibility of Unix, those who valued the graphical interface, logical layout, and tight feel of Apple's Macintosh, and those whose preference for less expensive hardware led them to adopt Microsoft's Windows, still a graphical interface to DOS. IBM's imminent acquisition of Lotus would make it the world's largest software company, capable of fielding a fully-IBM system, from the hardware, through the OS/2 operating system and an office suite built around Lotus' popular programs. WordPerfect remained the word processor of choice. E-mail was just becoming widespread, and America Online had recently become the leading provider of network access and content to home users.

Microsoft announced that the long-awaited Windows 95 would soon provide a coherent feel that previously had been available only to Mac users. But this soon-to-be-released program omitted a convenient way to access the Internet. This omission was hardly glaring; Internet connectivity was rare outside the academic world. A group of students, in fact, had only recently launched Mosaic, the first user-friendly browser, and founded Netscape to commercialize it. Yet another new company, Amazon.com, set out to exploit the Internet's untested retail potential.

Laptops were almost light enough to carry comfortably, but handheld computers remained a failure despite some high-profile attempts. A few gadget freaks had CD drives built into their computers, and some of them even used their drives to play music. Cell phones were clunky, unreliable, heavy, and mostly analog. The communications industry structure was still an artifact of the 1982 consent order breaking up Ma Bell, and questions about the property rights inherent in digital files rarely left the offices of copyright lawyers.

1995 thus began with various pieces of the revolution in place, action still needed on several key fronts, and many more audible promises than visible actions. The technologies central to the long-heralded convergence of computing and communications were improving; software announcements foreshadowed important innovations; and at least parts of the governing legal framework were in desperate need of an overhaul.

And then the revolution took off and the full-blown information sector emerged. By the end of 2000, Microsoft dominated personal computing with Windows and Office. Instant messaging had assumed many of the early uses of e-mail, particularly among teens and preteens. IBM's reduced consumer focus restored Microsoft to its title of world's largest software company. Netscape was a specter with a dwindling market share, having lost the "browser wars" to Microsoft; America Online—itself about to become AOL Time Warner[1]—had acquired Netscape two years earlier. Microsoft announced the imminent release of Windows XP, Office XP, and a barrage of accompanying initiatives. Napster circulated free music software, and MP3 files were ubiquitous. Linux and Apache established a significant open-source presence in the server world populated mostly by information technology (IT) professionals.

Laptops were light, easy to use, and outfitted for widely available public dataports. Personal Digital Assistants (PDAs) and wireless phones were everywhere, many homes had high-speed Internet access, and we looked forward to solving the last-mile broadband challenge. E-commerce was big business, and no e-commerce business was bigger than Amazon. The Telecommunications Act of 1996 had attempted to revamp the competitive environment for communications, and the Digital Millennium Copyright Act (DMCA) of 1998 allowed Congress to claim that it was updating copyright law for the digital age.

In between, we lived through THE BUBBLE, that unsustainable investment frenzy built upon air and faith, rather than grounded in fundamental analysis and due diligence. The Internet investment bubble was *the* central story of the information sector's formative years. For a while, it was everywhere. And though many of us enjoyed the ride, we soon came to appreciate the wise warnings emanating from the hallowed temples of academe—warnings that we had been all too eager to ignore. Yale economist Robert Shiller's best-selling *Irrational Exuberance*, fortuitously published as the bubble approached its peak, described aspects of investor psychology that seemed to be leading to a dangerous overvaluation of the American equity markets.[2] His concerns transcended the inevitable losses that misguided investors would absorb when the bubble burst. He feared that the overvaluation of publicly traded companies was skewing investment decisions. It was leading the country to overinvest in selected industries while ignoring crucial infrastructure needs and other socially important goods. He perceptively saw the bubble as more than simply a phenomenon of the stock market. He recognized it as a defining social phenomenon.

Shiller aptly characterized the crowd psychology driving the bubble as a naturally occurring *Ponzi scheme*, a dangerous type of scam named for the 1920 efforts of noted Boston con artist Charles Ponzi. Two key elements mark an "investment strategy" as a Ponzi scheme: an offer that sounds too good to be true, and a plausible explanation of its truth. Shiller focused on the dynamics of the investment community that allowed the scheme to flourish without really resolving the key motivational question: *What caused the bubble?* He left it to later analysts, armed with empirical data and informed hindsight, to determine what made the alchemical Internet-investment pitch plausible enough to hook investors.

Business journalist John Cassidy accepted part of the challenge.[3] He attributed the crowd psychology driving the bubble to journalism and finance—whose cognoscenti undoubtedly played a leadership role. But Cassidy's analysis can't answer the question because, like Shiller, he focused on crowd psychology to explain what kept the phenomenon rolling once it got started. He did not explain *why* the madness of the crowd began in the first place.

The answer lies in our *partial* absorption of the lessons of network economics. We learned the hard way that it can be dangerous to take half a lesson out of a temple and onto Wall Street. The bubble began when investors applied a fundamental misunderstanding of contemporary network economic theories to predict the rapid growth and dominance of new "pure play" companies. That misunderstanding set them on an elusive quest for "the next Microsoft," those inevitable monopolists of the Internet. The deflation began when those same investors discovered that empirical data couldn't sustain those theories as applied; they had omitted the critical concept of "lock in."

Along the way, we adopted and discarded an entire theory of Internet economics: the "New World" view.[4] According to New World thinkers, the economic laws that govern the physical world do not apply to the Internet. Instead, new economic laws emerge from three key beliefs: One, network industries, though relatively rare occurrences in the physical world, will be rampant on the Internet. Two, virtually all commerce will eventually gravitate to the Internet. Three, legacy systems will weigh down conventional brick-and-mortar companies and make it impossible for them to compete with new, nimble, Internet-savvy pure plays.

These beliefs combine to form a simple rule for New World investing. Successful first movers in an Internet space will inevitably monopolize that space. Because monopolists earn greater profits than do firms operating in a competitive environment (i.e., the monopoly rents), they're very solid investments—particularly if you can buy their shares *before* anyone else notices that they're poised to become monopolists. Equity markets value stocks based on their projected profits. If the market values a company assuming that it will earn a competitive return, and instead it earns a higher monopoly return, its price will rise and early investors will profit handsomely. So, when you think you've spotted a competitive company poised to become an inevitable monopolist, particularly if you've noticed it before the crowd, *buy early and don't worry too much about your entry point.*

New World investors developed this theory at a particularly opportune moment. The decline in defense spending following the end of the Cold War had forced many engineers to find new professional venues and removed what had been their most reliable source of employment. This "peace dividend" talent pool was huge, and the Internet stakes were large enough to attract a substantial number of players. Overall economic conditions were ideal for growth, and government economic policies simultaneously expanded opportunities, reduced risks, and motivated innovation. In this environment, it almost made sense for New World investors to use Web sites as lottery tickets. Their lottery powered history's greatest experiment in rapid private-sector infrastructure development, created a small class of new billionaires, and left many unhappy investors and creditors to grapple with worthless shares and unpaid bills.

It also left the rest of us with much to digest. We had to consider what we'd seen unfold in the economy and how it had rippled through American—and global—society. The greatest lesson of the American economy of the 1990s may be that economic growth is the best of all possible social programs. A combination of smart policies and dumb luck helped turn the United States into a richer, more tolerant, more civil society. The unrivaled growth of the 1990s meant that so much new money was floating around that people were willing to experiment and to share. But rather than mindlessly raising taxes to redistribute wealth, we *invested* in long-term future growth. We experimented with a number of novel social and educational programs that expanded the base from which future entrepreneurs will emerge, while at the same time retaining ample rewards for our current entrepreneurs.

The information sector was central to this growth. When it entered our businesses, it made us more productive. When it entered our homes, it created new opportunities for entertainment, education, community building, and home efficiency. When it entered global society, it introduced new opportunities for communication, collaboration, and the spread of ideas; it provided citizens of many countries with new and exciting opportunities to participate in their country's own development, governance, and growth. Above all, though, it got us excited about the future. The information sector's growth made us believe in a future that was fundamentally better—a future with greater opportunities, more winners, fewer losers, and better facilities to care for the few who fall to the bottom anyway. In short, the information sector's growth caused a blossoming of hope. Granted, we might have been better off had we tempered that hope with a bit more reason, but even so, the hope of a better future helped us strive for things that we otherwise might never have attempted.

The story assumed a different tenor when the bubble began to collapse. We learned that the information sector's products and profits wouldn't materialize as quickly as we'd expected. That dented our hope. We learned that some of our erstwhile heroes had lied to us. That dented it further. And then we learned the most painful lesson of all—the information sector's spread made it easier than ever for people who hate us to expose our vulnerabilities. Our dumb luck ran out. Fear replaced hope. Security replaced growth as our overriding concern. We stopped investing in our long-term societal future and shifted our dwindling savings instead into safer arenas closer to home.

Around the same time, our policies shifted to favor the safe, comfortable planning of dominant incumbents over the exhilarating chaos of entrepreneurial start-ups. We downplayed our investments in infrastructure and opportunity to emphasize, instead, increased incentives—though the incentive to invest in high-risk, high-payoff, long-term ventures hardly seemed to be lacking. The second stage of the information sector's tale unfolded glumly in this policy environment. The sector wound its way through some painful years, into the early stages of a potential recovery. It emerged with New World thinking discredited and with a view of the Internet as a "New Channel" on the rise.[5]

New Channel thinking rests upon a single modest belief: The Internet makes it cheaper for buyers and sellers to communicate with each other. As a result, the Internet alters the relative cost-effectiveness of various types of transactions—a change that's likely to play itself out in very different ways in different industries. In other words, there are few *Internet companies* out there. In reality, there are just a bunch of companies in different industries that have noticed a new *communication channel* and built it into their businesses.

We stand today at the beginnings of stage three. The only way that we can return to real hope and growth in this stage of the story is to assess what worked, what didn't, and why. We must devise policies consonant with those that fostered growth in the 1990s, but which also recognize our newfound sense of vulnerability and need for security. We must learn to trust again—and in particular, to trust the corporate innovators and entrepreneurs who make growth possible. We must make sure that short-term rewards remain significant enough to promote investment. We must focus that investment on the parts of the economy most likely to promote long-term, multiplicative productivity growth. We must spread the opportunities to take advantage of that growth as widely as possible—throughout the United States and around the world. The continued growth, maturation, and health of the information sector are critical to each of these tasks. At the same time, though, we must remain vigilant; the constant attempts to censor what we see, invade our privacy, damage our economy, and kill our people unfortunately *also* become easier as our information infrastructure improves.

These are all tough challenges, and there's plenty of work to go around. Governments, businesses, technologists, and scholars must work together to restore our trust, rekindle our hope, keep us safe, and let us grow. If we each do our part, we all stand to win, and the Internet *will* make us all rich. This enrichment will come neither as abruptly nor as easily as we once wished. We will all get a little bit richer one online transaction at a time, and we'll have to fend off those who would prevent our enrichment. But if we don't first believe that we can return to an era of hope and growth, we never will.

Positively You

The Internet is only the latest example of the complex interconnections that govern modern life. Earlier such networks include the electricity grid, the telephone system, the rail lines, and the road system. Each of these networks introduced challenging issues of technology, of law, and of public policy. It also helped move entire industries into the realm of "network economics."

From an economic perspective, the defining feature of a network is that the value of membership increases as the network grows. Riding the rails became less expensive and more valuable as a growing number of riders pushed the railroads to provide more comprehensive service. Telephones became more valuable as more people bought the phones necessary to take each other's calls. Large networks enhance the wealth and welfare of all of their members. Throughout much of human history, networks were few and far between. They began to appear in significant numbers only after the industrial revolution. Each new network brought additional sectors of the overall economy into the network economy and created new wealth that all network members shared. The information age accelerated the emergence of new networks, thereby making us all richer.

Many people looked for a way to capture, direct, and privatize that newly created wealth. One common idea was that anyone who controls a network should be able to collect enough tolls to generate substantial profits. There were good reasons for this belief, but there were also some fundamental problems with it. Toll collection on the information superhighway is only lucrative if consumers are "locked in" to the toll road.

If there's a viable toll-free alternative, consumers will take it—leaving the toll collector with an unused new toll road and a mound of construction debt.

Therein lies one of the Internet's many apparent paradoxes. The Internet creates extraordinary *public* value that's quite difficult to privatize. Frustrated investors *know* that there *must be* some way to make money from the Internet, but they remain largely baffled as to *how*. Investors who bid up Internet stocks understood the definitional growth component of network economics, but they paid insufficient attention to the lock in component. Most of their investments floundered. Microsoft, on the other hand, was much more attentive to lock in. Its investments in the Internet appear to be bearing fruit. As always, well-planned plunder is a safer road to riches than ill-conceived alchemy.

But alchemy and plunder may be set aside as artifacts of a gold rush. The key underlying question remains how to use the Internet to generate profits—perhaps not the obscene profits for which we all once hoped—but comfortable profits comparable to those generated by other successful companies. That question, in turn, suggests thinking not like *Internet* entrepreneurs, but simply like run-of-the-mill, hoping-to-succeed, willing-to-work-hard entrepreneurs.

And so, let's start with the obvious. If you want to build a profitable company, you'd better be able to answer three questions: What's your product? What makes your product special? How are you going to use that "special quality" to generate profits? Every company in every industry faces these questions in some form or another. Management must consider them when allocating resources and devising business plans, and investors must consider them as the first steps of due diligence. Despite rumors to the contrary, which flared during the bubble, these questions are at least as important for Internet ventures as they are for conventional firms. In fact, they may be even more important on the Internet than they are elsewhere because it's so easy to copy a Web site—not to mention the idea behind it.

The story of Tom Friedman, Jeff Bezos, Lyle Bowlin, and Scott Rosenberg provides an illustrative—and cautionary—tale. The first two of these names are well known; the latter two less so. But they all came together to demonstrate the perils of doing business on the Internet. Tom

Friedman is a well-respected columnist for the *New York Times* who has written extensively about the Internet's impact on social and commercial development. Jeff Bezos—a passive player in this particular tale—founded Amazon.com and pioneered a number of innovative Internet business techniques. He noticed, for example, that the retail price for books is much higher than the wholesale price. Traditional booksellers need much of that markup to cover their overhead; they must pay rent on their stores, keep shelves stocked with books that don't sell very quickly, and incur all of the expenses that generally accompany a retail operation. Their actual profits are rarely huge. Bezos realized that running his business over the Internet should reduce his overhead costs. That reduction would allow him to undercut retail prices and still turn a profit. Setting aside what we now know about the early profitability of Internet businesses in general and Amazon in particular, Bezos had thus constructed plausible answers to all three key questions. He had a well-defined product (books) to sell in a unique manner (over the Internet) that would generate profits (by cutting overhead, lowering prices, and increasing volume).

Bezos's story resonated among the book-buying public, the investment community, and beyond. At its peak, the story was so compelling that he was *Time* magazine's 1999 "Person of the Year." Months before Bezos earned that particular accolade, however, Friedman detected a flaw in the story. On February 26, 1999, Friedman's column "Amazon.you,"[6] asked: What's so special about selling books over the Internet? He introduced Lyle Bowlin, a professor of small business at the University of Northern Iowa and founder of Positively-you.com, a bookselling Web site. Bowlin, his wife, and his daughter ran Positively-you out of their spare bedroom. This arrangement let Positively-you cut its overhead even further than Amazon—according to Bowlin, down to about $150 a month—and thus to undercut Amazon's prices. Friedman's conclusion? "For about the cost of one share of Amazon.com, you can *be* Amazon.com."[7]

Not surprisingly, Friedman's column was good for Bowlin's business. Within ten days, Positively-you's business had grown by a factor of about thirty. Bowlin moved its operations out of the spare bedroom and into the formal dining room. Friedman responded with a follow-up column,

"KillingGoliath.com,"[8] in which he summarized Positively-you's success in a two-word reply directed at the skeptical readers who'd questioned "Amazon.you." No, not those two words. This was, after all, the op-ed page of the *New York Times*. Friedman's response was a fully capitalized "YOU'RE WRONG."[9]

That's where Scott Rosenberg entered the story. Rosenberg, the managing editor of Salon.com, was one of the skeptical experts to whom Friedman had directed his reply. In "Amazon vs. the Ants,"[10] Rosenberg explained that Friedman had captured only half the logic of the online marketplace. That half, the low cost of getting started, certainly allowed hobbyists like Bowlin to launch commercial ventures. The other half, in Rosenberg's view, was what set Amazon apart from Positively-you. He cited two fatal flaws with Positively-you's business model. The first flaw stemmed from scalability. Positively-you's overhead was lower than Amazon's precisely because it was a smaller operation. As business grew, Bowlin would have to relocate yet again, likely to a warehouse for which he might actually have to pay rent. He would also eventually run out of unpaid family members and need to hire employees. These costs would drive his overhead up and narrow if not eliminate any cost advantage that he maintained over Amazon. The second flaw dealt with the challenges and the expense of generating traffic comparable to Amazon's. Rosenberg simply assumed that Bowlin couldn't rely upon the substantial free publicity that he received by appearing in Friedman's columns. Rosenberg's conclusion? "If I were Amazon's Jeff Bezos, I wouldn't be too worried."[11]

Lyle Bowlin and Positively-you then proceeded to fall from public view for about a year. They reappeared March 3, 2000, in columns written by Friedman and by Rosenberg. Friedman's "Saga of an Online Pioneer"[12] told of Bowlin's attempt to leverage his early publicity into a real business. He raised $90,000, took a leave from his teaching position, rented office space, hired employees—and went out of business. Friedman considered Positively-you's failure instructive. He cited a number of lessons that he had learned about e-commerce. The two most significant of them were the difficulty of scaling costs and the challenge of driving traffic to a Web site.[13] Rosenberg's column basically said "I told you so," which, of course, he had.[14]

The Positively-you.com saga illustrates the Internet's tantalizing allure. It's so easy to open an Internet company, yet so difficult to succeed with one. So what's the secret? The "secret" lies in truly understanding the three key questions: What's your product? What makes your product special? How are you going to use that "special quality" to generate profits? Amazon's answers may sound deceptively simple. But that apparent simplicity masks some subtle insights.

All Internet companies start as software-development ventures. The bare minimum required for doing business on the Internet is a working Web site. A fully functioning and launched site, however, is little more than an idea, and ideas travel quickly. Any Web site based on a good idea is likely to be copied many times over. The only way to convert such an idea into a profit is to ensure that everyone attracted to your idea works through your site, rather than through a rival's knock-off. These needs all pose complex challenges.

In the Internet's early days, pioneers believed that they could meet these challenges with little deep thought, and a few may have been right. Most of them proved to be horribly wrong; the once-vibrant Internet economy was decimated by failure. The main lesson from that failure is that deeper thought is required. In order to deepen our thought, however, we must first identify what we're to think about. Once again, the three key questions of business development point us in the right direction. It's hardly a coincidence that the single company best poised to capitalize on the Internet is Microsoft, who delivered a product (Internet Explorer) in a special way (integrated into the Windows platform) as part of a strategy to generate profits (by maintaining and extending its monopoly of the platform market). Nor, for that matter, is it a coincidence that Napster, who delivered a popular product (digital music files) in a special way (shared freely among fans), but without a legitimate business strategy (it neither paid for the music files nor charged for its services), has already met its demise.

A profitable Internet company must develop software that embodies a powerful idea and then leverages it in an appropriate direction. Entrepreneurs maximize their prospects for success by building their companies around products that are well-defined, in some way special, and distributed in a manner designed to generate profits. Computer scientists study the first of these requirements, software development. The second, the protection of ideas, is the purview of intellectual-property (IP) lawyers. The third, leveraging, lies at the intersection of applied industrial economics and antitrust law. Deep thought about either Internet success or the future of the information sector translates into deep thought about all three sets of issues.

Technology, economics, law, and public policy interact cyclically in the information sector. Technology comes first: Innovations in information technology make it easier and cheaper for producers and consumers to exchange information. Economics takes over: Information innovations drive down the cost of transactions, save consumers money, and often suggest new business models that increase producer profits. Law enters the picture: Some of the new business models might be illegal, either because they leverage competitors out of business inappropriately or because they infringe on someone else's property rights. Policy resolves the dilemma: Government must decide which laws to tighten and which to liberalize—and thus which business models to encourage and which to prohibit. The cycle then repeats itself with a new set of incentives in place. Technologists move yet another industry into the information sector, consumers and producers benefit, aggrieved parties litigate, and governments legislate.

There's nothing new about this story; it predates digitization, computers, information products, and bit strings by at least several centuries. The influential Peruvian economist Hernando de Soto has spent more than twenty years investigating why capitalism has created so much wealth in the West while working only sporadically elsewhere. He's concluded that reasonable records and databases of property rights are a prerequisite for a viable capitalist economy. Physical "real property" like land and buildings is tough to convert into cash that can then be reinvested elsewhere. But *titles* to land and buildings, recognized by governments and enforceable by trustworthy courts, are widely accepted as collateral. Thus, for example, would-be entrepreneurs can mortgage their homes and receive investment capital with which to begin new businesses. De Soto has shown how, throughout the history of both the Western and developing worlds, entrenched interests have worked to prevent new, rising classes from converting their property into information—and from information into capital. He has also shown how the development of each new information system unleashed a new wave of entrepreneurs whose hard work catapulted society to its next, richer, level.[15]

In other words, development—and its consequent enrichment of each of society's members—first became possible when real estate morphed into a "property information sector." What de Soto didn't explain, though, is that what worked for real property has also worked for other property. Whenever we develop a new informational analog to an existing industry, the folks who are already successful in that industry fight the change. When they lose, as they eventually do, the information sector grows and we all become richer. But sometimes that eventuality can take a long time. Our challenge is to ensure that market dynamics prevail and that good ideas chase bad, so that the Internet and its consequent changes to the economics of information can enrich us all. To meet that public-policy challenge, we need to understand the basics of technology, economics, and law that underpin our marvelous new information infrastructure.

Guide for the Perplexed

The interactions among technology, economics, and law can be both intricate and confusing. Stated simply, technology *constrains what we can do*, legal rules *change the alternatives' relative costs*, and economic incentives *indicate which alternatives we are likely to choose*. Healthy industrial development is only possible if all three are aligned.

Mature industries based on well-understood technologies tend to change slowly. Our understanding of the underlying technologies generally leads to stable, reasonable laws and regulations that enable efficient companies to earn attractive profits without violating important public policies. Industries undergoing rapid, radical technological change rarely exhibit that type of stability. New technologies introduce new opportunities. Some attempts to exploit these new opportunities may yield enormous rewards, while others that appeared to be equally promising may lead to spectacular failures. Meanwhile, the existing legal environment—by definition a legacy of a different technological era—may be ill-equipped to deal with this brave new world. The inheritance is almost certain to include laws that prohibit beneficial advances, laws that permit harmful exploitation, and even laws that somehow manage to do both simultaneously.

In the late 1990s, technological advances in software, microprocessors, and communications disrupted conventional thinking. These advances catapulted the Internet from an esoteric research tool into the preeminent global infrastructure for commerce, entertainment, and communication. New technological possibilities seemed to arise every day, and every new technology spawned promises of obscene riches. Professionals immersed in relevant areas of economics and law suddenly had to rethink their most basic assumptions and attitudes; technology had invaded their realms. Technologists had to adjust many of their own assumptions and attitudes; hordes of lawyers, economists, financiers, investors, marketers, regulators, lobbyists, legislators, and onlookers invaded their laboratories. The professionals' confusion paled in comparison with that of the public at large. Claims about a new world, a new economy, and a new set of rules seemed to arrive daily. Too many people bestowed blind faith upon "experts" working from an unstable experience base. Opportunities and costs changed too quickly for the reflection and analysis required to form the basis of expert opinion.

Now that the situation has calmed down—at least a bit—an assessment of the technologies, the economic theories, and the legal doctrines that emerged during the recent information revolution is possible. Unfortunately, disentanglement is rarely easy, and translating esoteric, nuanced arcana into plain English is always a challenge. The information sector's emergence from the academic temples onto the front pages forced copyright lawyers to learn about oddities like "data encryption standards" and "file transfer protocols." Software specialists learned that much of their collegial behavior violated copyright law and often crossed the line into the even more ominous "misappropriation of trade secrets." Economists had to confront the relationship between intellectual property *policy* (which most of them understand intuitively) and intellectual property *law* (which many of them find baffling). The general public—which had no technical, economic, or legal background—had to assimilate all of these ideas, along with academic concepts like equity valuation, network economics, industrial organization, antitrust leveraging, monopoly maintenance, transaction costs, software design, user interfaces, Ponzi schemes, crowd psychology, and accounting conventions.

The sheer complexity of this kaleidoscopic information sector drove many to passive reliance upon the pronouncements of "experts." On one hand, there's something comforting about waking up in the morning to discover that Microsoft has automatically downloaded a software upgrade for you, that Merrill Lynch has found a new stock for your portfolio, and that Congress has changed the copyright laws to keep some important industries functioning as usual. It frees us up to go about our day without worrying—or even thinking—about any of these issues. But there's also something disconcerting about waking up with those discoveries. What if the upgrade conflicts with non-Microsoft programs that we use and enjoy? How do we know that Merrill Lynch's recommendation is objective—and what recourse do we have if it isn't? And exactly who represented *our* interests in these Congressional hearings? Whether these issues represent an improvement over the set that we avoided is, of course, a matter of personal taste. But it lands us back at exactly the same place. If we want to understand the ways in which the world is changing around us, we need a bit of background. And in particular, if we want to understand the ways in which the information sector emerged from its crypt one dark night in the mid-90s and wormed its way onto the front pages, we must first pass through the temples of law, economics, and computer science.

That quest defines our first true challenge. We must glean the key concepts from these fields, in plain English, and explore the ways in which their interactions shaped the information sector—and thus increasingly shape our lives.[16] Some concepts emerged from the temples of industrial organization (IO) economics and competition (or antitrust) law. The relevance of these concepts to the Microsoft trial is obvious: Microsoft stood accused of violating the antitrust laws. It helps to know why these laws exist, whom they protect and how, what the government believed that Microsoft had done wrong, and how Microsoft justified its behavior. These laws' relevance to other aspects of the information sector, though, is just as significant—if somewhat less direct. Day traders and Internet investors spent a great deal of time reading about the Microsoft trial. These readers invariably asked themselves two questions: Why won't the government leave Microsoft alone? and How do I identify and invest in "the next Microsoft"? Answers require at least some familiarity with the concepts of market structure, its natural workings, and the abilities of certain players to interfere with its smooth functioning.

These same temples also house the secrets that will allow the Internet to make us all rich. Their inquiries into "transaction costs," or the elements of pricing that owe less to the cost of production than to the cost of distribution, reveal the areas in which new business models oriented around the Internet can help both consumers and producers—while raising the ire of traditional distributors. This revelation sets the stage for the battles surrounding both Linux and Napster—and likely the entire future of the information sector.

But while IO and antitrust are the disciplines best suited to explain these concepts, they are also both established fields, first developed to study railroads, manufacturing, and smokestack industries. Much of the New Economy literature contended that old avenues of inquiry were inapplicable to the dynamic, creative, information sector. While that literature may have oversold the novelty of the situation, the shift from an industrial to an information economy did introduce a number of new concepts into these once stodgy fields, most notably "network economics." In a network industry, rational consumer behavior turns selected popular products into entrenched standards. A single player who owns that standard becomes very powerful, often able to disrupt the workings of the marketplace and retard innovation in ways that serve the owner's proprietary interests. One question that lingers among erstwhile dot-com advocates is why Microsoft was so successful while the dot-coms failed so miserably. Certainly, part of the answer lies in managerial competence and product quality. But those answers are only partial. Platform software (e.g., Windows) and many Internet spaces exhibit aspects of network growth. But only platform software allows the exploitation of consumers—which translates directly into high profit margins. Microsoft understood this distinction. The dot-coms did not.

So far, so good. But these ideas all deal with markets. Markets are meaningless in the absence of products. The information sector's products encompass various types of software. We must thus ask computer scientists: What is software? How does it evolve? What motivates software developers? and What rewards do they receive when their programs work?

Two critical ideas from artificial intelligence (AI) and software engineering provide some answers: translation and modular design. The "translation chain" embodies the various tasks that software developers tackle. It refers to the many steps required to enable those of us who speak human languages to communicate with silicon chips that notice when voltage levels change. One of computer science's truly marvelous accomplishments has been its incorporation of increasing amounts of the translation task into the computer, a chain of translations that links voltages to bits, to numbers, to words, to programming languages, to user interfaces, and eventually to us. Not too long ago, it took years of specialized training for a person to communicate with a computer. Now even preliterate children can use mice and touch screens to "talk" to microchips. Web browsers that incorporate color, pictures, and sound were an important link in that chain. But they were only the gloss built atop generations of previous work.

The conceptual links in the translation chain lead naturally to modular design. Software engineers understand that the most effective way to improve our computing experience is to link a new software module to the previous generation's interface. Graphical browsers, pictures, and sound hardly appeared out of nowhere. All of these innovations—like the innovations of preceding generations—arrived first as modular add-ons or as separate application programs that consumers could run on top of existing systems. But these add-ons were often clunky and full of bugs. Software developers eventually worked out the bugs, integrated the new ideas into the main software's translation chain, and presented slick unified products.

In most generations of software, engineers were responsible for integration decisions. They decided when an add-on product had matured enough to incorporate it into the translation chain. Sometimes they were right, and people bought their new integrated products rather than the old modular ones. Sometimes they were wrong, and their companies lost sales and profits to their competitors. But the Microsoft trial introduced a new twist. Suppose that strategic marketers, rather than software engineers, made the integration decisions? And furthermore, suppose that those marketers were in a position to foist their integrated products on the public whether consumers wanted them or not? Should consumers care? Should the government care? Should the law care? One of the most perplexing questions to emerge from the Microsoft trial thus remains: When is product integration a good thing? This question is likely to reappear in a number of legal battles over the next few years.

Translation chains and modularity are important concepts in the design of information products. But the very notion of an information product raises its own set of complexities. After all, software packages, Web sites, databases, and even music files are little more than interesting ideas that are now easy to copy, easy to circulate, and easy to broadcast. How can anyone truly "own" this type of product? And more to the point, why would anyone want to? How can anyone turn a profit by investing in product development and then watching it circulate freely? These questions lead us back into the realm of law, specifically IP law. IP law long has motivated invention and creativity by allowing inventors and authors to retain certain basic rights in their creations' use and distribution. In fact, the U.S. Constitution empowered Congress to create a body of laws that provided the appropriate motivation. Congress responded by codifying the laws of patents and copyrights.

The constitutional imprimatur notwithstanding, these IP rights create an odd sort of property. Their owners can't really watch them or police their use; many people violate IP rights with impunity. Usually all the "owners" can do is file an occasional lawsuit—and even then, an infringer's inability to pay often ends the litigation prematurely. The ability to sue, in turn, suggests that IP owners also can offer a valuable license defining the terms under which they promise not to sue; that's where they make much of their money.

But the information age has placed an enormous strain on the precepts of IP law. With each passing year, more and more products become digital bit strings, and more and more people learn how to infringe (particularly copyrights) in the privacy of their own homes. These changes infuriate the rights holders and threaten to erode the profitability of their operations—and reduced profitability implies reduced motivation implies reduced product development. Put bluntly, the ability to swap music files could reduce the amount of new music—at least according to one school of thought. This issue arose only at the periphery of the 1990s information sector, as the motivation behind an important change to the copyright laws known as the DMCA of 1998, and as the undercurrent of the battle over Napster. Its importance, however, grew quickly—and it will grow even further as the information sector spreads its tentacles throughout the economy. IP law thus promises to become the information sector's next great battleground.

Pillars of the three temples—the legal concepts of antitrust and IP, the microeconomic theories of IO, and the computer-science principles of artificial intelligence and software engineering—formed the framework for the information sector. We must therefore consider these foundations before we can truly understand the information sector's story.

2

Progress of Science and Useful Arts

The Legislators and the Innovators

Two hundred years after the founding fathers wrote the U.S. Constitution, the government that it created thrust the Internet from the temples of academe into the cold, cruel commercial world. The Constitution empowered Congress to "promote the progress of science and useful arts, by securing for limited times to authors and inventors the exclusive right to their respective writings and discoveries."[1] This IP clause made no reference to any specific form of protection. It simply stated a goal (the promotion of art and science) and a mechanism (the reservation of exclusive rights), leaving Congress to work out the details.

This charge defines the overriding objective of IP policy: to harness the profit motive to motivate innovation. Want to encourage inventors to invent and authors to write? Bribe 'em. Let them charge people to use their ideas and their innovations for long enough to keep them innovating, and then make them release their innovations into the public realm. From then on, the people may use the ideas free of charge.

Such bribery (or motivation) is not a bad idea, at least in theory, proving once again that the drafters of our Constitution were pretty savvy thinkers. But they left the details of IP *law* to Congress—and that's always a challenge. While policy goals are often straightforward, the operational laws intended to reach those goals can be rather complex. And so, while U.S. IP policy can be stated in a simple sentence, U.S. IP laws are based on a few long and detailed statutes. That distinction between idea and implementation has split the world of IP. A key issue that separates temple-dwelling IP scholars from those who practice IP

law is the significance the two groups place on IP policy. Good IP lawyers
know that IP law is what it is; we *presume* that Congress fulfilled the
Constitution's policy prescriptions. Legal IP scholars are less deferential.
They spend much time, and expend much ink, exploring Congressional
fidelity to the Constitution's goals. They often dislike what they find.

Our modern world differs from that of the Constitution in many ways.
The information sector wreaked havoc on the generally sensible system
that early Congresses had established. Those Congresses couldn't possibly have imagined words that actually *did* something. In their world,
authors drew upon words and grammars to create texts. Inventors
applied technical creativity to solve problems. The distinction between
them was clear. So what would they make of the computer programmer,
who draws upon words and grammars to solve challenging technical
problems? Is such a person an author or an inventor? And how should
the law motivate—or bribe—such a person? These questions rage as
matters of front-line controversy among IP scholars. They also reveal
how legal rules can alter economic incentives, which in turn determine
which technologies attract innovative fervor and investment.

But back to Congress. The Constitution, adopted in 1789, gave the
new Congress the power to bribe authors and inventors to encourage
innovation. Of course, that first Congress had a whole government to
build, and the Constitution never told Congress that it *had* to reserve
rights for authors and inventors—just that it could if it wanted to.
Nevertheless, Congress seemed to feel that a working IP system was a
priority item. That very first Congress deciding that authors and inventors each needed different incentives; it gave us both the Patent Act of
1790 (for inventors) and the Copyright Act of 1790 (for authors). While
each statute has been updated a handful of times, grown increasingly
more complex with each update, and granted stronger property rights
with each update, many of the broad outlines remain essentially as they
were more than 200 years ago.

Inventors with a new, useful, not-terribly-obvious way to solve a particular problem can apply to the Patent and Trademark Office (PTO). If
the PTO decides that a patent is warranted, it offers a deal: Publish a
detailed description of the clever innovation, and the government will
grant fairly broad rights to restrict its production, use, and sale for a

while (twenty years under current law). If anyone tries to infringe those rights, just take the matter to court.

The process for Authors is easier, though in theory the rights are not quite as good. An author or an artist who composes something original receives immediate copyright protection, even without registering it with the Copyright Office. That protection gives the copyright holder the exclusive right to copy, to distribute, to perform, or to display the work, as well as comparable rights over "derivative works" based on the original. Copyright protection, however, covers only the expression of the idea, not the idea itself. That means that we're all free to write novels about youthful wizards. (Good luck.)

The Copyright Act appears to offer authors something of value without extracting too much cost from society at large. But unlike the short-term life of patents, copyright protection currently lasts ninety-five years. Back in 1790, copyrights lasted only fourteen years. Then, slowly and incrementally, Congress made them longer and longer. They didn't hit ninety-five years until 1998, when the Sonny Bono Copyright Term Extension Act responded to the pressing needs of Disney, whose copyright protecting Mickey Mouse was about to expire. Now, the whole point of IP policy was supposed to be to motivate innovation. And it seems unlikely that, in the late 1920s, Walt Disney weighed his heirs' prospects for convincing Congress to extend copyright protection for an extra twenty years in deciding whether or not to create his cartoon mouse. So from that perspective, Congress does seem to have dropped the ball.

But to some, it appeared that Congress had done more than that. Some people believed that Congress had exceeded its constitutional charge. Eric Eldred, for example, had an information sector business (or perhaps more accurately, a serious hobby), republishing via HTML books whose copyrights had expired. Eldred had many good works to draw upon, but he'd been hoping to expand into the lost generation authors of the 1920s and 30s. Just as their works were about to enter the public domain, Congress ripped them from his hands. So Eldred enlisted the aid of IP crusader Larry Lessig, and together they sued the government, claiming that Congress's apparent willingness to keep ratcheting up the time limit whenever a certain mouse appeared destined to enter the public domain was tantamount to a *permanent* grant of rights. Such a deal violated not only Constitutional *policy*, but also the Constitution's actual wording; after all, the Constitution only authorized these rights for "a limited time."

Their crusade showed some initial promise. They convinced the Supreme Court to consider the issue—never a mean feat. But seven of the nine Justices decided that the Constitution gave Congress exceedingly broad flexibility, and that *any* time limit met the Constitutional requirement of a "limited time."[2] Nevertheless, Justices John Paul Stevens and Stephen Breyer did accept Lessig's arguments. They raised a number of issues at the heart of IP policy, opening a discussion of the relationship among our existing statutes, Congressional behavior in updating them, and the intended purpose of the IP clause. Justice Ruth Bader Ginsburg, who wrote for her six colleagues (and thus with the full force of the Court behind her), picked up the gauntlet that they had thrown. She rejected their arguments, explaining that the extension to ninety-five years was consistent with the original purpose: Because Congress changed the IP laws from time to time, innovators were on notice that their rights could change; this notice was part of their overall motivation. Her argument implies, of course, that innovators are also on notice that their rights could weaken (or even evaporate), should Congress decide to go that route. But because that particular question didn't arise in this case, she never addressed it explicitly. It remains a theoretical issue for scholars to debate another day.

Now, the significance of a debate between a court's majority and its dissenters differs depending on how close to the bench you stand. If you don't live in the legal world, it's little other than a curiosity. Such debates have no immediate impact on the law, which is as the majority says it is. But legal scholars recognize that these debates are often harbingers of things to come. Eldred and Lessig gave the Supreme Court an opportunity to begin debating the appropriate relationship between IP law and IP policy. Though they lost this particular battle, they helped elevate the discussion from one that engaged only law professors to one that engaged the Court. Creative IP scholars and lawyers are now poring through the Justices' words to find intriguing ambiguities, seeking ways to get the Supreme Court to consider deeper nuances in the relationship.

And given the number of questions raised during the information sector's formative years, not to mention those raised in other areas of active technological innovation, they seem likely to find some.

The Court's rejection of Eldred's claim encapsulates many basics of IP law. The Constitution set up a policy objective, Congress devised a few complicated statutes, and the law is what the statutes say it is. IP lawyers and judges are not tasked with assessing the relationship between the policy and the law; that's Congress's job. So unless someone like Lessig can convince the Supreme Court that the IP laws actually *violate* the Constitution, the laws remain as Congress writes them. A mere demonstration that the law in practice is likely to be inconsistent with the purposes of the Constitution is unlikely to be effective. Judges who inquire about Congressional fidelity to Constitutional policy are invariably labeled "activists" by anyone who disagrees with their conclusions. In other words, if we think that the deals that Congress offers authors and inventors don't serve the Constitution's goals or society's welfare, we have to lobby Congress to change them.

But before we write to our Representatives and Senators, we have more to learn about IP. For example, the entire IP system is an "opt in" system. Anyone, author or inventor who prefers to keep an innovation secret, is free to do so. The government won't offer him any special protection, but we will respect his choice. Inventors who choose not to share the secrets behind their inventions can keep them as "trade secrets." Courts protect trade secrets against industrial espionage and theft, but once someone else learns them—either independently or legitimately— the secret's out and there's not a damn thing the inventor can do about it. Not surprisingly, secrecy is more common among inventors than among authors. After all, I can still sell a machine based on a secret technology. I can't really imagine how or why anyone would buy a book with a secret text.

That is, I couldn't have imagined it until I heard of a special kind of "book": a computer program. Believe it or not, all three bodies of law protect commercial software. Software typically begins with a mathematical algorithm that may be patentable. The algorithm is implemented as copyrightable "source code" written in a high-level programming language, and then compiled into copyrightable "object code" lying further down the translation chain, closer to the machine's language and incomprehensible to human readers. Most software companies copyright and circulate this incomprehensible object code and retain the source code as a trade secret. As a result, the dominant legal protection for information products combines copyright and trade-secret law. Because trade-secret law is more a matter of espionage protection than actual IP rights, most of the discussion of information-sector IP focuses on copyright. But it's important to remember that the triple threat of patented algorithms, copyrighted and trade-secret protected source code, and copyrighted object code protect many software products in the market today.[4]

Did Congress meet the constitutional policy objective? The answer depends on your perspective. And from the perspective of the information sector, the rights protecting software look pretty damn powerful.

The Jeremiad of IP

Perhaps it's good that we offer software developers powerful protection. Maybe triple protection isn't terribly threatening, and maybe it motivates substantial innovative software development. More to the point, though, maybe it's an appropriate reward for a developer's successful investment first in a useful algorithm, then in functional source code, and finally in distributable object code. Why shouldn't she get some form of protection on each of the three?

Well, maybe because this particular combination seems to violate the bargain between innovator and public. It grants an innovator legal protection without granting the public new knowledge. It can also impede technological advancement. Competitors have little incentive to invest in improving ideas that someone else owns; the broader the protection offered to the first innovator in a field, the more concentrated the field is likely to become. That kind of industrial environment could mean that while several large, wealthy companies might compete on a first generation product, the competition would wither when one of them secured broad IP rights. The others would have little incentive to develop competing second and third generation improvements. Furthermore, the current combination of IP rights allows software monopolists to leverage their strength in ways that violate antitrust law.[5]

But that's jumping ahead. Before we conclude that Congress is failing to carry out its IP mission, that information sector companies are violating their deal with the public, and that reforming the IP system is a pressing need, we should get back to basics. Personally—and this may just be a bias from my legal training—I like to look at the Constitution whenever it has something relevant to say. The IP clause defines the first principles of IP, so whenever we want to understand something about our IP system, we should think about three basic issues: the profit motive, innovation, and disclosure. If the profits available to innovators push them to develop and to disclose important new ideas, then Congress has succeeded. But if not . . . well, then a call for reform might be in order.

So, considering profit, innovation, disclosure, and the information sector, how is America doing? We've certainly seen much innovation over the past two decades. The information sector exploded from a curiosity to a major part of the global economy: Microsoft put Windows on my desktop, Lotus taught me about spreadsheets, Netscape enabled me to surf the Web, Yahoo! posted information for me to read, Amazon sold me books, e-Bay introduced me to auction purchases, and Napster helped me download music. We've done well. But maybe, with a different set of IP rules, we could have done much better. We might have developed better technologies faster and paid less for them. We may be paying too much now for innovations that we should have had years ago.

The situation may get worse before it gets better. Larry Lessig outlined a bleak *Future of Ideas*.[6] He painted a picture of special interests run amok, fencing off entire realms of thought and expression from the public domain. Lessig sees these interest groups using IP laws, in particular the strong forms of protection available for digital products, to control speech and thought, and to turn the once-vibrant Internet into the sole province of the rich, connected, and protected. He also proposes some ways to address the problem including, but hardly limited to, Eldred's lawsuit.

Lessig seems to have arrived at this pessimism in a roundabout way. His first book, published only a few years earlier, was considerably more upbeat. In *Code and Other Laws of Cyberspace*,[7] he sang the glories of the Internet revolution, which he saw as unleashing wave after wave of creative energy. Between his two books, Lessig shifted his focus from technology—which he approached as an outsider—back to law—where he is an eminent insider. And what he found depressed him. Where he saw technology setting us free, he saw law reining us in—in singularly unhealthy ways.

Though *The Future of Ideas* outlined more fears than hopes, the world that Lessig foresees is hardly the scariest prediction. Jessica Litman's *Digital Copyright*, for example, foresees a dangerous path down which the information sector seems to be headed—and how it might get there while we all remain asleep at the wheel.

American ideas of freedom are bound up with a vision of information policy that counts information as a social wealth owned by all. We believe we are entitled to say what we think, to think what we want, and to learn whatever we're willing to explore. Part of the information ethos in the United States is that facts and ideas cannot be owned, suppressed, censored, or regulated; they are meant to be found, studied, passed along, and freely traded in the "marketplace of ideas."

In fact, information is regulated in this country as in others. . . . The almost utopian vision of a wired future seems to assume that the legal infrastructure of our information policy will continue to encourage us to speak, think, and learn as we will. But the technological marvel that makes this interconnection possible has other potentials as well. . . .

One of the most important devices being used to effect this transformation, ironically enough, is copyright law. . . . [T]o the extent that the public considers copyright law at all, it appears to think that the law is designed to benefit authors for creating new works and thus to promote the progress of knowledge and art. And, that's certainly the theory. . . .

In the current milieu, the policy arguments over the rationale for copyright owners' imperfect control have taken on immense practical significance. If the reason that authors' and their publishers' control over uses of their works has been narrowly confined is to enable consumers and future authors to make the broadest possible use of protected creations that is consistent with the copyright system's encouragement of authorship, then digital technology changes very little. . . . If, in contrast, the goal of copyright law is to place all feasible control over works of authorship firmly in the hands of copyright owners, new digital technology offers us the opportunity for the first time to come very close to perfecting the system. . . .

In 1998, copyright owners persuaded Congress to enhance their rights with a sheaf of new legal and technological controls. . . . If current trends continue unabated, we are likely to experience a violent collision between our expectations of freedom of expression and the enhanced copyright law.[8]

Litman believes that the information sector may expand into entirely new realms a copyright owner's ability to control his work. Authors now stand to gain total control over their works. And Congress's recent actions have been moving in that direction. The Sonny Bono Act wasn't the only major change in copyright law in 1998. The "persuasion" that Litman mentioned showed up in the Digital Millennium Copyright Act (DMCA); some of its more questionable provisions have already been used in ways that make many who dwell in the information sector more than a bit uncomfortable.

Take, for example, the surprising story of Dmitry Sklyarov, then a twenty-seven-year-old Russian programmer for ElcomSoft. In July 2001, Sklyarov traveled to Las Vegas to attend a conference. When he arrived, he was arrested and indicted on five counts, including criminal charges that carried a maximum penalty of twenty-five years in prison and $2.25 million in fines.[9] Under normal circumstances we might assume that he'd been smuggling drugs into the country and call it a day. But those weren't the charges. It seems that Sklyarov, on behalf of ElcomSoft, had written a program breaking the protections built into Adobe's Acrobat eBook reader. Now, we can debate whether or not he should have been allowed to develop such a program. We can debate whether or not the fine was reasonable, given his product's potential to harm Adobe's entire market. But when the U.S. government starts filing *criminal* charges for copyright infringement and threatens to throw people in jail for twenty-five years, I get squeamish. Suppose that you're a young programmer with an idea for a great software product that does a variety of things—including possibly cracking someone else's copy protection. Want to risk it? Maybe you'd prefer to hire a team of copyright and criminal lawyers to discuss the possible uses of your code and your likely legal liability. Or maybe you'd prefer to just forget the whole idea and keep working at the mall. Talk about chilling innovation!

Many technology users advocate outright rebellion. They seem to believe that if someone else's IP rights are in their way, they should be able to ignore them with impunity. This attitude leads to an anarchic disregard of property rights, which is unlikely to be very helpful in achieving the goals of IP policy: many innovators who don't get paid will eventually stop innovating. At the same time, some rights holders want to develop an authoritarian system to protect what they see as a natural right to IP—as opposed to a Congressionally authorized limited right. In their view, if repressive, regimented, social and economic regimes are necessary to protect IP rights, well then that's what we need. Some go further than that, contending that if the government can't protect their property for them, there's nothing wrong with a bit of vigilante justice.[10]

Anarchists, authoritarians, and vigilantes are all dangerous. If anyone of them gets control of our IP system, we'll all be in trouble—and you can bet that innovation would dwindle. Litman's concern that the authoritarians are gaining the upper hand may be right. But knowing that the legal authoritarians are losing the technology wars tempers my concern. Sure, monitoring, surveillance, and encryption software are all improving. But evasive technology is improving just as fast. This knowledge leaves me somewhat less concerned than Litman—though hardly unconcerned—about our prospects for becoming a fully authoritarian state. On the other hand, I'm more than a bit concerned that an incoherent combination of legal rules, economic incentives, and technological advances could bring the information sector's remarkable growth to a screeching halt.

IP rights have already played a central role in all of the information sector's key formative stories. An inappropriate allocation of incentives may have made Microsoft's anticompetitive behavior all but inevitable. The absence of comparable rights protecting most dot-coms doomed all but the best of them. The debate over the propriety of secret source code led to the open-source movement and to Linux. And Napster's introduction of peer-to-peer (P2P) file-sharing systems challenged our entire system of music copyrights.

Those stories may be just the beginning. The information sector reduces transaction costs by bringing producers and consumers closer together, which is good as long as you're a producer or a consumer. But people who make money as middlemen may prefer the status quo. They're likely to fight to keep their profits coming. And when their products are information, they're likely to find that IP law is both the battlefield and the weapon that they wield most often. Debates over IP—both law and policy—are likely to loom even larger in the information sector's future than they have in its past. We must understand what it is that we—as consumers represented by Congress—gave away to promote innovation, what we got in return, and whether or not we got a good deal. And remember: if we haven't, we've got the Constitution on our side.

As for Sklyarov, he was eventually released and allowed to return to Russia, on the condition that he agree to testify against ElcomSoft. He did, but the jury ruled in Elcomsoft's favor.[11] In the meantime, Adobe decided that having a programmer arrested on their behalf might not have been its best public relations move.

Back from the Abyss

Many contemporary IP scholars have come to lament Congress's granting progressively stronger IP protection to each new generation of innovators, and the feeling is hardly restricted to the legal world. Cultural historian Siva Vaidhyanathan, for example, has shown that modern copyright law has morphed into a highly restrictive set of property rights that hampers creativity and leads to a poverty of civic culture.[12] He raises a number of issues more common in the humanities than in law, such as the metaphysics of authorship and the expropriation of selected icons of the African-American oral tradition by (mostly white) Anglo-American performers and corporations.

Many of these critics' points are beyond dispute. Every revision of both the Copyright and the Patent Acts has strengthened the rights of the innovator. Congress has *never* surveyed the entire terrain and decided that it may have gone too far (although it has provided an occasional minor clarification). We have *never* seen either statute change because Congress decided that innovators were being overcompensated, that the overcompensation was deterring others from innovating, or that the public was paying too much for too little. And so, as the years go by and the statutes are updated, the rights grow stronger and stronger, the private rewards become bigger and bigger, and the public relinquishes more and more control over new, innovative ideas. None of these consequences serve the public interest.

Of course, none of these consequences *are intended to* serve the public interest. The point of IP law is to create *a deal* between the public and its innovators, to convince the public to accept restrictions on ideas already in circulation and to motivate innovators to put new ideas into circulation. IP scholars who focus on the increasing restrictions argue that the price is increasing. It is, but increasing prices aren't necessarily bad. The key is quality adjusted prices: Are we getting a better deal for our IP dollar despite the higher prices?

Vaidhyanathan's concerns about civic culture notwithstanding, it would be hard to argue that we don't have vibrant technology industries. Software and computers have redefined the ways we work, play, and communicate. More new music is being written, performed, and circulated today than ever before. The same is true of film, of theater, and even of literature. Newspapers and magazines cater to every possible taste and interest. Though our cultural elite may question the quality of much of this work, it does cater to popular tastes—not at all a bad way to reward "the public" for accepting higher prices. The bottom line is, we're paying more and getting more.

Are we getting a better deal, though? Napster, for one, pitted the rights of record companies (innovators holding copyrights poised to continue producing new music) against their artists' fans (members of the public wishing to disseminate music that had already been recorded). We do want the record companies to continue introducing, producing, and circulating new music, but we also want to be able to share the music that we enjoy without worrying about the nuances of IP law. These two undeniable "good things" may be in conflict. How do we resolve the conflict? We ask Congress to contemplate the IP clause and to craft an appropriate tradeoff. Or at least that's the theory.

Another example of our quandary arose from Microsoft's triple IP protection on Windows. The government went to great lengths to show how Microsoft abused that protection. Should we have never given Microsoft such strong protection? Maybe. Is the protection fine as a general matter, and the problem simply that as a monopolist Microsoft deserves heightened scrutiny in all of its dealings? Maybe. Should we take away that triple protection now, as a punishment for its abuse? Maybe. The Constitution gave Congress the primary role in answering these questions by inquiring whether the rights that we've offering innovators are promoting innovation. And if Congress is too busy, it could delegate part of the assessment to a regulatory agency, or even give the courts a bigger role in case-by-case consideration—much as it does antitrust. But it doesn't seem that anyone has ever even asked the question. In the words of respected copyright scholar Paul Goldstein.

Representatives and Senators may regularly invoke the principle that copyright owners bear the burden of persuading Congress of the need of bring new rights within the sweep of copyright, but Congress has never once required authors or publishers to demonstrate that, in fact, they need the new right as an incentive to produce literary and artistic works.[13]

Someone, somewhere, ought to be conducting the cost/benefit analysis to see how we're doing—and whether or not we could do better. Someone's not doing his job.

All of IP's critics appreciate the need for this analysis. The source of their frustration is that *no one* really looks at these questions. In fact, Litman contends that jockeying among special interest groups drove the entire history of copyright law. Congress hears many stories from industries pushing to change the IP laws. By and large, changes happen when the loudest industries—typically pushing for changes that would move the laws in different, and sometimes opposite, directions—hammer out a compromise. Congress frequently passes laws that quiet screaming interest groups—even if their effects on quieter interest groups is less than healthy. And therein lies the true source of the quandary: Congress has been conducting the wrong analyses, with unintended consequences that haven't served the public interest. Critics believe that Congress has abdicated its responsibility as protector of the public weal and become a shill for screaming interest groups.

That sort of lament may be fine for an IP scholar, but it can be a bit confusing in the real world. It's easy to say that Congress should conduct a different analysis. It's another to conclude that the world would be a better place if it reached a better balance between rights and freedom. And it's yet another to theorize what that better world might look like. So here's the challenge: How could we rejigger our IP rights to reduce public costs without reducing innovation? Stated another way, can we encourage all the same innovations—and maybe even more—while paying less for them?

Rise of the Reformers

Imagine an early information-sector entrepreneur who wrote some code and developed a product, then hired an attorney and asked him whether she should seek patent protection or copyright protection. After all, her product is a functional textual work. Since copyrights protect texts and patents protect functions, her lawyer likely would have been flummoxed. And he wouldn't have been alone.[14]

Back in the early days of computing, say the 1950s, the PTO refused to grant software patents while the Copyright Office copyrighted software. But it's not really their call. Congress took until 1980 to confirm that software was, in fact, copyrightable.[15] Then, in 1981 the Supreme Court found a software patent that it liked[16] but getting a software patent was still difficult. Software patents remained rare until the mid-1990s. In 1994, the Court of Appeals for the Federal Circuit, the appellate court uniquely charged with hearing all appeals in patent cases—and whose decisions about patent law only the Supreme Court can review—determined that the PTO had been too stingy in awarding software patents.[17] The trickle of software patents gave way to a stream. Four years later, the Federal Circuit opened the floodgates when it ruled that "business methods" applying algorithms to specific problems, in finance for example, also qualified for patent protection.[18]

The confusion about software IP rights continued, and confused states are inherently unstable. When Amazon.com managed to convince a District Court judge that it deserved the patent on one-click shopping,[19] the Federal Circuit recognized that protections may have gone too far. It overturned that ruling,[20] but not before Barnesandnoble.com had to change its shopping software in the middle of the 1999 holiday season. In the meantime, Amazon's one-click patent interfered with Internet retail development for fourteen critical months. The PTO reportedly began to reflect on whether its standards for business-method patents had become too permissive. The Supreme Court, the Federal Circuit, and Congress should all follow the PTO's lead.

The challenge of categorizing software thus posed some serious definitional problems that continue to cause controversy. But the underlying problem runs deeper than ambiguity at the edge of legal doctrine. Despite the availability of software patents, the combination of copyright and trade-secret law continues to protect most software. This protection has allowed software developers to exert their rights in new and disturbing ways.

Software just doesn't fit into any pre-existing IP category. Sure, it's somewhat like a book (in that it contains text that's pretty easy to copy), and it's somewhat like a machine (in that it does something), but it's also emphatically *not* like a book and *not* like a machine. If we offer copyright protection only when the source code is revealed, software developers will have no real protection and little incentive to create software. After all, copyrights protect expression, not ideas. Put another way, while a reinterpretation of a Harry Potter novel would probably bomb, Java code based on someone else's C code would probably run just fine. That renders the sort of protection that we normally offer to book authors worthless to software developers. But if we patent too many algorithms or business methods we risk shutting down the entire industry, and if we settle for the current combination of copyright and trade secret protection we're likely to be severely exploited in a marketplace laden with antitrust violations.

Patents and copyrights are what they are. No mechanism exists to allow a court to decide that the owners of a "software patent" possess a different sets of rights than the holders of a hypothetical alternative such as a "mechanical patent." They would both hold patents—and any new rules established to help software patents make more sense had better not cause confusion in any other industries. The same is true for copyrights. Of course, Congress could *create* a special category of IP rights for software, but convincing Congress to act is difficult and slow. Industry-specific categories of IP rights might be a logical step, but it would require a radical restructuring of our IP laws and could easily introduce its own set of problems.

A number of people have proposed more moderate reforms that might actually work without changing too many existing laws, which is good because unless and until we manage to convince Congress that our IP system is broken, a patent is a patent and a copyright is a copyright. And it's simply irrelevant that software is neither a book nor a machine.

But we pay our academics to shoot for the stars, and so their literature is replete with suggestions for software-specific IP rights (including my own humble contribution).[21] We owe perhaps the most significant of these contributions to a team of two IP scholars, Pam Samuelson and J. H. Reichman, and two technologists, Randy Davis and Mitch Kapor.

Their grandiose *Manifesto* roused the faithful of Columbia University's Law School at a 1994 symposium by "contribut[ing] a basic framework for constructing a new form of legal protection for program innovations."[22] The Manifesto tackled a critical issue that computer scientists had deferred to their social science colleagues: how to motivate and reward software developers.

The team began its work on the horns of a dilemma. Most programs don't meet the requirements for patents, so we need to give them copyrights. But copyrights don't protect ideas—such as the way that a computer program works—and programmers care about the ideas embodied in their code. So if we reward a programmer like we would any other author, we're not providing much motivation. But if we allow both copyright and trade-secret protection, then we're cutting ourselves out of the bargain—we're giving software developers legal protection without asking them to reveal anything.

The Manifesto proposed to parallel many of patent law's important motivators, but in ways and within a time frame appropriate for the information sector. It proposed requiring software developers to disclose their programs—including their source code—in exchange for short-term exclusive legal rights to their program's innovative behavior. So if, for example, you developed the first spreadsheet, the proposed IP rights would guarantee that you'd be the only spreadsheet vendor on the market—for a couple of years. By the time those rights expired, your source code and the idea it embodied would be in the public domain and you'd probably face competition.

In all honesty, disclosing source code makes enforcing any set of IP rights pretty difficult. But the challenge is not impossible to meet. For example, developers need not necessarily be forced to publish their source code immediately. We might be better off requiring developers to register their source code with the government in exchange for IP protection and deferring government publication for long enough to permit commercial development. But that's an implementation detail—critical no doubt, but tangential to the scheme's inner workings. The fundamental idea is to develop specialized software IP rights that mimic the patent system in many ways, but that differ from it in several others—notably the standards for granting protection and the timeframe of that protection. This radical proposal would command a great deal of Congressional attention, but it's certainly worth pondering.

Not all recommendations are quite that radical. The National Research Council favored a more tempered approach. Its 2000 study, *The Digital Dilemma*, concluded that although a clear need for new forms of IP protection exists, legislation would be premature.[23] The study recommended that Congress observe the various "experiments" already underway. It noted that various businesses were relying on combinations of contracts and technology to protect software, and that some judges were reinterpreting parts of IP law to make it relevant to the information sector. *The Digital Dilemma* was eminently moderate, despite the participation of some of the Manifesto's authors—and its approach is probably correct.

Even those of us who believe that our IP system will need a major overhaul someday soon, even those of us who believe that the current system hurts the information sector, even *we* don't necessarily believe that we know exactly what the best answers are today.[24] What's more, our certainty is irrelevant because until Congress is ready for an overhaul, our readiness, certainty, and necessity don't matter. So while IP theorists may be a bit radical, we're also realists in practice. And realism breeds moderation, which suggests looking at existing IP law to see which pieces of it may be useful with only a little bit of tweaking.

Julie Cohen and Mark Lemley, for example, argued that a large part of the problem with software patents today stems from the courts' reading them broadly.[25] In other words, if a new program looks like it *might* infringe an existing patent, the courts have been ruling in favor of the patent holder. That makes the patent pretty potent. Cohen and Lemley would curb that potency by ruling the other way. They would say that if a new program *might not* infringe, the courts should rule against the patent holder. In their view, proving infringement of a software patent should be difficult. That would leave a patent with a fair amount of value, though less than it has now. It would also free up large areas of innovation that developers wary of an existing patent's scope might otherwise avoid. Cohen and Lemley also made a few other suggestions about minor reinterpretations of existing laws that could help clear up difficult problems patent issues cause. They didn't address, however, the broader issue of patent/copyright/trade-secret protection; they said nothing about the challenge posed by software developers who misuse their triple protection to exploit consumers.

An existing bit of law might help address that, too. The Supreme Court realized that it was possible to "misuse" a patent as far back as 1917.[26] Imagine that way back then, you'd invented a wonderful "projector" that allowed people to show "moving pictures." You went to the PTO, filled out all the appropriate forms, published a description of your projector and how it worked, and received your patent. You're now the only one who can sell these projectors. That's the whole point of the patent; it motivated you to build the machine. You've got a nice little business going, but you decide to branch out. So you start making movies and try to sell them to your projector customers. But your projector customers prefer movies made by another studio. So you put a warning label on every projector you sell saying that showing anyone else's films violates the terms of sale. I buy your projector, ignore the warning, and show the hugely controversial but inevitably classic *The Birth of a Nation*.[27] You sue me for infringing your patent. Who wins?

According to the Supreme Court, I do. It seems that you took your perfectly legal patent right and tried to leverage it to take over an independent market that was supposed to have been competitive. You tried to exceed your patent rights, and in so doing, you misused them. What can the courts do about it? They can be pretty tough. They can refuse to enforce your patent until you can demonstrate that you've undone the damage and restored competition to the market for independent movies. You reduced the amount of competition to the detriment of movie consumers? Fix it. Once you can show that you've set the market back to where it should be, the courts will enforce your rights again. Until then, don't bother suing.

But that's *patent* law. Is there such a thing as "copyright misuse?" According to Brett Frischman and Dan Moylan, copyright misuse has existed for a long time, but no one talked about it much until fairly recently.[28] They explained that the courts couldn't foresee how anything protected by a copyright could give its owner the awesome power needed to misuse it—at least until we invented software. After all, if you take away my patented projector, I'd have to shut my theatre. But if you pull your copyrighted movie, I'd just run someone else's.

Software changed all that; it was both copyrighted and functional. Somewhere around 1990, the courts decided to start applying a doctrine of copyright misuse in the same way that they had long addressed patent misuse. The first few cases tread somewhat lightly and looked at narrow, specialized software for Computer-Aided Design and Computer-Aided Manufacturing (CAD/CAM), for medical practice management, and for technical equipment diagnosis and repair. The courts concluded that the companies that made the dominant software packages in each of these markets had tried to force their customers to either accept terms or to buy products that they didn't want. The courts ruled that these actions constituted copyright misuse and that they wouldn't enforce the copyrights until the misusers fixed the broken markets.[29]

While most IP scholars, and every court that's considered the issue, believe that copyright misuse is both important and real, we still haven't heard from the Supreme Court—who has final say on the matter. However, assuming that the Supreme Court notices that copyright misuse is a useful doctrine needed to cleanup potential problems, the voices of moderation appear to be correct. While after-the-fact tweaking and cleanup are hardly a substitute for aligning IP rights with technological and economic imperatives, they're not bad in the short run.

But maybe we could do better still—again without requiring Congressional action. An entire community of software developers actually *refuses* to maintain its source code as a trade secret; its members publish their source code where all can see it. Most people never notice this "open" source code, because most users just want software that works. But programmers and software developers can inspect this source code, extend it, modify it, and use it as a model for future software development. Open source developers, like proprietary software companies, circulate their software subject to licenses outlining conditions to which the "buyer" must agree. For most users, these terms are quite liberal. Not only is the software free, but you can do virtually anything you want with it as long as you don't distribute it. If you do distribute software, though, you'd better pay attention to the license's specifics. Some open-source licenses, notably the General Public License (GPL),[30] try to enforce the community ethos through a clever "copyleft" clause. Developers who incorporate *any* GPL-licensed code into their own software *must* release their new products under the GPL. Anything else would violate the terms of their license. But even the GPL isn't all that fierce. It reinforces an unusual business model, but it tends to be much less restrictive than most software licenses. And many other open-source licenses are less restrictive than the GPL; they even allow developers to incorporate open source code into their own products with secret source code.[31]

Fierce or not, copyleft represents a truly clever reassertion of the Constitutional bargain. Copyleft keeps knowledge in the public domain using only existing IP laws—a moderate approach that's somehow more radical than what the radicals propose. At least, so things appear; no one has yet tested copyleft in court. And though copylefting resolves the problem of dual copyright and trade secret, what of patents? Even if I had access to patented source code, I couldn't do anything with it. I couldn't use it without permission, I couldn't customize it, and I certainly couldn't sell my own interpretation of it. Software patents are powerful—and increasingly common. By some counts, the PTO has awarded hundreds of thousands of them over the past decade. How does the PTO know which ones to grant? The sad truth is, it doesn't. Patent examiners have a hard time determining which applications truly represent novel advances to the state of the art—the basic requirement for patent protection. And to make matters worse, the PTO isn't hiring enough computer scientists, mathematicians, or statisticians to allow them to make better decisions; applications to join the Patent Bar favor traditional scientific or engineering training.[32] The preponderance of improvidently awarded software patents alone could do more than simply complicate the free circulation of open source code; it could stunt the information sector's overall growth.

But that problem has yet to materialize fully—and perhaps, if we're lucky, it never will. In the meantime, we can add copyleft to a radical manifesto, a number of moderate modifications to current law, and the moderate application of misuse remedies as after-the-fact fixes. Our IP priests have thus met half of the challenge set for them by suggesting ways to cut public IP costs. Their proposals' likely impact on software quality will be addressed in a later discussion of the information sector's future in chapter 8.

Cry, the Beloved Clause

If you're an economist, you have to love the IP clause. After all, how many clauses in the Constitution set up an explicit economic analysis? Very few. But there's pretty widespread agreement that the IP clause is broken. IP analysts may disagree about whether the systems are too permissive or too restrictive, but if they agree about anything it's that we've got a problem (or at a bare minimum, that we're about to develop one).

The interplay of the technology, the law, and the economics of the information sector poses many potential challenges. Lessig's, Litman's, and even Vaidhyanathan's concerns went far beyond my own narrow focus on the market. Their worries go to the heart of civil society—to our ability to communicate freely. Others have voiced even broader concerns. Cass Sunstein worries that the Internet's customization will fragment society.[33] He sees us becoming a world of narrow people and groups, feeding only on the ideas and opinions to which we already subscribe, and filtering out all that could make us rethink our positions or consider alternative viewpoints. The Internet allows each of us to design customized media channels. Sunstein fears that once we successfully block all that we find offensive or irrelevant, we'll become islands unto ourselves. Can communities arise in such a world? Will democracy have any meaning? Will we continue to view tolerance as a virtue? Julie Cohen has asked if we'll still be able to read anonymously—and if not, what that may mean for the future of intellectual curiosity and development.[34]

These compelling questions point to a potential dark side of the information age. They raise the specter of reduced privacy, democracy, intellectual development, and free communication. The potential restriction of our Constitutional right to privacy[35] is certainly more frightening—and more fundamental to our identity as a free people—than are Congressional missteps on IP policy that hinder innovation. But those are topics for a different book, and essentially tangential to the role that IP law will play in shaping the future of the information sector. And what I see there is less than inspiring.

We're giving away a very powerful combination of rights that enables antisocial and anticompetitive behavior—largely by software developers misusing the rights we've given them. While it's certainly possible to simply grant the rights, to assume that innovators will wield their rights responsibly, and to clean up inappropriate uses with industrial-strength antitrust laws and misuse remedies, that sort of approach is exceedingly dangerous. An IP system that conferred appropriate rights and that minimized the rights-holders' ability to abuse them would serve us better. But the potential hazards of the *wrong* reform are equally obvious: they could destroy the current strengths of a thriving information sector while offering little of value in return. We need "moderate and cautious, but potentially radical" reform—a pretty tough challenge.

In thinking through such reforms, *The Digital Dilemma* is right. If we're going to consider reform proposals, we must project the full range of each proposal's costs and benefits. Our analysis must recognize that the costs inherent in an IP regime aren't restricted to the balance between risks and rewards that they offer innovators, or even to the societal costs and benefits of progress. They also include both the transaction costs inherent in running a policy regime and the potentially large one-time transition costs inherent in regime change. These transaction and transition costs can be significant, and they are relevant to the ultimate attractiveness of a proposed reform. They're distinct, however, from a consideration of the merits of a proposed regime change. Even if we can figure out how to fix things—and prove that our fix is really an improvement—we still may lose the argument if the method of getting from here to there is too difficult or too costly. Political economy analysis played a central role in shaping Litman's pessimismm, and it's precisely what makes the situation look so dark.

But darkness need not exist forever. We have some good legal doctrines to help us clean up our worst messes. Justice Ginsburg may (or may not) have put innovators on notice that their rights could weaken overnight, and we may find additional ways help ourselves along. The extent to which self-help is possible depends on how Congress allocates, and the courts interpret, the property rights underlying information products. For while technology will always delineate our opportunities, and while economic incentives will always dictate which we choose, our legal system will play a critical role in allocating the costs and the benefits of each alternative. The IP system's assignment of property rights will be at the center of the information sector's legal maelstrom. When we leave the confines of academic discourse to enter the real world, we'll see those legal issues arise in many contexts and in many ways. We'll revisit the Manifesto and copyright misuse when we contemplate Microsoft, open source when we meet Linux, and transaction costs and the very nature of IP rights when we consider Napster. The true battle lines over the information sector's future are just forming, as technology reduces transaction costs and traditional distributors fight—frequently using the weapons of IP and of public policy—to reintroduce them.

Soon IP rights will permeate everything that we say about the information sector, for information never truly can be owned. Information-sector businesses must all manipulate a legally constructed notion of ideas as property. And that, in turn, implies that every question that we ask about the way that things *are* will touch upon IP law, and every question we ask about the way that things *should be* will touch upon IP policy. We will only reach the information sector we seek—the one consistent with the Constitutional prescription of IP policy, the one that appropriately aligns the concerns of technology, economics, and law—if we consider the ways these factors interact in the real worlds of software development and investment in innovation.

3

Competition and Its Discontents

Capitalism Stripped Bare

Competition is the central pillar supporting modern American industrial policy. Consumers love having multiple suppliers compete for their business. But investors would rather own shares of monopoly suppliers who exploit their customers. Since most of us are both consumers and investors, we get tugged in both directions; we adore the hardworking competitors with whom we trade and the profitable exploiters in our portfolios. So it's not so strange that sometimes we get confused.

Industrial organization and antitrust, the economic and legal studies of competition, the discontents who attempt to destroy it, and the regulation that prevents its destruction, can guide us through our confusing loyalties. IO studies the ways that industries are organized—how large the firms are, how many of them compete (or how *concentrated* the industry is), and the impact that size and concentration have on competition, prices, innovation, and consumers. These economic studies suggest that only some industries are highly competitive. In others, a small number of firms are disproportionately powerful. That's where antitrust law comes in. Many branches of the law protect the small and weak from the large and powerful. Antitrust law fits neatly into that category. Over the years, IO economists have theorized and observed that some market structures provide dominant producers with enough power to exploit their many small customers. Antitrust law protects those consumers. Antitrust litigators, regulators, and enforcers police the free market system. They identify potentially dangerous concentrations of power, monitor the ways in which this power is used, terminate illicit exertions of power, and punish those who would callously exploit the consuming public.

The consuming public isn't always grateful. We'd prefer for the market cops to enforce the antitrust laws vigorously only against companies whose products we buy, but to ease up on the companies in our investment portfolios. The government, for example, sought to discipline Microsoft in the name of consumers of personal computers and software. Microsoft's shareholders, many of whom were also consumers of personal computers and software, were less than thrilled. These same investors, however, also discovered a new uncharted investment arena called cyberspace, found parallels to Microsoft in each of its spaces, and ran out to invest in the Internet's inevitable monopolists. The *consuming public* thereby abdicated its consumption role to recast itself as the *investing public*. This masquerade worked for a while and created enormous paper wealth; we valued small, weak companies as if they were huge, powerful, inevitable monopolists. But before long, most of us remembered that we actually consume more than we invest, and decided to treat all Internet companies outside our portfolios as if they were small and weak. Not surprisingly, that was the beginning of the end. It left us with regrets, remorse, and deflated portfolios. But more than that, it left us confused. And it's that confusion that IO and antitrust can address.

The story of the information sector is a story of capitalism, and competition is the cornerstone of capitalist systems. In the information sector, we're all hard-core capitalists—innovative, productive, and above all competitive. The information sector is capitalism stripped bare, capitalism in a pure, raw, uncut, unadulterated form. Or at least, it would be if not for some powerful discontents.

Capitalism's striptease for the information sector bares some of its most basic rules. First, profit is a powerful motivator. Second, buyers like to pay low prices for quality goods. They're happiest when many sellers offer high quality goods at low prices, each hoping to make the sale. This *competitive* state of the world maximizes consumer welfare—it's the best of all possible worlds for consumers. Third, sellers like to charge high prices for low-quality goods. They're happiest when they can destroy their competitors, dominate their industries, and force consumers to overpay for substandard goods. While consumers describe such overcharges with a more colorful term, IO calls this *rent extraction*. Antitrust economists and lawyers scrutinize such uncompetitive behavior very closely. Fourth, in most cases middlemen are between buyers and sellers, adding both costs and values to the transactions. Technology often allows producers and consumers to eliminate these middlemen; middlemen tend to fight against these advances. Fifth, and most remarkably, transactions close at the "right" price and resources flow to where they can be used most efficiently—as long as markets stay competitive.

So how realistic is it for markets to be "competitive," in the sense needed to keep prices right and resource allocation appropriate? The two places that come closest to the competitive ideal may be freshman economics texts and the information sector. Elementary textbooks generally assume markets where many small buyers face off against many small sellers. Individual buyers and sellers are all helpless in their desires to shape the market. Prices fall where they *should* fall, and any deviations caused by odd buyer or seller behavior are ephemeral. Prices always return to where they should be.

Suppose that you're a producer out to sell your goods at the highest price possible (that's the profit motive in action). You look at your production costs, multiply them by ten, and launch your product. Not bad, you think. All I need to do is sell it, and I've cleared a 900% profit. Your competitor gets the same idea, but since he'd be willing to settle for an 800% profit, your customers all run to him. You counter by reducing your price below his, he counters back, and so on and so forth until you've dropped your price to a penny above your costs. Your competitor drops his price to equal production costs. Checkmate. The best that you can do is match him. If you try going lower, you'll lose money on every sale. Prices simply can't drop any lower—unless and until someone discovers a more efficient method of production.

Now let's add a twist. Suppose that producers need to buy an expensive machine to enter the business, but that once they've got the machine, they can crank out finished products from inexpensive inputs. Now where should the price fall? Well, since the producer had to lay out the "fixed" cost of the machine just to get into the game, it's mostly irrelevant to his thinking going forward—though he would like to be able to recoup his initial expense at some point. This need to recoup total costs differentiates the producer's long-run thinking from his short-run calculations. So let's think about the short run first and worry about the long run later.

In the short run, the "variable" input costs needed to produce each additional unit at the margin dominate the producer's forward thinking—leading to a model known as "marginal cost pricing." Any finished unit that the producer can sell above his marginal input costs represents a profit on that unit. In many industries, marginal costs differ with the size of the production run. But there are exceptions. The cost of filling an additional seat on an airliner about to take off, or an additional container on a cargo ship set to sail, is close to zero—as long as there are vacancies on the plane or ship. Information products thus follow a pattern more common in transportation than in manufacturing. It's quite expensive to generate the first copy of a program, but every copy thereafter is virtually cost-free. And unlike planes or ships, information products face no capacity constraint; it's meaningless for them to be "full." This observation actually leads to the special-case model of freshman textbooks—the constant variable cost model. For large numbers of information-sector producers, marginal costs equal average variable costs. Under any case of the marginal-cost pricing model, though, market dynamics set prices. Competition pushes prices down toward marginal cost, and the profit motive keeps prices from falling below marginal cost. These considerations dictate that a product's price should equal its marginal cost of production—at least as a theoretical matter in a perfectly competitive market and until we start thinking about the long run.

From the other side, buyers determine sales volumes. Think about lining up buyers in order of their enthusiasm. The most eager buyers are willing to pay the most for the product; the least eager are willing to pay the least. The seller, of course, doesn't known which buyers are most eager, and therefore fixes a single price for all potential buyers. And since the seller wants to produce one unit for each buyer willing to cover his input costs on that marginal unit, everything just falls into place. The price will drop to the marginal cost of production, and every buyer willing to pay that price will be satisfied.

Let's take a concrete example. A good software-development team requires at least a bit of equipment and many smart people who could be earning good money elsewhere. Other information products, such as digitized songs or movies, can be even more expensive to produce. The fixed costs of these products are large, but the creation of a second copy of a bit string is close to free. Information-sector products thus tend to have high fixed costs and zero marginal costs. And therein lies the first key to the economics of the information sector: digital products should all be free.

Now, *that* prediction can't survive for long, but the simplified textbook model has more to add before either the real world or the long run impose a touch of realism on its less-plausible predictions. Even theoretical prices don't quite fall to the producer's marginal costs. While buyers (or consumers) and sellers (or producers) are always essential, they typically need help transacting their business. Sometimes, for example, the buyer calls the seller to place her order, and the seller ships the product ordered. In that case, a phone company and a trucking company entered the fray, and both deserve to be compensated. Where will the money come from? Since competition already drove the producer's price to its bare minimum, the consumer must foot the bill. In other words, the consumer's price just rose above the producer's marginal cost. But the least willing consumers—those who were willing to pay only the producer's marginal cost of production—would prefer to let the deal fall through than to absorb this extra cost. In the presence of such transaction costs, consumers lose because prices rise and producers lose because sales volumes decline.

The myriad transaction costs prevent our real world from achieving the competitive ideal. Phone bills and shipping costs are but two of the more obvious. Many transaction costs stem from the difficulty of collecting information. Producers may not know exactly what features consumers want. Consumers may not know which vendor is offering the best price. The necessary information costs can make transactions much more expensive. But these costs all drop—dramatically—in the information sector. And therein lies the second key: the information sector reduces transaction costs.

Ronald Coase won the 1991 Nobel Prize in Economics for pushing transaction costs onto economists' radars. His famous Coase theorem suggests that in the absence of transaction costs, all resources would flow to where the overall economy achieved maximum efficiency.[1] So any reductions in transaction costs should be great for the economy and should make everyone happy. But then again, *nothing* ever makes *everyone* happy. While eliminating transaction costs would certainly help producers and consumers, the phone company and the trucking company would be less than thrilled. After all, they provide important services, they employ a fair number of people, and they *live* for transaction costs. Reduced transaction costs reduce their revenues. And therein lies our third key: middlemen will fight against information technology to reimpose transaction costs.

But let's not get too upset at these callous middlemen. After all, many of them exist for valid reasons, provide valuable services, and are pillars of our economy. Many of them are even pillars of the information sector. Because a basic problem lingers in the world beyond the textbook—the theoretical prediction of free digital goods. If charging for information products is impossible, information producers must find a new way to recoup their investment in product development. Somewhere along the line, producers *must* recoup their fixed costs. Otherwise, no one would ever invest, and we'd never get any good information products. That's where we bring producers' long-run thinking back into the equation. Transaction costs provide a way out of the dilemma. We've used the law to impose an artificial transaction cost known as an IP right. We gave information producers the right to sue anyone who uses their creations without permission. That legally imposed transaction cost means that everyone but the innovator must face an additional cost: either a license or a potential lawsuit. IP rights thus give innovators a distinct cost advantage over their rivals, and they make it impossible for competitors to bid the innovator's prices down to *the innovator's* marginal costs. They thus allow at least some information producers to keep their prices above their marginal costs—and suggest that information products need not be free, after all. Legally induced transaction costs, in the form of IP licenses, may enable the entire information sector.

But we passed these laws long ago, back when copying and circulating information products was still expensive. Technology protected information producers from most people, and the law protected them from a few rich competitors. The information sector devastated their technological protection. While large corporations can still sue each other, they hate hailing small buyers into court; it's rarely worth the trouble, and it makes them look bad (though they'll do it when backed into a corner). And that's precisely how the information sector strips capitalism bare. It creates a world of information products that come as close to the textbook model as anything that we've ever seen. The information sector points toward a world without transaction costs, where prices *should* fall at the marginal cost of production, and where that marginal cost of production is zero. It also points us toward a world in which the producers whose business models make sense only because the law protected their IP rights are likely to become increasingly unhappy with technological progress.

The Market Cops

Transaction costs are only one reason that real prices typically remain above the marginal cost of production. The rarity of perfect competition also plays a role. In many industries, a small number of sellers exhibit a fair degree of power in setting prices. IO also studies these industries, and these are precisely the industries that interest antitrust.

Oligopolies are markets dominated by a small number of large sellers. Oligopolists generally know a great deal about their competitors' identities and behavior. Because they can observe each other's production, prices, marketing, etc., they also can send each other subtle (or at times, not so subtle) signals. An oligopolist, for example, might try to raise his prices. His competitors can either match the increase so that everyone earns a higher profit on each item sold, or keep their prices low and steal his customers. But they know that if they take the second route, he'll cut his price and win back his customers. So they decide—quite rationally— to match the price increase. If the market had many vendors, someone would *eventually* bid the price back down toward marginal costs, but in an oligopoly market, prices can stabilize above costs; oligopolists can thus extract "rents" above competitive profit levels from their many small customers.

Contemporary IO models the interactions among oligopolists as games. Game theorists recognize that when the same players repeatedly show up to play the same games, they learn something about each other and about the game. The players learn how to signal each other—and how to interpret the signals that they receive. Such signals often convince oligopolists to "meet" a price increase "suggested" by a competitor. Two different names describe this behavior: *conscious parallelism* (a neutral-sounding term) and *tacit collusion* (which definitely sounds negative). By either name, it's a legal way for an oligopolist to increase her profits at the expense of her customers.[2]

But oligopolists are hardly in the best possible position to exploit their customers fully, because truly disgusted customers always have other choices. Maximum exploitative power requires the elimination of all possible alternatives. *Monopolies* are markets with only a single seller. All that a monopolist has to do to extract rents is raise prices. No signal, no response, no delay, no risk. After all, the customers rave nowhere else to go. Their only other choice is to "do without" and exit the market. From the monopolist's perspective, the downside of high prices is that every price increase chases away some consumers and reduces sales volumes. At some point, the volume reductions will be great enough to make the price increase unprofitable; the monopolist is then better off making a smaller per-sale profit on a larger sales volume.

Monopolists also worry about the threat just over the horizon. Markets populated by disgruntled consumers paying exorbitant prices for shoddy products in order to generate consistent obscene profits for an unpopular incumbent monopolist must look attractive to *someone*. Eventually someone would see this market as an opportunity. This threat is often enough to convince the incumbent monopolist to temper its behavior—if for no reason other than to avoid "inviting entry" of a new competitor.

Most people other than devout antitrust priests find it hard to swallow that this crass exploitation of the consuming public by an incumbent monopolist *is perfectly legal*.[3] Monopolists who defeat their competitors using nothing more than a legal combination of product quality, savvy marketing, and dumb luck can then turn around and extract whatever rents consumers are willing to pay.

Fortunately, most markets aren't prone to monopolization. IO studies the relationship between a market's basic characteristics and the structure that emerges as it matures. Only markets exhibiting certain characteristics are likely to become highly concentrated. By and large, it's only possible to *become* a monopolist in markets with reasonably high *barriers to entry*, costs that a company must bear to enter a new market that incumbent producers need not bear.[4] Sometimes entry is as easy as posting a sign announcing that you're open for business. A monopolist that dominates such a market won't be able to exploit too many consumers without attracting entry. In most markets, though, entry is a bit more expensive than that. New entrants may need to invest in capital equipment, to develop sophisticated products, or to seek regulatory clearance. Investments of this sort are often *sunk*; a failed entry attempt leads to a permanent loss. Entrants also may have to project a significant sales volume to recoup those sunk costs; failure to reach projections also leads to a loss. This combination of high fixed start-up costs (the investments needed to go into business) and a high minimum viable scale (the smallest amount of business needed to turn a profit) is often enough to deter would-be entrants and to maintain a durable monopoly. In such markets, monopolists can raise prices significantly without inviting entrants to risk sinking costs.

New entrants also may have to sink costs to attract customers. In many settings, consumers have sunk their own costs buying their existing equipment and learning how to use it. An entrant who expects to induce consumers to switch to his new product will have to compensate them somehow. Such "switching costs" also form a barrier to entry that can help maintain a durable monopoly. Once again, it's perfectly legal for a monopolist who finds herself protected by such barriers to exploit consumers—as long as the barriers are "natural" artifacts of the market, and not artificial constructs that the monopolist devised to protect her own profits. And therein lies the fourth key: monopoly rents can only be as high as the barriers to entry.

This spectrum of market structures, from perfect competition through concentrated oligopoly to unitary monopoly, frames the IO view of the world. Players in these different types of markets interact in different ways. All of the interactions discussed so far are legal—even if some are unpalatable. But oligopolists have opportunities that competitive firms lack, and monopolists possess even broader opportunities than that.

Sometimes their behavior crosses the line from smart-and-legal into illicit cheating—say, by creating artificial barriers to entry to inflate their rents. Such behavior disrupts the natural flow of the market. Only legal intervention can correct it.

Such necessary intervention is squarely in the realm of antitrust law. Modern antitrust adheres to the *consumer welfare standard* captured by a somewhat idealized market dynamic: Because monopolists earn the largest possible profits, every seller in every market would like to become a monopolist. The profit motive tells us that. But a competitor only can become a monopolist by winning customers away from its competitors— and the only way to do that is to offer the best, least expensive, most desirable products on the market. Thus, the greater the competition, the greater the race to improve the product. Such races serve the best interests of consumers and reward the most efficient producers.

These races also highlight the futility of trying to cheat in a competitive market. A seller who offers an unattractive combination of price and quality will lose potential customers to a competitor striving to become dominant. Markets of this sort are essentially self-policing. Market forces push producers toward both greater efficiency (i.e., cost reductions), and appropriate pricing. As a result, antitrust law isn't much concerned with behavior in competitive markets. Attempts to cheat tend to be suicidal. The winners in a competitive market are the producers whose products best reflect a fair combination of price and quality.

As these efficient producers grow, inefficient competitors shrink and eventually disappear; in some industries, the market may dwindle to few enough players to qualify as an oligopoly. Prices in an oligopoly market, as noted above, tend to be higher than they would be in a competitive market, thanks to signaling. But some oligopolists might notice that signaling is awkward and inexact. They may come up with a better way to raise prices. Why not just collude? Why not, to put the matter bluntly, work together as a CARTEL!

The truth is, there's no internal reason not to take this approach. At least, the basic rules of capitalism suggest that this approach is highly rational; it allows sellers to reduce product quality, increase price, and follow the dictates of their internalized profit motives. Cartelization is *great* for cartel members. Only consumers lose. Left to the brutal nature of the marketplace, consumers would have no protection from cartels—other than to rely on human nature and to wait for the cartel members to begin cheating on each other. This sort of internal dissent happens all the time in cartels. OPEC and the world oil market provide a high-profile case in point. OPEC members periodically get their act together and drive up oil prices. Eventually they all start to cheat, and prices fall. Cartel theorists recognize that this sort of behavior is endemic, and that relatively few oligopolies really lend themselves to stable cartels. But cartels need not be long-lived to be destructive; OPEC's 1973 embargo sent the global economy into a tailspin in less than a year.

So consumers need more than the basic rules of economics to protect them from rational oligopolists. At times, they also need the market cops, who have two big guns—the Sherman Act and the Clayton Act—and a couple of smaller, less important ones. The market cops watch for four types of particularly suspicious behavior: oligopolists behaving as if they were a cartel, oligopolists trying to merge to become something closer to a monopoly, monopolists trying to leverage their monopolies into competitive parts of the market, and monopolists constructing artificial barriers to protect their monopoly positions. They also police a number of other attempts to interfere with the smooth functioning of competitive markets, but those four are by and large the most important.

Our market cops thus restrict most of their antitrust inquiries to oligopoly and monopoly markets, and they generally scrutinize the behavior of monopolists more closely than that of oligopolists. After all, whatever incentive an oligopolist might have to collude with competitors, form a cartel, and exploit consumers, the monopolist has in spades. And because the monopolist doesn't need to coordinate her behavior with her competitors, monopolies are much more stable. In fact, without the market cops looking over the monopolist's shoulder, she has few limits on her power—particularly if she monopolizes a product that consumers consider to be essential and that's protected by high barriers to entry.

In its few short years of existence, the information sector has demanded a fairly active police presence—largely, though not exclusively, concerning the behavior of an unruly young monopolist accused *both* of leveraging its platform software monopoly into previously competitive markets and of constructing barriers to prevent the introduction of competing platforms. But before examining Microsoft, we should think about monopolies in general. Antitrust law recognizes that even a legal metamorphosis from competitor to monopolist changes incentives and behavior. A monopolist has two basic goals—neither of which is to provide top-flight product value. First, a monopolist must make sure that consumers continue to want its products. Second, a monopolist must make sure that no new competition emerges to challenge its monopoly. One approach might be to continue to release better, cheaper versions of the monopolized product. But that approach is both difficult and risky; it requires investing in research and development that might fail. A variety of other approaches are also possible—few of which actually benefit consumers. Monopolists could attempt to sign large numbers of exclusive contracts, threaten distributors who carry a new entrant's competing products, introduce secret product features that make their monopoly products incompatible with competitors' products, bundle monopoly products with new innovations that had previously been sold in competitive markets, etc. In other words, monopolists have an incentive to create artificial barriers to entry that protect their profit streams.

These barrier-creating techniques raise some of the toughest issues in antitrust analysis. After all, there's nothing inherently wrong with exclusive contracts (the only thing that makes franchising possible) and integrated products (an important way to design and deliver product improvements). As a result, market cops must be trained to differentiate between good and bad uses of select business practices.

Antitrust is thus a highly context-specific body of law. A few activities are always prohibited, known as the *"per se* offenses." Everything else is evaluated on a case-by-case basis, or "subject to the rule of reason." Most antitrust analyses begin by identifying market structure. If the market is competitive, self-policing market forces provide all the discipline that we need. In oligopoly markets, the matter is less clear. Oligopolists receive greater scrutiny than do out-and-out competitors because it's *possible though difficult* for them to cheat. Monopolized markets are rarely self-correcting; cheating is often not only *possible*, but also *easy*, which is why market cops spend so much time scrutinizing monopolists' behavior. While the status of *being* a monopolist is hardly

illegal—and may prove a history of superior product development—
monopolists have both the ability and the incentive to cheat the market
and to exploit consumers. The only way to balance these incentives is
through the law. And therein lies the fifth key: the more concentrated
the market, the more important it is to maintain an active police
presence.

We've now collected five keys to information economics: digital products should all be free; the information sector reduces transaction costs;
middlemen will fight against information technology to reimpose transaction costs; monopoly rents can only be as high as the barriers to entry;
and the more concentrated the market, the more important it is to maintain an active police presence. These keys, while general and applicable
to all of the economy's sectors, are particularly important when unlock-
ing the mysteries of network economics.

The Luck of the Irish

I don't remember when I first encountered network economics, but I do
remember when I first noticed that it had entered the interest of a broad
public. M. Mitchell Waldrop's *Complexity: The Emerging Science at the
Edge of Order and Chaos* became a bestseller in 1993.[5] Waldrop opened
with the story of Brian Arthur, Catholic son of Belfast, sitting alone and
dejected in a strange Silicon Valley bar on St. Patrick's Day 1987. But
Arthur was not just any son of Eire; he was a chaired Professor of
Economics at Stanford bemoaning the poor reception that his ideas
had received from his colleagues at Berkeley. Those ideas laid the groundwork for a New Economics based on *increasing returns*, one of the
central concepts of network economics.

Waldrop was hardly the first one to bring these ideas beyond the
temple walls; Arthur had done that himself a few years earlier in the
pages of *Scientific American*.[6] Arthur explained that "classic" economics derived from the insights of late nineteenth century thinkers. At that
time, agriculture, mining, and basic manufacturing dominated the world
economy, and the most advanced areas of scientific inquiry still lay primarily in Newtonian mechanics. Classical economics tend to reflect those
sources, by considering, for example:

the competition between water power and coal to drive electrical generators. As hydroelectric plants take more of the market, engineers must exploit more costly dam sites, thus increasing the chance that a coal-fired plant will be cheaper. As coal plants take more of the market they bid up the price of coal . . . thus tipping the balance toward hydro. The two end up sharing the market in a predictable proportion that best exploits the potentials of each.[7]

In other words, if coal is expensive I'll build a hydro plant, and if hydro is expensive I'll go for coal. Classical economics predicts that our energy supply should include some of each—and empirical experience bears that out.

Stated more generally, the classical paradigm predicts that if two technologies perform the same basic task, and if each one appears to be superior under some but not all sets of circumstances, different people will make different choices and both technologies should survive. Real world experience with real world technologies and products validates that prediction. In my own home, I operate at least three lightbulb technologies (incandescent, fluorescent, and compact fluorescent), two telephone technologies (fixed and mobile), two shaving technologies (manual and electric), and three coffee-making technologies (drip, percolation, and French press).

But I also remember when I owned a Mac running Mac OS, a PC-clone running DOS, and a Sun workstation running Unix—and when my local video rental store stocked both VHS and Beta videocassettes. The classical predictions didn't seem to work there. That bothered a small group of economists to which Arthur belonged. They noticed that some products, particularly though not exclusively new technology products, seemed to behave differently. In these settings, two roughly comparable products that perform more-or-less the same task, introduced around the same time, appeared to gain adherents in roughly equal numbers. But after a relatively brief introductory period, one emerged as the clear market leader. And then, suddenly and without any apparent explanation, the other dwindled to a niche market—or disappeared altogether. The rivalry between VHS and Beta illustrated the point nicely, and conventional wisdom concerning Beta's technical superiority drove it home even further. If conventional wisdom were true, the market got it wrong! It tipped the wrong way, and locked consumers into the weaker

VHS technology. And therein lies a problem, because capitalism's basic rules taught us that *markets don't get things wrong*!

But neither Arthur nor those economists who shared his concerns were heretics. They weren't interested in squelching economic research, but rather in expanding its horizons. They sought both additional examples and an explanatory theory. Arthur glommed onto the example of clocks running "clockwise" almost by accident. While "everyone knows" that clocks are numbered with the 12 at the top, the 1 to its right, and numbers falling sequentially to the right, there's no clear reason why they shouldn't be numbered sequentially to the left (or even, for that matter, with the 12 on the bottom). In response to a question after one of his lectures, Arthur casually predicted that other conventions should have existed at some point—and shortly thereafter, a listener sent him a photo of a clock numbered "counterclockwise."[8]

Perhaps an even simpler example comes in written languages. There's no particular reason that my cursor traverses the screen from left to right. Ancient inscriptions didn't necessarily adhere to *any* convention; Biblical era tombstones and coins arranged letters to form aesthetically pleasing shapes. Eventually, the Canaanites, the Judeans, the Israelites, the Arameans, and the Arabs all decided to orient their writing from right to left. The Greeks made the equally arbitrary decision to proceed from left to right. The Romans followed the Greeks's lead with Latin, and we pretty much picked it up from there—hence my cursor. But historical precedent doesn't make a decision any less arbitrary—or even irreversible. When Mustafa Kemal Ataturk founded modern Turkey, he switched written Turkish from the Arabic to the Latin alphabet—thereby reorienting the language. Ataturk thus chose a standard, imposed it on his people, and quickly drove out the old standard.

The most widely discussed example of this phenomenon, though, occurred with an important nineteenth century innovation: the typewriter. Our current QWERTY keyboard, named for the first six letters in the top row (counting arbitrarily from left to right) is hardly the most obvious organization of the alphabet. In fact, during the first few decades of typewriters, QWERTY competed with other keyboard designs. How did it win? According to Waldrop:

An engineer named Christopher Scholes designed the QWERTY layout in 1873 specifically to slow typists down; the typewriting machines of the day tended to jam if the typist went too fast. But then the Remington Sewing Machine Company mass-produced a typewriter using the QWERTY keyboard, which meant that lots of typists began to learn the system, which meant that other typewriter companies began to offer the QWERTY keyboard, which meant that still more typists began to learn it, et cetera, et cetera. . . . And now that QWERTY is a standard used by millions of people, it's essentially locked in forever.[9]

The pattern holds time after time after time. A vendor in a competitive market introduces a new product. Through some combination of product quality, outside events, and luck, the right decision-maker adopts it at the right time. Suddenly, it becomes the "must adopt" product, the *de facto* standard, and frequently the only player left in the game. Sometimes this victory occurs because the product is clearly superior to all of its competitors. Frequently its superiority (or lack thereof) is irrelevant. The market tips and the victor emerges.

Arthur proposed an explanation of such "increasing returns." In an increasing returns world, the strong get stronger, the weak get weaker, and markets tip to a standard. This phenomenon arises infrequently— that is, it doesn't explain most markets—but often enough to be of broad general interest. Of even greater interest, though, is *where* it tends to occur when it does occur. Arthur's increasing returns tend to cluster in cutting-edge technologies, and in particular in knowledge-based industries. They're thus critical to the information sector.

Of course, referring to the idea as "Arthur's increasing returns" represents a severe injustice to the many other economists who explored the same ideas at the same time. Arthur himself noted that:

In the last few years I *and other economic theorists* at Stanford, the Santa Fe Institute, *and elsewhere* have been developing a view of the economy based on positive feedbacks. Increasing-return economics has roots in economic thinking that go back for seventy or more years, but its application to the economy as a whole is largely new.[10]

He even credited Alfred Marshall—among the most influential of those classical 1890s economists—with the critical underlying observation that "a firm that by good fortune gained a high proportion of the market early on would be best able to best its rivals; 'whichever firm first gets off to a good start' would corner the market."[11] Even the contemporary version of the ideas preceded St. Patrick's Day 1987. Jeffrey Rohlfs (re?)introduced them at least as early as 1974;[12] Paul David introduced the QWERTY story to the modern economic literature in 1985;[13] and Michael Katz and Carl Shapiro published seminal articles in two of the most prestigious scholarly economics journals in the mid 1980s.[14]

More to the point, though, Arthur's despondency over his poor reception at Berkeley notwithstanding, his was hardly a lone voice in the wilderness. True voices in the wilderness *do not* become chaired professors at Stanford or affiliates of the Santa Fe Institute—as Arthur already was back on that doleful St. Patrick's Day. While one particular Berkeley seminar may have been a flop, economists were hardly shunning his ideas about network effects.

Few voices speak louder about a theory's growing acceptance than those of its critics. About the time that Arthur revealed his ideas in *Scientific American*, Stan Liebowitz and Stephen Margolis decided to debunk the QWERTY story. In *The Fable of the Keys*, they reviewed the history of typewriters and explained that QWERTY's emergence was little more than the normal functioning of the market.[15] They contended that the QWERTY keyboard was simply the best of the various designs, and that it defeated its competitors the old-fashioned way: by being the superior product. Whether their historical analysis is right or wrong, their apparent need to attack both the example and its underlying ideas suggests that far from being obscure, network economics was well on its way into the mainstream by 1990.

So why did Waldrop choose to open his book with Arthur's story? And why did I choose to incorporate his opening into my own introduction of network economics? As to Waldrop's motivation, I can only guess. His book described some cutting-edge interdisciplinary work underway at the Santa Fe Institute—exciting work that unified seemingly anomalous observations in economics, physics, biology, politics, and a number of other fields. He described the scientists who brought that work together to create the emerging science of complexity. Arthur was the key economist *in that group*. I can only surmise that these concerns guided Waldrop to push Arthur beyond the temple walls and into his opening chapter. Then again, many decisions appear to be rational in hindsight when they were, in fact, arbitrary.

My own decision was entirely utilitarian. Waldrop had already performed the heavy lifting. He had laid out a wonderful story about an early thinker of network economics. I adopted his opening because it was accessible, and credited Arthur with these ideas because Waldrop had already given him that credit. In the words of one early network theorist: "For unto every one that hath shall be given, and he shall have abundance: but from him that hath not shall be taken away even that which he hath."[16] Stated somewhat more prosaically, my reference to "Arthur's increasing returns" was positive feedback in action.

No Exit

So far, I've used three technical terms almost interchangeably: *network economics*, *positive feedback*, and *increasing returns*. I've also glossed over another term critical to the economics of the information sector: *lock-in*. Believe it or not, these two seemingly minor sins—one of commission and one of omission—may have played central roles in the information sector's formative years.[17] And so, if we're going to understand those years, we'll need to know what network economics is, how it relates to positive feedback, increasing returns, and the equally misused terms *virtuous cycle*, *Metcalfe's Law*, and *tipping to a standard*, and why lock-in must never be forgotten.

Research on network economics began with the observation that most—but not all—purchases follow a familiar pattern. A consumer selects a product, pays for it, and uses it. If she uses it often and enjoys it, it's valuable; if not, it's less valuable. In either case, no one else's actions much matter to the product's value. The minute that she bought it, her relationship with the manufacturer, the seller, and the realm of other potential buyers ended. But for an increasing number of technological products, those relationships persist. For such products, the value of ownership grows with the number of people who own compatible products, effectively creating a community of consumers with interlinked value functions.

These interconnected value functions form a communal "network" of owners—each of whom is a "member" of the network. The larger the network, the more valuable the membership. The "returns" on my investment in membership "increase" as the network grows. The value of my chair, for example, is unaffected by the number of other people who own comparable chairs; the value of my phone increases when new people buy phones. Telephones are thus network goods, while chairs are not.

Of course, in order to extract value from my phone, I not only need to know other people who own phones, but other people who own compatible, interconnected phones. When I choose a telephone—or analogously, a design for a rail car, or a computer, or an operating system, or a word processor—I need to know not only how well the specific phone works, but also how well the associated network works. Because the functioning of the network depends in large part upon its size, membership in a large network is more valuable than membership in a smaller network defined by an essentially comparable product. Thus, it's rational for me to choose the most popular phone—thereby increasing its popularity.

That choice means that I've bought more than just a phone. It means that I've bought into someone else's dream (about phones). In fact, I've become an investor in their network, to the tune of at least a phone and likely some training. And I'm not done yet; I may need further investment to add equipment and/or amenities to my phone. I've also developed a vested interest in enhancing the network's value; if I can convince my friends and family to join my network, the value of *my* investment will increase. And so, I'm likely to become an evangelical marketer spreading the gospel of my network—helping to further a dream that someone else may own.

When I evangelize my new network, I provide the network owner with *positive feedback*. When I convince my friends not only to join my network, but also to convert their own friends to our network, our orgiastic outpouring of zeal creates a *virtuous cycle* in which growth leads to more growth and value enhances value. How fast will the value increase? According to Metcalfe's Law, the network's value is proportional to the number of members, squared.[18] While this "law" is far from binding on most real world networks, it does embody the key insight driving the entire analysis of network industries, namely that the value of membership increases rapidly as the network grows.

Imprecision aside, a virtuous cycle, once started, will continue until so many rational consumers join the largest network that it becomes the only reasonable choice. Whereas I may once have debated the relative merits of competing telephone standards, new consumers will be spared the agony of deliberation and choice: anything other than the dominant network will have become either obsolete or relegated to a niche. The market will have "tipped to a (de facto) standard." This dynamic, whereby increasing returns lead to positive feedback forming a virtuous cycle of growth that eventually tips the market to a standard is what differentiates network industries from their more conventional counterparts.

The subtle differences among these terms—increasing returns, positive feedback, Metcalfe's Law, virtuous cycles, and tipping to a standard—will help us understand how Microsoft succeeded while the dot-coms failed. Each describes a somewhat different aspect of a network industry's almost organic growth, and they are collectively termed *network effects*. Furthermore, because each of these effects enhances the value of *my* network membership based entirely on events beyond my control, some economists prefer to call them *network externalities*. Finally, *network economics* is the economic study of industries exhibiting these effects. So, at least nine different terms describe the same basic growth phenomenon!

Lock-in is different. Rather than describing network growth, it enables that growth. Lock-in was always central to network economics. Waldrop talked about it. David talked about it. Arthur talked about it. Even Liebowitz and Margolis talked about it (though critically, and not by name). But they didn't talk about it much because, in all honesty, it didn't seem to be that interesting. Networks grow until they tip to a standard. Consumers are then locked in to a single choice. The exciting part is the growth! Organic growth fueled by increasing returns ran counter to much of classical economic theory. Now there's excitement. To early network economists struggling to mainstream their growth theories born of empirical anomalies, lock-in was little more than a logical consequence, a mundane afterthought. But not everyone saw lock-in as mundane. Some IO economists considered it to be a pernicious effect that allowed monopolists to exploit consumers. They set out to convince the Supreme Court to pay attention to the relationships among monopolists and their locked-in customers.

When Congress passed the key antitrust statutes, it basically told the courts to decide which business practices to prohibit. The Supreme Court introduced the distinction between *per se* and *rule of reason* offenses, and it laid the groundwork for differentiating legal from illegal uses of selected business practices. But antitrust law is fluid. From time to time, a group of economists and attorneys approach the Supreme Court armed with new theories about markets, about potential market failures, and about the consequences of those potential failures on competition, competitors, and consumers. An important wave of antitrust theorists swept into Washington from the University of Chicago along with the Reagan administration in the early 1980s. This Chicago School, inspired by Robert Bork's *The Antitrust Paradox*, revolutionized antitrust law.[19] The Chicagoans believed—correctly—that the courts had banned many benign, and even some beneficial, business practices. They explained that markets were more robust than the then-existing antitrust laws implied, and that they were perfectly capable of policing themselves. Chicago School economists felt that market magic would deter or punish anticompetitive behavior in virtually all markets, and that antitrust enforcement was rarely warranted. They gained many converts, including the government agencies that enforce the antitrust laws and the courts that interpret them.

A decade or so later, the Chicago School reforms had become the status quo. A new wave of economists and attorneys arrived to challenge their supremacy. This Post-Chicago School agreed with many Chicagoan tenets. It too believed in the magic of markets and agreed that many of the recently legalized activities should never have been prohibited. But Post-Chicagoans also believed that the Chicago School had pushed too far in the other direction. Whereas the Chicagoans arrived in Washington to find a rigid, repressive antitrust regime choking productive, efficient companies, their revolution sent our large corporations slouching toward Gomorrah, where they exploited American consumers without fear of the market cops.

The corrective counterrevolution began with a chance encounter between some Post-Chicago economists and some Independent Service

Organizations (ISOs) who repair copying machines. Together they challenged Kodak, who though best known for its cameras, also makes copying machines.[20] Now copying machines—it's worth noting—are not network products, which is why Kodak could remain in the market with a small share and still compete against much larger players like Xerox. But, of course, Kodak's machines occasionally needed repairs. Consumers with broken Kodak copiers could call Kodak, who would send a technician, supply replacement parts, and charge a high price—or they could call an ISO, who would send a technician, buy the necessary replacement parts from Kodak, and charge a lower price. Then Kodak changed the rules. Kodak announced that it was no longer willing to sell spare parts to ISOs. Consumers who needed service would have no alternative to Kodak's high prices. They couldn't turn to ISOs, because the ISOs couldn't get parts. And they couldn't abandon their expensive copiers, because the purchase price and their personnel training had locked them in; their switching costs created a sizable barrier to any competing copier manufacturer attempting to win away their business.

Sunk switching costs locked in these consumers, Kodak chose to exploit them, the ISOs sued to protect their businesses, and the Post-Chicagoans supported the ISOs with cutting-edge economic theories. Kodak, of course, insisted that it had done nothing wrong—and adherents of the Chicago School agreed. In fact, one of the most influential Chicagoans, Justice Antonin Scalia, wrote an impassioned dissent insisting that Kodak's exploitation of "wretched" locked-in consumers was overblown, that market forces would prevail, and that a victory for the ISOs would hurt the economy as a whole.[21] But Scalia's arguments failed to sway the majority of the Court and the Post-Chicago School scored its first major victory.[22]

Over the next few years, the courts came to realize that though the Chicagoans had rightly forced them to reconsider the degree to which markets could police themselves, they had dropped the restraints too far. The Post-Chicagoans taught them to scrutinize monopolists' behavior more carefully, and to appreciate that natural market forces and natural barriers to entry can often insulate monopolists—and even some oligopolists—from the sorts of consumer feedback that are supposed to make markets work. Entrenched incumbents learn to exploit consumers and then work to preserve the barriers enabling the exploitation. The Post-Chicagoans insisted that such barrier preservation—often accompanied by artificial barrier creation—constituted cheating that market forces would not correct in a timely manner, and that only rigorous market cops could prevent. Six years after the Supreme Court ruled against Kodak, the government sued Microsoft, and showed how a monopolist blessed with the natural barriers of network growth and lock-in can leverage them even further to create artificial barriers capable of devastating the information sector.

The Wretched of the Networks

The years between Kodak and Microsoft were hardly quiet times in either IO or antitrust. Network economics and lock-in exploded into the real worlds of business and management—and in particular, into the businesses of the information sector. Carl Shapiro and Hal Varian captured that emergence in *Information Rules: A Strategic Guide to the Network Economy*.[23] Whereas Waldrop had written about the science and scientists of network economics, Shapiro and Varian made the material relevant to the managers and businesses toiling away in network industries. And managers have a limited tolerance for new theories. The only way to get their attention is to answer that critical question: *How is this theory going to make me money?*

Shapiro and Varian revealed that in network industries, the answer is lock-in. They told corporate managers how to recognize the network nature of their businesses, how to maximize their prospects for emerging as the owners of the *de facto* standard, and how to maximize their profits. Of course, as good Post-Chicago economists, they also cautioned their readers not to run afoul of the antitrust laws.[24] That cautionary note reiterates the distinction between natural and artificial commercial advantages. There's nothing inappropriate about a company exploiting natural barriers to charge consumers higher prices, nor is there anything wrong with exploiting natural lock-in to do the same. In fact, in some industries the ability to overcharge after securing a naturally advantageous position is the only way to motivate investment in product development. If the antitrust laws spared consumers from having to overspend after one firm secured a comfortable position through an appropriate combination of product quality, timing, and luck, there might not be any products for us to consume.

Lock-in in a network industry can allow an erstwhile competitive company to become a monopolist protected by a "network barrier to entry." Tipping to a standard suggests that whatever standard emerges will be a monopoly. There are two main types of standards—open and proprietary—with a number of variations on each theme and a few hybrids lying in between. No one owns an open standard, though someone is usually in charge of maintaining it. That maintainer, typically either a trade association or a government agency, solicits input from across the industry—producers, consumers, and interested onlookers alike—and convenes a panel of experts who decide upon the accepted standard. The maintainer discloses the entire standard to the public, makes sure that it contains no hidden secrets, and if necessary controls the flow of royalties to companies who relinquished private property to help build this open standard. Networks that emerge around widely accepted standards are notoriously hard to displace.

A network based upon an industry open standard is likely to be a monopoly only in some senses. It's certainly likely to restrict consumer choice. Producers rarely push technologies that compete with industry open standards. Instead, they produce competitive products that conform to the standard; competition *within* the standard replaces competition *for* the standard. The standard is thus a "monopoly" network, though open standards are rarely *called* monopolies, because they raise a different set of antitrust concerns than do true monopolies.

Proprietary standards are different. When a single, private entity controls a network standard, keeps at least part of it secret, and "closes" it to the rest of the world, the network barrier to entry will secure the owner's true monopoly. In order to displace the monopolist, new competitors will have to produce a superior *network*. That challenge can be daunting—and it provides the network monopolist with ample opportunity to exploit consumers.

How much exploitation is possible? In a network industry, switching imposes even more costs than it would in a nonnetwork setting. If I ever switch out of a network, I'll lose the external value of membership—the value that I gained from all of the other members. So a new entrant who wants me to switch to his network is going to have to compensate me for my loss. Because if anything even close to Metcalfe's Law holds, that loss will be quite large. A network monopolist's position is pretty comfortable.

The incumbent monopolist has a distinct cost advantage over all would-be competitors. New entrants are unlikely to displace the incumbent unless either switching costs are low or their new products are so far superior that they can absorb the switching costs and still be profitable. A monopolist faced with the first situation is in a weak position. Monopolies of simple products with low switching costs don't really have locked-in customers to exploit. Such "weak" network properties—network growth without lock-in—may be interesting as a matter of industry dynamics, and they could still drive business strategy, but they're unlikely to make either a firm or its investors obscenely rich. Most dotcoms fell prey to this trap; they rushed to monopolize Internet spaces without lock-in, only to discover that profits were elusive.

Monopolists in the second camp face a different challenge. Their products exhibit the "strong" network properties of network growth coupled with lock-in. Owners of such standards can extract significant rents as long as no one produces a vastly superior product. Such superiority, however, rarely arises through a direct challenge. It usually occurs when an innovator develops a fundamentally new technology capable of displacing the old standard.[25] The incumbent wishing to protect its network monopoly must constantly monitor technological developments and either co-opt them or cut them short before the threat materializes. Owners of monopoly networks are thus wary of innovation. Their first choice is to own all innovation relevant to their networks. Their second is to control it, and to direct all third-party innovation toward their networks. Their third is to squelch it. Network owners are happier when technology fails to progress than when it progresses in the "wrong" direction and leads to a competing network—which is, in turn, the worst thing that can happen to a network monopolist.

The first strategy is extraordinarily difficult to implement. Just ask Ma Bell, who owned *everything connected to the telephone network* well into the 1950s. An entrepreneurial innovator invented a small plastic cup that you could screw onto your phone's mouthpiece. With a Hush-a-Phone in place, you could talk into the cup to gain a modicum of privacy even in a crowded office. Ma Bell went ballistic. She threatened to cut off the telephone service of any business that allowed its workers to tamper with their telephones in this outrageous manner. She claimed that Hush-a-Phone users threatened the integrity of the telephone network and thus imperiled national security. The Federal Communications Commission (FCC) agreed. Fortunately, the federal judges who heard the appeal had a bit more sense.[26] They reversed the FCC and allowed anyone to connect physical (i.e., *not* electrical) devices to a telephone handset. Hush-a-Phone was the first chink in Ma Bell's armor. It began the erosion of her total power over the phone network. A few decades and several landmark lawsuits later, the government dissolved most of the rest of her "natural" monopoly. But in its heyday, AT&T owned the telephone network and everything connected to it—and the government was willing to enforce that monopoly. It's hard to imagine how anyone could gain that sort of power without a government guarantee.

In the information sector, Apple tried to apply the first strategy throughout the 1980s; it didn't work out well. Apple refused to share its hardware specifications with other software computer manufacturers, and insisted that only Apple could develop equipment compatible with the Apple network. But too much pent-up innovation existed for Apple to shut it down. IBM and Microsoft tried variants of the second strategy, though with notably different results; they chose to control and to direct innovation, rather than to own it. IBM published the specifications for its PC architecture, and allowed all interested manufacturers to build compatible components. On the software side, Microsoft kept some things secret, but revealed enough for third party software developers to write programs that ran on Microsoft's platforms—thereby enhancing the value of Microsoft's network. By the 1990s, IBM's architecture had become the de facto PC standard, but IBM had lost the ability to control it. Microsoft, and to a lesser extent Intel, had gained control of the "WINTEL" standard: the basic IBM architecture running a Windows platform on an Intel chip. Microsoft's inheritance of IBM's mantle, coupled with its own 1980s strategy of encouraging third-party development, positioned it well to shift into the third, innovation squelching, strategy to prevent products like Navigator and Java from emerging as full-blown competitors.

The battles over network standards in strong network industries can be brutal. But even the weak network story can be brutal, particularly when it's the subject of massive confusion—as we learned the hard way during the bubble, when confusion reigned supreme. The investor chat rooms that helped to power the bubble buzzed incessantly with misapplications of several reputable theories—notably the "Gorilla Game,"[27] the "Telecosm,"[28] and "disruptive technologies"[29]—each of which allegedly provided a scholarly patina to the disscussants' simplistic investment "analyses." The most egregiously misapplied theory, however, was none other than network economics. Shapiro and Varian had written *Information Rules* for managers, not for casual equity investors; the book extracted practical lessons from economics and presented them as strategic advice to companies in technology industries characterized by varying degrees of network effects. Lock-in was the key to many of these lessons. Companies gain flexibility, negotiating strength, and pricing power when dealing with locked-in consumers—often gaining enough to warrant offering those consumers sweetheart up-front deals to lock themselves in.

Investors who recast this sound strategic *management* advice as strategic *investment* advice did an astoundingly poor job. They compounded their error by misinterpreting the daily accounts of the Microsoft trial. They "learned" that network growth combined with Microsoft's large market share to make Microsoft's profits inevitable. Investors fell in love with the idea that networks exhibit organic growth, and concluded that inevitable profitability was widespread. All that it took was the early identification of a network industry—say, a newly opened Internet space. Because that first mover into that space would inevitably emerge as the monopolist, profits and returns would flow as a matter of course. And therein lay the critical error.

The observation of network-driven growth should mark the *starting point* of industry analysis, not an entire theory. Two early network economists, Stan Besen and Joe Farrell, for example, had explained that

a final characteristic of network markets is that history matters. Outcomes in other markets can often be explained by contemporaneous consumer preferences and producer technologies, but network market equilibria often cannot be understood without knowing the pattern of technology adoption in earlier periods. Because buyers want compatibility with the installed base, better products that arrive later may be unable to displace poorer, but earlier standards.[30]

Chat room investors tended to ignore the caveat "a final characteristic," and viewed tipping as *the only* important characteristic in network markets. That misconception led them to equate all network growth with monopoly rents and first movers with inevitable monopolists.

Even scholars who undoubtedly knew better tended to oversimplify, at least when addressing the public. Business School Professors Michael Cusumano (of MIT) and David Yoffie (of Harvard), for example, blurred a number of related yet distinct terms:

Web commerce also exploded from nothing in 1993 to $22 Billion in 1998, with predictions of hundreds of billions of dollars early in the next century. This rapid expansion of the network is a classic example of what economists describe as "positive feedback loops," "increasing returns," and "network externalities." Behind the jargon, the dynamics are easy to follow. As more people and organizations connect to the Internet, more people and organizations create more tools and applications that make the Internet even more useful. And the more users, as well as tools and applications, there are, the more valuable connecting to the Internet becomes. As a result, more people start connecting, more tools and applications appear, and even more people sign on, ad infinitum. The technology community likes to describe this phenomenon as Metcalfe's Law, which states that the usefulness of a network, like the Internet, grows exponentially as the number of users grows.[31]

Among nonacademics, the confusion was even more obvious. A well-written Motley Fool posting, for example, explained that

market share is important because the software industry exhibits increasing returns, a phenomenon explained by W. Brian Arthur of the Santa Fe Institute. His theory states that once a company gets a market share lead, it gets farther ahead while competitors fall farther behind. This happens because technology buyers are conservative and they demand technologies that are standard and work effectively with the rest of their infrastructure. As more copies of a leader's software are sold, it increases the likelihood of its becoming the standard, causing even more copies of software to be sold and reinforcing the growth cycle.[32]

Chat room residents viewed network growth as a sufficient condition for dominance and monopoly profits. No one much bothered to mention lock-in.[33] The investment community came to believe that the Internet— the ultimate network—*had* to be a network industry, and that network effects were rampant. Investors then embarked on a wholly understandable quest for the next Microsoft.[34]

Investors seeking the next Microsoft found positive feedback everywhere. On the Internet, positive feedback meant that the more people posting information to a site (or the more products offered for sale on a site), the more people who would look to that site for the information. The more people known to be looking to a site, the more eager information providers or vendors would be to post to that site. These mutually reinforcing growth trends would inevitably lead to a robust durable monopoly. These investors found a chimeric "Internet barrier to entry" that mirrored Microsoft's highly effective applications barrier to entry. This belief in widespread network effects guided investment strategies throughout the bubble. But the circumstances surrounding Microsoft's dominance were unique, and grounded in the peculiarities of platform software.[35] The misapplication of network economics, and the attempt to exploit growth without lock-in, was doomed to fail—as indeed it did.

And so, while Microsoft rose, the dot-coms sank. The lessons of IO and antitrust—playing themselves out as the information sector paraded across the front page—no longer seemed quite as abstract as they first appeared to be.

4

The Artificial Science

A Laureate's Lament

The late Herb Simon, winner of the 1978 Nobel Prize in Economics for his pioneering work in organization theory and long-time Professor of Computer Science and Psychology at Carnegie Mellon University, was a man at home in many different temples. But that doesn't mean that he was at peace with their inner workings. Nor was he bashful about sharing his concerns. He did so, for example, in keynote speeches at MIT in 1968 and at Berkeley in 1980. He then followed them up by first writing and then updating *The Sciences of the Artificial*.[1]

His concern was that the natural sciences had edged the artificial sciences out of their rightful role in professional education—in engineering, architecture, business, education, law, and medicine—to the point that the very term "artificial science" sounds odd. Though the artifacts of artificial science shape our everyday lives and social interactions, professional educators weren't giving them the respect that they deserved. Fortunately, Simon's expertise in conquering organizational challenges also led him to detect a solution stirring.

A science of artificial phenomena is always in imminent danger of dissolving and vanishing. The peculiar properties of the [artificial] artifact lie on the thin interface between the natural laws within it and the natural laws without. What can we say about it? . . . The artificial world is centered precisely between the inner and outer environments; it is concerned with attaining goals by adapting the former to the latter. The proper study of those who are concerned with the artificial is the way in which the adaptation of means to environments is brought about—and central to that is the process of design itself. The professional schools will reassume their professional responsibilities just to the degree that they can discover a science of design, a body of intellectually tough analytic, partly formalizable, partly empirical, teachable doctrine about the design process . . . [S]uch a science of design not only is possible but is actually emerging at the present time. It has already begun to penetrate the engineering schools, particularly through programs in computer science.[2]

Decades of experience have proven Simon half right; his diagnosis was correct, his prognosis flawed. The artifacts of artificial science remain central to our lives as social creatures. At least two of them—markets and computers—have emerged as central features of everyday life. In addition to everything else that they've done for the modern world, they combined to give us the information sector. But academic computer science programs hardly developed in the direction that Simon predicted. The luminaries of academic computer science chose to burnish the engineering credentials implied by "computing" and to abdicate the social responsibilities implied by "information."[3] Both the teaching and research emphases of most computer science departments (typically located in schools of engineering) stress the construction of faster, slicker machines and the software needed to make them soar. Social impact issues, studies of the ways that people use computers, or inquiries governing the artificial interface between the natural sciences of silicon-based computing machines and carbon-based computing users, have been pushed to (and often beyond) the periphery of the field.

The information sector lies *precisely* at that interface. It exists as an interface artifact of artificial science. While this interface artifact assumes many faces and goes by many names, four of its most famous personae played critical roles in the information sector's formative years: Windows, Linux, Napster, and the World Wide Web. Windows and Linux are interface artifacts that separate human users from their own personal computers. Napster is an interface artifact that sits on a computer network and separates two human users from each other. And the World Wide Web is an interface artifact that separates human users from the vast resources of the Internet. The study of the information sector is the study of these and similar interface artifacts—and of the ways that they relate to the disparate worlds between which they sit. Of course, no one wanders around talking about the artificial interface artifacts of the information sector. We call them software. The information sector is all about software: what it is, how it evolves, and how its developers are motivated and rewarded. Therein lies the answer to Simon's query—the things that we can say about software explains why it is a "doctrine about the design process," and thus a proper artificial science.

Software is an internal computing matter. Software is a set of instructions that guide electrical impulses inside a computer. The natural sciences used to study computers answer the questions about software's identity. Computer scientists study the phenomena of software and computers; they've derived a complex and elegant science that is of direct interest primarily to those who choose careers in computing. The public is generally content viewing their outputs as black boxes without understanding their inner workings.

How software developers are motivated and rewarded is a human matter. Computer scientists rarely trouble themselves with such issues; they prefer to leave these concerns to their colleagues in economics, psychology, management, or business. These issues are essentially matters of human cognitive psychology—appropriately described by the natural sciences.[4]

But how software evolves—therein lies the interface question. Evolution itself, though perhaps the quintessential internal response to the changing needs of survival, is inherently an interface phenomenon. All organisms exist within an environment with which they must interact. Sometimes the environment changes. When that occurs, the organism must either adapt or die. At other times, the organism changes first. It gains new abilities to interact with its environment. When it applies those abilities, the environment may change, too. Either way, natural forces act upon the inside organism and the outside environment, and something curious occurs at the interface where they interact.

Two organisms and two environments define the information sector. In a stunning bit of symmetry, each organism defines the environment in which the other must survive. The first organism is human; the computer's requirements define its environment. That selfsame computer is the second organism; it must exist in an environment comprehensible to the human. Failure by either party will lead to mutual irrelevance; neither can survive in the information sector alone. A human unable to interact with the computing environment loses the benefits of modern technology, while a computer unable to interact with the human environment is a worthless box. Their existence as functioning, productive organisms of the information sector is entirely symbiotic.

Software defines the interface between these symbiotes. It must adapt and evolve in response to their needs. Changes in human aptitudes or even tastes may force one sort of evolution. Changes in computer capabilities may lead to a second. And whichever organism changes first may—through the evolution of the software at the interface—impel the other into its own evolutionary change, in a potentially perpetual cycle of adaptation and growth.

The only way to understand software evolution is to explore the nature of software itself. First and foremost, all software derives from a single goal: the desire to increase the range of activities with which a computer can prove to be helpful. This goal leads to a view of software development as *translation*. Computer scientists face a daunting task. A computer is a machine capable of determining when voltage levels rise and fall. A potential computer user is a person who expresses himself or herself in an imprecise human language (usually English, or increasingly, Chinese). An actual computer user also believes that the computer will help solve some task. For that to happen, though, the user's thoughts must be translated into sequences of voltage levels, manipulated by the computer, and then translated back into the user's language. The implicit translation chain defines the fundamental challenge of computer science.

Anyone with even a cursory exposure to computers realizes that there are actually two series of translations in this chain. Responsibility for the first half lies with the human user, who must learn some combination of a restricted lexicon (e.g., a programming language), Boolean logic (i.e., stringing keywords together using "AND"s and "OR"s), and graphical manipulation (e.g., mouse clicks) to talk to the machine. Responsibility for the second half lies with engineers and programmers. Their work begins by representing high and low voltage levels as 1s and 0s, respectively. They then group these binary digits ("bits") together to generate more interesting numbers that encode words. Of course, only a small subset of these words is meaningful to the computer—those that it can use to manipulate yet other voltage levels. This limited lexicon and grammar form the basis of a low-level computer language (e.g., an assembly language), with which a talented programming language designer can develop a "higher level" language.

While people always needed a full translation chain to use computers, the locus of technical and commercial attention has shifted as computers have matured. In the 1960s, virtually all computer users were technically trained professionals personally proficient in Fortran, COBOL, ALGOL, LISP, or some other specialized language that bore only a cosmetic relationship to English. By the 1990s, these once-popular computer languages had given way to more sophisticated, object-oriented languages like C++ and Java—which *still* bore only a cosmetic relationship to English. Of greater significance, though, advances between the 1960s and 1990s enabled humans with *no* understanding of these odd-looking dialects to communicate with computers. It's now possible to become an accomplished computer user without knowing any machine language more technical than the Boolean inputs to a search engine or a set of point-and-click instructions. Computer engineers began this shift by developing technologies that increased hardware power. Computer scientists and programmers then availed themselves of that power to advance the translation chain progressively closer to English. This progression defined software's evolutionary path; Simon's artificial interface grew incrementally beyond the computing environment into realms that had previously been the sole province of humans.

The bridge connecting the human and computer organisms is thus constructed of one translation chain built "up" from voltage levels into increasingly complex languages that look more and more like English, and one translation chain built "down" from English to look more and more like math. These chains meet at a level known as the "user interface," literally the point at which the user interfaces with the machine, but also the artificial interface artifact that Simon urged us to study.

Origin of a Specie

A computer—above all else—computes. The part of the translation chain between voltage levels and mathematical computation was the easiest part to write. From there, things became harder. The only way to get a computer to help with any other task is to translate that task into computation. Much of this work has its roots in artificial intelligence (AI). AI's practitioners interview human users to identify tasks ripe for translation into computation, and then develop the techniques necessary to effect those translations.

Their work began with a "simple" challenge first issued in 1950: translate chess into computation.[5] Looking back, it may be hard to remember just how young the computing world was in 1950, but when Claude Shannon, a prominent communications researcher at Bell Labs, proposed chess as the first not-strictly-computational task that anyone ever asked a computer to solve, he had to explain that he planned to write a set of instructions that would "program" the computer to play chess, rather than to build a special chess-playing machine.[6]

Shannon approached the challenge through game theory. Several years earlier, a group of mathematicians and mathematical economists led by John von Neumann had shown how to translate games like chess into mathematical constructs called "game trees." They had also explained the algorithmic steps needed to "solve" the mathematical equation implicit in the game tree, and to devise the optimal moves to make under any possible circumstance.[7] If Shannon could implement von Neumann's algorithm, he could teach his computer to play *perfect* chess. But there was a problem. While the game-theoretic algorithms were *theoretical* breakthroughs, and the game tree model gave Shannon a sturdy platform upon which to base his work, von Neumann's pointers to chess-playing perfection suffered from a glaring lack of efficiency. Had Shannon implemented them in 1950, his computer would still be thinking about its first move—for about another 10^{100} centuries. Shannon wisely chose another route to computational chess.

He decided to forego optimality, to settle instead for a program that would make pretty good moves much of the time. He augmented his computational algorithm with heuristics, shortcuts that embody tidbits of wisdom in an attempt to do pretty well, while making relatively few mistakes. Heuristics were radical at the time. Back when computers performed only computational tasks, tolerance for errors was limited. Programs that returned the wrong answer—even if only on rare occasions—were "bad." Shannon's consideration of computer chess taught him an immediate lesson about the evolution of the interface: If it was going to grow upward in any meaningful way, it would have to take risks. It would need principles that allowed it to issue educated guesses, even at the expense of an occasional mistake. His inquiry gave birth to the concept of heuristic programming.

Sound esoteric? Well, it was in 1950, but today it's not. In fact, heuristic programming lies at the cutting edge of e-commerce. Heuristics are what allow Amazon to guess what books you may want to buy based on your past purchases. They're what allow Yahoo! Music to know that I (and perhaps I alone) enjoy segueing from Yoko Ono to the Weavers. They're also what allow the same program to posit erroneous connections, such as suggesting that if I like Simon and Garfunkel, I'd probably also like Mary J. Blige.

But Shannon had no way of knowing where his inquiry would lead some fifty years in the future. He wanted to integrate heuristics with algorithms to teach his computer how to play chess. He started by studying the game-theoretic algorithm for chess perfection. The underlying idea was fairly straightforward: Think about all of White's possible openings. Now think about all of Black's possible responses to each of White's possible openings. Now think about all of White's possible responses to each of Black's possible responses to each of White's possible openings. Now keep on going until you've generated all possible chess games. Then look at all the games that have finished. It's pretty clear which ones White won, which ones Black won, and which were stalemates. Now look at all the next-to-last moves. The player who made that move would prefer a win to a draw and a draw to a loss—so we can tell how the game would end if we could only get to that next-to-last move. Then look at the next-to-next-to-last moves. Again, whoever got to make that move would prefer a win to a draw and a draw to a loss. So we can tell how the game would end if we could only get to the next-to-next-to-last moves. And so on and so on and so on (and so on). We can work our way back up from each possible ending to the opening moves, and know how each opening will end. (You can see why this might take 10^{100} centuries). Simple. Complex, inefficient, and heavy on the bookkeeping, but conceptually quite simple—and alliteratively named "minimax."

Shannon saw two possible shortcuts that kept at least some of mimimax's flavor: he could either look ahead only a few moves (rather than all of them), or he could consider only selected openings and responses (rather than all of them). Strategies of the first sort represent "brute force searches" of the game tree. They don't really need to think about what they're doing. The key lies in bookkeeping. They simply consider every possible alternate path until they run out of either time or memory space. When they reach a "horizon" lying several moves in the future, they apply heuristic information encoded by a programmer who knows something about chess to estimate the probability that each point on their horizon will lead to a win, apply the minimax algorithm to those estimates, and make the move that appears to be best. Strategies of the second sort define "selective searches." They embody a good deal more heuristic information. While they may enumerate all possible openings, they don't waste their time considering responses to stupid openings. This immediate rejection of the foolish allows them to save a great deal of time, effort, and bookkeeping. It allows them to look many more moves into the future than brute force searches before applying their horizon heuristics. It also means that they damn well better be right. The heuristics that they use to "prune" moves by immediate rejection need to embody a good deal more chess expertise than their horizon heuristics.

Shannon's inquiry into chess programming led him to define both categories of search strategies. Over the years, a number of researchers followed his lead, expanded his concepts, and turned them into powerful, generally useful algorithms. How general? And how useful? The current incarnation of these algorithms powers every commercial search that the Web has ever seen. Google, Yahoo!, Lycos, Alta Vista, HotBot, and even Lexis/Nexis—all can trace their intellectual underpinnings back to Shannon's initial inquiry into computer chess. The evolutionary processes that he unleashed in his desire to find a not-strictly-computational use of his computer laid the groundwork for the information sector to absorb reference lookups into the realm of computing.

But again, Shannon wasn't looking to revolutionize library science. He just wanted to play chess. And the truth is, he wasn't even really interested in that; his primary interest lay in using his computer to model human decision making. As a result, he outlined the pros and cons of both brute force and selective searches, programmed his computer to play pretty poor chess, and wrote an important and influential article about the experience. But his article had thrown down more gauntlets than he may have realized. At least two important groups of challengers arose to pick them up: the chess programmers and the AI researchers.

The chess programmers more or less missed Shannon's point. Shannon had explained that his interest in chess was essentially incidental; he was primarily interested in helping software evolve from its strictly computational roots into the broader world of decision making. He viewed chess as an excellent first step in the right direction. The chess programmers arrived with a different agenda. They liked chess. They wanted their computers to play chess. In fact, they wanted their computers to play world-class chess. They wanted to build the world's first automated chess champion. Because many of the chess programmers were also prominent chess players, they liked to believe that excellence in chess required extraordinary intelligence, keen insight, and carefully honed acumen. They were thus not terribly enamored of brute force searches. No, they preferred selective search strategies that would allow them to teach the computer what they had mastered themselves—how to tell with but a quick glance which moves were so stupid that they weren't worth considering. It was a great plan. The best human chess players would train great automated chess players. The chess programmers set out to evolve the interface between the human and the computing worlds by incorporating chess within the computational environment.

But they were wrong. And not because they were slouches at chess. They were just wrong. Take Mikhail Botvinnik, for example. Botvinnik was the greatest chess player of his time; he held the world championship for fourteen of sixteen years between 1948 and 1963. He was also a chess programmer. He developed a technique that he called the "chess master's method," and taught it to his computer, which he named PIONEER. Regrettably, PIONEER never learned how to play competitive chess. But Botvinnik was not beyond taking advantage of a lucky coincidence. His chess master's method actually embodied some sophisticated, generalizable approaches to reasoning and decision making. Botvinnik put these approaches to use in his day job; the reconfigured PIONEER planned maintenance repair schedules for power stations across the Soviet Union.[8] Nevertheless, Botvinnik's experience did demonstrate an important type of software evolution: he helped to convert scheduling into a computational task and thereby moved the translation frontier upward.

But it was Hans Berliner, a correspondence chess champion and a Professor at Carnegie Mellon, who proved to be the most important of the chess programmers. Berliner extolled the virtues of selective strategies and derided the simple fools who advocated brute force approaches. He emerged as the most articulate priest of computer chess, developed several chess programs embodying his ideas, and entered virtually every available computer chess tournament. His programs never won, but defeat is effective in focusing the mind. After one-too-many brute force programs defeated his selective searchers, Berliner experienced an epiphany; in the mid-1970s, he began extolling the virtues of brute force approaches and deriding the simple fools who advocated selective searches. As luck would have it, he was right this time. By the mid-1980s he had assembled a team of students who stood Shannon's original idea on its head. They built dedicated chess-playing machines named Hitech and Deep Thought.[9] And Deep Thought was an excellent chess player. In fact, it was a good enough chess player for IBM to hire it and rename it Deep Blue. Deep Blue's evolution continued at IBM, as it drew more and more chess knowledge out of the human environment, across the software interface, and into the computing environment. In 1997, Deep Blue met world chess champion Gary Kasparov for the second time—and won the match.[10]

And so, nearly fifty years after Claude Shannon set out to translate chess into a computational problem to enable software to evolve into the realm of chess, Gary Kasparov found himself losing a match to a fully evolved chess machine. Even those who *missed* Shannon's basic point managed to make an important contribution to software's evolution. That left only those who joined Shannon's original quest to model human decision making: the pioneering researchers of AI.

Survival of the Fittest

John McCarthy first coined the term "artificial intelligence" for a 1956 summer research project at Dartmouth University. From that prominent beginning, he became the most influential of the early advocates vying to define AI's research agenda. McCarthy's authority enabled him to send AI in some of its most important directions—but also to some of its most wasteful dead ends.

The stated purpose of the summer project—which McCarthy organized with Shannon, Marvin Minsky, and Nathan Rochester—was

to proceed on the basis of the conjecture that every aspect of learning or any other feature of intelligence can in principle be so precisely described that a machine can be made to simulate it. An attempt will be made to find how to make machines use language, form abstractions and concepts, solve kinds of problems now reserved for humans, and improve themselves.[11]

McCarthy and his colleagues wanted to translate complex tasks into precise computational problems, and thereby to evolve computers into arenas previously reserved for humans. They had framed the problem brilliantly. They recognized that computers were creations capable of evolution, growth, and self-improvement—if only someone could teach them the precise steps needed to evolve, to grow, and to improve.

McCarthy's careful early ministrations and innovations nurtured AI throughout its infancy. But alas, he failed to appreciate the true complexity of evolution. His 1956 proposal also asserted that: "we think that a significant advance can be made in one or more of these problems if a carefully selected group of scientists work on it together for a summer."[12] This estimate was way, way, *way* off. The agenda outlined in that proposal continues to command the attention of research scientists today—and appears likely to do so throughout the foreseeable future.

McCarthy apparently failed to learn from that early faux pas. In 1969, he and Patrick Hayes published an influential article insisting that probability theory was "epistemologically inadequate" for dealing with the challenges of AI.[13] In lay terms, McCarthy and Hayes argued that the branch of mathematics specifically devoted to helping people make decisions in uncertain environments was inappropriate for translating uncertain human environments into computational terms. They advised their followers *to avoid* the only known branch of mathematics capable of solving the problems that they were trying to solve. Many heeded their advice. For close to two decades, orthodox AI insisted that intelligence—

both natural and artificial—was strictly a matter of manipulating "symbols," and that numeric, mathematical, or quantitative reasoning was inapropos.

Fortunately, not everyone followed that orthodoxy. Expert systems researchers were AI pragmatists who managed to get the basics of software evolution right despite AI's ban on mathematics. They followed in Shannon's footsteps by translating specific, narrow, not-strictly-computational tasks into mathematical models. The tasks that they chose turned out to be much less complex than chess; they investigated banalities like diagnosing cardiopulmonary diseases or prospecting for molybdenum.[14] Their basic approach was simple. They identified genuine human experts, interviewed them, and built huge databases of the lessons that they learned during these interviews. They encoded their entire database as a collection of "if . . . then . . . else . . . " rules, and generated some surprisingly insightful conclusions. While this original formulation was much too simplistic to capture more than a few special problems, it did demonstrate another important point about software evolution. Computing organisms require education to grow. This lesson echoes what Berliner learned along the way from correspondence chess to Deep Blue: General principles and strategic acuity reach their limits in a vacuum. Growth, evolution, and eventual excellence also require detailed information.

In addition to just raw information, though, growth and evolution require mechanisms for reasoning, particularly in the presence of uncertainty. And the scientific discipline devoted to uncertain reasoning is none other than statistics, which McCarthy and Hayes had banned from AI. Nevertheless, and despite the ban, various probabilists and statisticians continued to explore the role that their tools could play in translating conceptual tasks into computational ones—thereby evolving the translation frontier upward.

Their work arrived at AI from two different directions. One school rejected the claimed inadequacy of probability theory outright. Its members demonstrated that the best way to evolve computers is to translate tasks involving uncertain reasoning into the only mathematical language capable of manipulating uncertain quantities in a logical manner: probability theory. This work, most of which applied Bayesian approaches to probabilistic modeling and decision making, drew together scholars of computer science, management science, operations research, cognitive psychology, behavioral economics, and statistics.[15] Their systems combined the knowledge-intensive approach of expert systems with the more flexible and powerful structured interviewing techniques of decision analysis. These systems, and the principles behind them, began to emerge from the labs and enter the commercial arena in the late 1980s.[16]

A second school developed a set of *neural networks* capable of "learning" statistical relationships;[17] Star Trek's writers were so enamored of this work that they credited Lt. Commander Data's android intelligence to his neural network. And though neural networks have yet to approach Trekkie dreams, they did make a huge contribution to software's evolution. They demonstrated how a system could learn to reason while acquiring knowledge. Suppose that a software system began by making arbitrary connections—along the lines of directing all Simon and Garfunkel fans toward Mary J. Blige. If it noted my rejection of that link, it might then update two of its internal databases to incorporate this information: its database on me personally, and its database on Simon and Garfunkel fans generally. The more feedback it gets about its suggestions, the more it learns which links work and which don't. Eventually, it learns to connect my current book and music choices with apt future recommendations. Thus, while these neural networks might not yet pilot starships, they can direct commerce—not a bad start.

Eventually, even the priests of orthodox AI had to admit that they'd been wrong. They incorporated numeric reasoning back into their work. The innovations of expert systems, Bayesian decision analysis, and neural networks, had done more than fundamentally reshape the faith. They had also made major contributions to the evolution of the translation frontier by translating task after task from imprecise English into precise computation—even if the computational outputs were occasionally wrong.

The tenacity of these unorthodox scholars had brought down the ruling order, in the research world's version of survival of the fittest. As the 1990s dawned, AI's leading lights realized how to help software evolve in promising, important directions. That realization set the stage for some important evolutionary advances. The Internet would soon bring these newly evolved delights to our desktops and living rooms, and we would soon come to marvel at our noble ancestors who had somehow managed to navigate the unwired world of the pre-information age.

A Theory of Evolution

Artificial science. Evolutionary software. Chess. AI. Brute force vs. selective search. Probability theory vs. symbolic reasoning. Neural networks and Bayesian models. Much to digest, but they define the scientific underpinnings of the information sector and the principles underlying all of the information products that are coming to govern our lives.

AI's founders were amazingly insightful. Simon, Shannon, and McCarthy were all around during the earliest years of computing. Yet they not only saw that a computer could evolve beyond its limited role as a computational machine into a general intelligent aide, they also saw how to do it! By 1970, they and a small number of colleagues had outlined virtually every important AI research topic. Their ability to recognize these challenges from the starting gate is truly impressive—though their consistent inability to appreciate the full complexity of the issues that they identified may be equally impressive. Their insights at the dawn of the computer age helped launch the information sector. Its growth since then has been mostly a matter of evolution, and the scientific study of that evolution has centered on AI. AI remains the area of computer science most interested in shifting challenging tasks from the human environment, across the interface, and into the computing environment. It also remains the only scientific field to actually boast about being "artificial" in the sense that Simon first intended, and thus the one most relevant to the study of Simon's artificial interface artifacts.

AI remains a multidisciplinary field, where psychologists, linguists, and management scientists mingle freely with mathematicians, statisticians, and electrical engineers. The first three groups study the human organisms and labor to understand the human environment; the last three serve the realm of the silicon-based voltage-reading creatures. They collaborate in AI to shift the barrier separating their worlds. AI improves the quality of the human/computer symbiosis, slowly, incrementally, one task at a time, through the evolutionary process guiding the generational development of increasingly sophisticated software.

But evolution is science. And as everyone knows, science alone doesn't put products on the shelves or equities in our portfolios. Academics of all stripes are notoriously poor product developers; they tend to get distracted by interesting theoretical challenges and philosophical puzzles. Consumers, on the other hand, prefer things that actually work, that perform useful tasks, and in the case of software, that make their computing experiences faster, easier, more productive, and more enjoyable. This consumer preference helped to push many of AI's evolutionary ideas out of the university and into the commercial world, where they landed in the lap of software developers and software companies.

The science that had motivated AI researchers thus plays itself out as software engineering. As always, this shift from science to engineering engenders a significant shift in emphasis. Whereas AI's artificial scientists want to understand the mechanisms underlying software evolution, the practical engineers of software development are more concerned with harnessing those mechanisms. Good software engineers don't worry about the comparative theoretical purity behind selective or brute-force searches, information-intensive databases or general principles of problem solving, mathematical probability theory or abstract symbol manipulation. They learn about all of these techniques, develop broad toolkits, and use whichever combination appears best suited to the task at hand. In other words, software engineers shifted from Simon's focus on the study of design processes to the more mundane task of actual design. That shift simplified a huge number of complex scientific issues that turned out to be purely tangential to the task of evolutionary software design.

Software engineering has its own notables, though they tend to be more focused and pragmatic than are AI researchers. They also tend to work for companies devoted to product development rather than for universities. Fred Brooks, for example, worked for IBM back in the days that Big Blue dominated the world of computing. He served as a project manager first for the IBM System/360 family of computers, and then for the massive OS/360 operating system. These were critical positions; IBM's 360 family was one of the dominant mainframes from the 1960s into the 1980s. Brooks thus possessed ample experience managing large teams of both hardware engineers and computer programmers focused on meeting cutting-edge technological challenges. More to the point, though, Brooks had to figure out how to manage these teams. He began with a general knowledge of management techniques, but he soon realized that coordinating a software design team posed unique challenges. Fortunately, Brooks chose to share his lessons in a series of essays. Once again, the insights of a pioneer proved to be remarkable. *The Mythical Man-Month* may be the only computing book from the 1970s that software engineers continue to study; Brooks's analysis holds up even as the world of software has changed around it.[18] In fact, his twentieth-anniversary edition affirmed all of his basic messages and most of his subsidiary lessons.[19]

Some of Brooks's revelations remain central to the information sector—and in particular to understanding the Microsoft trial. He explained that complex software has a lot in common with a large number of other products, and showed how to tweak some standard management models to accommodate software design. Two textbook design principles, modular design and cost/benefit analysis, explain all but the most technical aspects of software design. Suppose that some creative software developer figures out the math necessary to translate a vague, qualitative task into formal computation. That task would then be ripe for automation. The developer should, in theory, be able to evolve a software implementation of her model that will eventually impel the frontier upward. But how should she approach that challenge? The standard approach is to write a new program that runs on top of the existing interface—and that in turn presents a slightly modified interface to users. In other words, she should write an *application* to run atop her existing *platform*. In order to run on the platform, of course, the application must learn the platform's language—not the language that the platform uses to communicate with humans, but rather a special language that the platform uses to communicate with applications designed to run upon it. This language, known as the platform's application programming interface, or API, enables independent developers to write applications that sit atop platforms without knowing much at all about the platform's inner workings.[20]

This new application is, in some sense, dangling off the edge of the preexisting frontier—perhaps communicating directly with users, perhaps allowing other programs to build upon it to dangle off the frontier still further, and perhaps both. This location presents some advantages and some disadvantages—in other words, it sets up a cost/benefit analysis. Perhaps the greatest benefit of having things dangling off the edge of the frontier is that they are easy to fix. If someone discovers a bug in the application or devises some clever way to improve it, he can snap the application off the frontier, modify it, and reconnect it without disturbing any of the translators between the hardware and the platform. Applications treated as experimental modules need not interfere with the smooth workings of either the platform or of the many translations beneath it.

These simple principles of cost/benefit analysis and modular design are among the keys to software engineering. They were prominent in Brooks's work, we've been teaching them in elementary programming classes for decades, and they retain their importance at the highest levels of commercial development. Some form of high-level schematic describing different computational tasks and the interrelationships among them has guided every program ever written. Each of these computational tasks defines a module within the larger program—a module that managers can then parcel out to individual programmers or teams. But the principle of modularity doesn't end at a program's boundaries. A standalone application program defines a module within a suite of interoperable software—which may, in turn, define a module within an overall computing system, etc. Modules nest within modules as the system grows. Modules at any level turn software into a sort of jigsaw puzzle; pieces developed to perform specific tasks fit together to form a coherent whole.

But modularity can also have a downside—particularly in terms of applications sitting on top of platforms. The downward translation sequence is time-consuming and a drain on the computer's resources. Every additional translation layer reduces the efficiency of the computing and slows things down—a concern that may have been much more important in the early days of computing than it is today, but one that still remains relevant. Extra translation layers also introduce seams into the system—and seams are where any product's problems are most likely to occur. Simon's interface artifacts raise their heads yet again. The natural science internal to the application must pass through the artificial science at the seam into the natural science internal to the platform, and vice versa. The very description of the process suggests potential instability. If, instead, the platform could evolve to subsume the application, then coordination, stability, and efficiency might all be improved.

So much for Simon and science. Back in Brooks's world of practical software engineering, "integration" forms the flip side of modularity. If the developer could integrate the application into the platform, the combined product might run faster and more fluidly. This realization brings us back to the cost/benefit analysis—or perhaps more precisely, to the classic engineering trade-off of design efficiency vs. operational efficiency. A modular application running on top of the platform is easy to design, to fix, and to improve, but it may function less efficiently than it would were it integrated into the platform. Integration thus increases efficiency at the expense of complicating and increasing the expense of modification.

Virtually all engineers face these sorts of trade-offs, and while they may disagree about the specific point at which to integrate an application into a platform, the general principle is well understood. Developers should launch their new innovations as modular applications; new applications tend to contain large numbers of bugs, and modules are easy to fix and to improve. Beyond bugs, though, new applications—and in particular, powerful important applications—tend to motivate waves of innovation. Second- and third-generation releases typically embody not only fixes, but also new features, including some that the developers hadn't even imagined at the time of their first release. Premature integration can do more than simply complicate bug fixes; it can make it harder for developers to grasp the full potential of their products and to develop new and innovative features.

After a while, though, every application's functionality tends to stabilize. Fixes and improvements become much less frequent, innovative features become few and far between, and efficiency concerns loom larger. Such an application is ripe for integration into the platform from a software-engineering perspective. While other factors may argue in favor of maintaining the application as a stand-alone module, the dual fears of causing collateral damage to a stable platform and of impeding innovative improvements shouldn't apply to mature applications. Software engineers may well decide that the potential improvements to the application's efficiency outweigh both the effort of integration and the potential decreases in the platform's efficiency (after all, the larger the platform, the less efficient it is). They may decide to integrate the application's functionality into the platform—thereby evolving the platform further from the machine and closer to humans.

This integration, of course, saves only a single translation. As the erstwhile application's functionality becomes increasingly robust, computer engineers may decide to migrate it even further downward—into machine language, and possibly even into the hardware, where much of Deep Blue's intelligence resides. With each migration downward the efficiency of the application's functionality may increase, but the complexity, cost, and systemic disruption of an upgrade will certainly skyrocket. While good software engineers may debate whether or not a specific application warrants the trade-off, the underlying principle of modular design remains as it was even before Brooks articulated it.

Mutation of a Sector

Integration, translation, and modular design long have been critical to the information sector. That slow evolutionary process mutated to give us the full-blown Internet only about a decade ago. As with most useful mutations, however, the real story began back in the dim recesses of memory. In the late 1960s, a group of academic researchers working on projects sponsored by the Advanced Research Projects Administration (ARPA) of the U.S. Department of Defense (DoD) devised a novel approach to communicating and to sharing data; they built a long-range network of high-speed mainframe computers located at selected universities around the United States.[21] This network, originally known as the ARPANET, grew to encompass many universities and research institutions, as well as research activities outside the ambit of DoD programs. By the late 1980s the ARPANET had become an important backbone for the American—and global—research world. In the early 1990s the federal government withdrew its support for the network's governance and turned it over to a small number of private-sector firms. The network, no longer sponsored by ARPA was renamed the Internet.

The spread of computing and networks throughout the 1980s and early 1990s wasn't restricted to the research world. At least two other important sectors also witnessed rampant computerization: offices and homes. Office automation began with selected administrative, accounting, and word-processing capabilities, then progressed to place a PC on every desk, and eventually interconnected all of those computers via a local area network (LAN). Companies with multiple locations began to network these LANs together to create private, often nationwide (or even global) networks. During this same period, many homes acquired their first PCs, primarily to perform business-like tasks—home finances, writing, homework, etc.—but soon discovered that simply owning a computer created an unexpected set of opportunities. Private-sector companies bet that home consumers would appreciate the benefits of e-mail, information sharing, and connectivity to their proprietary networks via modems and telephone lines.

The 1990s thus began with widespread computing connected to a number of separate, often proprietary, networks. Two further innovations were necessary before that world could evolve into its current form. Perhaps the single greatest weakness of the research-oriented Internet lay in indexing. As a matter of technology, any user on a network could access any file residing anywhere on the network. As a practical matter, there was no systematic way for users to know which files were available, what information they contained, or where they were located. Put another way, the natural science on both sides of the divide was fine; what we lacked was one of Simon's carefully designed interface artifacts. In 1989 Tim Berners-Lee, a researcher at the European Laboratory for Particle Physics (CERN) in Geneva filled that gap. He developed an indexing scheme that gained rapid and widespread acceptance.[22]

Berners-Lee's system combined a text-formatting system called HTML (the Hypertext Markup Language), a communication standard called HTTP (the Hypertext Transfer Protocol), and an addressing scheme to locate "Web sites" called a URL (Universal Resource Locator). This combination essentially broadcast every file's content and location to every user on the network. Broadcasts are only valuable, however, in the presence of receivers. These receivers, known as browsers, allowed users to locate files indexed by URL. The combination of browsers and search engines—programs that search files' keyword lists and return their URLs—enabled full-scale navigation of the Internet. Navigability soon made the original Internet so popular that previously proprietary networks felt compelled to join. They too adopted URLs, enabled keyword indexing, and revised their network protocols to be compatible with those of the ARPA-originated Internet. The World Wide Web was born.

Of course, Berners-Lee didn't create the Web tabula rasa. He built upon many layers of research contributions to provide some critical missing pieces. He himself recognized that Vannevar Bush—head of the U.S. Office of Scientific Research during World War II—foresaw something like the Web as early as 1945. Bush had hoped to build the Memex, a machine that would combine binary coding, instant photography, and other technologies either available or foreseeable in the 1940s, to index and to cross-reference texts stored as microfilm. Twenty years later, Ted Nelson coined the term "hypertext" and predicted that computers would soon allow people to write in this nonlinear format. His futuristic machine of 1965, Xanadu, would publish all of the world's information as hypertext.

But the basic ideas underlying hypertexts and hyperlinks predate even Memex and Xanadu—by more than a few centuries. Journalist Jonathan Rosen demonstrated how the arcane techniques of biblical exegesis embodied in the Babylonian Talmud presaged the Web long ago, in the great Jewish academies of what is now Iraq, in the centuries before the Arab invasion.

I have often thought, contemplating a page of the Talmud, that it bears a certain uncanny resemblance to a home page on the Internet, where nothing is whole in itself but where icons and text boxes are doorways through which visitors pass into an infinity of cross-referenced texts and conversations. Consider a page of the Talmud. There are a few lines of Mishnah, the conversation the Rabbis conducted . . . stemming from the Bible. . . . Underneath these few lines being the Gemarah, the conversation *later* Rabbis had about the conversations *earlier* Rabbis had in the Mishnah. . . . Running in a slender slip down the inside of the page is the commentary of Rashi, the medieval exegete, commenting on both the Mishnah and the Gemarah, and the biblical passages (also indexed elsewhere on the page) that inspired the original conversation. Rising up on the other side . . .

are the tosefists . . . who comment on Rashi's work, as well as on everything Rashi commented on himself. The page is also cross-referenced to other passages of the Talmud, to various medieval codes of Jewish law . . .[23]

Rosen's parallels between Talmudic cross-referencing and hypertext are instructive. Not because huge numbers of Web surfers are likely to access the Talmud—though they could[24]—but rather because they illustrate an important point about technological development and innovation. Talmudic study developed slowly, over the course of centuries. While the discussions themselves included many cross-references, the true challenge arose in designing an appropriate layout. How could printers assemble all of these commentaries-upon-commentaries in a manner that successive generations of scholars could access? It took a certain amount of ingenuity, but they did it. They devised a layout that anyone could follow. Anyone, that is, with suitable Talmudic training. No wonder "exegesis" sounds arcane! The beauty of the Web is that it made this type of nonlinear indexing available to the broad public. And while some still find the Web a daunting place filled with strange dead ends, pop-up ads, irrelevant links, frustrating searches, and unwelcome solicitations, the training necessary to bring them up to speed falls *far* short of the training needed to educate a Talmudic scholar. First the Internet and then the Web democratized a form of nonlinear thinking that was, for ages, the sole province of an esoteric priesthood.

It was Berners-Lee's contributions that made that final step possible: HTML, HTTP, and URL made casual exegesis a reality for millions—so casual, in fact, that we relabeled it "surfing." They also completed the Internet's basic plumbing. The PC revolution had placed computers on every desktop, in all but the least-affluent American homes, and in many public places. The networking revolution had ensured that most of these computers were at least equipped to join a network. URLs and browsers made it easy to share information. The convergence of multiple networks to the single global Internet, no longer focused on scholarly research, guaranteed widespread interconnection. Anyone with information to share could be reasonably certain that he could direct it to his intended audience—if only he could get the members of that audience to request it. Information sharing had suddenly become easy and cheap. Network usage by businesses and consumers would soon dwarf usage by researchers. The Internet was about to adopt an entirely new complexion—a focus on the commercial sector. The stage would soon be set for the explosion of e-commerce into the public consciousness.

As it turned out, the Internet puzzle was still one crucial piece shy of a commercial explosion. The newly complexioned Internet gave businesses and consumers a fundamentally new, low-cost way to exchange information. But relatively few companies felt the need to rush into the online world, and relatively few consumers clamored for such access; total goods sold on the Internet during 1996 reportedly fell below $3 billion. The source of this casual disregard was obvious. Once again, the initial research focus of the Internet had colored the way that the technology had matured—and the features that excited technologically oriented researchers (a.k.a., geeks) didn't necessarily excite typical companies and consumers.

Early browsers contained inelegant textual interfaces useful for the retrieval of text and data files. These browsers became popular among academic researchers, college students, and technophiles but failed to capture the imagination of the public at large.[25] In 1993, a group of students at the University of Illinois developed Mosaic, the first platform-independent, user-friendly, graphics-enabled browser. In 1994, several key members of the Mosaic team (led by Marc Andreessen) moved to the Silicon Valley and joined forces with tech-industry veterans (notably Jim Clark, the founder of Silicon Graphics)[26] to form a company dedicated to the improvement and commercialization of Mosaic: Netscape. Netscape's founding marked the beginning of the full-blown information sector. Everyone "knew" that the Internet was a surefire technological advance and that Netscape would essentially own it. Anyone who wanted to access the Internet would have to pass through Netscape's browser or use Netscape's services.

Not only was Netscape's IPO a precursor of the bubble to come,[27] but its flagship product, Navigator—a modular design sitting atop established translation frontiers, in the spirit of Brooks—motivated the first serious analysis of the new interfaces to the Internet—a design analysis in the spirit of Simon. Cusumano and Yoffie studied the people and ideas that drove Netscape's stratospheric rise. They interviewed many of Netscape's key employees, studied the company's strategic coups and missteps, and contemplated the meaning of *Competing on Internet Time.*[28]

But Netscape's strategic maneuvering was only part of their analysis. The other—and ultimately the more important—part of the "competition" came out of Redmond, Washington. On Pearl Harbor Day—December 7, 1995—Bill Gates announced that Microsoft was redefining itself around the Internet, redesigning all of its software products to be Web-centric, and developing a browser that would be free forever. The news that Microsoft "got" the Internet spread like wildfire through the tech-investment community; some routes to the Internet might no longer pass through Netscape's browser. Netscape soon lost half of its market cap. Microsoft had fired the opening shots of the "browser wars" and set the stage for the trial that would soon share the front pages with the Netscape-inspired bubble.

The browser wars redefined the terrain of network-connectivity providers. As late as 1995, the network world consisted of the research-oriented Internet and a number of separate private and/or proprietary commercial networks. Netscape's Navigator, and soon thereafter Microsoft's Internet Explorer, made the Internet too attractive for anyone to sustain a stand-alone proprietary model. By the end of 1996, even the largest proprietary networks recognized that the Internet age mandated a new business plan. AOL linked its previously proprietary network to the Internet, adopted the advertising slogan "The Internet and More," began offering some of its proprietary content to nonmembers, and changed its fee structure from a base-plus-usage system to a flat fee for unlimited use.[29]

Meanwhile, as AOL labored to redefine home connectivity and content provision in the Internet age, the browser wars raged—until Netscape conceded in late 1998. Netscape's leaders realized that they lacked the resources to compete with Microsoft's tactics—many of which violated the antitrust laws and reminded tech investors why it's good to be a monopolist—and sought a richer partner. AOL acquired Netscape, and Microsoft's Internet Explorer became the dominant gateway to the Internet. The true irony in Netscape's defeat, though, was not its choice of adoptive parents, but rather its timing. Netscape's demise as a stand-alone entity in November 1998 marked the first failure of an inevitable

Internet monopolist—at almost precisely the moment that investors launched the next wave of Internet IPOs to stratospheric valuations.

But those tales, exciting as they were, only obscured the real trends that had finally mutated into a vibrant information sector. Every time that AI translates a new task from the qualitative world of humans to the computational world of machines, the information sector's potential grows. Every time that software engineering implements that translation as a software product, the information sector's actual reach grows. Software's evolutionary stage thus defines the information sector's size, shape, scope, and importance.

That evolution has been rapid and profound. From its humble beginnings as a tool that allowed select government scientists to crunch large numerical problems, the information sector has evolved into the dominant communication platform of the global economy. It has shaken our beliefs about correspondence, about reference libraries, about financial services, about shopping, and about the availability, utility, and ubiquity of information—both critical and frivolous. And it's about to take over the world of entertainment.

Napster's peer-to-peer (P2P) file sharing has already shaken the music industry's self-image. Jazz greats Louis Armstrong and Ella Fitzgerald never thought of themselves as "content creators." Grateful Dead lyricist John Perry Barlow and Metallica drummer Lars Ulrich very clearly do. Ulrich testified in front of the Senate Judiciary Committee about the need to protect his bit strings; he described P2P as "old fashioned trafficking in stolen goods."[30] Barlow rose to Napster's defense. He contended that P2P opened exciting new vistas for artists, enhanced their ability to serve their fan bases, and increased the economic welfare of artists, though likely at the expense of the record labels and production companies: "I do not believe that the kid in Ohio is injuring my economic interests by sharing my music with another fan in Los Angeles, Tokyo, or Dublin. Deadheads have been sharing our songs with each other for decades, and it did nothing but increase the demand for our work."[31] Barlow put his activism where his mouth is by helping to found the cyberlibertarian Electronic Frontier Foundation.[32]

That sort of evolutionary encroachment relates to the artificial science. A series of scientific queries first introduced to allow Shannon's computer to play chess evolved in a matter of decades to enable kids around the world to steal from Metallica while enriching the Dead. It also framed a critical strand of the information sector. The browser wars and the P2P wars reappear later, in chapters 5 and 7, respectively. For the moment, though, they both illustrate the roles that the artificial science of software evolution and its practical counterpart of software engineering played in the information sector's emergence from the ivory tower and onto the front pages.

Beyond the Temples

The information sector jumped into the real world with a splash. For a while, though, the real world hardly seemed real. Warnings of irrational exuberance notwithstanding,[33] alchemists, charlatans, and Ponzi schemers drove crowd psychology to believe in the New World. At its peak, a New World company called Pixelon announced that it had cracked some of the toughest challenges in computer graphics. Though the high-profile Pixelon raised more than $20 million in the fall of 1999 and hosted a star-studded Vegas extravaganza, the whole thing was a fraud. Pixelon CEO Michael Fenne was actually convicted felon David Kim Stanley, an old-time con man who realized that Internet investors were even easier marks than elderly churchgoers.[34] Something was clearly amiss.

It was only a matter of time before investors started to notice that they had been caught in a Ponzi scheme. The network growth pitch had sounded good. Its connection to Microsoft related recent successes to future ones, and grounded the *reasons* for both in academic theory. Listeners unaware of what constituted a "technology company," why Internet pure plays weren't really technology investments, and precisely what network economics established—in other words, most investors—found the argument enticing. It enticed enough of them to get the Ponzi scheme rolling; crowd psychology took over from there. As the bubble grew, the balance between investors seeking a rational explanation and those simply jumping on the bandwagon may have shifted, but the presumption of a plausible justification grounded in cutting-edge economic theory remained critical throughout. And it might very well have worked, except for one tiny problem: the cutting-edge theory was inapplicable to Internet pure plays.

The network economics pitch justifying the bubble had always focused on network growth. But growth alone is insufficient for a company to exhibit the type of strong network effects that helped Microsoft. In order for even a firm controlling a network to reap monopoly profits, it must have some way of *staying* a monopolist when it raises its prices; it needs to lock its consumers in and its competitors out. Investors considering an "inevitable" network monopolist thus need to determine whether entry barriers exist. If they don't, any price increase will anger customers and invite competitive entry. Monopolists unprotected by entry barriers are thus faced with a quandary; they can raise prices and lose their monopoly, or they can keep prices low and remain unprofitable monopolists. Either way, investors would be well advised to consider alternative investments.

The key to the bubble was thus that few, if any, Internet companies were able to lock in enough customers to become profitable. Insufficient attention to the actual conditions of entry and the ease of consumer switching led investors to overestimate barriers to entry. These widespread misconceptions created both the tech-stock boom and the New World paradigm—and doomed them both to become merely interesting historical footnotes.

The challenge of locking-in consumers manifested itself as a lack of customer loyalty—even to successfully branded first movers. Consumers—many of whom were also the very investors decrying the disloyalty—began to compare prices across competing sites, effectively forcing e-tailers to bid away whatever slim margins they may have been attempting to earn. The theoretical predictions of marginal cost pricing and of zero profits throughout the information sector began to raise their ugly heads. Shopping "bots" emerged to help consumers compare prices by accessing the information on multiple sellers' sites and reporting it back to a consumer accessing the bot site. Some bots even allowed consumers to make their purchases without ever visiting the seller's site— thereby reducing the number of hits to that site and consequently the seller's potential to gain revenue by selling advertising space. Some sellers—or sites representing sellers—responded by posting virtual "No

Bots Allowed" signs. E-Bay, for example, hung such a sign, and then (successfully) sued Bidder's Edge's offending bot for trespassing.[35] While this apparent "disloyalty" was really nothing more than a case of rational consumers availing themselves of the Internet's reduced information costs and the inherent lack of lock-in and of switching costs, it helped expose the shortcomings of the New World paradigm's assumption of rampant network effects.

When investors began to grasp these issues, they also began to understand that there was no such thing as "an Internet company," and in particular that it was meaningless to think of a company as "an e-tailer." Companies simply used the Internet in differing degrees to sell a wide array of goods. Online vendors competed with off-line vendors for the same consumer dollars. This understanding would soon lead to the New Channel paradigm. Before that was possible, however, one other "detail" had to be resolved. Internet investors had to realize the full scope of their error. The first *visible* sign came when prominent e-tailers' (also known as B2C, or business-to-consumer, companies), including Toysrus.com, announced days before Christmas 1999 that they could not guarantee delivery in time for the holiday.[36] E-tail stocks quickly fell out of favor.[37] By the end of January 2000, equity prices had fallen far below their highs, and in some cases below their IPO values. From there, the bubble's burst spiraled outward. E-tailers unable to pay for Web development and software renegotiated deals with their suppliers or simply refused to pay—at times even suing for breaches of vague contractual responsibilities.[38]

The combination of unpaid bills and increased skepticism hit hardest at small, highly leveraged service providers. In many cases, the hit came as they were contemplating their own IPOs, giving them the unenviable choice of either stopping work, writing off large portions of their receivables, and risking litigation with deadbeat clients, or continuing work, aging their receivables, and hoping for a B2C upturn. Accounting conventions made their choice easy. They continued work and hoped that a rapid turnaround would make their aging invoices collectable. Most of them also decided to postpone their IPOs until that day arrived. As a result—and because most of them are still awaiting that day—IPOs were delayed and eventually cancelled, valuations of public companies dropped, and the disillusionment with New World thinking spread from B2C firms to Web developers and Internet-focused software companies.[39] The disillusionment spiral continued. It moved horizontally to B2B (business-to-business), vertically to more conventional software firms, and outward into Web-hosting companies, computer hardware, chip and component makers, optical equipment firms, etc.

Companies in traditional businesses that had oriented themselves toward Internet and New Economy companies felt the pain as well; Internet magazines folded and law firms with strong technology groups disbanded. By the middle of 2002, the unwind had reached pipeline company–cum–bandwidth trader Enron, and large, debt-laden telecommunications firms like Global Crossing and WorldCom. In all three cases, questionable accounting practices and allegations of outright fraud compounded the issue. The lack of public diligence to the financials of the firms in which we had invested had given their accountants a false sense of omnipotence. We queried their auditors and learned that oversight had been virtually nonexistent. That revelation brought down the once-venerable firm of Arthur Andersen & Co. The "tech wreck" changed the perception of the Internet among investors, analysts, industry observers, and the public at large. It also provided the empirical data necessary to discredit the New World view,[40] and to set the survivors on the path towards more realistic New Channel thinking.

In the first true public display of the real world information sector, then, we misconstrued network economics to miscast Internet companies as inevitable monopolists. More significantly, though, we became excited, hopeful, and focused on growth. But while the economy as a whole and the information sector in particular experienced stunning and sustained growth, our portfolios didn't fare quite as well. The priests had lost control of their creation—and left investors holding the bag—as information products completed their transition from laboratory experiments to major players in the global economy. We the investing public were not alone, it seems, in realizing that we had much more to learn.

5

Mortal Combat

Life on the Street

The Internet is hardly the only important figure in the information sector, but it was the most blessed. Unlike the Internet's coddled youth as a plaything for the funded and sagacious, the software industry endured a rough and tumble childhood on the mean streets of competitive commerce. It began life as a scrappy fighter seeking respect in a hardware-dominated world. By the mid-1990s, it had matured to overtake the lumbering mainframes that had both tormented it and protected it during its formative years. But the scars of its troubled youth remained. Many of the key players of its early days, shining, rising stars in their time, had met their untimely demise. Yet even so, some were spared and even thrived.

One software company in particular emerged as the kingpin, dominating first operating systems—those critical programs that defined the translation frontier—then the graphical interfaces to those operating systems. From that position of strength, it expanded to take over a broad swath of the applications terrain. Its operating system evolved upward, as its graphical interfaces finally stabilized to allow safe integration into the underlying operating system. This evolved product at the translation frontier took the name "platform."

At just about the time that the evolved platform first appeared, the kingpin of software, toughened, scarred, and cocky, first encountered the Internet naïf wandering gingerly into the world of commerce. The kingpin was perplexed; never had he encountered such crude gullibility. It seemed that the Internet had come to town intending to wade in the dirty waters of commerce without getting soiled. She had arrived with an ethic of openness and sharing, and asked for little beyond Mountain Dew and a foosball table. The kingpin ignored her; life in the city would teach the Internet a lesson.

But the kingpin's savvy scouts noticed that this bumpkin of an Internet, despite her obvious naivety, was not without a certain charm—or a certain potential. They noticed an adoring public showering her with fawning adoration, admiration, and above all, money. And so the kingpin took a second look, and he saw the Internet in a new light. He saw the potential that the Internet carried, and he knew then and there that he had to have her. "I will make this Internet my own!" he bellowed. "I will give her my name and dress her in my clothes, and soon none will recall where my domain used to end and that of the Internet used to begin. And I will be kingpin not only of the software industry, but of the Internet as well."

And so the kingpin set out to remake the Internet in his own image. He employed the very same methods that had served him so well on his way to the top. And once again, he littered the streets with the bodies that he left behind. Almost without our noticing it, the Internet began to appear dressed in the kingpin's clothes. We almost lost sight of her, as she moved behind the kingpin's gates to be glimpsed only through his windows. No longer did the Internet romp through the mosaic of software styles that she had enjoyed in her carefree youth. And though the selfsame government that had given the Internet life and trusted her to find fame and fortune in the city of commerce moved to challenge the kingpin of software, its efforts may have been too little and too late. For more and more, the Internet came to resemble the kingpin, until one day we found ourselves looking from kingpin to Internet, and from Internet to kingpin, and from kingpin to Internet again; but already it was impossible to say which was which.

Birth of a Behemoth

Microsoft wasn't always Microsoft. And when I say that, I mean more than just that its original name was Micro-Soft. The heartwarming tale of two high school friends who left college to found the world's most successful company has been told many times and has inspired many imitators; the dot-com world was overrun with them. But even long after Micro-Soft became Microsoft, it *still* wasn't today's Microsoft, the behemoth from Redmond, scourge of the software world. Throughout the 1980s and into the 90s, Microsoft competed with other companies producing software for personal computers. By the mid-1990s, Microsoft was the unchallenged kingpin of PC software. How did it get there?

An uncanny knack for launching the right product at the right time took it part of the way. In fact, some contend that marketing is *the only* area in which Microsoft excels. But, you may be wondering, why are we talking about product quality and marketing skills? What of increasing returns, positive feedback, and virtuous cycles? What of tipping to a standard and lock-in? Didn't Microsoft's Windows simply become the *de facto* standard for PC operating systems? Why wouldn't that alone be enough to guarantee Microsoft's dominance and to relegate all others to remote corners of the computing world, if not to outright oblivion?

All fine questions. But before we even get to network economics, we must answer two more basic questions—how a software monopolist emerged from the pack, and why it was Microsoft. Competitive markets are supposed to be robust. It should be virtually impossible to cheat your way into becoming a monopolist. The Bork-inspired Chicago School even revolutionized antitrust law by arguing that virtually all markets would regulate themselves through the competitive process, and that antitrust enforcement should be extremely rare. And yet, by the late 1990s, Robert Bork himself had come to believe that Microsoft had beaten the system to become a marauding monopolist. Roughly twenty years after *The Antitrust Paradox* took Washington by storm with its advocacy of government abstinence from antitrust enforcement, Bork agreed to help represent Netscape in support of the government's case against Microsoft. But that, too, lay in the future.

Long before any of those events occurred, Microsoft became a monopolist by being the strongest player in a market protected by reasonably high barriers. Economists are well aware of the human penchant for monopolization. They know that every entrant wants to compete, that every competitor wants to join an oligopolistic cartel, and that every oligopolist wants to destroy his competitors to become a monopolist. But they also know that only markets protected by barriers to entry are prone to monopolization. In the absence of such barriers, a monopolist's attempt to raise prices and to extract added profits from consumers will invite new entrants. The relationship among entry barriers, switching costs, and profitability doomed the dot-coms. But software has at least two natural protective barriers, and both are highest in platforms.

The first barrier derives from the nature of software itself, and from the difficulty inherent in profiting from the sale of a product that lends itself to unauthorized reproduction—the zero-price prediction that haunts the information sector. A software company must invest time and effort in software development, but once the first copy goes out the door, competitors can copy it and circulate it at virtually no cost. The barrier thus arises because the software business appears to be inherently unprofitable. This "unprofitability" barrier presented itself in the early days of software, gained resolution to some extent, but continues to rematerialize; outright software piracy remains a huge issue in the international arena, and the outcry over P2P file swapping continues to roil the entertainment industry. This barrier is also fundamental, so anyone interested in profiting from an information product must devise a way around it. Many people believe that in the absence of IP rights, no one would ever develop software. We thus decided, as a matter of industrial policy, to award IP rights to software developers. But not everyone agrees with this view. Others argue that we were wrong to consider software marketable in the first place. They prefer to view software as a calling card designed to promote documentation, customization, support, and service businesses—all of which require expertise that is harder to "steal." In the contemporary software industry, the first solution has led to powerful products like Windows, Acrobat, and Quicken; the second to powerful products like Linux and Apache. But either way, all software developers know that the barrier is real and are unlikely to enter the marketplace until they see a way around it—and toward profitability.

The second natural barrier in software markets, and the one that's both of greater significance today and of more direct relevance to Microsoft's position as a monopolist, lies in the network nature of the operating systems market. But that's a barrier for a mature industry. There may be no way to reach the network barrier to entry until we've resolved the unprofitability barrier. How did this industry ever develope? Why didn't rampant piracy stop it dead in its tracks? After all, how could anyone—much less a start-up software firm—police and enforce IP rights that are so easy to ignore?

A historical detour may provide some answers. Back in the 1950s, 60s, and 70s, the way to make money in the computer business was to sell computers: big, expensive, precision equipment that only governments, universities, and big businesses could afford. These machines often filled an entire room, and access to that "computer room" was strictly controlled. Most users—and becoming an authorized user was far from trivial—wrote their programs on paper. Then, confident that the program would work, a users would present her work to a keypunch operator who would help her produce a stack of coded punch cards. The user would then walk the punched cards over to the computer window and hand them to a computer operator, who would interact with the actual computing machine. The user would break for dinner, maybe take in a movie, and return later to pick up her output. And that's if she were lucky. Such was the world of "batch processing."

Now, this little blast from the past may bring fits of nostalgia to some, peals of laughter to others, but it's unlikely to make anyone jump up and scream: *Man, if I were around back then, I would have started a software company!* And by and large, nobody did. The task of writing software fell to the computer companies, who saw it primarily as a component of the computing systems that they were selling. Their products consisted of many working parts; some were hardware and others software. Occasionally, a hardware manufacturer might allow a small company—or even a couple of college kids—to develop software under contract. For the most part, software was just a component of a computing system.

But technology marches on, and by the mid-1970s the machines had become smaller and less expensive, the programming community had grown beyond its original retinue of well-trained nerds with company-issued pocket protectors, and the wonderful world of punch cards had begun to fade into the era of the dumb terminal. All of a sudden, programmers could sit at individual computer screens and observe their interactions with the still-hidden computing machine. A few companies, such as Radio Shack, even made small stand-alone "personal" computing machines. Suddenly, we had developed a class of software users—people who might even be willing to buy software that didn't come with their machines.

Of course, no one could have seen this niche as a decent way to make money. After all, everyone who owned a computer knew how to write his own programs. Hobbyists *bought* computers to write code; that's what made them hobbyists. And those who wanted to use others' programs could copy them easily. The unprofitability barrier made the prospects for a software industry look bleak.

No decent-sized company was likely to dedicate the resources necessary to engage in such a risky line of business. The prospects for profitability just seemed to be too slim. And so the challenge fell to a couple of kids. Back in 1975, when keypunches, terminals, and personal computers coexisted, Paul Allen showed Bill Gates a copy of *Popular Electronics* with a cover story describing the MITS Altair 8800, a $360 computing kit. The two crafted code exciting enough to earn them a contract writing Altair software. And so, in the balance of risks taken in the name of innovation, Gates dropped out of Harvard to found Micro-Soft, Allen moonlighted at Micro-Soft while keeping his job at MITS, and MITS ponied up the princely sum of $3,000, agreed to share the royalties with the kids and their little startup, and (I guess) looked the other way as Allen moonlighted.[1]

At the beginning, MITS appeared to have the best of the deal. Micro-Soft's software became reasonably popular reasonably quickly, and it probably helped improve Altair sales. That made MITS happy, but it didn't really help the young Mr. Gates; Micro-soft was having a hard time collecting its royalties. Much to Gates's chagrin, few people were willing to pay for software that they could easily copy from their friends. Fortunately for the future of his company, Gates wasn't bashful. On February 3, 1976, Gates penned an open letter challenging the governing ethos of the small-but-growing hobbyist community.

To me, the most critical thing in the hobby market right now is the lack of good software courses, books and software itself. Without good software and an owner who understands programming, a hobby computer is wasted. Will quality software be written for the hobby market?

Almost a year ago, Paul Allen and myself, expecting the hobby market to expand, hired Monte Davidoff and developed Altair BASIC. Though the initial work took only two months, the three of us have spent most of the last year documenting, improving and adding features to BASIC. . . . The value of the computer time we have used exceeds $40,000.

The feedback we have gotten from the hundreds of people who say they are using BASIC has all been positive. Two surprising things are apparent, however, 1) Most of these "users" never bought BASIC (less than 10% of all Altair owners have bought BASIC), and 2) The amount of royalties we have received from sales to hobbyists makes the time spent on Altair BASIC worth less than $2 an hour.

Why is this? As the majority of hobbyists must be aware, most of you steal your software. Hardware must be paid for, but software is something to share. Who cares if the people who worked on it get paid? Is this fair? . . . One thing you do is prevent good software from being written. . . . Most directly, the thing you do is theft.[2]

Gates's lament is a wonderfully articulate expression of a fundamental problem. He had inadvertently developed a business model that would later inspire an entire generation of dot-coms: Build your market first and worry about profits later. Unlike his followers on the Internet, though, Gates recognized the model's folly. He knew that if he could collect royalties from only one out of every ten "customers," he would have to charge an exorbitant royalty rate just to break even—and that, high price in turn, would drive even more hobbyists to theft. How could anyone expect to make money in such a cockamamy business?

While it was tough for a couple of years, the young company flowered beyond its maiden contract with Altair, lost its hyphen, moved to Washington State, and built itself up to a couple of dozen employees and a few million in annual revenues. While a few other software companies managed to spring up, the business model still looked shaky. Software was just too hard to steal. In 1981, Microsoft got its big break. IBM, with the help of Intel, was about to foray into the world of personal computing. But IBM had designed all of its software to power mainframes. It was unsuitable for a machine designed for home users, hobbyists, and small businesses. IBM needed an operating system to power its new machine. In one of those occasional fateful decisions that determine the course of industrial history, IBM outsourced the task and licensed MS-DOS (Microsoft Disk Operating System) to serve as its operating system.

Microsoft suddenly had a captive audience—everyone whose IBM computer came equipped with MS-DOS—and captives can't be thieves. An entire world of IBM customers would have no opportunity to avoid paying Microsoft's royalties. Microsoft was thus able to clear that first fateful barrier of easy theft; its guaranteed royalties were large enough to both recoup its fixed development costs and to turn a profit. Any further sales that it could make before rampant piracy set in were gravy.

So that explains Microsoft. How did anyone else enter this nascent software industry? Though IBM was the biggest of the hardware manufacturers, it was far from the only one. At that time, consumers configured their own systems. They were able to choose from among a number of hardware companies, and the hardware choice restricted their operating systems choices. MS-DOS was popular, but it wasn't even the only version of DOS, and DOS wasn't the only operating system. The operating system choice, in turn, delimited the range of available software—at least some of which came preloaded onto the system. Once again, software sold with hardware provided software companies at least some security. The software companies also began offering documentation and services to their paying clients, effectively expanding their product offerings beyond the easily stolen software itself. And then, to a large extent, the community ethos changed. Consumers came to share Gates's belief that unauthorized copying of software was theft. At least many American consumers came to share that belief. In other parts of the world, different beliefs dominate even today. By some estimates, for example, piracy accounts for over ninety percent of all software in China—roughly the same proportion of the market that motivated Gates's open letter.

And so, the software industry cleared its first barrier and emerged to play a small role in a computing world still dominated by hardware. And Microsoft, through its partnership with IBM, stood poised to become the biggest player in that new industry.

From Playground to Battleground

So what exactly is the software industry? Computer science may have taught us about the underlying evolutionary science, and maybe even some basic principles of software design, but it was silent on the commercial end. What is it that software companies actually do? And even more importantly, given how easy it is to steal their products, how do they manage to turn a profit? The priests of computer science were silent on this matter for a reason. The answer lies beyond their temple—in the realm of IP, where Congress was charged with crafting industrial policy to motivate software developers and to shape the market.

Because software evolves, developers must constantly change their focus to help each generation's users achieve increasingly sophisticated tasks. The aspects of software, of software engineering, and of software management that appear central to the field's definition change every few years. At any given point in time, though, three key questions define the software industry: What types of software comprise the contemporary commercial industry? Which of the industry's characteristics drive consumer preferences? and How can firms profit from developing software? If these questions sound familiar, they should. They echo the questions in the discussion of Lyle Bowlin's drive to unseat Amazon.com: Of course, back then we asked them in their generic form: What's your product? What makes your product special? How are you going to use that "special quality" to generate profits? Here we see them in their software-specific incarnation. But their underlying truth remains untouched. If you want to make money, you need both a product responsive to consumer needs and a business plan capable of generating profits. Software companies must rethink all three questions every time that the translation frontier evolves to define a new generation of software.

The two broad categories of commercial software are platforms and applications. Platform programs sit at the translation frontier separating the human environment from the computing environment. Human users communicate with the platform directly; the platform begins the translation downward to voltage levels. When the machine responds to trigger the upward translation chain, the platform conveys the response back to the user. The best-known examples of platforms are operating systems, such as DOS, Windows, OS/2, Unix, and Linux. Sometimes, though, users need more help translating their concerns down to voltage-level queries. They enlist the aid of application programs, whose specific capabilities allow them to function as modular additions sitting atop the platform. Popular types of application programs include word processors, spreadsheets, and games.

As software evolves, each generation incorporates new technological innovations to shift the translation frontier further away from voltage and closer to English. Much as this evolution shifts the balance between hardware and software, it also shifts the balance between platforms and applications. Each technological generation incorporates more tasks that had been required to translate down from English into the chain growing upward from voltage. These shifts migrate tasks from applications to platforms to hardware and impel software development toward increasingly natural input languages and interfaces. As a result, the boundaries between platforms and applications shift with each successive generation of technology. These boundaries have changed multiple times within the brief history of the software industry. Commercial opportunities follow that technological lead; again, technology creates opportunities and economic incentives indicate which opportunities businesses choose to pursue.

Under any generation of the technology, successful communication between the platform and the applications is critical; without this last remaining translation, the entire system is useless. Platform developers help application developers learn to communicate with their platforms by publishing dictionaries and grammars. These translation aides are the platform's application programming interfaces (APIs).

Despite the consistent (and ongoing) changes that the software industry encounters as technology advances, some basic things never seem to change. Almost all computers have always housed exactly one platform but many applications. And virtually all users have always looked for computer systems that can accomplish a broad range of tasks. Users have thus tended to select a platform first, and to accept the de facto restriction to applications that can communicate with the platform they select.

That user decision shifts our attention from computer science to network economics. The choice of platforms defines both the virtual networks of the software world and the second great entry barrier of the software market. The "applications barrier to entry" is a two-sided network effect. It arises because rational applications developers write programs that run on the largest platform network, thereby making it even more attractive to users. Users, in turn, purchase the platform that hosts the largest collection of interesting applications, that choice minimizes the de facto restrictions that they need accept. The two trends reinforce each other, making the largest platform subject to strong network effects. As Microsoft and the dot-coms all learned, this barrier works only when developers and/or consumers commit to network membership by sinking switching costs. The Internet barrier to entry proved spurious; Microsoft's applications barrier to entry is quite real.

Much as the unprofitability barrier complicated the software industry's birth, this network barrier threatens its continued health. One of the great questions hovering over the information sector is how to navigate around this barrier. Our best antitrust experts tried to answer it and failed. They proved conclusively at trial that the network barrier was real, that its misuse constituted a grave danger, that Microsoft controlled it, and that Microsoft had misused it. And yet, Microsoft emerged still firmly in control of the platform market and the entry barrier that it implies. In the future, others may rise to meet the challenge; perhaps our IP experts will succeed where their predecessors failed.

But even if they do, that story would lie in the future. We're still looking at the eternal: the invariant forces that shape the software industry as it evolves from one generation of technology to the next. The critical lessons here are that network barriers to entry are ubiquitous and that the hurdles they impose become higher as the products become more complex and the market nears saturation. What's more, these barriers are natural consequences of rational behavior; independent developers and individual consumers make only the decisions that maximize their return—at least in the short run. And while consumer decisions drive developer decisions and vice versa, the platform developer can sit back and watch the value of its platform grow exponentially through the independent unpaid efforts of developers and consumers.

Well, perhaps "unpaid" is a bit extreme. After all, given how much a platform owner can gain from building a big network, a little signing bonus might be in order. The applications barrier to entry creates some interesting incentives. On the one hand, platform development is tough work. Software companies that develop powerful platforms want—and deserve—compensation for their efforts. Logically, a good platform should be expensive. As a platform becomes more expensive, though, fewer users will buy it. Fewer users buying it reduces the applications it will attract. And the fewer applications it attracts, the less valuable the network becomes. Thus, paradoxically, the more expensive the platform, the less valuable the network. But the flip side is also true. If the platform were both powerful and free, it would be everywhere—at least in theory. Users would install it (there would be no need to "buy" it), applications developers would write to its APIs, and its network would become quite valuable. But with no price tag, the platform developer would either have to find an alternative revenue source or go the way of so many dot-coms.

This second model lies at the heart of the "free software" or "open source" movement, in many ways the hobbyists' response to Gates's open letter. Gates had posited that in the absence of profitability, no one would write good software. After all, why would anyone invest the time and effort necessary to develop software if they couldn't sell it? The hobbyists behind the open source movement had an answer: pride of authorship. But their other answers might be more compelling to those who don't think like artists: first, a huge talent pool of programmers sharing their abilities freely should produce some pretty powerful software; second, good software creates service-sector opportunities that developers are best positioned to win. Now in all honesty, plenty of people find even these rationales to be wanting, including those like Gates himself who consider this model of software development to be the antithesis of capitalism. But some good capitalists, including those running IBM and Sun, disagree. They contend that open-source development is an important part of a competitive software industry.

From the perspective of entry barriers, though, open source promises an alternative revenue stream to platform developers who choose to grow their networks by circulating their software free of charge. It thus has the potential to resolve the ultimate paradox of network businesses: the inverse relationship between platform price and network value. Shapiro and Varian outlined this resolution as a unique business strategy available only in network industries:[3] Take a loss to build your network, then generate revenues from locked-in customers in your aftermarket. But first, *make sure that you've locked in your customers.* Otherwise, you're headed down the path of dot-com doom.

That said, adventures in the aftermarket can be tricky—as Kodak learned during the post-Chicago counterrevolution. But most aftermarket strategies are not problematic. After all, consumers should understand that they will be locked into a network defined by whichever platform they choose. As long as the platform owner is honest about the kinds of aftermarket costs that consumers are likely to incur and about the kinds of opportunities that they're likely to find to address those needs, the market cops need show no concern.[4]

Apple and Microsoft both dealt with this network paradox back in the 1980s. While they approached it in different ways, both companies realized that platform pricing was much harder than application pricing, precisely because of the relative sizes of the aftermarket. The weaker network barriers in applications markets allow software companies to operate like other companies in other industries, who try to set their prices to maximize profits through the optimal combination of unit prices and volume sales.

Strategic considerations highlight the differences between the incentives of platform developers and those of application developers. They also split the software industry into two arenas with distinct incentive patterns. The most likely source of revenue to a platform developer comes from the sale of network access and related support and services. The most likely source of revenue to an application developer comes from software sales. At the moment, Microsoft is kingpin of both worlds. It rules the platform world with Windows and reigns over an important part of the applications world with Office.[5]

Microsoft won the office-software battle despite a protracted government investigation that progressed through much of the early 1990s. But little awareness of Microsoft's tactics in office applications markets worked its way into the public consciousness. After all, these actions occurred long before the information sector took up residence on the front page. By the time that the papers made big news of Microsoft's attempt to use Windows to make the Internet its own and thereby to emerge as the undisputed kingpin of the information sector, the software playground in which the youthful Micro-Soft had merrily launched Altair BASIC had become a deadly battleground bloodied from Microsoft's many victories.

Leader of the Pack

Behavior in battle is often controversial—and Microsoft's has been no exception. In certain circles, it's not at all uncommon to see the names "Bill Gates" and "Mephistopheles" linked. Yet every trip along the road to perfidy begins with but a few simple steps. For Microsoft, the first step was Gates's decision—from day one—to focus on the consumer market rather than on the cutting edge of the software world. The second step was Microsoft's ability to keep abreast of cutting-edge developments while building downstream consumer products. The third was Microsoft's consistent incorporation of ideas gleaned from others into its own products. From there, Microsoft's descent to the inner circle followed quickly. In the eyes of many software developers, Microsoft stole other people's ideas, developed weaker versions of them, wrapped them in its own product line, and took credit for them.

Of course, not everyone shares that opinion, even within the technical community. To many, Gates's business model was pure genius. Consumer demand drove Microsoft's entire product line. Whereas most engineers like to invent gadgets that excite other engineers, Gates looked for products struggling to earn a toehold in the consumer world, like the MITS Altair or the IBM PC, and supplied the missing piece. He scoured the market for newly launched ideas with potential and devised ways to turn them into popular products. He catapulted consumer computing decades ahead of where it might have been without him. Gates's supporters are confident that Microsoft and its leader belong to Paradiso, not Inferno. A Google search shows Gates's name linked far more often with God and Jesus than with Mephistopheles—and only a small fraction of these hits relate to the wonderful efforts of the Bill and Melinda Gates Foundation to improve the health of the world's poorest people.[6]

In all likelihood, the truth lies somewhere in between (as it always does). But the debate, if not its intensity, does raise an interesting question: How good are Microsoft's products? It's fair to suppose that they must be pretty good to have buried their competitors. After all, if a competing platform were better than Windows, wouldn't it have become the standard? The answer lies back in the temple of network economics.

Liebowitz and Margolis, the skeptics who claimed the inherent superiority of the QWERTY keyboard, contend that inferior products never get locked in. They moved beyond typewriters to argue that VHS offered consumers a better combination of price and quality than Beta—challenging another classic example of lock in. Then they turned to software. In *Winners, Losers, and Microsoft*,[7] they claimed that Microsoft's consistently superior products led to its many victories—and that superior competing products led to Microsoft's few losses.

Build a better mousetrap and the world will beat a path to your door. This, surely, is one path to success. There's nothing mysterious or underhanded about the success of a company that provides consumers with a product that gives more bang for the buck than its competitors. . . . But the possibility of lock-in suggests that there may be other paths to market determination. . . . If and when there is lock-in, a product succeeds in spite of inferior quality. . . . One interesting market to study is the software market, which is often alleged to exhibit network effects, lock-in, leveraging, and tipping. . . . Microsoft, by any reckoning, is a tremendously successful company, but why is it so successful? Does it just build better mousetraps? Or, as some have claimed, are its products only mediocre? Has it achieved its large market share in spite of its mediocre products, by lock-in and luck, or through the leveraging of its ownership of the operating system? Our data provide clear answers to these questions. Good products win. Microsoft's success derives from good business decisions and superior products.[8]

Their data analyses make a compelling case that Microsoft was more responsive to market demands than were its competitors, that Microsoft provided superior combinations of price and quality, and that the market rewarded those efforts by granting Microsoft market leadership—particularly in the spreadsheet and word-processor markets whose data they studied. Nevertheless, their analyses also misconstrued some basic claims of network economics, most of the government's allegations in its antitrust case, and the reason that Microsoft's leveraging of its Windows monopoly threatens innovation and creativity across the world of software.

Growing from just one of many competitors into a monopolist is tough. And that's where Liebowitz and Margolis made a critical mistake. Their analysis of market data and product reports stressed the quality of Microsoft's products, the savvy of its marketing department, and the wisdom of its business strategies. But even if Microsoft's successful products were far superior to those of its competitors, it's hard to see how Microsoft could have *monopolized* these markets in the absence of network effects. Suppose, for example, that several consecutive generations of Microsoft Excel were better than the concurrent releases of Lotus 1-2-3. It seems unlikely that the quality gap would have been sufficient to knock Lotus down to a niche without a bit of help. That help likely came from Excel's working more smoothly with Windows. That edge represents a leveraging effect; Microsoft pushed from its monopoly in platforms to gain a second monopoly in spreadsheets (and a third in word processors). But even superior quality and leverage shouldn't have been enough for Microsoft to monopolize a market—other than one that tipped to a standard. What's more, Liebowitz and Margolis completely ignored the nature of lock in; though Microsoft's products may have been unrivaled at the time that they locked in consumers, there's no guarantee that superior rivals wouldn't emerge. Microsoft needed to create artificial barriers to stave off that possibility. Therein lay the antitrust violation and the harm to consumers.

But Liebowitz and Margolis were hardly alone in ignoring (or avoiding) this point. They were joined by the editorial pages of the *Wall Street Journal*—a consistent vociferous critic of the government's case—and by the many callers to talk radio who asked: "Why can't the government just leave Microsoft alone? They broke up the phone company and now look at the mess we're in." Questions of this sort suggest how poorly the scholars of both network economics and antitrust have educated the general public. The breakup of AT&T was extremely beneficial to consumers; prices plummeted, service offerings soared, and the only real downside has been an annoying telemarketing campaign.

In a deeper sense, though, these talk-radio callers had correctly detected parallels to the telephone monopoly. Ma Bell had given us the best, most reliable, most comprehensive, least expensive communications system in the history of the planet. Who could have been blamed for thinking that it might not be a good idea to tamper with such a good thing? The same was true of Microsoft. Windows was—and remains—the best, least expensive, easiest to use, most widely accepted, most reliable platform software standard the world has ever seen. Were we really sure that we wanted market cops tampering with a good thing like Windows—or with the valuable, admired company that developed it?

Yes. We were sure. Windows may have become the de facto standard because Microsoft's remarkable knack for releasing the right product at the right time positioned it to have the most popular platform at the time that the market tipped to a standard. That quirk of timing arose in part through a combination of product quality, marketing savvy, and luck— the factors typically necessary to catapult a strong competitor to monopoly status. But in the case of Windows, quality, savvy, and luck were not all Microsoft had going for it. Microsoft also had reached a strategic decision to skirt the borders of both IP law and antitrust law. And the genesis of that strategy takes us back to our historical detour.

By the mid-1980s, several competing versions of DOS were available; Microsoft's MS-DOS was the most popular of them. Meanwhile, the overlords of IBM's Big Blue Empire continued collaborating with Microsoft to develop the operating system of the future, OS/2, the platform that would simultaneously supplant DOS and cripple the Mac— thereby restoring the empire to the full reach of its glory. Microsoft's little secret was that while it was intent on maintaining the empire's integrity, it planned on staging a coup. Microsoft realized that the world of computing needed livelier, younger leadership—and it had only one candidate in mind. But circa 1985, no one outside of Microsoft knew that (though some may have suspected it).

Between about 1985 and 1987, a couple of important new products hit the market. One was DR-DOS, first released by Digital Research in 1987. DR-DOS was fast, efficient, clean, and it allowed you to run *any* program originally written for MS-DOS. Digital Research, in fact, claimed that DR-DOS was superior to MS-DOS. Microsoft didn't debate the point; its confidence in OS/2 had led it to more-or-less ignore MS-DOS's development.[9] DR-DOS thus threatened Microsoft's bread-and-butter product. DR-DOS and MS-DOS presented identical translation frontiers. The two could talk to all of the same machines, they spoke the same API dialect, and they could converse fluently with all of the same applications.

Throughout the rest of the 1980s and on into the 90s, Microsoft faced real competition in the DOS market. At one point, DR-DOS captured ten percent of the U.S. market—and did even better overseas.[10] And DR-DOS's reputation for superior quality just grew. In August 1990, for example, *BYTE* magazine glowed that:

The latest incarnation of DR DOS, Digital Research's MS-DOS clone, is an innovative and intriguing operating system that's thoughtfully designed. Version 5.0 is also packed with the extra features that Microsoft's own operating system should have (and might eventually have if the long-rumored MS-DOS 5.0 becomes a reality). As the people at DRI make very clear, its not pronounced Doctor DOS, although the analogy isn't far off the mark, since it indeed cures many (but not all) of MS-DOS's shortcomings.[11]

Several months later, in its "Awards for Technical Excellence" issue, *PC Magazine* gushed:

Digital Research is the microcomputer operating system company that predates Microsoft. As if to prove it hasn't lost its touch, DR DOS 5.0 does all the things you wish MS-DOS did. Its features include . . . full compatibility with MS DOS. . . . Everybody's DOS should be this advanced.[12]

Microsoft was hurting—and worried. Gates himself lamented that: "DOS being fairly cloned has had a dramatic impact on our pricing for DOS. I wonder if we would have it around 30–40% higher if it wasn't cloned. I bet we would!"[13]

Microsoft fought back—on two fronts. The first lay somewhere in that netherworld between marketing and propaganda. Microsoft issued a number of strategic announcements about products and improvements that it was on the verge of releasing—products that might prove to be incompatible with DR-DOS. This practice, known in the industry as releasing "vaporware," is an insidious way to frighten customers away from powerful competing products without really offering them an alternative.[14]

The second front was even more insidious. It involved that second important product launched in the mid-1980s—Microsoft Windows. Windows 1.0, launched in 1985, adhered to the gospel of modularity; it was a graphical interface that sat on top of DOS. DOS continued to define the translation frontier, and thus the network; Windows was an application that communicated with DOS. It was, of course, a special type of application, because in addition to talking directly to users (as most applications do), Windows also exposed its own set of APIs to communicate with other applications. Such special applications are "middleware" between the platform and the more conventional applications. True applications perform a task. They communicate with the platform at one end and the human user at the other. True platforms, on the other hand, embody full downward-translation chains. Middleware communicates only with the platform at one end—it relies on the platform for the rest of the downward chain—yet with another application at the other end. The gospel of modularity implies that developers should launch potential platform innovations as middleware, where they're easy to fix, to modify, and to improve without interfering with the platform. Each generation's middleware programs provide candidates for migration downward in the next evolutionary stage of the platform's development.

Microsoft set out to monopolize the DOS market by growing a network around its proprietary Windows APIs. Independent application developers who wanted to take advantage of Windows' graphical capabilities could write programs that spoke the Windows API language. Many developers chose not to go the Windows route. Programs that spoke directly to DOS tended to remain faster and more robust—if less attractive and less user-friendly—than those that communicated with DOS only through Windows. Nevertheless, many other independent developers— as well as Microsoft's own application team—did learn and use the Windows APIs. Many consumers appreciated this new combination of an inexpensive machine with the look and feel of a Mac. Windows-based applications came to represent a significant chunk of the market.

This burgeoning demand for Windows products within the DOS market posed a quandary for Digital Research. One of DR-DOS's biggest selling points was that it could talk to all of the same programs as MS-DOS. In order to maintain that feature, DR-DOS needed to be able to talk to all of the Windows-based programs. Either Digital Research could write its own program that spoke the Windows API language, or DR-DOS could talk to Microsoft's Windows. For obvious reasons, the first approach would have been more lucrative (after all, Digital Research might have picked up a significant chunk of the growing Windows market), but the second was easier—or at least, it should have been.

Microsoft ensured that neither could occur. Gates himself "doubt[ed Digital Research] will be able to clone Windows. It is very difficult to do technically, we have made it a moving target and we have some visual copyright and patent protection. I believe people underestimate the impact DR-DOS has had on us in terms of pricing."[15] This sort of security blanket combines the good and the bad. Microsoft's ability to design and to develop a technically sophisticated product serves consumers well. It's a perfect illustration of how IP rights motivate innovation; the Constitution would be proud. Microsoft's decision to "make it a moving target," on the other hand, serves no purpose other than to keep competitors out of the market. From the perspective of consumers, it's a potential disaster. It diverts Microsoft's time from product improvement to market protection. It prevents Digital Research (or anyone else) from designing a product that's not only compatible with Windows, but that might even be superior to it. And, as Gates noted, it helps Microsoft keeps its price up. The net effect is that consumers in May 1989—when Gates wrote this e-mail—were paying more for a weaker version of Windows than had Microsoft been willing to work with only its IP rights and market forces.

In the face of these obstacles, Digital Research eventually fell out of the market. It sold DR-DOS to Novell, who eventually sold it to Caldera. In 1996, Caldera filed suit against Microsoft, alleging violations of the antitrust laws. Microsoft asked the court to dismiss the charges, but in late 1999 the court refused. In early 2000, Microsoft and Caldera reached an undisclosed settlement. That means that Caldera never proved its claims in court, and Microsoft can still legally claim that it did nothing inappropriate to wrong either DR-DOS or consumers. Along the way, though, a fairly sizable collection of the documents that Microsoft had had to turn over during the litigation made their way to the public; the e-mails quoted above were but a small sample.

So much for Microsoft's skirting the antitrust laws. What of the IP laws? Here, despite arguably skirting the law, Microsoft did not violate it. The similarities between Windows' graphics and those on the Mac desktop were hard to miss. They both used windows, icons, and mouse-driven point-and-click commands. Some of the icons even looked alike. Apple sued, claiming that the similarities were so close that they infringed its copyrights. It turns out that this type of claim is one of the toughest challenges for IP law to navigate. After all, if IP law allows me to take your product, tweak it in some minor way, and market it as my own, your IP rights aren't worth very much. That type of rule would under-protect your rights and promote far too little innovation. If, on the other hand, my new product isn't allowed to bear any similarity at all to any existing product, pretty much anything I do will infringe *someone's* rights. That won't motivate much innovation either. The framers of the IP clause would hang their heads in shame at either scheme. They would tell Congress to do better. But Congress would have to punt, because the question of "how similar is too similar?" isn't really a question of either policy or law; it's a question of fact. The courts need to consider each case independently.

Fortunately for the judges asked to look at these two complex pro-grams, others had already faced similar challenges. These judges found a test for software copyright infringement that had been floating around the courts for a couple of years, adapted it to the facts at hand, and com-pared the two platforms.[16] They started with a list of all of the similar-ities. Then they divided their list into three categories: similarities that occurred because the design decisions were obvious; similarities that arose from Microsoft's earlier relationship as a contractor to Apple; and similarities that arose because Microsoft infringed Apple's IP rights. When they finished partitioning their list, they noticed that the first two categories were quite long. The third was empty. The courts ruled in Microsoft's favor. And the final piece fell into place.[17]

Microsoft had launched Windows in 1985 into a competitive oligop-oly: a small number of large players paid attention to each other's moves and attempted to steal each other's customers. Hardware and software manufacturers both competed to add new features while keeping their prices down. Consumers choosing a system had to consider the manu-facturer's reputation, the features it offered, and the price—with Apple providing a unique and somewhat extreme case of price/quality trade-offs. Software manufacturers also faced some difficult decisions about compatibility. To some extent, they all wanted their new systems to be "backward compatible" with those of their competitors, so that they could attract customers who used to favor their competitors. On the other hand, they *did not* like it when their competitors applied a similar strategy to win away their own customers.

Windows changed all that. Not immediately, of course; early versions of Windows weren't very good products. But when the powerful Windows 3.0 appeared in early 1990, independent software developers helped Microsoft build a sizable collection of applications that spoke only the Windows API language. Microsoft had earned its first true applications barrier to entry. IBM's OS/2 was doomed from the starting gate. And the days of the Mac as a serious general-purpose rival were numbered. Windows had thus achieved its two main objectives: it shrank the Mac's share of the market and marginalized all competing successors to DOS. Between early 1991 and mid-1993, Microsoft's stock doubled in price. IBM and Apple each lost about two-thirds of their market value.

Microsoft's 1994 IP victory over Apple was indeed the last piece to fall in place. And with that, we finally understand how Microsoft became kingpin of the software industry. Quality, savvy, luck, timing, and a strategic decision to skirt the edges of the law all played a role. But whatever the balance among these factors, their combination worked like a charm. Microsoft was finally free to turn to its next great challenges: the technical challenge of integrating Windows graphics and MS-DOS to create a single, smooth, next-generation platform to assume its proud role at the translation frontier; and the business challenge of maintaining the monopoly position that it had worked so hard to achieve.

Enter the Leviathan

It's good to be a monopolist. But it's not without a downside. Lest we forget, just about the time that a monopolist's party gets good, the market cops show up. Competitive businesses don't have to worry much about antitrust enforcers. Oligopolists learn to look over one shoulder to see if they're coming. Monopolists need to set aside a guest room because they're moving in.

Of course, it's never quite clear when an oligopolist moves from first among equals to first and only. And even with perfect hindsight, it's not possible to know precisely when it happened to Microsoft. But the market cops arrived permanently somewhere around 1990. The company had become a monopolist, and normal market forces could no longer constrain its behavior.

So what can we expect from a monopolist? Economic theory rests on the belief that people—or corporations—behave rationally. And corporations are much easier to analyze than people because their values are much less complex. Human rationality tends to incorporate love, compassion, power, sex, religion, tribal attachment, and whatnot (mostly whatnot). Corporations don't (or at least aren't supposed to) worry about any of those things. The raison d'être of the corporation is the maximization of profits, but maximizing profits is a tough job. Corporate decision makers need to balance short-term concerns against long-term prospects, they need to remain constantly vigilant of developments in their industries and of their competitors' actions, and they need to manage their reputations among both their customer base and the public at large. No single formula is always appropriate. These sorts of concerns, in different combinations, motivate all corporate behavior, whether the corporations in question are small competitors, key oligopolists, or dominant monopolists.

IO reveals a number of truths about monopoly markets. First, prices are higher in monopoly markets than in competitive markets. Second, monopolists have less incentive to invest in research, development, innovation, and product improvement than do competitive firms. That's not to say, of course, that monopolists have no such incentives. After all, if their products never changed, their sales would be limited to new customers and replacements. If they develop occasional upgrades, they can keep selling bits and pieces to their existing customer base. Third, monopolists tend toward both confidence and paranoia. Confidence can lead them to treat customers with contempt. After all, when you have a monopoly, your customers have no choices other than to buy from you or do without. But above all, paranoia may be the key to understanding monopolists' behavior. A monopolist tends to believe that any potentially competitive product could undermine its entire market position, deprive it not only of its monopoly but also of its profitability, and spell its demise as surely as it vanquished those who preceded it. Not all such fears are irrational, but differentiating false threats from real ones can be tough—and so some monopolists spew venom on any and all competitors, threatening suppliers, distributors, customers, and even society at large with doom and destruction should the threat materialize.

Good IO experts would tell you that none of this is necessary, and they could point to instances of monopolized industries in which fairly little of it did happen. But none of the bullying is unusual, and all of it is predictable. We fully expect a rational monopolist to raise its prices, to slow innovation to the point at which it can manage appropriately timed upgrades, to reduce its emphasis on customer service and consumer relations, and to work hard to deter potential competitors from entering its markets. Is this behavior appropriate? Well, some of it is. In fact, conventional wisdom agues that in many industries we need to promise possible monopoly rents just to motivate up-front innovation. This type of motivation is prevalent in technology industries, and in particular among companies that rely upon IP rights for protection—including both much of the information sector and pharmaceuticals. We may *need* industries with this profile for modern society to function. If so, the offer of eventual monopoly profits in such industries fulfills the Constitution's charge to Congress in the IP clause. It dangles a valuable profit stream in front of salivating competitors to motivate intense competition.

But such motivation hardly means that anything goes. Monopolists have much power, and their fear of competition can lead them to abuse it. Our modern economy is complex. As hard as it is for a new company to develop a new product capable of dethroning a monopolist, it's even harder to imagine such a company working in a vacuum. Any entrant needs access to distributors, to advertisers, to co-contractors, and to consumers, almost all of whom already have a relationship with the monopolist. And that means that the monopolist can flex its muscles. Some companies, for example, might be skeptical of a monopolist's challenger but willing to give the challenger a chance to prove itself. But if the monopolist is aware of the situation, it can give them an ultimatum and force them to choose between it and the entrant. And if the entrant develops an exciting new product that consumers want, the monopolist could develop a knock-off, give it away, and use a vaporware announcement to promise that later generations of its knock-off would be superior. Besides, the monopolist can always point to a longstanding relationship with its customers; there's no way of knowing whether the entrant's products would cause system failure, cancer, or plagues of locusts. And if anything does go wrong with the competitor's product, the monopolist is likely to blame consumers who used the entrant's products for their foolhardy disregard of the monopolist's many warnings not to do so (if not the even more problematic disregard of the fine print in some license or contract). If that fails, the monopolist can start building time bombs—like Windows's moving targets designed to serve no purpose other than to create incompatibilities with DR-DOS. Finally, the monopolist can even threaten consumers directly; a typical threat might warn that adding a competing $10 item to the monopolist's $1000 system would void the warranty.

That sort of behavior is completely unacceptable. And it's particularly insidious for two reasons. First, if the monopolist is entrenched and its industry is central to the economy, market forces are unlikely to constrain it, and the breadth of such behavior's impact can be astounding. Second, consumers shorn of options tend to forget that options *could* exist. They tend to think that things are the way they're supposed to be, even the only way they could be. The thought of change to some unknown setup makes them nervous, and they don't see the problem with having only a single provider. That's how most of us deal with our local phone company, our local cable company, and many government offices. It's also how most of us think of our local platform-software monopolist. And it explains the tremendous public support that Microsoft was able to garner during its trial.

Most of us don't think hard about infrastructure. We like it when it improves, bitch constantly when it breaks, but become very nervous when anyone threatens to shake things up and to inject a little creativity—which, admittedly, may cause disruptions before it makes improvements (and could even fail). But in all honesty, we prefer not to think about it. Pity. For as *The Economist* noted in November 2002:

What is striking is how little innovation there has been in the bits of the market that Microsoft dominates, and how much where it has little influence. Operating systems, web browsers and word-processing software all look much as they did five years ago. But not many people are using five-year-old mobile phones, handheld computers or music-sharing software.[18]

Microsoft may have given us a good platform standard, but that hardly means that we couldn't have done better.

Setting Microsoft aside for a moment, the games monopolists play look like they should be effective. So why do only *some* monopolists play them? After all, if they can do it, and it tends to work, why don't *all* monopolists at least try it? Aren't these games rational steps toward maximizing profits? The answers lie in an analysis of risk. Remember that once the market cops identify a monopolist, they move in to monitor its behavior. And they let everyone else in the industry keep an eye on the monopolist for them, too. Market cops are always willing to listen to inside dirt. They do tend to listen with a bit of skepticism—after all, competitors want to knock down the monopolist, whether its behavior is appropriate or not—but tips could actually lead to something. Market cops can move to enforce the antitrust laws, and at least in the United States, everyone else in the industry can bring private lawsuits to try to do the same. If competitors are sitting on the fence, we let them *treble* their damages and add on their legal fees when assessing what the monopolist might owe them—all to convince them to help the market cops enforce the antitrust laws. And these suits aren't mutually exclusive. The government and private parties can *both* sue a monopolist for the same antitrust violations. As a result, getting caught violating the antitrust laws can be expensive. Even entering the gray area at the periphery of the law can be expensive. After all, none can know where "questionable" behavior will fall. The decision to skirt the law thus combines high reward and high risk. Get away with it and you'll rule the world. Get caught and you're screwed. Monopolists must weigh the likely costs and benefits before deciding to push the law to its limits.

Sometime in the early 1990s, Microsoft became a monopolist. From that day on, the market cops were responsible for scrutinizing Microsoft's behavior. They found a savvy, rational monopolist unafraid to take the risks inherent in skirting the law, which told them that in the case of this new platform monopolist, they needed to pay particularly close attention.

The market cops that entered the fray have many faces and speak many languages. Most developed nations—often at the behest of the United States in years gone by—have a government agency charged with enforcing antitrust law. Over the years, Microsoft has raised eyebrows at several agencies not typically known as brutal enforcers—say the Fair Trade Commissions of Japan and Taiwan—as well as at some that are developing a reputation for careful scrutiny and zealous enforcement, notably the European Union's DG Comp (formerly known as DG IV). In fact, though the events of Microsoft's U.S. trial are much better known, the EU has been the primary focus of antitrust scrutiny of Microsoft since at least late 2002. In the United States, two government agencies share antitrust enforcement authority: the Federal Trade Commission (FTC), an independent agency, and the Antitrust Division of the Department of Justice (DoJ), part of the executive branch. Both agencies have had the dubious pleasure of working with Microsoft.

Of course, scrutinizing a monopolist's behavior is one thing, but bringing charges against it is another. Antitrust lawyers know that it's not illegal to *be* a monopolist. Sometimes companies violate the antitrust laws on their way to becoming monopolists, and sometimes their position as monopolists gives them the ability to violate the antitrust laws after they've achieved their lofty status. But just being a monopolist? No problem at all. Being a monopolist is an existential state, not a crime against consumers—at least not in the United States.

The market cops scrutinizing Microsoft weren't supposed to do much unless and until they detected a specific way that Microsoft's behavior might have violated the antitrust laws. Once they saw something suspicious, they could launch an investigation. And if the investigation revealed what they believed to be an actual violation, they could file a lawsuit; they then could try to convince a judge or a jury that the monopolist had violated the antitrust laws and harmed consumers. Then, no matter the trial's outcome, the losing side—or, in more cases than you might want to believe, both sides—could file an appeal, and ask another court to review the trial judge's conduct and conclusions. Then, depending on this appellate review's outcome, the case could continue to bounce around the courts for a while, possibly leading to another trial and further appeals.

Sometimes, of course, these matters do end, and some court or another issues a final judgment either telling the monopolist what to do or telling the government to back off. Most of the time, though, exhaustion sets in, and the monopolist and the government reach an agreement. In the resulting "consent order" (an oxymoron if I ever heard one), the monopolist agrees to modify its future behavior in some way or another, and the government agrees that if the monopolist performs as promised, it will consider the issue on the table resolved.

But wait! There's more! Somewhere along the line, someone realized that some corporation large and rich enough to be nettlesome monopolist might also be able to exert undue influence on a government agency, and there's no telling what an unduly influenced agency might do. And so, we require the government and the monopolist to convince a federal judge that the consent order serves the public interest. The overwhelming majority of these Tunney Act proceedings are straightforward. The monopolist and the government go to the judge *together*, and both argue for the consent order. No one argues the other side. So unless the judge sees something egregious in the order, she okays it. Rubber stamp. Next case. The consent order then becomes a binding contract between the monopolist and the government. If the monopolist violates the contract, the government can sue the monopolist under contract law—never mind the antitrust laws. Contract cases are *much* more straightforward than antitrust cases. They move faster, they involve fewer complicated issues, their trials are simpler, *and they actually end*!

That's the general story of antitrust battles. Microsoft, somehow or another, managed to make every step of the process unusual.

King Kong vs. Godzilla

Microsoft fought its way from two guys in a dorm room to kingpin of the software industry. The government sent in its finest market cops to keep an eye on the company. They found something suspicious in Microsoft's behavior with respect to DR-DOS and decided to delve a bit further. The battle was joined.

The long, tortuous road to Armageddon began simply. The market cops arrived in Redmond intent upon watching Microsoft's every move. And just in case they happened to miss anything, the rest of the software world stood poised and ready to point it out to them. But what were they looking for? Virtually all of the charges ever brought against

Microsoft fall into one of two broad categories: maintenance of monopoly or leveraging. Microsoft has tried to erect barriers to prevent potential entrants from challenging its sovereignty of the translation frontier, thereby *maintaining its monopoly* of the platform. Microsoft has also used its platform monopoly to gain an unfair advantage over competitors in software markets beyond the platform, thereby *leveraging* its platform monopoly into other software markets. Sometimes the same activity accomplishes both goals.

In 1990, members of the FTC staff, encouraged by application software developers banging down their doors demanding that *something* be done to stop the behemoth from Redmond, began to scrutinize Microsoft's burial of DR-DOS.

While the feds of the FTC staff were busy investigating Microsoft's *past* destruction of DR-DOS to maintain its operating system monopoly, Microsoft was busy leveraging that monopoly to take over various applications markets. Competing application developers were understandably more concerned about their own fate in the very near future than the fate of a departed compatriot of the recent past. Even this early in the game, the market cops had to deal with both maintenance of monopoly and leveraging.

The FTC staff stayed engaged for about three years before presenting its recommendations to the five actual commissioners of the FTC. The rule is that if a majority of the commissioners vote to file a complaint, the FTC sues. If not, the FTC doesn't file a suit—no matter how strong the staff thinks the case is. The commissioners met. When it came to Microsoft, one recused himself. The other four deadlocked 2–2; no majority, no lawsuit. But they did agree to hold another vote after taking a bit more time to think things through. And so, after much lobbying and jockeying for position, they did. But the deadlock remained. The FTC couldn't go forward without a majority. The matter seemed about to die, which is what typically happens when the FTC decides not to sue a company that it's been investigating. But this was Microsoft, and so the standard rules didn't apply.

The matter didn't die; the DoJ picked it up and continued the investigation. While it was ongoing, though, the applications end of the software market went through some significant changes. Borland, best known for its Quattro Pro spreadsheet, and WordPerfect, best known for its eponymous word processor, both capitulated. Lotus, manufacturer of the popular programs Notes and 1-2-3, was reeling; IBM would soon acquire the company. Novell had shrunk to a bit player in the PC-applications market. The competitors who had been lobbying the feds to prevent Microsoft from leveraging its operating system monopoly into the applications software market had all but disappeared. By the middle of 1994, Microsoft was an applications kingpin. And still, the investigation continued.

That left both the DoJ market cops and their targets at Microsoft wondering what to do with the summer. They decided to spend part of it in Europe. It seems that while the American antitrust agencies were scrutinizing Microsoft's behavior, their European counterparts were doing the same. DG IV shared many of the DoJ's concerns and wanted Microsoft to take many of the same actions. In late June 1994, Microsoft, the DoJ, and DG IV decided to see if they could reach a transatlantic settlement. Teams of lawyers worked on the wording of a consent order through much of July. And just when they thought they had something that everyone could live with. Bill Gates refused to consent. Round and round the negotiations went. Each time, Gates (who had no prior exposure to antitrust law) objected to some little nuance in the wording. And each time he sent his lawyers back to argue that his proposed wording better captured the intent of the agreement.

Finally, the dust settled. The lawyers had crafted an agreement that everyone could sign. The final sticking point had been Microsoft's insistence that customers who wanted to buy one product, say MS-DOS, also had to buy another, say Windows or Word. Microsoft was willing to concede that point and stop the marketing practice. But Microsoft simply couldn't agree to stop its software's evolution. After all, as everyone versed in software engineering knows, when an application becomes robust, its developers can integrate it into the platform without worrying about harming the platform's performance. That's how functions traverse the long arduous journey from isolated modules dangling off the frontier down the translation chain toward the hardware. Microsoft couldn't agree to freeze its software in time; evolution would come to a dead halt. The market cops of two continents were willing to concede that point. And with those concessions in place, so was the framework for a consent order. Microsoft agreed not to "bundle," but retained the right to "integrate." Everyone signed. Gates the antitrust neophyte had waved a basic rite of software engineering in front of the erudite market cops and outsmarted them all. The government investigation of Microsoft was finally over.

Or was it? The courts still had to clear the consent decree, but Tunney Act proceedings are typically rubber stamps. Sure, a judge could object to the order, but in practice they don't. And besides, everyone involved knew that there was no possible hint of undue influence. The DoJ team disliked Microsoft, they had fought over virtually every word of the consent order, and a foreign government had also been involved. Who could possibly believe that the government had not done its very best to protect consumers?

Well, Stanley Sporkin, for one. Under normal circumstances, one lone dissenter might not amount to much, but this involved Microsoft. And, more to the point, Stanley Sporkin was the federal judge presiding over the Tunney Act hearing. Judge Sporkin concluded that the consent decree wouldn't constrain Microsoft effectively. He threw it out. In February 1995, the government's hard-fought deal with Microsoft was no more.

Or was it? The government and Microsoft had discovered a common enemy. Microsoft's lawyers joined Deputy Assistant Attorney General Joel Klein to oppose Judge Sporkin's ruling; they appealed his decision to the Court of Appeals for the D.C. Circuit, where they fared better. In June 1995, a panel of three appellate judges disagreed with Judge Sporkin—vehemently. They yanked Sporkin from the case and replaced him with a randomly chosen colleague, Judge Thomas Penfield Jackson, a Reagan appointee with a pro-business reputation. In August 1995, at a second Tunney Act proceeding, Judge Jackson reinstated the consent order. Microsoft was now contractually bound to stop bundling products together but free to integrate previously distinct products into a single, new, next-generation incarnation. That same month, Microsoft launched its important, new flagship product: Windows 95.

Eyes on the Prize

Microsoft launched Windows 95 amidst much fanfare. And the hoopla was well deserved. Though the company's perpetual critics derided the product for its lack of technical excellence, they were, quite simply, wrong. Windows 95, technological shortcomings notwithstanding, was a hugely important evolutionary step in the translation frontier's upward migration. While the Windows 3.x series was both usable and popular, it always felt like an alien add-on, a lively graphical throw rug clumsily covering the supportive DOS floor. Windows 95 was the first graphically oriented operating system that felt like it belonged to the IBM-inspired, Intel-based, PC architecture.

Alas, the public afforded Microsoft not a moment to rest on its laurels. For no sooner had it launched Windows 95 than the public began to clamor for easy Internet access and Web browsers. Now this particular consumer demand hardly caught Microsoft by surprise. In fact, Microsoft released a set of Internet access tools, including Internet Explorer 1.0 and MSN (Microsoft's first attempt to compete with AOL) concurrent with the Windows 95 launch. But no one really took these products seriously— particularly the Internet Explorer browser. Microsoft knew that its future lay with Windows. The Internet properties could develop into valuable divisions at some point, but they were hardly central to the company's growth strategy. More to the point, though, the public wasn't terribly interested. They were happy using software circulated by their Internet service providers (ISPs) for access to gateways other than MSN. And they were even happier eschewing Internet Explorer for competing browsers, notably but not solely Netscape's Navigator.

At some point between August 24, 1995, when Microsoft first shipped Windows 95, and December 7, 1995, when Bill Gates gave his now-famous Pearl Harbor Day speech, Microsoft experienced an epiphany. Microsoft would "embrace and extend" the Internet's standards. Under this brilliantly deceptive strategy, Microsoft would proclaim publicly and loudly that it wanted to work with the rest of the software industry to develop the best possible standards for the Internet. It would thus "embrace" existing developments and "extend" them in new and exciting directions. Of course, Microsoft didn't disclose that any extensions Microsoft developed would be proprietary. What else could they be? Gates had been a strong proponent of software IP rights as far back as 1976. Why would anyone imagine that he would do anything else? Microsoft didn't tell anybody that its products combined open standards, which anyone could share, with little optimization tweaks that Microsoft threw in to ensure that all embraced-and-extended products worked best with Windows. But the important point is that the software ran well on Windows—the platform of the largest network in the market. Who could object to that? The tactic was brilliant—and effective. Within a few short years it had eviscerated the market for two of the most exciting and innovative software products of the mid-1990s: Navigator and Java. Microsoft combined its strategic focus on the Internet with its embrace-and-extend tactic to brutal effect. By the time Windows 95 gave way to the platform's next important evolution—the fully integrated desktop/browser of Windows XP—Microsoft had reemerged as fully in charge of the translation frontier. If a human wanted to communicate with a microchip, she had to go through Microsoft. And that's just how Bill Gates always thought it should be.

As luck would have it, a fair amount has been written about these browser wars. This material gave me the opportunity to test some academic lessons in the real world. It allowed me to see how real software companies put the various principles of software engineering into practice. It also provided insights into what actually drove Microsoft's behavior—the combination of marketing, product development, and business strategy that guided monopolist behavior.

Various authors offered various takes on the matter. *Competing on Internet Time* took the perspective of management science. Cusumano and Yoffie spent a good deal of time getting to know key players at both Microsoft and Netscape, followed the battle as it unfolded, and tried to distill the strategic approaches that worked from those that failed.[19] And while they did explain a good deal about strategy in fast-moving software markets, they didn't dwell much on one of the differences between the two companies that I found most fascinating. Netscape was about twenty years behind Microsoft on the corporate personality development scale. Microsoft started in the mid-1970s as an ambitious company led by talented technologists intent on propelling discovery and innovation forward. That description also fit Netscape in the mid-1990s. But Microsoft matured in some dangerous directions. Within ten years, it had become a creative, consumer-focused software company interested *both* in developing new products and in knocking out its competitors.

Ten years after that, it was destroying both products and markets to ensure that all software innovation was shoehorned through Windows. That was the Microsoft that Netscape faced, and I wanted to understand how that deadly transition had occurred. Cusumano and Yoffie, while interesting, were of little help in that investigation. I had to turn elsewhere.

David Bank, who spent many years covering Microsoft for the *Wall Street Journal* gave me the answers in his insightful description of the internal struggles for Microsoft's soul. Microsoft is a big place, full of people with definite ideas and nonnegligible egos. At various points in the company's history, it made strategic choices that favored some products over others. As you might guess, every product had its internal backers, and every strategic juncture led to a vociferous debate—frequently resolved way up at the top. Bank's *Breaking Windows* revealed the nature of those debates.[20] In particular, it answered one nagging technical question that continued to bother me through everything else that I had heard or read about the browser wars. One of the issues that never seems to have come up—not in the trial, not in the press, not anywhere—was that Internet Explorer was integrated into Windows so early in its development that it violated the principle of modularity. Its evolution was out of step with everything that we know about software development. An internal debate must have addressed the wisdom of integrating Internet Explorer into Windows that early.

Now in all fairness, the trial did raise a related question, namely whether Windows and Internet Explorer were one product or two. While this distinction may be meaningless to computer scientists, it can have a fair amount of legal significance. Tying, a form of leveraging illegal under the antitrust laws, occurs when a monopolist refuses to sell consumers its popular "must have" product unless they also buy some other junk that they may or may not want. If the junk that I don't want is part of the product I need, I'm stuck. But if the two are distinct products, then we have a tying claim—and a violation of the antitrust laws.

No one questioned, for example, Microsoft's right to insist that I buy the parts of Windows that display icons if I wanted to buy the rest of the program. Had I called Microsoft and asked them to ship me a reduced-cost version of Windows that simply displayed the words "recycle bin" on the desktop where the picture of the bin normally sits, Microsoft would have been well within its rights to refuse—and the government would have backed Microsoft. On the other hand, if Microsoft refused to sell me Windows unless I also agreed to buy its keyboard when, quite frankly, I wanted to use a competing Logitech keyboard, that would have been an obvious case of tying—a not-too-subtle attempt to drive Logitech out of the keyboard business. But where was Internet Explorer? It seemed to be somewhere in between. If it was an independent product distinct from Windows, Microsoft's insistence on packaging them together was illegal tying. If it was simply an integrated function of Windows, there was no real problem. So like those involved in the trial, I found the one-product-or-two question fascinating.

But because of my techie roots, I was also unsatisfied with that debate. I still wanted to know why and how Microsoft decided to integrate this product when it did. Evolutionary integration is usually slow. Any good software designer knows enough to keep new functions as application modules as long as possible, and to integrate them downward into the platform slowly and deliberately. Microsoft followed this principle with Windows. It took ten years to migrate Windows from a middleware application down to a part of the platform—and another six to finish the job, because until Windows XP's 2001 release the integration was not seamless. Internet Explorer made it into the platform from its initial launch—and most objective software engineers probably would tell you that it was incorporated prematurely. In other words, Windows and Internet Explorer *should have been two products* at the time of the trial, whether they were or not.

But techie question or not, the issue of premature integration has just as much legal significance as the direct question about tying. One of Microsoft's most devastating defenses to all of the charges levied against it was always: "Hey, we're just a bunch of dumb software engineers making engineering decisions. Don't you want us to develop good products to sell to consumers?" Judges *hate* to second-guess business decisions. Questions about the timing of product integration are engineering questions. No judge in the country would try to examine the internal workings of Microsoft's engineering and design teams to decide whether or not they made the right decisions about modular design, product integration, or the evolution of the platform sitting at the translation frontier. And since they knew Judge Jackson wouldn't do that, the attorneys spent less time than they might have looking into it, leaving me with this annoying, nagging question: Why did the integration happen prematurely?

My guess was that somewhere inside Microsoft, a battle had emerged between two factions. One faction liked designing neat software in accord with reasonable principles of software engineering. The other faction understood network economics, lock-in, and the importance of maintaining a monopoly on the platform. At meetings, I guessed, the first faction always insisted that its approach would lead to better products; the second faction always countered that its approach would lead to bigger profits. That's where the profit motive entered the conference room and resolved the debate. A corporation behaving as corporations are supposed to behave would always take the second course.

I surmised that strategic marketing, not engineering excellence, had driven Microsoft's decision to integrate Internet Explorer into Windows prematurely. And any competent judge would know how to interpret that preference. Intent is often important in the law, and it's certainly important in complex antitrust trials. The government exerted a good deal of time and effort showing that Microsoft *intended* to control the market by strong-arming distributors and competitors. A strategic decision to integrate a product prematurely in order to leverage a monopoly in the desktop platform market into the browser *is not* an engineering decision. It's an economic decision to engage in behavior that runs explicitly counter to the antitrust laws.[21]

So it seems that my little techie question could have had some intense legal consequences as well. But I couldn't find the answer anywhere—until I found *Breaking Windows*. Bank described a deeply entrenched culture of strategic market manipulation at Microsoft. He didn't describe a *single* instance of engineering concerns overriding market strategy. In fact, he related a widespread view among Microsoft's own developers that "the company sacrificed innovation for 'strategy,' the complex set of hooks and lock-in techniques that Gates invariably insisted on to steer customers toward Microsoft's end-to-end product line and keep them from being able to competitive products—and which customers hated for the very same reason. . . . The 'strategy tax' could be deeply demoralizing."[22] Monopolistic business strategy, not software engineering, guided Microsoft's product-design decisions. That's hardly surprising. A corporation owes its first duty to the considerations of the market. Its entire raison d'être is to extract maximum profits from the market and to shower them upon its shareholders. Bank demonstrated that Microsoft never let product quality stand in the way of strategic concerns; Microsoft simply deferred quality considerations until it had resolved the more important strategic issues.

Given the choice between spending a few months improving a product selling in a competitive environment and dedicating those months to securing the market, Microsoft will always choose to secure the market. With the market secure, Microsoft will return to improve the product. Eventually, consumers will have exactly one technically competent product on the market—Microsoft's. The product may arrive later than it should, and there will only be one choice, but if it works reasonably well, who would complain? Certainly not most consumers; they continue to believe that things should be as they are because, after all, when were they ever better? No, no one other than the government and its market cops are likely to complain.

So Microsoft set out to do what it did best, and it left the government to worry about problems and complaints. Microsoft acted like a monopolist. Microsoft came up with a number of clever techniques designed to make Netscape either play ball or die—where playing ball, of course, meant playing by Gates's rules. Microsoft tried honey. It tried vinegar. It tried making Netscape some offers it couldn't refuse. But Netscape did refuse, and Microsoft seethed. But Netscape was neither cowed nor amused. Its key technical leader, Marc Andreessen, made a number of public comments displaying the sort of brashness that the software world had not seen since, well, since a certain young Mr. Gates had made his presence known some twenty years earlier; for example, Andreessen reportedly boasted of his plans to turn Navigator into a platform and thereby to reduce Microsoft's newly released crown jewel to a "slightly buggy set of device drivers." Netscape's chairman, Silicon Valley veteran Jim Clark, took a slightly subtler approach. He asked his attorney, Gary

Reback, to let the government know what was going on and to see if they were interested in reopening their file on Microsoft.

Clark was hardly alone in believing that government action was needed. Many of the biggest names in Silicon Valley agreed with him. Sun's CEO Scott McNealy quickly emerged as one of Microsoft's harshest critics. Though Reback wrote his letter two-and-a-half years before McNealy spoke at the 1999 World Economic Forum in Davos, Switzerland, his concerns were known early on. In Davos, McNealy told the audience (which included Bill Gates) that "Microsoft is a planned economy. Left unfettered, unscrutinized, [and] unchecked, monopoly power can be leveraged into other businesses."[23] But as far back as May 1996, when a reporter asked McNealy whether or not he was concerned that Microsoft might abuse its license of Sun's platform-independent Java language to develop a proprietary standard, he replied "We're always worried people will try and hijack the standards on the network and make something that says, 'Looks best under such-and-such a browser,' or, 'Only runs under Explorer,' or 'Only runs and gets access to the following database from our browser.'"[24] At the time, though, he believed that the openness of the Internet architecture would protect Java. He was wrong. About a year later, Sun sued Microsoft for corrupting the integrity of Java by developing precisely such a version.

Industry support is one thing, though. While the Antitrust Division isn't a particularly political agency, it is part of the executive branch. Joel Klein, by then promoted to Assistant Attorney General for Antitrust, knew that if he moved against a company as big, as prominent, as rich, and as important as Microsoft, there would be fallout somewhere. His bosses, Janet Reno and Bill Clinton, would end up taking at least some of the heat. He needed political cover. Senator Orrin Hatch of Utah (proud home of Novell), the staunchly conservative Republican Chairman of the Senate Judiciary Committee whose primary relationship with the Clinton administration had been to block its judicial nominees, gave Klein the cover he needed when Hatch came out in favor of investigating Microsoft. The attorneys general of twenty states gave Klein even more cover. Klein had broad, bipartisan political backing to go with that of much of the high-tech industry. Thus insulated, he braced himself for the final battle.

This Time It's Personal

The birth of the information sector set the stage for a second cycle of market-cop involvement which looked very much like the first. In 1990, Microsoft had been consolidating its monopoly of the platform market and leveraging its way into various applications markets. When competitors in those applications markets alerted the feds, the feds launched an investigation, but the time the investigation was over, the competitors had faded into history. Microsoft had promised not to do it again. A few short years later, the Internet opened whole new vistas to explore, and Microsoft set out to leverage its monopoly into the browser market—the gateway to the Internet. Its Internet competitors alerted the feds and asked them to launch an investigation. Could this one possibly work better than the first? Could this one take action before Microsoft had vanquished its competitors and reduced consumer "choice" to a single product—its own?

The challenge fell to Klein, who had one great time-saving device that his predecessors had lacked. The consent order that he had personally helped convince Judge Jackson to approve gave the government a contract with Microsoft. Klein didn't need to prove a complex antitrust violation. He sued Microsoft for violating the order's terms by bundling Internet Explorer with Windows. Microsoft claimed that the products were integrated, not bundled; the order's plain language gave it "unfettered liberty" to integrate products at will. Klein was not amused. He saw this dodge as an end run around the order's intent—an order in whose ability to protect the public he had taken a personal stake.

Judge Jackson shared both Klein's concern and his personal stake. By the end of 1997, he had ruled against Microsoft, explaining that:

contrary to Microsoft's claim to absolute discretion to dictate the composition of its operating system software, it appears not unlikely, as a matter of contract, that Microsoft's "unfettered liberty" to impose its idea of what had been "integrated" into its operating systems stops at least at the point at which it would violate established antitrust law.[25]

But he didn't stop with a mere explanation. Jackson also ordered Microsoft to comply with the consent order by distributing independent versions of both Windows 95 and Internet Explorer. From that point on, consumers would be able to buy the existing integrated product, a stand-alone Windows 95, or a standalone Internet Explorer—whichever best suited their needs. Even worse from Microsoft's perspective, Jackson also made the order binding on successor programs to Windows 95. And with Windows 98 set to ship within six months with an even more tightly bound browser, Microsoft felt the heat. Jackson, meanwhile, knew that he would be seeing a lot more of Microsoft. He hired Larry Lessig, the reformist IP scholar, as his "special master" and advisor on technology and the law.

How would computer scientists feel about this ruling? Did Jackson ignore one of their basic tenets? On the surface, it looked as though he had frozen the translation frontier and announced that Internet Explorer would never be able to migrate down into Windows. But in reality, all that Jackson had done was insist that Microsoft give consumers a choice. If consumers overwhelmingly preferred the integrated product, the independent set would soon fade into oblivion and the evolution of the translation frontier would proceed apace. What might make consumers prefer one set over the other? Well, since it would certainly be cheaper and more convenient to buy them together than separately, the key issues would likely be usefulness and product quality. As the Internet moved into more and more areas of computing, Internet Explorer's usefulness would increase. Fewer and fewer consumers would configure computers without browsers. Product quality, though, would flow from the tenets of evolutionary software design. If Internet Explorer were ready for migration down into the platform, the integrated product would be seamless and efficient. If, on the other hand, Internet Explorer's migration were premature, its bugs could threaten the working of the entire platform, complicate fixes and upgrades, and generally frustrate consumers. Jackson's ruling thus effectively insisted that the market alone be allowed to determine whether or when Internet Explorer's functionality was mature enough to migrate downward. It was a legal ruling that nonetheless remained true to the principles of both market economics and software engineering.

But Microsoft wasn't interested in playing by the rules of the competitive marketplace. Jackson's order meant that Microsoft might have a harder time freezing out Navigator—and that was, after all, Microsoft's entire strategy. So Microsoft devised a curious tactic, one that only a company with a monopolist's confidence would conceive, and one that only a company with a monopolist's paranoia would dare. Microsoft complied with the letter of Jackson's order. It released independent versions of its two products. There was only one slight problem. They didn't work. Microsoft foisted broken products on consumers to show Jackson that he had no business poking around its product-design decisions. What Microsoft had lost in unfettered liberty it reclaimed as unfettered chutzpah. No one was fooled. The *San Jose Mercury News* termed it "compliance with a raised middle finger."[26]

Jackson was not amused. In open court, he asked Microsoft's David Cole: "It seemed absolutely clear to you that I entered an order that required you to distribute a product that would not work? Is that what you're telling me?" Cole replied: "In plain English, yes . . . We followed that order. It wasn't my place to consider the consequences of that."[27] Microsoft had just raised the personal stakes for Jackson.

But Microsoft did more than just raise its middle finger and the personal stakes. It also took the appropriate route to complain about a ruling that it considered unjust by appealing. The case went back to the same three judges on the D.C. Circuit with whom Microsoft had been lucky before. Its luck held out. The appellate court ruled that Microsoft had not violated the terms of the consent order, overruled Jackson, let Microsoft ship Windows 98 as intended, and fired Lessig. But it *did not* rule out the possibility that Microsoft's behavior violated the antitrust laws. And so, with the very real possibility of an antitrust violation still on the table, Klein and his backers were still in the picture.

A word of warning: Watching a trial can make you feel dirty. The trial itself may be a clean show in a pristine courtroom, but that show is only staged late in the game. Most of the work goes on long before the trial, during "discovery," which is the litigation equivalent of a strip search. During discovery, an opponent pokes and prods, inquires and investigates, and asks questions that must be answered, in addition to forcing busy executives to give up days upon days of valuable time; refusal to cooperate is likely to lead to being held in contempt of court. Microsoft and its key executives undoubtedly felt violated as government lawyers seized and reviewed years of internal communiqués and e-mails, and forced them into videotaped depositions for hour after hour. The government then selected its personal favorites and put on a show, staged by the talented David Boies. The voyeurs swept in—and, I confess, I was among them—to learn what the government had gleaned from its search and what had actually been going on for the past few years of the information sector.

But the most important of the voyeurs resided in the press corps. The misconception of network economics in the chat rooms, after all, couldn't have materialized in a vacuum. The press supplied day-by-day details and revelations and introduced the various characters in this morality play: lead government litigator David Boies, lead Microsoft litigator John Warden, the various witnesses with whom they sparred, and Judge Jackson himself. We met them all the same way that we'd met Johnny Cochrane, Kato Kaelin, and Judge Lance Ito half a decade earlier: through the good graces of the press. Press coverage was abundant. Joel Brinkley and Steven Lohr, who covered the trial for *The New York Times*, for example, prepared an anthology of that coverage. Between mid-October 1998 and mid-June 2000, the *Times* dedicated enough ink to the trial to fill a 325-page book.[28] And that was just the *Times*.

Then there was Ken Auletta. He was privy not only to the trial performance, but also to the Judge's thinking. While the trial was pending, Jackson granted Auletta several interviews—an apparent breach of judicial ethics that would come back to haunt him later. Auletta combined the insights gleaned from these interviews with his own observations of the trial to compose *World War 3.0*, a comprehensive description of the players and the events, as they unfolded both in the courtroom and across an anxious world tuned in to that courtroom.[29] He and his colleagues in the press corps allowed us all to become eager voyeurs to the very last "trial of the (twentieth) century."

Armageddon

The trial began in October 1998, promising to answer many lingering questions about the software industry, the Internet, and their convergence into the information sector. By the end of November, AOL had announced its intention to acquire Netscape—answering at least one burning question in the negative. Netscape couldn't hold out long enough for the government to stop Microsoft from disrupting its market.

The trial ranged far and wide. The government outlined how Microsoft had destroyed Netscape, but it didn't stop there. It showed how Microsoft had crippled Sun's Java—a language that allowed programmers to write a single program that would communicate with *any* platform—by "extending" it into a Windows-only version. It showed how Microsoft had forced IBM to terminate the last vestiges of OS/2. It showed how Microsoft had forced Intel to squelch a nascent software-development effort; how Microsoft had threatened Apple with extinction in order to eliminate it first as a credible platform challenger and then as a potential Netscape ally; how Microsoft had coerced computer manufacturers and ISPs to choke off Navigator's best distribution channels; how Microsoft had bribed Web developers to tweak their Web pages to appear best (or only) when accessed through Internet Explorer. Overall, the government showed how Microsoft had engaged in tactic after tactic that reduced consumer choice throughout the worlds of software, computing, and the Internet.

The government claimed that Microsoft had engaged in all of these actions both to maintain its platform monopoly and to leverage that monopoly into additional software markets. Microsoft, the government claimed, was intent on retaining its sole proprietorship of the translation frontier, so that all communications between humans and machines would have to pass through a Microsoft translator. As the controller of the only usable frontier, Microsoft would own the gateway to the Internet—and the gateway to the microchip. All human/computer communication would have to begin and end by paying homage to Microsoft. And as god of the gateways, Microsoft would be able to charge whatever it chose for either access to its network or for its uniquely compatible aftermarket products and services. Microsoft could reduce its prices when necessary to ward off an occasional challenge, raise them when it decided that short-term revenues were paramount, and generally maintain them at whatever level was necessary to convince consumers to continue deepening their switching costs, thereby deterring competitive entry. Microsoft was the toll keeper of the information superhighway—that same elusive goal that sent so many investors chasing the Internet's inevitable monopolists. Microsoft, the government explained, had learned much about network economics and had used its lessons to brilliant, brutal effect; Microsoft never shied from a fight, never fought fairly, and never moved on until its product was the only real choice on the table. Because it could leverage its platform monopoly to engulf whatever middleware threat promised to define the next-generation platform, Microsoft typically succeeded. And few consumers either noticed or cared.

The government's case seemed devastating. And for the most part, Microsoft didn't deny the actions that the government described; it simply disagreed about their propriety, their underlying motives, and their effect on consumers. Where the government saw cheating, anticompetitive behavior, and consumer harm, Microsoft asserted laissez-faire capitalism, superior product development, brilliant marketing, and shrewd negotiating.

The trial ended in mid-July 1999. In November, Judge Jackson issued his "findings of fact." He agreed with the government on almost everything. But in an unusual move, he didn't say anything at all about the law. Now, judges split many of their opinions into "findings of fact" and "findings of law," particularly in complicated cases. The former set is essentially a story. The judge basically says, "Okay. I heard two versions. I've seen both presentations, I've looked at all of the evidence, and here's what I think really happened." Once he's done that, the judge can turn to the law. Usually, though, these two sets of findings are part of the same document. But this was Microsoft, so the usual rules didn't apply. Judge Jackson issued his findings of fact in November; they included ample indication of his leanings on the law:

Microsoft took actions that could only have been advantageous if they operated to reinforce monopoly power. These actions are described below. . . .[30]

Microsoft focused its antipathy on two incarnations of middleware that, working together, had the potential to weaken the applications barrier severely without the assistance of any other middleware. These were Netscape's Web browser and Sun's implementation of the Java technologies. . . .[31]

The combined efforts of Netscape and Sun threatened to hasten the demise of the applications barrier to entry, opening the way for non-Microsoft operating systems to emerge as acceptable substitutes for Windows. By stimulating the development of network-centric Java applications accessible to users through browser products, the collaboration of Netscape and Sun also heralded the day when vendors of information appliances and network computers could present users with viable alternatives to PCs themselves. Nevertheless, these middleware technologies have a long way to go before they might imperil the applications barrier to entry. Windows 98 exposes nearly ten thousand APIs, whereas the combined APIs of Navigator and the Java class libraries, together representing the greatest hope for proponents of middleware, total less than a thousand. Decision-makers at Microsoft are apprehensive of potential as well as present threats, though, and in 1995 the implications of the symbiosis between Navigator and Sun's Java implementation were not lost on executives at Microsoft, who viewed Netscape's cooperation with Sun as a further reason to dread the increasing use of Navigator. . . .[32]

Once it became clear to senior executives at Microsoft that Netscape would not abandon its efforts to develop Navigator into a platform, Microsoft focused its efforts on ensuring that few developers would write their applications to rely on the APIs that Navigator exposed. Developers would only write to the APIs exposed by Navigator in numbers large enough to threaten the applications barrier if they believed that Navigator would emerge as the standard software employed to browse the Web. If Microsoft could demonstrate that Navigator would not become the standard, because Microsoft's own browser would attract just as much if not more usage, then developers would continue to focus their efforts on a platform that enjoyed enduring ubiquity: the 32-bit Windows API set. Microsoft thus set out to maximize Internet Explorer's share of browser usage at Navigator's expense. . . .[33]

Not much subtlety in there. Despite the absence of a ruling on the law, Jackson couldn't possibly have left Microsoft with any doubt as to which way the wind was blowing.

Jackson even took the opportunity to address the most controversial question of all—and the one on which Microsoft had likely been pinning its greatest hopes: *Did Microsoft really do anything that harmed consumers?* After all, it's one thing to say that Microsoft harmed Netscape or Sun or IBM. And that's bad, particularly if you held shares in Netscape or Sun or IBM, but what's it to us consumers? What has Microsoft ever done to hurt us? Microsoft claimed that all of its actions had both the intent and the effect of helping consumers—and many of its supporters agreed. Jackson, however, did not.

Now, Microsoft's effect on consumers is likely to remain one of the trial's great open questions, to be debated for decades to come.[34] What's more, even if Microsoft *did* harm consumers, it still might not deserve to lose the case; courts are only empowered to redress certain types of harm. But the question of consumer harm remains central to understanding the trial, the debate around it, and the information sector itself. Finding an answer requires a trick that also reveals why that answer is so elusive: We must imagine what the software market would look like today had Microsoft not violated the antitrust laws. Now, if we're all better off in that picture then, yes, Microsoft harmed consumers. If not, not.

In my picture, Microsoft did maintain prices above their competitive levels—but that was only a small part of the harm. The bigger problem was that Microsoft forced a standard on the public. In so doing, it impeded innovative product development and retarded the information sector's natural growth. To be fair, even an enforced standard has its advantages, though they're small compensation for reducing what should have been an exciting, competitive, innovative software market into one controlled by the Microsoft commissariat. I don't like centrally planned software features because I believe in the power of markets. Let developers compete and let the market decide.

Of course, not everyone agrees with me. Many callers to radio shows, debunkers of network myths, Microsoft's economists, and the editors of the *Wall Street Journal* all take a different view. Perhaps they find huge comfort in knowing that never again will they have trouble translating programs between formats—at least as long as Windows reigns supreme. More likely, they also believe that many of Microsoft's flagship products were technically superior to those of their competitors, that Microsoft won its many dominant positions by being responsive to consumer needs and desires—not through monopoly leveraging, and that Microsoft has pushed software prices down, rather than up. And I can't *prove* that they're wrong any more than they can prove that I'm wrong. So we're still stuck in a sort of stalemate.

But in the final analysis, the only imagined present that really mattered was Jackson's—and he pictured a market that Microsoft had distorted badly. In his view, Microsoft's positive contributions paled in comparison to its intentional violations of the antitrust laws. And so, with the release of Jackson's findings of fact, Microsoft knew that it was on the verge of being ruled a monopolist and ordered to do something that it would consider odious. But Jackson had split his ruling, at least in part, because he didn't want to have to do that. Had he ruled against Microsoft, he would have needed to devise an appropriate penalty—and that promised to be messy. Jackson hoped to spare himself—and everyone else—the agony of a remedy hearing. He wanted this case to settle. And so he went to Chicago, to enlist the help of Richard Posner, a prominent judge on the Court of Appeals for the Seventh Circuit, a respected Adjunct Professor of Law at the University of Chicago, and generally acknowledged as among the finest living scholars of antitrust. Jackson convinced Posner to mediate.

But Posner, despite being a judge, a professor, and a respected scholar, had somehow retained at least a modicum of common sense and innate wisdom. After four months of trying to reconcile the irresistible force from Washington with the immovable object of Redmond (or was it the other way around?), he withdrew. He realized, correctly, that no settlement was possible. In April 2000 Jackson issued his findings of law. He elevated Microsoft from the status of mere monopolist to the rather rarified infamy of adjudicated monopolist.

That legal ruling set the stage for the next question: What sort of remedy could Jackson impose that would fix things? A good remedy should do a number of different things. It should *punish* Microsoft for behaving in an anticompetitive manner. It should *preclude* Microsoft from repeating that behavior. It should *deter* anyone else from following Microsoft's lead. It should *restore* competitive balance to the markets. And it should be *fair* and proportional to the nature of Microsoft's transgressions. What remedy could achieve all of that?

Antitrust remedies typically fall into one of two broad camps: structural and behavioral.[35] Remedies in most cases are behavioral. The court tells the defendant to stop doing whatever it has been doing, orders it to pay some money, and everyone calls it a day. But here, the challenge lay in figuring out what set of instructions could possibly preclude Microsoft from repeating its behavior. After all, from DR-DOS through the applications markets and on into Navigator, Microsoft was a proven recidivist. How do you fine a company that's essentially minting money? How do you stop a company from what is essentially rational (if illegal) behavior designed to maximize profits using the tools at its disposal? Is it possible to do more than to nudge such a firm so that rather than crossing the line of antitrust legality, it merely skirts that line from the inside—until, that is, it finds another direction in which to push outward? And above all, *how do you fix a market that has been so badly broken that the only remaining player is your adjudicated monopolist?*

These questions convinced many observers that no behavioral remedy could possibly work. As long as Microsoft retained sole proprietary ownership of the Windows APIs, it would be able to leverage its way into virtually any software market that it chose to conquer—and it was a pretty safe bet that Microsoft would choose to conquer any middleware threat that might force it to share the next generation of the translation frontier with a competitor, or even worse, with the world at large in the form of (shudder) an open standard. These observers argued that Jackson had to do something unusual to inject competition back into the platform market. They argued for a radical restructuring of the software industry; surgery that would change Microsoft's corporate structure. Such structural remedies would break Microsoft into a number of competing companies.

Any such structural approach would certainly prevent *Microsoft* from repeating its behavior, and seems sufficiently draconian to have a serious deterrent effect on other monopolists (including the companies to emerge from the breakup). The remaining questions were thus whether this remedy was fair and whether or not it would fix the market effectively. Effectiveness, of course, would depend on the specific breakup ordered. Many of the outside scholars and observers who had proposed intricate breakups, for example, questioned the plan ultimately submitted by the DoJ, which split the operating system company from the applications company—but left the Windows monopoly intact. Many of them had favored creating multiple (typically 3) Windows companies, nicknamed the "Baby Bills," who would then compete directly with each other.

The DoJ, however, felt that no such division of the Windows monopoly was necessary. And so, in the spirit of Aristophanes' toast at Plato's Symposium, the jealous gods of the DoJ moved to sever the happy Microsoft into two natural halves—a platform company ("Winco") and an applications company ("Appco")—reasoning that they would each wander the software world seeking to recreate their missing halves. When Appco recreated a Windows competitor and Winco recreated an

Office competitor, competition would reign throughout the land, and consumers would benefit.

Jackson agreed. On June 7, 2000, he ordered Microsoft broken into Winco and Appco. He also subjected Microsoft to a number of conduct restrictions. Finally, he put all of these remedies on hold until an appellate court had had a chance to review them—on the off chance that Microsoft might want to appeal.

Not With a Bang, but a Whimper

Microsoft did appeal—within the week, which was probably good, because no one had fully addressed an unspoken but critical question: who would determine how to divide Microsoft's greatest asset—its people—between Winco and Appco?

If the breakup order had gone through, something along the following lines would have unfolded: Jackson would have given Microsoft about six months to craft a divestiture plan. Six months later Microsoft would have presented its plan, and the DoJ would have opposed it. Jackson would have agreed and rejected it, and Microsoft would have appealed. A few months later, the appellate court would have refused to interfere and shipped the case back to Jackson, who would have given Microsoft detailed instructions for its next divestiture plan, ordering it to give personnel and organizational information to DoJ so that DoJ could devise an alternate plan. Then they would both have come back to court in six months to present their plans to Jackson who would . . . what? Meanwhile, Microsoft would have been up to its old tricks, continuing its leveraging tactics to push its dominance even further across the Internet. Bottom line: Breaking up is hard to do.

The 1984 breakup of AT&T worked because, in the final analysis, AT&T agreed to work with the government to develop a divestiture plan, and because Judge Harold Greene agreed to become "the AT&T judge." And AT&T's business lent itself to some obvious geographical divisions. Earlier antitrust breakups, like Standard Oil, more-or-less severed the companies along divisional seams left over from earlier mergers. But Microsoft had grown as a single organic company. No one had ever broken up such a company before without the full cooperation of both management and the board. No one knew how to do it. So all in all, it may not be horrible that we never got there.

But that doesn't mean that we shouldn't have tried. Even more importantly, it doesn't mean that a behavioral remedy would have been better. All of the problems that motivated the drive towards radical surgery were still in place. Without a structural remedy, Microsoft would retain most of its weapons, its incentives would be largely unaltered, and the market would remain its private playground. Klein's DoJ, its supporters, and Jackson, had done a great job appreciating the shortcomings of behavioral remedies. They were less thorough thinking through the practical implications of structural remedies.

Microsoft's appeal returned the case, once again, to the D.C. Circuit Court of Appeals. This time they agreed to hear the case *en banc*, which means that all of the Court's judges (except for a few who recused themselves) participated in the proceeding. It took them a little more than a year, but their unanimous conclusion gave us all something to read over 2001's Fourth of July holiday. They accepted Jackson's findings of fact. They agreed with him about some points of law, disagreed with him about others. In yet another legal area, the application of tying law to the specific case of platform software, they decided to change the rules governing the legal analysis. Then they concluded that since they had just made up a new rule, Jackson couldn't possibly have followed it correctly. They thus ordered a new trial on the government's tying claim (just one of the government's several leveraging theories). Finally, and on this point they were trivially correct, they noted that since Microsoft was now guilty of fewer violations than Jackson had thought it to be when issuing his breakup order, the court also needed to be revisit the remedy.

When the dust settled, a few things were clear. Microsoft was still an adjudicated monopolist; it had violated the laws pertaining to the maintenance of a monopoly. The breakup order was off the table, at least for a while. We were going to have another trial. And Judge Jackson was off the case. The appellate court had been particularly harsh with Jackson, accusing him of appearing to violate the canons of judicial ethics. Among his many faux pas, he had spoken to the press in the midst of the trial. Microsoft had outlasted its second judge. The court held yet another lottery to pick a new judge. Judge Colleen Kollar-Kotelly drew the short straw.

She began her tour of duty armed with the Court of Appeals's sage, if incomprehensible, advice:

As a general matter, a district court is afforded broad discretion to enter that relief it calculates will best remedy the conduct it has found to be unlawful. This is no less true in antitrust cases. And divestiture is a common form of relief in successful antitrust prosecutions: it is indeed "the most important of antitrust remedies."

On remand, the District Court must reconsider whether the use of the structural remedy of divestiture is appropriate with respect to Microsoft. . . .

In devising an appropriate remedy, the District Court also should consider whether plaintiffs have established a sufficient causal connection between Microsoft's anticompetitive conduct and its dominant position in the OS market. . . . Absent such causation, the antitrust defendant's unlawful behavior should be remedied by "an injunction against continuation of that conduct." . . .

While we do not undertake to dictate to the District Court the precise form that relief should take on remand, we note again that it should be tailored to fit the wrong creating the occasion for the remedy.[36]

In other words, the punishment (and we're not going to tell you what it should be) should *both* prevent Microsoft from repeating its past behavior *and* be fair given the specifics of Microsoft's actual liability.

To make Kollar-Kotelly's assignment even tougher, this time Microsoft had done more than simply outlast a judge. Microsoft had outlasted an entire administration. The market cops who moved to Redmond during the Bush *père* administration had begun an investigation that lingered through the entire Clinton administration and fell into the lap of the Bush *fils* administration, who most definitely did not want it. Nevertheless, Attorney General John Ashcroft appointed a strong team to take over. Charles James, the man who inherited Joel Klein's mantle of Assistant Attorney General for Antitrust, was a respected antitrust lawyer. He replaced David Boies—who had used the break in the Microsoft trial to argue on behalf of the Gore campaign both in Florida and in front of the Supreme Court—with Phil Beck, an equally talented litigator who had argued on behalf of the Bush campaign in Florida. Seems only fair. But on September 6, 2001, before Beck could begin litigation, the new DoJ announced that it would neither seek a structural remedy nor pursue the tying claim.

Judge Kollar-Kotelly had an almost impossible task. She was charged with crafting a remedy that was fair, proportional, and related to the maintenance of monopoly violations for which Microsoft had actually been ruled liable, but that also prevented Microsoft from repeating behavior that combined those violations with various leveraging actions that were no longer on the table. She was in a no-win situation with a defendant who was somehow poison—the Court of Appeals had already slapped around two of her senior colleagues, Judges Sporkin and Jackson, for trying to curb Microsoft's monopolistic excesses.

The DoJ announcement on September 6, 2001, was also the last interesting movement on this case. More will occur again in the future, but likely in a different political climate, within a different general framework, and with a different cast of characters. But this next round may be a few years off. In September 2001, Microsoft and the DoJ still had a clock to run out, even though we all knew that the game was over. Sure, Judge Kollar-Kotelly wouldn't issue her final ruling for almost fourteen months. And while newspaper stories continued and events kept unfolding, none of that mattered. The game was over; all that remained was a long, boring, and anticlimactic final act. Microsoft clearly was going to get away with a slap on the wrist. The only question was how hard a slap.

But even an anticlimax deserves to be told. The DoJ, Microsoft, and half of the states quickly agreed upon a behavioral consent order. When it came time for the Tunney Act hearing, they all asked Judge Kollar-Kotelly to sign the order. Nine other states sought tougher behavioral restrictions; they wanted to save the market from Windows 2000 and Windows XP, products that Microsoft hadn't even launched until after the trial. This rare, bitterly contested Tunney Act hearing proved, once again, that nothing involving Microsoft ever unfolds as expected.

Judge Kollar-Kotelly held a long hearing, took months to deliberate, and on November 1, 2002, issued a lengthy, detailed opinion—basically rubber stamping the consent order and telling the remaining states to go away. Most of them did, though Massachusetts and West Virginia fought on. Anticlimactic. This case had finished back on September 6, 2001; the last fourteen months were just filler.

Once the Bush DoJ had dropped the possibility of corporate capital punishment, all that was left was a behavioral remedy. But behavioral remedies couldn't possibly be effective. They couldn't truly punish Microsoft, they couldn't prevent it from repeating its behavior, and they most certainly couldn't restore competition to *any* of the markets that Microsoft had destroyed. And as to their deterrent effect, suppose that the young Bill Gates back in the early 1980s had a dream showing how Microsoft's future would unfold—its emergence as the platform software monopolist followed by its antitrust conviction and the terms of the settlement agreement. When he awoke, would he be likely to let things unfold as they did, or reform his ways and change the future? Answer: He'd be out of his mind to change a damn thing.

And so, though Judge Kollar-Kotelly's order is unlikely to have much of an impact on the information sector, it probably represented the most prudent course of action she could have taken given the many constraints she faced. She accepted the deal that Microsoft had cut with the DoJ subject to only a very few, very minor changes and wrote a lengthy, detailed explanation describing the relationship between the violations and the penalties. She thus met *one* of the Court of Appeals's instructions: the remedy was proportional to the specific narrow violations that the government had proved. Since it's not clear that she *could have* hit both instructions simultaneously, doing a good job on one front can't really be all that bad.

Or can it? After all, not only is her order shorn of deterrent effect, but the opposite is true. In the future, anyone who *can* emulate Microsoft's behavior, *will*. The Bush DoJ showed Internet investors that while they may have been mistaken about the Internet barrier to entry, they were dead-on right in their quest for the next Microsoft. If you can find it, invest. Heavily. Because the next Microsoft will leverage its monopoly successfully, it will transfer rents from consumers to shareholders, and it will get away with a slap on the wrist. Therein lies the ultimate message of the Microsoft trial to the public. Thus educated, we must wonder about the future of the information sector, soon to be a wholly owned subsidiary of Microsoft. Yes, this is the way that the trial ends. Not with a bang, but a whimper.

Déjà vu

Quite a story. But where does it leave us? And perhaps even more importantly, where does it leave Microsoft? Quite possibly stronger than ever. Sure, Microsoft incurred bad publicity and monstrous legal fees. But the trial also focused a stellar array of antitrust experts on Microsoft's business practices. Their analyses gave Microsoft a wealth of useful information about network effects and monopoly leveraging. And Microsoft applied those analyses wisely—before even hearing from Kollar-Kotelly.

Microsoft hit the ground running in late 2001, almost immediately after reaching its agreement with the DoJ. Before the year was out, Microsoft's Windows XP evolved the translation frontier upward to subsume a media player and an instant messenger, and it launched several initiatives to reshape the Internet in its own image: Passport to ease e-commerce; the ambitious if somewhat amorphous .Net initiative that combines "a set of Microsoft software technologies for connecting your world of information, people, systems, and devices";[37] and a "Hailstorm" of announcements about forthcoming products and services. The company made a major push into the server market, where it tried to leverage its way from the desktop into the back office—a computing environment that remains competitive. Microsoft also reportedly issued a series of threats: to impose a permanent cost disadvantage on corporate customers who failed to upgrade to Windows XP—and its counterpart in the applications world, Office XP—on *Microsoft's* schedule, and to tell consumers that all third-party software was incompatible with XP unless the developers gave Microsoft a copy of their source code. It's unclear how many of these announcements and/or threats Microsoft ever carried out, but their combined effect demonstrates the extent to which the company felt unshackled by its agreement with DoJ.

But of all of these initiatives, one stands out. The Windows Media Player (WMP) "integrated" into Windows XP demonstrated just how much Microsoft had learned in the temple of network economics. Think back for a moment to what actually happened in the browser wars, and to why it was so important for Microsoft to win them. By 1995, Windows was secure as the translation frontier between human users and their desktop hardware. Netscape and Sun had created versions of their products that ran on top of various platforms—Windows, Mac OS, Unix, Linux, even DOS—and that made it pleasant and easy for people to use the Internet. All of a sudden, human users had two different reasons to talk to hardware, and two different interfaces through which to talk. When they wanted to do business- or office-like tasks, they'd ask Windows to translate. When they wanted to use the Internet, they'd ask Navigator to translate. People could suddenly talk to their hardware without a Microsoft translator. That made Microsoft nervous.

What made Microsoft even more nervous was the thought that some folks using Netscape Navigator's interface on a "thin client" or an "Internet appliance" that wasn't set up to do office work might want to access an Internet-based word processor or spreadsheet. If that happened, not only would people be able to talk to their hardware without Microsoft, but they'd be able to do office-like tasks without using *either* Microsoft's Office suite or Microsoft's platform. In other words, competition could reemerge in both halves of the translation chain; new applications closer to humans could sit atop Navigator, and new platforms or utilities closer to hardware could create parallel paths from interface to microchip. That threat—no matter how remote—was untenable, so Microsoft stopped it.

Perhaps the most negative consequence of Microsoft's behavior in the browser wars was thus that it rendered this parallel translation frontier stillborn. And so today, instead of having two competing translation frontiers with enough different features to reveal which were best for which tasks, we have one monopoly frontier: Microsoft's integrated Windows/Internet Explorer. That platform evolves not in response to market forces, but rather in response to Microsoft's paternalistic judgments about appropriate evolution. As long as Microsoft is right, we're all fine. And when Microsoft is wrong? Who'll know? Most consumers will persist in their Panglossian belief that we must truly be in the best of all possible worlds—after all, it's the one that Microsoft created.

Microsoft integrated WMP into Windows for a similar set of reasons. Before WMP, most people used the industry open standard of MP3 to encode music files. But Microsoft created its own proprietary format, WMA. While WMP will play MP3 files, it will only rip WMA files. The average user who buys a new computer with WMP already installed is likely to develop a large collection of music files encoded in a format that *only* WMP can play—threatening competing products from Real Networks and Apple. Leveraging the platform outward, embracing and extending, wrapping a technology developed elsewhere into Windows and claiming it as Microsoft's own—we've seen it all before. Microsoft learned its lessons well. Many of the initiatives launched with Windows XP do the same thing. Its integrated instant messenger threatened AOL and Yahoo!, and Passport was created to translate all of our shopping needs to the hardware.

And that was all *before* Kollar-Kotelly approved the agreement in November 2002. But as we've seen, antitrust inquiries rarely fade into oblivion. In June 2003, the remaining states, Microsoft, and various amici (scholarly "friends of the court") filed their briefs appealing Kollar-Kotelly's ruling. At about the same time, Microsoft settled its lawsuit with AOL—a suit that AOL had brought seeking compensation for the damage that Microsoft had inflicted upon its subsidiary, Netscape—and these two giants of the information sector promised to play nicely with each other. That agreement left some of AOL's former playmates out in the cold; Real Networks's stock dropped roughly ten percent the day after Microsoft and AOL announced their deal. Various other private lawsuits seeking compensation from Microsoft for the damage it inflicted on the information sector's products and consumers linger on. And then, in August 2003, roughly four years into their own investigation of Microsoft's behavior— including its releases of Windows versions through XP—regulators in the EU announced plans to impose behavioral restrictions on Microsoft in both the media-player and server markets. The action shifted back to Brussels. *Plus ça change, plus c'est la même chose.*

Today Microsoft is both better armed and better informed about the power of monopoly leveraging than it was a decade ago, and its opponents are spent, disarmed, discouraged, and looking about for help wherever they may find it. One of these days, we'll start calling the events to date "the first Microsoft trial," because it's almost inconceivable that there won't be a second. Microsoft retains control of a bottleneck monopoly and a large staff now well versed in monopoly leveraging. The company will retain antitrust lawyers who make sure that it complies with the letter of Judge Kollar-Kotelly's order while likely working hard to violate its spirit. And this, despite her explicit admonition that:

During this litigation, promises have been made on behalf of Microsoft that the company will change its predatory practices which have been part of its competitive strategy in order to comply with the remedial decree. The Court will hold Microsoft's directors, particularly those who testified before this Court, responsible for implementing each provision of this remedial decree. Let it not be said of Microsoft that "a prince never lacks legitimate reasons to break his promise," for this Court will exercise its full panoply of powers to ensure that the letter and spirit of this remedial decree are carried out.[38]

But the temptation to be Machiavellian is just too great. The trial has done little either to reduce Microsoft's capabilities or to change its incentives, and leveraging up to the legal limits constitutes highly rational behavior for a powerful monopolist. Thus, Microsoft will return to court because it's a well-run company that will attempt to exploit its assets to yield maximum profits. Because of heightened government scrutiny, Microsoft is likely to take pains to avoid crossing into territory that's clearly illegal. But it will continue to flirt with the gray area. When the dust of the current proceedings finally settles, Microsoft will undoubtedly survey the tech terrain, spot new threats, and take the rational steps needed to squelch them. At the same time, political winds will change again—and the second Microsoft trial will begin. And perhaps, some years after that, so will the third and the fourth and the fifth.

In case you think I'm kidding about all those trials, I have three words for you: United Shoe Machinery.[39] Several competing manufacturers of shoemaking equipment merged to create this monolith of the manufacturing age in 1899. Twelve years later the government realized that United Shoe Machinery was an abusive monopolist and went to court seeking its breakup. It took until 1918 to reach the Supreme Court, which refused the government's request. Almost thirty years later the government tried again, and spent the better part of six years in court seeking its breakup—but achieved only limited behavioral relief. But 1953's behavioral relief proved inadequate. The Supreme Court ordered United Shoe Machinery broken up in 1968—about fifty-six years after the government's first complaint. On the United Shoe Machinery clock, then, we should break up Microsoft around 2050—unless antitrust law kicks into Internet time.

But whenever those future Microsoft trials occur, the new judge will face the same challenges that plagued Judges Jackson and Kollar-Kotelly.

Structural remedies will continue to be tough to implement, and behavioral remedies will never promise more than unlikely prospects for effectiveness. And Microsoft is counting on that. Microsoft may accept minimal restrictions unlikely to have much of an impact on the way that it does business, but it will *never* accede to a fundamental change. In 2003 and 2004, when things were relatively quiet for Microsoft in the world of American antitrust, the company remained engaged in negotiations with its friends across the Atlantic, the market cops of DG Comp. By that time, DG Comp had spent the better part of *five* years investigating the impact on European consumers of Microsoft's behavior, including the launch of Windows XP, the integration of WMP into Windows, and the push into the server market. The European market cops detailed a list of specific complaints and threatened to sue. To no one's surprise, settlement negotiations fell through. Mario Monti, the EU Competition Commissioner, explained that the parties had "made substantial progress towards resolving the problems which have arisen in the past . . . but we were unable to agree on commitments for future conduct."[40] Brad Smith, Microsoft's General Counsel, agreed that the problem was not the past, but rather crafting a "single formula" for dealing with future complaints.[41] The EU reportedly wanted Microsoft to accept limits on its right to integrate—a formula that any good Microsoft watcher could tell you the company would never accept.[42] Microsoft knows full well that governments are afraid of tampering with its successes, and that nothing short of a radical remedy can fix the markets that it's broken. So DG Comp did what it could. It announced behavioral remedies and fined Microsoft just under a half-billion euros. Microsoft appealed. And on it goes. . . .

That inherent quandary facing market cops and courts alike reveals, once again, the relationship among technology, law, and economics—and stresses the importance of diagnosing problems correctly and of selecting appropriate tools before trying to fix them. The market cops detected a problem in the software markets; they traced that problem to Microsoft. But Microsoft's anticompetitive actions were an effect; no one spent much time seeking the deeper cause. Microsoft behaved as it did because it could, and because it was rational to do so. It could because we gave it strong IP protection on its software without forcing it to promote human knowledge. The technology of compilation made it possible to circulate object code while keeping the knowledge-laden source code secret. The law of copyright gave that object code immense value. Economic incentives simply dictated that Microsoft use its rights to maximize corporate profits.

The market cops then tried to use antitrust remedies to fix the effect while leaving the cause untouched. It's hardly surprising that they failed. Perhaps next time they'll look beyond effect, to cause. The only way to fix the markets that Microsoft has broken—and will continue to break if it behaves rationally—is to change Microsoft's incentives. The only way to change Microsoft's incentives is to change its powers and the rights that underpin them. And the only way to change those rights is to realize that they are, at heart, IP rights, and that we need to seek advice from the priests of IP. Perhaps we should have paid more attention to their jeremiad.

And so, the trial, like the bubble, was fundamentally a tale of misdirection. Internet investors chased network growth without considering lock in. Market cops chased antitrust remedies without considering IP rights. Both tales were doomed to end poorly—at least for the general public. We need to rethink both of these stories in a new light—a light that shines more brightly over the open-source bazaar and the song of music. These stories demonstrate more clearly the ways that the information sector's reduced transaction costs let consumers pay less and producers sell more—but that also render traditional distribution channels less lucrative, and thereby motivate traditional distributors to try to reimpose the transaction costs.

That framework allows us to recast both the bubble and the trial. The bubble collapsed because distribution revenues could never materialize without lock in, and dot-com intermediaries could thus never become profitable. At trial, we learned that Microsoft's violation of the principle of modularity (among its other transgressions) choked its rivals' distribution channels and thereby raised their transaction costs. Microsoft subverted its role as a software developer to its more lucrative role as a software distributor. The dot-coms lost because they had no transaction costs to impose; Microsoft won because its IP rights and network barriers to entry enabled it to reimpose transaction costs on everyone but itself.

That new framework also points toward the information sector's future. The bubble's New World paradigm gave way to more sober New Channel thinking, while Microsoft's continued anticompetitive behavior may stir policymakers to consider the messages of IP reformists. And these reassessments will inform the key debate over industrial policy in an information age—the debate over transaction costs. Where do we want to reduce them to benefit consumers and producers? And where do we want to impose them to serve other important public-policy objectives?

Those questions will shape the future, as we continue our transition into the information age, and as the information sector continues to absorb large swaths of the economy. If we navigate this transition successfully, the information sector will make us rich one transaction at a time. And if we don't, things may remain as they are: an information sector whose only inevitable monopolist is Microsoft.

6

Fresh from the Source

Glory Days

I was never much of a hacker. Sure, I spent more than my share of time writing code—often until sunrise. I dined at the finest of campus vending machines, wore my hair and beard long, bushy, and wild, dwelt in a world populated almost entirely by men, dressed like a wannabe hippie, and (surprisingly) rarely dated. But I never fell in love with programming, and so I had no choice but to move on.

I'm talking about hacking because while the bubble and the trial dominated the front pages, the rest of our information workers managed to keep themselves busy—hacking. Back in the bubble's IPO heyday, Red Hat finished its first trading day up more than 500 percent, and the VA Linux (now VA Software) IPO soared to about 800 percent of its offering price (still a record). But these companies weren't dot-coms; they were (as the latter's name implies), Linux companies. And it's simply not possible to understand Linux without knowing at least something about hacking.

Hackers aren't criminals, and hacking isn't a criminal activity. While some hackers might like to think of themselves as engineers, they're really artists. And like many artist communities, hackers do tend towards the subversive—but that's a far cry from the criminal.

hacker   *n.* [originally, someone who makes furniture with an axe] 1. A person who enjoys exploring the details of programmable systems and how to stretch their capabilities, as opposed to most users, who prefer to learn only the minimum necessary. 2. One who programs enthusiastically (even obsessively) or who enjoys programming rather than just theorizing about programming. . . . 4. A person who is good at programming quickly. 5. An expert at a particular program, or one who frequently does work using it or on it; as in "a Unix hacker." ... 8. [deprecated] A malicious meddler who tries to discover sensitive information by poking around. ... The correct term for this sense is *cracker*. ... The term "hacker" also ... implies that the person described is seen to subscribe to some version of the *hacker ethic*.

cracker   *n.* One who breaks security on a system. Coined ca. 1985 by hackers in defense against journalistic misuse of *hacker*. ... There is far less overlap between hackerdom and crackerdom than the *mundane* reader misled by sensationalistic journalism might expect. Crackers tend to gather in small, tight-knit, very secretive groups that have little overlap with the huge, open poly-culture [of hackerdom]; though crackers often like to describe *themselves* as hackers, most true hackers consider them a separate and lower form of life.

hacker ethic   *n.* 1. The belief that information-sharing is a powerful positive good, and that it is an ethical duty of hackers to share their expertise. ... Almost all hackers are actively willing to share technical tricks, software, and (where possible) computing resources with other hackers. Huge cooperative networks such as ... [the] Internet can function without central control because of this trait; they both rely on and reinforce a sense of community that may be hackerdom's most valuable intangible asset.

mundane   *n.* [from SF fandom] ... 2. A person who is not in the computer industry. In this sense, most often used as an adjectival modifier.[1]

Hackerdom has always been a positive environment driven by creativity, productivity, a love of cleverness, and a penchant for jargon—not for destruction. And Linux is the sort of project that could have emerged only from hacker culture.

Linux is a powerful operating system developed under the open-source model. Linux defines a translation frontier that allows humans and microprocessors to communicate without passing through Microsoft's platform bottleneck. That makes Microsoft nervous, even though, at least at the moment, most Linux users are IT professionals who use it to power servers rather than individual desktops. And Linux is *very* popular among IT professionals—popular enough to make it into the news every now and again.[2] In fact, whether you know it or not, your own IT manager could be running Linux on your servers.

If you find a committed Linux user and give him even a modicum of encouragement, she'd tell you both what Linux is and why it's superior to any of its competitors. If she's a true hacker, though, you probably won't understand her answer, because she's likely to tell you that: "Linux is a freely distributable Unix clone for 386/486/Pentium based PCs."[3]

Many of the mundane, who would be the only ones to ask such a question, might find this response somewhat less than edifying.

Unix is an important operating system first developed at Bell Labs in the late 1960s and early 70s. Unix's popularity among hackers stemmed from its combination of simplicity, transparency, flexibility, and power. The revolutionary symbiosis between the Unix operating system and the C programming language enabled computer scientists to navigate multiple layers of the translation chain—from a bit above the hardware all the way up to the actual frontier—using a single language. But Unix also had its limitations. Most users have very little interest in accessing translation layers beneath the frontier. In fact, every upward evolution of the frontier convinces a new batch of *potential* users that they can overcome their technophobia to become *actual* users. And they are unlikely to want to pop the hood to see how it works. To new users, Unix looked like a slightly more confusing version of DOS, because like DOS, Unix is a line-command (rather than a graphical) operating system. But the daunting operating system was fine for its purpose. Most versions of Unix were designed to run on minicomputers and workstations, machines that were both much more powerful and much more expensive than the contemporaneous PCs that most casual users favored.

Those differences divided the computing world well into the 1990s. Users who wanted to solve everyday tasks opted for inexpensive PCs, mostly built around IBM's architecture, Intel's chips, and DOS/Windows (or the slightly more expensive and user-friendly Mac). Users at companies or universities able to afford cutting-edge equipment and who wanted to understand their machines gravitated toward Unix. By the early 90s, the performance gap was narrowing. Intel's 386 chip was powerful, and a number of people who'd always insisted on expensive computers were beginning to play with PCs. Some of them thought that it would be nice to have a Unix-like system that ran on an Intel machine. Linus Torvalds, a student at the University of Helsinki, did something about it. He wrote the first central component—known as the kernel—of such an operating system and named it Linux.

And so, two paragraphs of deconstruction later, we're able to parse *most* of the hacker definition of Linux. All that's left is the "freely distributable" part. And that's a story in and of itself . . .

Freedom, Speech, and Beer

I met Richard M. Stallman in 1990, at a conference "reception" consisting mostly of chips and free beer. Even then, Stallman was a celebrity hacker: the "free software" guy. Years earlier, Stallman had been a member of MIT's AI Lab when it got an early Xerox laser writer. While everyone in the lab was excited about the new toy, some were also annoyed at the frequency of paper jams. Stallman decided to write a utility to make the printer notify users of a jam. He went to the source code to add this fairly simple new routine, but the source code wasn't there. He couldn't find it anywhere. He finally called Xerox, *who would-n't give it to him!* He was appalled. His printer didn't work the way that he needed it to work, he knew how to fix it, and Xerox refused to fix it for him and refused to let him fix it himself. Xerox's exertion of IP rights over the source code meant that Stallman's printer *would never work the way that he wanted it to work.* Shortly thereafter, Stallman founded both the Free Software Foundation (FSF), dedicated to the proposition that all hackers must share their source code, and Project GNU (a recursive acronym that stands for "GNU's Not Unix"), under whose auspices he developed a number of free software products.

But Stallman's notion of "free" software isn't quite what you might imagine. He has explained that: " 'Free software' is a matter of liberty, not price. To understand the concept, you should think of 'free' as in 'free speech,' not as in 'free beer.' "[4] To Stallman:

A program is free software, for you, a particular user, if:

You have the freedom to run the program, for any purpose;

You have the freedom to modify the program to suit your needs. (To make this freedom effective in practice, you must have access to the source code, since making changes in a program without having the source code is exceedingly difficult).

You have the freedom to redistribute copies, either gratis or for a fee;

You have the freedom to distribute modified versions of the program, so that the community can benefit from your improvements.

Since "free" refers to freedom, not to price, there is no contradiction between selling copies and free software. In fact, the freedom to sell copies is crucial: collections of free software sold on CD-ROMs are important for the community, and selling them is an important way to raise funds for free software development.[5]

Now, I'd seen most of this material before I met Stallman, but I hadn't paid much attention to it. At the time, I thought that he was just the "free software guy," a talented hacker who'd written a few useful software tools. But he was more than that.

Richard Stallman and Bill Gates are yin and yang. Like Gates, Stallman sees software development in starkly moralistic terms. Whereas Gates was an early vocal advocate of keeping software proprietary to reward developers, Stallman argues that ethical developers *must* share their software freely. In a curious way, Gates and Stallman straddle the IP clause. The Constitution authorized Congress to give innovators limited rights to motivate them to share their innovations with the world. Stallman sees the sharing as paramount; Gates tends to focus on the motivation. Whereas Gates admonished hobbyists about their casual attitude that "hardware must be paid for, but software is something to share. Who cares if the people who worked on it get paid?"[6] Stallman paraphrased this admonition as "If you share with your neighbor, you are a pirate."[7] His reply? "I don't think that people should ever make promises not to share with their neighbor."[8] But their debate runs even deeper. Gates focused on motivation: developers unable to sell their object code would write less software, and what they did write would be of lower quality. Stallman stressed the aggregate nature of knowledge: developers who don't share their source code waste time reinventing the wheel.

In Stallman's free-software world, a developer gets an idea, writes a program, and posts it where other hackers can see it, grab it, and play with it. They like it and wish it did more. Being hackers, they soon figure out how to get it to do more, and post the improved version. And so an open-source project evolves. Shared source code thus leads to better software faster than proprietary code. Which is all well and good, as long as we can populate the world with people who've identified problems that they themselves would like to solve, who are willing to share their solutions, and who have both the free time and the inclination to pursue paths that they consider neat or cool. As Gates might ask: *Have you people forgotten about the profit motive?*

The answer is "not entirely." Even Stallman recognized that "collections of free software sold on CD-ROMs are important for the community." The FSF's original revenue model, in fact, charged hackers a nominal fee to circulate free software. Granted, it wasn't much of a business model, but it was a start.

From its earliest days, the hackers of the free-software movement generated powerful tools, directed almost exclusively at software developers. A few companies eventually emerged to help circulate this software. These companies also offered training and consulting services. In other words, these "software companies" viewed software as a service industry, rather than as a manufacturing industry. Rather than providing services to make people want to buy their software, they provided software to make people need their services. The idea was intriguing, but the market remained small. The efforts of proprietary-software companies like Microsoft, Apple, Lotus, Novell, and Oracle continued to dwarf the efforts of the community creating free software.

Then something radical happened. The Internet enabled hackers to share their projects throughout the *entire global hacker community*. Sharing was no longer restricted to a single lab, a single university, or even the major U.S. research universities. Suddenly, any hacker with a good idea could post it and share the development burden with every hacker on the planet. The free-software community suddenly was able to harness far more talent than any single proprietary software company.

The community began to develop structure. The "hacker ethic" grew and gained further definition. Hackerdom adopted procedures to ensure that contributors were credited, that free software remained free, and that all contributed enhancements were compatible not only with the official release, but with each other. The culture developed both folkways and mores. And a collection of private companies began to tie their fortunes to this "free" software.

Linus Torvalds, who had launched the Linux kernel in the early 1990s, moved from Helsinki to the Silicon Valley and emerged as a major player. Torvalds remains responsible for each "official" release of Linux. He posts that release on a Web site from which anyone can download it and play with it. Various developers around the world devise improvements and send them back to Torvalds. He posts them so that still other hackers can review, critique, and possibly improve them further. Periodically he incorporates selected enhancements into a new version—and announces a new "official" Linux release.

Linux quickly surpassed Unix as the hacker operating system of choice, and a number of longstanding Unix companies shifted or diversified into Linux. Perhaps most significantly, though, Linux emerged as the primary competitor to Microsoft's Windows. It was quite a competitor, not in a market-share sense of course, but in a philosophical sense. It's hard to imagine two systems more different. Windows exemplified Gates's emphasis on proprietary rights in closely held source code; Linux embodied Stallman's emphasis on source code shared freely. Windows's evolution integrated new features tightly within the code; Linux took the gospel of modularity to an extreme. Windows was sold as a single product, with auxiliary warranties and support contracts also made available; Linux was "distributed" by companies that assembled collections of free software modules and that offered installation advice and support. And perhaps most significant of all, Windows conformed to Microsoft's tastes and strategic designs, increased its sales through various leveraging strategies, and included both technological and contractual features to complicate interoperability with non-Microsoft software; Linux distributors offered their clients customized installations, sold the product strictly on its merits, and worked hard to ensure interoperability with all software, whether free or proprietary.

Meanwhile, Stallman had taken steps to keep free software free. He was particularly concerned with the embrace-and-extend concept that Microsoft had used to neutralize Java—back when embrace-and-extend was little more than a concept, and long before Microsoft learned to use it so effectively. Stallman realized that nothing prevented anyone from taking free-software source code, tweaking it a bit, adding a couple of features, keeping their new, modified source code secret, and selling it as a proprietary product. If someone succeeded in distributing a proprietary version rather widely, consumers might get hooked on it, independent developers might begin to write to its proprietary APIs, and the software would no longer be free. Stallman realized that he must create a way to prevent that from occurring. And so he did. He and the FSF crafted the general public license (GPL), and invented copyleft.

GPL's copyleft gives users permission to modify and redistribute copylefted materials however they see fit, but if they incorporate any copylefted materials into their own work, the combined product must be subject to the same GPL. Any program that contains *any* GPL code thus must be subject to the GPL—or it infringes the copyrights inherent in the original licensed product. As you might imagine, copyleft provisions are controversial. Various IP scholars have debated the provisions' finer points, and Bill Gates has described them as being anticapitalist. To date, no one has challenged them in court—which means that no one is positive that they're enforceable. And while the GPL hardly protects all free software (the community also uses several other licenses, most of which don't contain copyleft provisions), it does protect Linux. And that's made a number of people nervous—mostly because of a misconception that copyleft restricts users, rather than just software distributors. In reality, if you develop and distribute software, the GPL gives you many more rights than you'd get from anyone else, but it's not without its own set of restrictions. So here's some free legal advice for software companies: *Don't accept any licenses that your lawyers can't explain to your programmers!* For everyone else, though, the lesson is even easier: just ignore it. If you don't distribute software, copylefting can't hurt you. It can only help—by allowing hackers to build better software faster.

But more than just copylefting and the GPL make people nervous about free software. In fact the key item making people nervous about free software can be summarized in two simple words: Richard Stallman.

Apostle to the Gentiles

True believers, moralists, radicals, and revolutionaries have a way of coming off as a bit intense, at times even extreme. Stallman is no exception. For every time that he insisted that he wasn't opposed to commercial software, he stated twice that he stood for free software. And when someone runs around telling people that they can make money on free software, they tend to get a bit confused—even when they realize that newspapers, magazines, and TV stations manage to make money from free speech. Some sales pitches are simply doomed to failure.

But movements never stand still. They either become increasingly radical or they work themselves closer to the mainstream. In the case of free software, the latter occurred. A group of stalwarts decided to recast their ideas in more mainstream terms. Michael Tiemann, for one, noted that though "on the surface, [The GNU Manifesto] read like a socialist polemic, ... I saw a business plan in disguise."[9] Nevertheless, he conceded that most people who read something that sounds like a socialist polemic see socialism—not business plans. And with Bill Gates breathing down your neck *encouraging* you to find socialism, you're likely to find it.

In early 1997, a few of these pragmatists decided to change the sales pitch. Eric Raymond, in particular, had become concerned that Stallman's emphasis on freedom was putting off "conservative business people." Now, Raymond is hardly a conservative business person—he describes himself as both an "anarchist" and a "gun-nut,"[10] a combination that makes *me* more than a bit nervous—but he was able to notice that Stallman's ideas weren't playing particularly well among the moneymakers of the tech world. The word *free* both confused and spooked too many people. Raymond set out to coin a *marketable* phrase that captured many of the same concepts as "free software." He settled on "open source."

Raymond's hacking prowess and *The New Hacker's Dictionary* (first published in 1991) had long since qualified him as a demigod.

demigod   *n*. A hacker with years of experience, a world-wide reputation, and a major role in the development of at least one design, tool, or game used by or known to more than half of the hacker community. To qualify as a genuine demigod, the person must recognizably identify with the hacker community and have helped shape it.[11]

By early 1997, though, Raymond's greatest influence was emanating from his essays.[12] *A Brief History of Hackerdom* set him up as the anthropological chronicler of hacker culture. But it was his essay "The Cathedral and the Bazaar" (later the book title of his collected essays) that truly began to move his work beyond the rather cloistered confines of hackerdom and into the Real World. This essay addressed an issue that had long haunted hackerdom: the apparent lack of empirical support for Stallman's ideas.

By 1997, many people knew about free software, the FSF, the political discourses that surrounded it, and the software projects developed by its adherents. But no one took the movement terribly seriously—at least not in the commercial arena. Most folks viewed it as a collection of anarchists, socialists, and radical libertarians who lacked the social graces necessary to leave the computer lab. No one was particularly surprised that this talented if offbeat crowd had developed some good software. But the movement's products targeted mainly hackers; its focus remained on reputation-building within a narrow community, not on serving consumers who dwelt in the Real World.

Real World   *n.* 1. Those institutions at which "programming" may be used in the same sentence as "FORTRAN," "COBOL," "RPG," "IBM," "DBASE," etc. Places where programs do such commercially necessary but uninspiring things as generating payroll checks and invoices. 2. The location of non-programmers and activities not related to programming. 3. A bizarre dimension in which the standard dress is shirt and tie and in which a person's working hours are defined as 9 to 5. . . . 4. Anywhere outside a university. "Poor fellow, he's left MIT and gone into the Real World." Used pejoratively by those not in residence there. In conversation, talking of someone who has entered the Real World is not unlike speaking of a deceased person. . . . See also *fear and loathing, mundane,* and *uninteresting.*[13]

And so, once again, an offbeat academic from Cambridge, Massachusetts, had devised an extreme philosophy, insisted that software marketing was a political statement, left his university to be completely unconstrained by its capitalist taints, started a movement, attracted a following, and occasionally came up with a point that proved to be useful at the margins. No big deal. This sort of thing happens all the time.

Of course, the founding academic insisted that his ideas were not outlandish. Stallman contended that his approach to software development would lead to better, less expensive, more useful software than anything that a proprietary software company could develop. He spent over a decade pushing this idea. But he faced the one problem that most often trips up movements born of philosophical purity: *it wasn't working.* The free-software movement was developing small-scale hacker tools. The world of proprietary software was redefining the way that people across the world lived and worked. By the mid-1990s, it seemed clear which development model was likely to have the greatest long-term impact. Well-funded proprietary software had relegated free software to a developmental niche.

Then along came Linux. Suddenly, the world's second most important platform was a free software project. And to those who were *really* paying attention, the situation was even stranger. A free-software project called Apache dominates the back rooms of the Web; roughly 60 percent of all Web servers worldwide use it today.[14] Even back in 1997, when most people had just started noticing the Web, roughly 40 percent of all Web servers were already running Apache. People began to wonder if this movement was more important than just a dream of a crackpot academic backed by a couple of kids. Conventional wisdom suggested that *the model shouldn't work!* Developers weren't being motivated, coordination and control were inadequate, and the source code was out in the open where anyone could tamper with it. *It wasn't supposed to produce anything more than an occasional curiosity!* Clearly, something was afoot. *The Cathedral and the Bazaar* was an insider's attempt to make sense of it all.

Linux is subversive. Who would have thought even five years ago (1991) that a world-class operating system could coalesce as if by magic out of part-time hacking by several thousand developers scattered all over the planet, connected only by the tenuous strands of the Internet?

Certainly not I. By the time Linux swam onto my radar screen in early 1993, I had already been involved in Unix and open-source development for ten years. . . . I thought I knew how it was done.

Linux overturned much of what I thought I knew. I had been preaching the Unix gospel of small tools, rapid prototyping and evolutionary programming for years. But I also believed there was a certain critical complexity above which a more centralized, a priori approach was required. I believed that the most important software (operating systems and really large tools . . .) needed to be built like cathedrals, carefully crafted by individual wizards or small bands of mages working in splendid isolation, with no beta to be released before its time.

Linus Torvalds's style of development—release early and often, delegate everything you can, be open to the point of promiscuity—came as a surprise. No quiet, reverent cathedral-building here—rather, the Linux community seemed to resemble a great babbling bazaar of differing agendas and approaches . . . out of which a coherent and stable system could seemingly emerge only by a succession of miracles.

The fact that this bazaar style seemed to work, and work well, came as a distinct shock. As I learned my way around, I worked hard not just at individual projects, but also at trying to understand why the Linux world not only didn't fly apart in confusion but seemed to go from strength to strength at a speed barely imaginable to cathedral-builders.

By mid-1996 I thought I was beginning to understand.[15]

And with that inkling of an understanding, Raymond set out to explain two different concepts to two divergent, yet equally skeptical, markets.

On the one hand, he had to convince the already faithful that his shift in emphasis wouldn't undermine their values. On the other, he also became the apostle to the gentiles, explaining the miracles of free-software—now-open source—development to a hostile business world.

Fortunately for Raymond, he was not alone in either task. Bruce Perens, a long-time free-software activist who had already developed a "social contract" for Linux users, helped Raymond found the Open Source Initiative (OSI). The OSI adapted Perens's guidelines—already quite popular throughout the community—into the Open Source Definition (OSD).

Open source doesn't just mean access to the source code. The distribution terms of open-source software must comply with the following criteria:

1. Free Redistribution
... The license shall not require a royalty or other fee for such sale.

2. Source Code
The program must include source code, and must allow distribution in source code as well as compiled form. . . . Deliberately obfuscated source code is not allowed. . . .

3. Derived Works
The license must allow modifications and derived works, and must allow them to be distributed under the same terms as the license of the original software.

4. Integrity of The Author's Source Code . . .

5. No Discrimination Against Persons or Groups . . .

6. No Discrimination Against Fields of Endeavor
... For example, it may not restrict the program from being used in a business, or from being used for genetic research.

7. Distribution of License
The rights attached to the program must apply to all to whom the program is redistributed without the need for execution of an additional license by those parties.

8. License Must Not Be Specific to a Product . . .

9. The License Must Not Restrict Other Software
... For example, the license must not insist that all other programs distributed on the same medium must be open-source software.

10. No provision of the license may be predicated on any individual technology or style of interface.[16]

The OSD is *not* a software contract; it's a set of guidelines for contract designers to consider when developing or adopting open-source contracts. The OSI offers certification to software projects whose underlying contracts adhere to the OSD's rules.

While a number of the OSD's rules continue to generate debate among both hackers and IP scholars, its most significant feature may be an omission: Copyleft isn't required. The OSI chose to make copyleft optional to better accommodate squeamish conservative business people afraid that a low-level programmer who incorporates a few open-source subroutines into a large proprietary product could force them to reveal their IP—analogous to the fear that some low-level programmer might steal a competitor's trade secret and open your company to massive liability, and no harder to police with standard due diligence. Nevertheless, forces antithetical to open-source development had sowed the fear of copyleft throughout the private sector. Raymond, Perens, and the rest of the OSI's founders decided that copyleft was too controversial a provision to require; much to Stallman's chagrin, they dropped it before making their overtures to the business community.

Cathedrals and Bazaars

Raymond received substantial backing (which, in the open-source world, means moral support) from the business people of the fledgling Linux industry, mostly graduates of the free-software movement who had braved the waters of the Real World by commercializing, distributing, and servicing Linux and related software. From their perspective, Raymond's explanation was more than just plausible—it was evocative. The business community would instinctively understand both "cathedrals" and "bazaars." Cathedrals are designed top down. An architect draws a set of plans and explains them to the builder. The builder parcels the work among foremen, who then delegate it to workers. The organizational structure is hierarchical, and someone always maintains an overarching view of where the project is heading and what it will look like when it's completed. Discoveries and complications along the way may lead to some design changes, but even those changes must work their way down the hierarchy.

This basic management style proved to be popular far beyond the somewhat narrow confines of the cathedral construction community. When Fred Brooks revisited *The Mythical Man-Month* in the mid-1990s to update the lessons that he had first learned about software engineering in the 1960s, he concluded that:

Today I am more convinced than ever. Conceptual integrity is central to product quality. Having a system architect is the most important single step toward conceptual integrity. These principles are by no means limited to software systems, but to the design of any complex construct, whether a computer, an airplane, a Strategic Defense Initiative, a Global Positioning System.[17]

Three months after Brooks penned those words in March 1995, the Netscape IPO put the Web on our collective radar screens. The PC revolution gave way to the Internet revolution. Software development clicked into hyperdrive. Linux grew from a hobbyist's project into a powerful product. And leading software engineers began to rethink development. Roughly two years after Brooks concluded that a systems architect was more important than ever, Raymond first presented the bazaar model of software development.

To appreciate the radical nature of the bazaar model, picture the "organized chaos" of an Arab souk. Shouting abounds, prices are negotiable, sales pitches are everywhere, and all deals emerge from intense haggling and bargaining. The experience can be a bit disorienting; it's hard to get a holistic view of the souk.

A complex software system based on similar principles seems unlikely to work. But "conservative business people" know well that situations like the souk truly are capitalism stripped bare—and as such, they produce aggregate rational behavior. With one little metaphor and a slight change in terminology, we've moved from the quasi socialist-sounding ideals underlying free software to the rawest known form of capitalist markets to describe open-source software—*and we haven't changed a damn thing*!

Remember the unrealistic textbook model in which "market forces" drive infinite numbers of buyers and sellers toward aggregate rationality, set the prices in the right place, align supply with demand, and allocate resources in the best possible manner? Well, we just found it. The bazaar model is the basis of modern microeconomic price theory. Rationality is the property that emerges from the apparent chaos of the bazaar. And it turns out that the notion of rationality as an "emergent" property is not unique unto bazaars; it's reflected in the "tipping to a standard" that network scientists have detected in physics, chemistry, biology, and elsewhere.[18] And as we've already seen, these ideas had worked their way far beyond academia by the mid-1990s. Why not into the world of software development?

Raymond's bazaar model couldn't dispense with the architect *entirely*. But it could cut the architect's role in half and rename it the "maintainer."[19] Whereas an architect disseminates a holistic view of the completed project and then watches its pieces coalesce, the maintainer is only in charge of coalescence. The maintainer, of course, was often the one who came up with the original idea for the system and go things started—but in the world of open source, even that wasn't necessary. The community developed protocols for handing off maintenance responsibilities, or even for claiming the role of the maintainer on a project that had somehow fallen into disrepair.[20] Maintainers collect submissions, decide which to accept and which to reject, monitor bugs, release patches as needed, interact with other projects, and announce new "official" releases. Maintainers are usually individuals—Torvalds, as noted, maintains Linux—though they can also be committees or even companies. The software system is what emerges from the apparently chaotic submissions to the maintainer.

If it's immediately obvious to you why someone would want to become a maintainer, you may grok hacker culture yet.

grok *vt.* [from the novel *Stranger in a Strange Land*, by Robert A. Heinlein, where it is a Martian word meaning literally "to drink" and metaphorically "to be one with"] The emphatic form is *grok in fullness*. 1. To understand, usually in a global sense. Connotes intimate and exhaustive knowledge.[21]

After all, becoming a maintainer is the best way to become a demigod. If not, you might accept one of the other theories as to what motivates hackers. These theories include reputation within the community, resume enhancement beyond the community, and participation in what anthropologists call a "gift culture." Suffice it to say, though, that while maintainers will never be as wealthy as Bill Gates, they are likely to find ample, rewarding, and high-compensation opportunities to customize software and to consult.

In other words, the open-source movement may not be as offbeat as it sounded at first. The bazaar model embodies plausible approaches

to both product development and commercialization. And with a particularly delicious twist of irony, the downgrading of the architect to a
mere maintainer puts the capitalist shoe on the other foot. While Gates
may deride Stallman's free-software movement as socialist (or at the very
least, as anticapitalist), the open-source community may now respond
by echoing Scott McNealy's charge that Microsoft's cathedral-style
design is central planning.

And so there you have it. When the Internet expanded the open-source
community to the entire world, it made the souk big enough for its emergent properties to possess real power and value. This expansion suggests
that the information sector's next few chapters may be shaped less by
competition among companies than by competition among philosophies,
approaches, product-development strategies, and business models. It also
gives us a number of different ways to characterize this competition. At
the obvious level, it pits secret source code against open source. At the
metaphoric level, it's cathedrals vs. bazaars. At the pejorative level,
socialism squares off against central planning. Perhaps the most useful
characterization, though, is that the established "product-oriented"
vision of the software industry faces a challenge from a newer "service-
oriented" vision of the industry.

The long and the short of it is that a valid business model *does* exist
behind open source. The first ones to see the model were those, like
Tiemann, who already lived inside the community. Open-source hackers
founded companies like Cygnus Solutions, Red Hat, and VA Software,
so it's not surprising that they adopted its implicit business model. The
real question was whether anyone *outside* the community would ever
come on board. The answer came less than a year after Raymond first
released *The Cathedral and the Bazaar*, courtesy of Netscape.

On January 23, 1998, Netscape made two announcements. The first, as reported
by C|Net: "In an unprecedented move, Netscape Communications will give away
its Navigator browser, confirming rumors over the last several weeks."

The second: "It also will give away the source code for the next generations
of its Communicator suite."

The decision to give away the browser came as no surprise, but the release of
the source code stunned the industry. It hit the pages of newspapers around the
world, and even the Open Source community was surprised at the move. Never
before had a major software company opened up its proprietary code. What was
Netscape up to now?

We had decided to change the playing field, and not for the first time. Always known for thinking outside the box, this time Netscape was taking the commitment to building a better Internet to a new level. . . .

As fast and surprising as the announcement seemed to both insiders and outsiders, it reflected several converging tracks of thought. Netscape executives were discussing a whitepaper . . . advocat[ing] that Netscape free its source . . . citing Eric Raymond's paper, "The Cathedral and the Bazaar." . . .

In the engineering pit, there was a similar view. Many Netscape employees had experience working with Open Source.[22]

In other words, Netscape's *management*, not its hacker base, decided to open the source code. Management cited Raymond's work as the dispositive influence and hired him as a consultant. He helped them understand not only how to set up an open-source development project, but also what rights they would need to reserve in order to keep both their existing business commitments and those that they anticipated making in the future. Thus was born Mozilla, the open-source version of Netscape's browser.[23]

How did the Real World view Netscape's bold move? Well, Cusumano and Yoffie, whose chronicle of the browser wars gave them inside access to both Microsoft and Netscape, seemed to think that it was the right strategic move at the right time. They, of course, didn't speak of cathedrals and bazaars—they weren't hackers. They employed their own set of management metaphors to report the browser wars in terms of "sumo strategy" and "judo strategy"; the former pits strength against strength, while the latter attempts to turn an opponent's own strength against it. They saw Netscape's decision to open its source code as "classic judo. Netscape management recognized that flexibility was critical: Without the resources to fight Microsoft directly, it had to find a creative way to compete. . . . It also needed huge external resources to offset Microsoft's size and financial strength. Once again, it hoped to find these resources on the Net."[24] In other words, the hacker community allowed Netscape to "hire" a huge numbers of new developers by giving them something other than cash. Netscape gave them innovative technology with which to play. The plan worked—to a point. Mozilla.org (the organizational maintainer of the open-source Mozilla browser) began to receive new and imaginative contributions within six weeks of opening its source.

But we already know how the story ended. While Netscape was trying to leverage the hacker community, Microsoft found more effective ways to leverage its own strength in Windows—and succeeded in blocking Netscape from virtually all reasonable distribution outlets. Shorn of its ability to distribute its product easily, and faced with Microsoft's premature integration of browsing capabilities into the platform, Netscape conceded defeat before 1998 was out. Its decision to open its source code to developers couldn't prevent Microsoft from blocking its path to consumers. The open-source community had lost its first great opportunity to demonstrate the superiority of its development and business models. At the same time, though, Netscape *did* provide the community with high-profile exposure, and may have made a number of people consider Linux and Apache more seriously than they might have otherwise.

Furthermore, no matter how things may have looked to the Real World, the computer industry understood what had happened. Other computer companies were well aware of Microsoft's business tactics, and while they recognized that open-source was not, in and of itself, a strong enough model to overcome monopoly leveraging, that hardly made it a bad strategy. They began to explore its ramifications themselves, and began to contemplate ways to make money in the growing Linux and Apache markets—a trend that accelerated with the introduction of the GNOME and KDE desktops that provide a graphical interface to Linux in a role similar to the one that early versions of Windows played for DOS. Some, like Sun, developed open-source versions of important products, such as its office suite, StarOffice.[25] IBM opened the source to some of its products, and sells a sizable collection of both secret and open-source applications that run on Linux. Hewlett-Packard (HP) opened the source to some of its printer drivers, and established an entire Linux Systems Division to coordinate its open-source strategy. Finally, when Merrill Lynch identified itself as part of the open-source community, the notion that open-source development was antithetical to capitalism began to ring more than a bit hollow.

With important tech companies like Sun, IBM, and HP incorporating open-source into their strategic plans, the battle no longer appears to be Richard Stallman against the world. While much of the world has yet to adopt Stallman's more radical proposals—and may view even some of

Raymond's "pragmatism" as a bit extreme—large parts of the commercial software world clearly are drifting toward open-source and may even leave Microsoft standing out in the crowd. David Stutz, for example, generated a fair amount of controversy when he retired from Microsoft in February 2003 and immediately posted an essay on his Web site contending that Microsoft's refusal to embrace open-source was eroding the value of its products.[26] The looming battle appears to pit Bill Gates against the world. And though Stallman was easy to marginalize, the antagonists in this new battle may be evenly matched.

Parishioners, Purchasers, and Parliamentarians

Stallman spread the gospel among the hackers. Raymond evangelized the tech-savvy parts of the business community. But the ultimate battle between open-source and trade-secret-protected software will take place in the minds and wallets of consumers, and it's not at all clear who's been talking to them. The open-source "movement" is, above all else, a movement of software developers. Hackers wrote most of the open-source literature for other hackers. Even Raymond pitched primarily to the parts of the business world involved in software design. After all, cathedrals and bazaars are *design* metaphors. Why should a user care *how* her software was crafted—as long as it works? Yet it is the mundanes who ultimately will determine whether open-source succeeds or fails. Will they choose to worship at the cathedral or to shop at the bazaar? This question, rather than anything posed by Stallman or Raymond or even Gates, will determine the future shape of software development.

Ironically, it's pretty tough for anyone outside hackerdom to understand open source; most attempts to navigate the literature are likely to veer quickly into issues that aren't relevant to anyone whose interests lie beyond computer programming or software marketing. Yet, at least three other groups *should* be interested in the movement and its products: software users, potential investors, and government decision makers.

Users' interests should be clear, though they're likely to differ for different types of users. Broadly speaking, computers today serve two purposes. Individuals use their desktop computers for a variety of interactive tasks such as word processing, calculating, e-mail, and Web browsing; organizations also use servers to "serve up" information or services. Because Windows dominates today's desktop so decisively, relatively few individual consumers consider alternative platforms that would secure their membership in a competing network. Apple provides the only real alternative, and attempts to generate a popular Linux-based consumer system appear to remain at least a few years in the future. But organizational consumers and their IT managers also work with servers. Server hardware is often larger, more powerful, and more expensive than desktop machines, and sever software emphasizes different sets of attributes; stability, robustness, and ease of customization are often more important than the availability of a particular user interface. While Windows NT is popular on some types of servers, Microsoft hardly dominates the server market; Linux and Apache are probably the two most important server-software products. Institutional consumers thus already need to understand open-source products; individual consumers may need to learn about them soon.

Investors' interests may be somewhat harder to discern, but the relevant definition of an investor goes far beyond equity shareholders. Because platform software is a network industry, every user becomes an investor in every network that she chooses to join. Everyone running a copy of Windows on her computer has a vested interest in the ongoing maintenance, development, and support of the Windows platform and of the applications that run upon it. That means that she's also interested in seeing Microsoft survive and thrive. Everyone running a copy of Linux on her computer has an analogous interest in the maintenance, development, and support of Linux. But because Linux was born of a "movement," or a "community," rather than of a company, it's harder to know how to translate that interest into practice. As a result, anyone interested in "investing" in open-source software—whether that investment comes in the form of a cash outlay or simply a commitment to invest time and effort in the use of the product—needs to understand the open-source movement well enough to be confident in its survival.

Government decision makers possess both sets of interests—those common to users and those common to investors. Government procurement decisions don't really differ from those of private-sector organizations of comparable size and complexity. But while corporate responsibility is to maximize shareholder value, government responsibility is to maximize public welfare. At least some government decision makers, typically those charged with setting broad policy rather than those empowered to make narrow procurement decisions, must integrate their duty to the public into their overall thinking about the future of computing.

Such considerations tend to rise to the fore only at critical junctures in an industry's development. The relatively recent emergence of open-source systems into powerful and important products suggests that the software industry may stand today at such a juncture. Legislators around the world have begun to inquire about the implications of this new model of software development not only to their own computing environments, but to the future of their domestic software and technology industries. Linux, Apache, and a small number of other open-source success stories thus represent far more than simply new entries into the competitive software arena, to be considered for adoption and evaluated as are all other software systems. They redefine what it means to be a "software company," and thus provide policy makers with a rare opportunity to contemplate the direction in which they would like to move industrial policy and economic development.

And then there's always the leviathan in the room. Because governments tend to be not only software users, but also the single largest users in their jurisdictions, their decisions can help provide a way around Microsoft's formidable applications barrier to entry. If a single very large user adopted a new platform, developers would follow—precisely because the new applications market serving the entrant would reopen niches that had already converged to a standard in the dominant platform's more mature applications market. To pick just two obvious examples, multiple competing graphical desktops and office suites run on Linux. In the proprietary world, Microsoft owns both standards. Developers who felt that the new network defined a sufficient market would write applications to sell into it. Those applications, in turn, would entice new users—who would then attract additional developers, etc. A competing platform standard could emerge, and it would almost certainly define an open standard.

Governments may be the only users large enough to trigger the rebirth of full-blown competition among software networks. The existence of competing networks, though, would mean more than simply a reintroduction of consumer choice. It would also complicate the relationships among the various players in the computing and software industries—the original equipment manufacturers (OEMs) who build the hardware, the competing platform developers, the independent software vendors (ISVs) who write application programs, and consumers. Various companies may attempt to use copyright law, patent law, and contract law to manipulate the market to their advantage. Government decision makers can also influence which of these attempts succeed and which ones fail.

Government decision makers thus face a tough challenge. They have to consider all of the issues that drive consumer software purchases, including costs, service, reliability, and product quality.[27] But they also face a unique set of concerns relating to issues like national security and economic development. From a national security perspective, the openness or secrecy of source code, particularly for critical infrastructure software like a platform, can affect a cracker's ability to wreak havoc with national infrastructure. Furthermore, some governments might feel uncomfortable trusting their critical infrastructure to a private company's secrets—particularly when the company is foreign.

Beyond security, different countries have different concerns. China, for example, has a big (and widely reported) problem with software piracy. By most estimates, a full 90 percent of the software in China in 2002 violated *someone's* copyright (mostly, though not exclusively, Microsoft's). While China may be the last place on earth likely to worry about IP rights as a matter of governing theory, it's also a country trying to integrate its markets with the rest of the world.[28] Over the next few years, China will have to conform its economy to WTO rules, and the WTO has insisted upon better IP enforcement. A *great* way to combat piracy is to make people prefer legal software to pirated software. And open-source packages are *ideal* for that goal because users can circulate them freely without infringing anyone's IP rights. Red Flag Software is a government-owned company that promotes the distribution of open-source software throughout China; the Chinese government reportedly even has toyed with the idea of requiring open-source software for all government machines.

China is hardly alone. Legislators across Europe, Asia, and Latin America reportedly have introduced open-source legislation—though most have been little other than posturing by minority parties or back-benchers trying to grab headlines. These bills have run the full gamut, from truly intrusive command-and-control to more benign statements of preference. In some cases, for example, legislators have tried to ban proprietary software from government computers—a horrible idea that would block government's access to powerful applications for which no viable open-source alternative exists. Others have advocated requiring open-source platforms on all government computers, with no preference among applications—showing a bit more pragmatism and flexibility, but hardly enough. The most reasonable of them—and the only idea that could work without threatening to cripple government functioning—simply express a preference for open-source where available, and require procurement agents to justify selecting proprietary software over an open-source competitor.

Procurement legislation of even this measured sort is rather unusual. By and large, commercial considerations should guide government's commercial decisions. The elevation of social concerns risks causing more harm than good by hampering government efficiency. At the same time though, most people recognize that governments *should* consider industrial and economic development. Governments at all levels representing economies at all stages of development need to ensure that they've created environments that foster sustainable education, training, innovation, jobs, and commerce.

We've already missed the appropriate arena for debating software policy. The proprietary model of software development is only possible because IP law allows developers to protect their source code as a trade secret while simultaneously circulating their copyrighted object code. In other words, we adopted an *industrial policy* that enabled some business models that otherwise wouldn't have been viable. Unfortunately, we didn't debate this policy before we adopted it; we neglected to weigh its benefits against its costs, evaluate its impact on innovation, or project its contributions to scientific knowledge. No U.S. Congress—a body charged with this analysis—ever considered triple protection explicitly. And American courts are *required* to presume that Congress actually reached a reasoned conclusion, despite knowing that such a presumption is entirely fictional. We thus made a critical policy decision without ever evaluating either its merits or its implications—and then foisted it upon the rest of the world, where it may cause even more harm than it does in the United States. While procurement is hardly a good place to make industrial policy, for many governments it may be the only place left.

Our "decision" to award triple protection had a particularly adverse effect on the market for platform software. Platform software is an unusual product for a number of reasons. First, it's a network product prone to lock-in, high switching costs, and tipping to a standard. Second, it's a critical component of the public's information infrastructure. Third, a single private company owns its de facto standard. Fourth, that private owner operates the standard as a proprietary product. Fifth, the standard and its private owner are dominant worldwide.

This combination is unique. For the most part, those relatively few products that both tip to a network standard and play critical infrastructure roles are subject to some form of government control—either through direct government ownership or through regulations restricting the behavior of a "natural monopolist." These monopolists generally do pretty well for themselves and for their investors—though not always quite as well for their customers. But they do recognize that part of the price of being a monopolist is that they need to reserve that guest room for the market cops; we often designate entire regulatory agencies to police them.

The information sector's growth turned platform software into a critical infrastructure product. But for the first time, the provider is a private company unconstrained by *either* market forces or government regulation. Microsoft can set its prices wherever it wants, include whatever terms it wants in its contracts or licenses, and leverage its dominance in platform software into any middleware markets that it chooses. If anyone has a problem with Microsoft's moves, they can call in the market cops—but we've already seen how well that works. Technology gave Microsoft the ability to integrate new products into its platform, IP law protected its distribution channels, contract law permitted its licenses, and its economic incentives drove it to squelch all innovation that it couldn't direct through Windows.

Our inattention to industrial, software, and IP policy thus gave Microsoft an unregulated infrastructure monopoly, the ability to channel innovation in directions likely to serve its monopoly, and broad discretion about the directions in which its monopoly grows. Software should evolve as innovation above the platform diverges in competing directions, and eventually converge to a de facto standard when competing vendors copy each other's successful innovations. When convergence leads to stable, widely understood technology, developers can integrate the application safely into the platform to begin its slow journey down the translation chain. But we've given Microsoft the power to tamper with that evolution; the platform now evolves how, where, and when Microsoft wants it to evolve. And as Microsoft directs the platform's evolution, its creeping infrastructure monopoly becomes increasingly central to our lives. As far as I can tell, no private company has *ever* had this level of power over a product that is so central, while receiving so little government oversight.

Could open-source procurement legislation circumvent the applications barrier to entry? And even more to the point, should it try? Windows is a classic cathedral program. And though it might never have become dominant if we had a functioning bazaar, our information infrastructure wasn't quite capable of generating emergent systems as complex as a platform when Microsoft launched and nurtured Windows. In a curious way, Windows may be a victim of its own success. Its topdown construction helped create an infrastructure that enabled open source to match its raw power, while also embodying a number of other attributes that better serve the public's interests. The looming clash between these approaches to infrastructure could thus have a profound effect on more than just the information sector; it could help shape the future of economic and industrial development.

Governments worldwide will have to decide whether they want industrial policies that favor worshippers or shoppers—or policies that are indifferent between them. Existing policies play strongly in favor of cathedrals; if unchanged, we may all end up worshipping whether we want to or not. The debate over procurement legislation raises the possibility of leveling the playing field. Good legislation could give us a choice. Open-source platforms would lead to an open standard for software development, and force future developers to compete strictly on the merits of their products, not on their ability to leverage strategically from one software product market into another. That sort of open standard for infrastructure would lead to a more neutral, market-driven evolution of the rest of the software industry. Innovators and entrepreneurs could focus on software features enabled by technology, rather than on those motivated by Microsoft's business strategies. But bad legislation could destroy what we already have; it could force us into the bazaar even when we'd prefer to be lining the pews. Public policy may thus prove to be as important to the information sector's maturation as it was to its birth. And as long as we remain unwilling to revisit our default decisions about software IP rights, procurement may be the only arena in which policy movement is possible.

From Perú with Love

The world of software may be in the midst of redefining itself. As with all such industrial transitions, new entrants and powerful incumbents tend to forecast polar extreme outcomes. Proponents of open-source see uniformity flourishing throughout the world of computing, product quality skyrocketing with prices plummeting, education improving, and consumers and software developers all benefiting. Companies that have prospered under the prevailing industry model preach caution and risk aversion. They contend that open-source code threatens to reduce incentives for excellence and to devastate the environment of competitive innovation that has moved computing from esoteric laboratories to the center of our lives in but a few short decades.

The need for policy makers to understand which parts of these diametrically opposed visions are most likely to prove true should be obvious; promoting the wrong model of software development could ripple through the entire economy. At the same time, though, some of the rash legislative proposals threaten to cripple governments' abilities to provide effective constituent service. Government software adoption is a subtle process that needs to balance standard commercial concerns related to software quality and operating costs with political nuances, including competition among agencies and preferences for local, regional, or national developers. Bold policy pronouncements may provide useful guidelines and statements of preference, but they should never interfere with the smooth functioning of government.

And therein lies the task for government officials around the world: learn about the debate over open source, and try to harness its innovations to further your own industrial and economic development.

In March 2002, Peruvian Congressman Edgar Villanueva Nuñez introduced a bill that would mandate the use of open-source software on government computers. Microsoft wasn't pleased. Juan Alberto González, the General Manager of Microsoft Perú, drafted a letter to the congressman describing the evils that his bill would unintentionally unleash upon the fragile Peruvian economy, including collapsing domestic software markets, spiraling costs and systems migration nightmares.

First of all, we want to thank you for the chance you gave us to inform you about our work in this country for benefit of the public sector. . . .

The bill [that you introduced] makes it compulsory for all public bodies to use only free software, that is to say open source software, which breaches the principles of equality before the law, that of nondiscrimination and the right of free private enterprise, freedom of industry and of contract, protected by the constitution. . . .

So, by compelling the State to favor a business model based entirely on open source, the bill would only discourage the local and international manufacturing companies, which are the ones which really undertake important expenditures . . . as opposed to a model of open source software which tends to have an ever weaker economic impact, since it mainly creates jobs in the service sector.

The bill imposes the use of open-source software without considering the dangers that this can bring from the point of view of security, guarantee, and possible violation of the intellectual property rights of third parties.

The bill uses the concept of open-source software incorrectly, since it does not necessarily imply that the software is free or of zero cost, and so arrives at mistaken conclusions regarding State savings, with no cost-benefit analysis to validate its position. . . .

The bill demotivates the creativity of the Peruvian software industry. . . .

Open source software, since it can be distributed without charge, does not allow the generation of income for its developers through exports. . . .

If open source software satisfies all the requirements of State bodies, why do you need a law to adopt it? Shouldn't it be the market that decides freely which products give most benefits or value?[29]

Congressman Villanueva provided Sr. González with an insightful and detailed response.

First of all, I thank you for your letter of March 25, 2002, in which you state the official position of Microsoft relative to Bill Number 1609, Free Software in Public Administration, which is indubitably inspired by the desire for Perú to find a suitable place in the global technological context. In the same spirit, and convinced that we will find the best solutions through an exchange of clear and open ideas, I will take this opportunity to reply to the comments included in your letter.

While acknowledging that opinions such as yours constitute a significant contribution, it would have been even more worthwhile for me if, rather than formulating objections of a general nature (which we will analyze in detail later) you had gathered solid arguments for the advantages that proprietary software could bring to the Peruvian State, and to its citizens in general, since this would have allowed a more enlightening exchange in respect of each of our positions. . . .

It is also necessary to make it clear that the aim of the Bill we are discussing is not directly related to the amount of direct savings that can by made by using free software in state institutions. That is in any case a marginal aggregate value, but in no way is it the chief focus of the Bill. The basic principles that inspire the Bill are linked to the basic guarantees of a state of law, such as:

Free access to public information by the citizen.

Permanence of public data.

Security of the State and citizens.

To guarantee the free access of citizens to public information, it is indispensable that the encoding of data is not tied to a single provider.

The use of standard and open formats gives a guarantee of this free access, if necessary through the creation of compatible free software.

To guarantee the permanence of public data, it is necessary that the usability and maintenance of the software does not depend on the goodwill of the suppliers, or on the monopoly conditions imposed by them. For this reason the State needs systems the development of which can be guaranteed due to the availability of the source code.

To guarantee national security or the security of the State, it is indispensable to be able to rely on systems without elements that allow control from a distance or the undesired transmission of information to third parties. Systems with source code freely accessible to the public are required to allow their inspection by the State itself, by the citizens, and by a large number of independent experts throughout the world. Our proposal brings further security, since the knowledge of the source code will eliminate the growing number of programs with *spy code*.

In the same way, our proposal strengthens the security of the citizens, both in their role as legitimate owners of information managed by the state, and in their role as consumers. In this second case, by allowing the growth of a widespread availability of free software not containing *spy code* able to put at risk privacy and individual freedoms.

In this sense, the Bill is limited to establishing the conditions under which the state bodies will obtain software in the future, that is, in a way compatible with these basic principles.

From reading the Bill it will be clear that once passed:

• the law does not forbid the production of proprietary software
• the law does not forbid the sale of proprietary software
• the law does not specify which concrete software to use
• the law does not dictate the supplier from whom software will be bought
• the law does not limit the terms under which a software product can be licensed.

What the Bill does express clearly is that, for software to be acceptable for the state it is not enough that it is technically capable of fulfilling a task, but that further the contractual conditions must satisfy a series of requirements regarding the license, without which the State cannot guarantee the citizen adequate processing of his data, watching over its integrity, confidentiality, and accessibility throughout time, as these are very critical aspects for its normal functioning.

We agree, Sr. González, that information and communication technology have a significant impact on the quality of life of the citizens (whether it be positive or negative). We surely also agree that the basic values I have pointed out above are fundamental in a democratic state like Perú. So we are very interested to know of any other way of guaranteeing these principles, other than through the use of free software in the terms defined by the Bill.

As for the observations you have made, we will now go on to analyze them in detail.

[Almost 5,000 words later]

I wish you the greatest respect, and would like to repeat that my office will always be open for you to expound your point of view to whatever level of detail you consider suitable.[30]

Congressman Villanueva drafted his letter in April 2002. Multiple translations made it to the Web almost immediately, and the Congressman is reportedly well on his way to becoming a demigod. For all I know, the congressman could be a hacker—or, for that matter, an ex-hacker, an aspiring hacker, or even a recovering hacker.[31] Even if that were the case, as a member of the Peruvian Congress, he would hardly be a stereotypical hacker. What's more, his proposal is likely to be a bit too draconian to actually generate all of the benefits that he would like to see; though Sr. González undoubtedly erred in the other direction, many of his points were fundamentally sound. Nevertheless, this entire exchange serves as an important reminder that the information sector is a global phenomenon that relates to important ideals of liberty and openness—not just to those of property and development. It's also a reminder that government matters. Government decisions could help determine whether, in the information sector's future, we'll worship at the cathedrals of proprietary software, shop in open-source bazaars, or flit happily between devotion and consumption without ever having to choose one over the other.

This conclusion thus brings us full circle: government always played a critical role in the information sector, and government *still* has a critical role to play. Government developed the information sector's basic plumbing and turned it over to the private sector. Once there, it became easier and cheaper for the world's hackers to communicate and to exchange ideas, effectively reducing transaction costs enough to enable complex software development by bazaar. That product-development model then led to new business models, largely focused on add-on products or on service, support, and customization. Consumers win, because it provides them with better software and delivers it faster. Producers win because they can participate in product development while sinking only a fraction of the development costs. And that innovative explosion all occurred without the government. But that doesn't mean that governmental involvement can no longer serve a purpose. Because amidst all those winners, Microsoft and the smaller companies that follow its business model stand poised to lose—and no one sensible ever loses without fighting. Open-source threatens Microsoft's role as the head of the world's largest software-distribution chain by promising to undermine distribution profits. Microsoft is thus fighting back using all of the weapons at its disposal—IP rights, restrictive licenses, existing relationships throughout the software industry, and innuendo about copylefting. Microsoft possesses many of these weapons only because the government set industrial policy without really considering its implications.

The tension between Linux and Windows, or more accurately the tension between open-source and trade-secret-protected platforms, is precisely the tension at the heart of the future of the information sector; it pits reduced transaction costs against distributors whose revenue streams are about to run dry. It's hardly surprising that it hit software—the industry with the longest history in the information sector—first. But software won't be the last place it hits. Government policy makers must understand what happens each time a new industry undergoes the metamorphosis into an information industry, because each one is likely to introduce its own unique set of issues. Consider, for instance, what happened to the music industry. . . .

7

The Computer Ate My Industry

Real Good for Free

Way back in 1970, long before musicians knew that they were "digital content creators," Joni Mitchell wrote a song comparing her life as a star entertainer to that of a street performer. While she earns a fortune playing to packed audiences, he sets up shop near a lunch cart, where he plays "real good, for free." Joni's record label bundled this subversive message with several of her other songs as an album, and released it to the public. To this day, the record companies continue to collect royalties from consumers who purchase the album, perform the song, or quote its lyrics.[1]

Why "subversive?" Because we've always had this great concept of music that was real good for free. Some music you pay for, and some music is free. Free music is just out there for the taking. Someone put "his" music into the public domain, and you wandered by. No charge, unless you feel like throwing a couple of coins into the hat. Except for one little problem. It's not strictly true. One of the great dilemmas of the music business is that while a few well-paid superstars and a large number of street performers play music for us to enjoy, only some of them perform it legally. Odds are pretty good that Joni Mitchell's street performer played at least one copyrighted song, and that when he got home and tallied the day's take, he didn't forward the appropriate royalties. In other words, he was a thief.

Now, it's one thing to look the other way at this blatant disrespect for property rights, but it's another to actually lament the plight of these talented musical thieves—in a copyrighted song, no less. In many ways, it breeds contempt for the entire notion of proprietary music. Our star performers and major record labels have long fostered this sort of cultural contempt; in many ways, it's good for business. But it is cultural contempt—and as the record companies have learned, it can come back to bite you. After all, if some street-performing clarinetist can co-opt copyrighted music for personal financial gain with the full approval of the record companies, how could it possibly be wrong for me to treat the music in my CD collection as if it were my own? And if I can treat it as if it were my own, how could it possibly be wrong to share it with a few of my closest friends—or even with a few million of my closest friends?

We'd all like our music to be real good for free. But it isn't. It isn't because it costs money to compose music and it costs money to produce music. Until fairly recently, it also cost money to distribute music. But the information sector changed that. These days, music is nothing more than a bit string. Anyone can copy and move digital music around the Internet—hence around the world—at pretty close to zero cost. The people who own the rights to distribute it no longer control the channels of distribution.

The music business, like the software business, found that the Internet had altered a critical element of its production and distribution model. But unlike the software industry, which had always been in the information sector and was at least somewhat adept at navigating technological change, music and its people dwelt in a different world. Music thus became the first mature industry that the information sector swallowed.[2] Its players are still reeling from the change. The copyright owners—led by the record companies—are fighting to regain control of distribution. Many of their battles have taken place on the IP front, where they've convinced some judges to uphold the rights that they sought to protect, and some politicians to introduce bills that would strengthen those rights. They've also faced defeats on the IP front, because neither all judges nor all politicians have agreed with their arguments. The combatants have met on the technology front. The record companies have sought to reimpose control by developing technologies that complicate copying and circulation. A world of technically adept music fans have countered by either developing or adapting technology that cracked the security systems and eased distribution.

Music's future is thus likely to look quite different from its recent past. No one can be certain what direction it will take. Will the record companies find better ways to reassert control over distribution, or will technology force them to relinquish their distribution rights and to turn elsewhere for profits? Will ubiquitous music available on demand from wireless devices become a subscription service—and if so, who will be in charge of collecting fees and of distributing them among the many holders of music copyrights? Will recorded music become little more than a way to promote live performances—or to sell products? Will corporate sponsors become the primary "patrons of the arts," putting talented musicians on salary to develop Top 40 jingles? Will our IP laws become increasingly expansive, and the penalties for infringement increasingly harsh? Or will they become less restrictive to accommodate the easy, cheap distribution enabled by new technologies? And if our IP laws do change, how will we handle the overlap period, in which one set of rights protects valuable "old" music while a different set protects "new" music?

These are some of the questions that we'll have to answer over the next few years—or decades. But they're also far more than that. The future of the music industry will reveal how we handle ourselves when the information sector takes over a mature industry. We must try to understand how music slipped into the information sector, and consider how we should respond now that it's there to stay.

The Music Never Stopped

They're a band beyond description
Like Jehovah's favorite choir
People joining hand in hand
While the music plays the band
Lord they're setting us on fire
Crazy rooster crowing midnight
Balls of lightning roll along
Old men sing about their dreams
Women laugh and children scream
And the band keeps playing on
Keep on dancing through to daylight
Greet the morning air with song

No one's noticed but the band's all packed and gone
Was it ever here at all?
But they kept on dancing
Come on children, come on children
Come on clap your hands
Well the cool breeze came on Tuesday
And the corn's a bumper crop
And the fields are full of dancing
Full of singing and romancing
The music never stopped.[3]

Let's back up a bit, to a time when the music business seemed lucrative and the perils of digitization appeared to be far in the future. In fact, let's back up even more than that, all the way to a somewhat hypothetical beginning lost in the mists of time.

The music business has been around for a long time. It's in the Bible, in Greek mythology, and in just about every aboriginal culture that we've ever uncovered. Throughout most of its history, though, the underlying business model was pretty simple. Most musicians played for handouts. A few performers would get together to play, a handful of patrons would gather to listen, and if they liked what they heard they'd offer the players coins or food or sex or something else of value. Then everyone would pack up and go home, and there would be no more music until someone else decided to perform. A few musicians may have been lucky enough to secure steady work, serving as temple trumpeters or singers, court musicians, or some such important role. While they may have performed for a salary, the model was essentially the same: they played, people listened, and then everyone went home.

That began to change when someone figured out how to transcribe musical compositions. These "music writers" encoded notes and intonations; anyone who saw what they had written and knew how to read their musical language could recreate a performance. Their handwritten code created an entirely new "thing." It certainly wasn't music—it didn't require performers, and you couldn't listen to it. Instead, it was a set of instructions that explained to people how to produce a reasonably reliable reproduction of some earlier musical performance. In other words, it was information about music, the first step toward converting music into an information industry.

But these handwritten music codes did more than that. They opened up new business models. Suddenly, people could compose "records" of what music was supposed to sound like. "Distributors" could move those records around, and multiple performers could learn to translate a composer's conception into actual music. Patrons, fans, and listeners continued to pay performers under the two old models but new people could also get into the act. After all, composition was a value-added skill—and thus warranted compensation. So, for that matter, were transcription and distribution.

This new industry grew around specialized talents. Some folks composed, others transcribed multiple copies of the compositions, and still others distributed those copies. Way down at the opposite ends of this chain lay the two original—and still the only two indispensable—members of the music community, the performers and the listeners. Now, I don't know precisely how the composers, transcribers, distributors, and performers split the revenues from this new business, and in truth I don't much care. What I *do* care about is that two parallel "music businesses" developed; one converted music into information and distributed it as information, while the second converted that information back into music. Those are, in fact, distinct businesses that require distinct business models, though some folks undoubtedly contributed to both, and some of the revenue models may have integrated them into a single operation.

Both parts of the industry improved over time. Instruments got better, performers spent more time training, and published music improved to help standardize that training. Meanwhile, the printing press replaced transcription and distribution became easier and more lucrative. Of course, not everyone could enter this lucrative business. To begin with, it required owning a printing press—a fairly significant capital investment beyond the reach of most consumers. But even that expense came down over time; by the nineteenth century a fair number of printing presses were in operation. The nineteenth century is a good place to pick up the story because it brings us into the era of American commerce and lets us consider the country's music businesses, and it lands us at a juncture where technology was poised to take another great leap forward.

By that time, entrants into the music-publishing business also had to contend with IP rights. Congress presumably had decided that it could promote musical innovation by granting composers time-limited copyrights on their compositions. Music publishers had to pay for those rights to distribute those compositions as sheet music. Consumers could thus choose between published sheet music of "old" unprotected compositions or "new" protected compositions, which likely sold at a premium. Publishers could justify this premium in two ways. First, their costs were higher—after all, they had to pay the composer. Second, because they owned the rights to the composition, they were its exclusive publishers. The market for old sheet music was much more competitive; anyone with a printing press and a distribution network could enter.

Then technological innovation added a new complication. Someone invented a mechanical device that could play music *all by itself!* For the first time in the history of music, a consumer could go out, buy a "box," install it at home, and flip a switch to hear music. No publication, no circulation, no performers. Places like saloons and dance halls, where people got together to listen to music, were sure to make it a hit. The music publishers, incensed, claimed that the newfangled technology would put them all out of business. After all, who would spend money on printed, coded music that only a trained musician could interpret when they could get music from a box?

These middlemen whose businesses relied upon printing and distributing copies of music encoded as information turned to Congress for help. After a bit of tinkering with the copyright laws, and the addition of a few special rules governing musical IP rights, Congress found a way to allow both the traditional distributors and their new competitors to make money selling music. So Congress, acting pursuant to its powers under the IP clause, made the world safe for *the player piano*. The world of music would never be the same.

The player piano was but the first of many technological innovations to alter the music industry. Player pianos were really primitive musical computers. To play music, they required a piano roll, which looked more than a bit like the punch cards used in computer rooms into the 1980s. These rolls of paper held coded music, not in some written form, but rather in the binary language of "paper and holes." This language, which bore little resemblance to anything that human would recognize as music, told a piano-shaped input/output device how to decode them into music.

Voila! Music was now entirely within the information sector. Of course, the rest of the music business kept on going. Player pianos were hardly the cheapest devices on the planet, and entering the piano-roll business still required a respectable capital investment. Equipment and distribution limited competition, kept prices at levels capable of generating profits, and overall made for a nice little business. At the same time, the fidelity of music reproduced by player pianos was less than stellar. While adequate for saloons, it was hardly up to symphonic standards. And something about a live performance—whether amateur or professional—was just more *fun*. In other words, plenty of room existed for an expanding music business that included live performances, instructions distributed for live performers, and mechanical "recordings" and devices. But nothing comes free.

The player piano marked the beginning of the modern expansion of IP rights.[4] Every few decades, a new technology threatens the business model of music distribution—and a familiar pattern follows. The scions of music information appeal to Congress for stronger IP protection. The promoters of the new technology and a handful of early-adopting consumers oppose them. Congress listens to both sides, tells them to work out a compromise, and then buys into whatever deal they work out. Invariably, that deal contains something for the music information business, something for the new technologists, something for the early adopters, and (SURPRISE!) nothing for everyone not sitting at the table.

So far, no one in Congress has ever bothered to ask whether any of these new deals were consistent with the Constitutional charge to promote innovation. By and large, any bill that's supported by every vocal group, that's likely to hurt only those who aren't paying attention to it, and whose damage is likely to be long-term and diffuse, will win overwhelming majorities of both the House and the Senate. And so, the IP rights protecting music—and often the IP rights protecting many other industries, as well—grow stronger and longer with time, without any explicit analysis of either their costs to society or their benefits in promoting innovation. And with each such increase, the Jeremiahs grow more numerous and their lamentations grow louder—until, as we learned in chapter 2, the Supreme Court agreed to let Larry Lessig argue that they had gone too far. But his arguments proved unconvincing. Justice Ginsburg, writing for a 7-2 majority of the Court, explained to him—and to us—in no uncertain terms that Congress can pretty much do whatever it damn pleases to *strengthen* IP rights, and even to strengthen them *retroactively*.[5] Despite a pointed challenge by Justice Stevens, she never told us whether Congress retained the same unfettered discretion to weaken rights retroactively.[6]

But I digress. Back in the music-information business, technology developed better and better ways to record music. Some of them required significant capital outlays—like recording studios. Others let individuals make decent copies at home—like cassette decks. Every now and then a technology even enabled capturing pictures as well, thereby dragging the movie industry along for the ride. The VCR, for example, was presumed to make it impossible for anyone to make any money as a filmmaker. The Hollywood studios sued Sony for "contributory infringement," claiming that its Betamax helped individual consumers copy copyrighted movies and TV shows from broadcast TV onto videocassettes. Because Sony gave the infringers the tools that they needed to commit their heinous acts, Sony had contributed to them—hence, contributory infringement. The studios insisted that the courts ban VCRs from the consumer market, or at the very least, sell only players without recording capabilities.

The Supreme Court refused. The Court agreed that the Betamax certainly gave consumers the *ability* to make unauthorized copies, but noted that not all uses of those copies necessarily infringed the studios' rights.[7] Copyright law contains a provision known as "fair use," which shows that we never gave copyright owners absolute or unfettered rights over their creations. Now, no one knows exactly what constitutes a fair use and what doesn't, or where to draw the line between them. So every now and then, we have to go to court to see what's fair and what isn't. For example, we've learned that it's "fair" for a teacher to copy a couple of pages from a book—including this one—and give them to her students.

But it's *not* fair for her to copy the entire book and to sell it to her students.[8] The Supreme Court told the studios that the same was true with TV programs. It's "fair" for me to tape *Sex and the City*, watch it later ("time shifting"), rewind it, and review key passages to gain insights into contemporary sociology. But I cannot "fairly" show that tape later on a big screen TV in a bar, charge admission, and turn it into a public performance. And so, the Supreme Court reasoned that since consumers had legitimate noninfringing reasons to want VCR technology, they were entitled to own it. If some users decided to misuse the technology by infringing the studios' rights, that wasn't Sony's fault—or problem. Once again, technology opened new alternatives, the law explained which of these alternatives would actually become inexpensive, and economic incentives motivated the studios to devise new business models consistent with technology and law. The studios responded, and Hollywood recovered.

More and more of the entertainment business came to hinge on information—and no part of entertainment made the transition faster than music. This transition happened in several stages, but each stage followed a common pattern. First someone figured out how to convert entertainment into finer gradations of information. Next, someone else devised a way to record and to transmit that information using expensive technology—and the folks who owned that technology learned how to profit from transmission or distribution. Then the cost of manipulating that information plummeted and widespread entry became easy. Rampant competition (at times from consumers in their own homes) drove down distribution prices. The distributors needed some way to keep their profits up, so they turned to IP law. Sometimes they got what they wanted; other times they had to change their business models.

Yet somehow, through it all, the middlemen known as the record companies and the movie studios persevered. In stage after stage, facing technology after technology, the record companies have used their talent scouts to find exciting new performers, their expensive equipment to enhance and to capture the performances, and their distribution networks to spread these recordings among the performer's fan base—and somehow, no matter what technology threw in their path, the music never stopped. Nor, for that matter, did the profits.

Dire Wolf

I sat down to my supper
T'was a bottle of red whiskey
I said my prayers and went to bed
That's the last they saw of me . . .
Don't murder me
I beg of you don't murder me
Please
Don't murder me
When I awoke, the Dire Wolf
Six hundred pounds of sin
Was grinnin' at my window
All I said was "come on in"[9]

By the mid-1990s, the music business was in dire trouble. A wolf in digital clothing was grinning through its window, and the record companies knew that it was simply a matter of time. Because when the information sector swallowed the music business, it undermined the entire technological basis of prevailing business models.[10] Record company executives appreciated the threat; they just had no idea what to do. They recognized that

The railroads should have been GM and Ford and Chrysler, but they didn't think that anyone would want to travel off the tracks . . . The telephone companies should have been the cellular phone companies, but they couldn't imagine anyone wanting to talk on the phone in their cars. And then, of course, the networks are the best example most recently. They also should have owned the cable industry but they couldn't imagine what anyone would want to do watching all those channels. . . . It was possible [the recording industry was] heading there if we were not moving quickly enough in a coordinated fashion. . . . Artists are probably just going to have to figure out how to go on tour or sell their underwear once they've recorded this song because there's no way to sell music on the Internet. The Internet is all about everything being free.[11]

Business models predicated on the idea that it's expensive to copy and to distribute music are unsustainable in a world of cheap, easy copying and distribution. Technology creates too many new opportunities, and economic incentives suggest that people will take them. The law provides the only possible recourse to those clinging to outdated business models. But the law would have to work extremely hard to keep the old models afloat. And sooner or later—likely not much later—the law will have to give up. Otherwise, the legal tactics that we employ to protect music will start looking like those that we use in the drug wars. Remember Dmitry Sklyarov? The twenty-seven-year-old Russian programmer threatened with twenty-five years in prison and $2.25 million in fines for cracking the protection on Adobe's software? Well, maybe it's not a coincidence that his sounds like a story we usually tell about drug smugglers. Maybe it's a harbinger of future IP enforcement. But the truth is, I don't think it is. I think that we'll roll back some of the more absurd approaches to IP enforcement before we get there. At least, I hope that we will. Otherwise, the twenty-first century could become a pretty scary place.

We've already experienced enough of the music industry's misadventures in the information sector to know that change is afoot. Everyone understands that the music business ten, twenty, fifty years from now will look very different from the industry to which we've grown accustomed. But no one knows precisely what it will look like, who will win, who will lose, or what the transition will entail. The issues are so confusing that I've heard numerous reports of meetings in which the debates pitch AOL and Sony Electronics (the technologists) against Time Warner and Sony Music (the record labels). Someone at Time Warner (formerly AOL Time Warner) and someone at Sony must be feeling more than a bit schizophrenic. How did it all happen?

For centuries, we had two distinct but related music businesses. In the "pure music" business, performers played, fans listened, and then everybody went home. In the "music information" business, someone sitting atop a distribution chain encoded music as information, copied the code onto a physical medium, circulated that medium, and then let consumers decode the information back into music using either specialized knowledge or a device capable of "playback." Of these businesses, the pure-music side has been incredibly robust. We now have larger arenas, amplified sound systems, and projection TV screens, but by and large a concert is a concert. The information sector hasn't much altered the pure music business, nor is it likely to, despite the promise of "live" concerts delivered through streaming media. Live music—that is live music where the performer and listener are in the same room at the same time—is *fun*, and talented performers can generate an enthusiastic if ephemeral sense of community among their listeners. Anyone who ever saw the Dead (or for those a bit younger, Phish) can attest to the strength of that community. People are likely to be enjoying live performances millennia into the future.

But the music-information business essentially redefines itself every time a new technology comes along. Sometimes we force the businesses to deal with the new technology. At other times, the businesses not only embrace the new technology, but force it upon us whether we want it or not. CDs were a prime example of this approach. Once upon a time, the record companies sold most music encoded on 12-inch vinyl LPs. At some earlier date, a performer had gone to a record company's studio, and actually played some music. The record company's expensive equipment encoded the music as an analog waveform, record company sound engineers manipulated the waveform to enhance its production quality, and still more of the record company's expensive equipment imprinted the enhanced waveform on vinyl discs—and then made many, many copies. In other words, this vinyl LP was a joint production of the songwriters who wrote the music, the performers who played it, and the record company that enhanced, encoded, and recorded it. The record company's distribution network then circulated the LPs among record stores, where fans paid money for them.

Fans took the LP home and treated it as if it were their own, despite the many IP rights latent in it. Fans' record players decoded the analog information and played it back through an amplifier. Fans could listen to this earlier performance in their own homes, at times of their own choosing, as often as they desired, and with as many guests as they cared to invite. They even could share or trade LPs. But LPs have their weaknesses. LPs are fragile and soft. They scratch easily, pick up static, and dust interferes with playback. Vibrations from, say, dancing makes record players shake and skip. Plus, LPs are pretty big and not terribly dense; it is tough to fit an hour's worth of music on two sides of a disc the size of a pizza. From the record companies' perspective, LPs presented an even more disturbing limitation: they didn't generate large enough profits to keep executives happy. And so, when pioneers in chemistry, materials, and lasers devised CD technology, the record companies jumped.

The basic idea was simple. A new digital code replaced the old analog waveforms. Recall that computers communicate by shifting voltages from low to high (or vice versa), and that computer engineers begin the arduous translation chain by encoding these shifts as 0s and 1s, respectively. Light can do the same thing—particularly when using lasers. The binary language of 0s and 1s can also encode dark and light, using the same concept of holes and disk that worked so well in paper piano rolls. CD players are thus computers based on optics and lasers rather than on electron flows.

That said, many steps are needed between envisioning laser encoding and selling a consumer product. A programmer must finish the translation chain to relate sounds to bits. Record company's studios must replace their expensive analog equipment with new equipment that translates musical performances into binary code. Sound engineers must learn to work with this new equipment. Expensive imprinting and copying equipment must be swapped for laser-based machines that make CDs instead of LPs. And, of course, record stores must choose to carry these CDs and consumers must choose to buy them.

This challenge brings us back to network economics. For CDs to succeed, consumers not only had to buy CDs, they also had to buy CD players to enable them to decode the binary language and turn it back into music. In other words, the electronics companies manufacturing CD players and the record companies selling CDs needed to displace an entrenched network standard. Fortunately for them, a couple of advantages helped them meet this challenge. First, their new digital technology was superior in a number of ways. The discs and players were more robust, and the fidelity of the playback was higher. Second, these new CD players were compatible with large parts of music fans' home systems; they could plug into existing stereo receivers, tape decks, and speakers using an open standard for connectivity. Third—and this was critical—the companies pushing the new technology also controlled the old technology. That dual control allowed them to play with pricing, at least once they figured out how to manufacture CDs and CD players at a cost that consumers were willing to bear.

The first few CDs released didn't sell particularly well. But by the mid-1980s, the price of CD players had dropped into an acceptable range for consumer electronics, and people began to buy them in substantial numbers. Meanwhile, the record companies decided to price CDs at roughly double the price of LPs, raising their profit margins on each unit sold. Then came the coup de grâce. Prices were low enough and penetration was broad enough to embolden the vendors. They dropped the old technology and shifted almost entirely to the new—a move that was fairly smooth because they controlled both. Eventually the record companies decided to sell only CDs, and the electronics companies stopped manufacturing new record players (in both cases, with a few minor exceptions). For all but a few diehards, the age of the LP was over.

The music-information business had gone through a major transformation. Fans received higher-quality playback, electronics companies sold more capital equipment to recording studios and more components to consumers, and record companies watched their margins soar. Everyone was pleased. While no one was paying attention, though, fans around the world amassed large collections of digitally encoded music. Our living rooms and dens became veritable libraries of bits, as discs with tiny little holes sat silently waiting for us to decode them back into music. The record companies were thrilled; fans didn't much care. And for perhaps the first time in a century, the music business navigated a technological transformation without help from Congress or major changes to the IP laws. Everybody won. Or so it seemed. But danger lurked just around the corner.

Crucify

I've been looking for a savior in these dirty streets
Looking for a savior beneath these dirty sheets
I've been raising up my hands
Drive another nail in just what god needs one more victim
Why do we crucify ourselves
Every day
I crucify myself
Nothing I do is good enough for you
Crucify myself
Every day
And my heart is sick of being in chains[12]

The record companies had inadvertently crucified themselves by forcing music fans to replace their analog music with new digitally encoded music. Whereas analog waveforms can take on an infinite number of shapes, digital codes can only be 1s and 0s. Digital codes are therefore much easier to copy and to read than are analog codes. Those tiny 1 and 0s turned the record companies from victors into victims.

Technology rarely sits still. While the record companies were busy making money selling digital music, the computer industry was just as busy developing new and better ways to store and to manipulate digital information. Specifically, computer engineers realized that optical CDs could encode all sorts of information, not just music—and that they could hold significant numbers of bits. They developed the codes, encoding machines, and decoding machines necessary to replace diskettes with data CDs as the primary software distribution mechanism. Of course, consumers had to buy yet another bit of technology to translate the CDs back into the voltage language that their machines understood: a CD-ROM drive.

ROM is an old computer term that stands for "read only memory." When the computer industry launched CD-ROM drives, imprinting a CD was still expensive. Only large companies could circulate CD-ROMs because *encoding* something on a CD required expensive capital equipment. But *decoding* a CD was much less expensive. Electronics companies had spent more than a decade turning these decoders into inexpensive stereo components. Redirecting their efforts to achieve the easier translation necessary for a computer took much less work. They built these CD-ROM drives, sold them at a reasonable price, and sold their more expensive encoding equipment to software companies.

Now, electronics companies are no slouches, and they understood that network economics was likely to haunt them here, too. Most computer users had drives that read diskettes, not CDs, so software companies would have to continue circulating their software on diskettes. Why would anyone be willing to buy a CD-ROM drive simply to save the effort of loading a few diskettes into a diskette drive? The payoff didn't seem to be worth the price—so few software companies would clamor for the more expensive imprinting equipment. But the electronics companies realized that most computer users already owned a collection of CDs—ones that happened to contain encoded music, rather than encoded data. Computers had long made sounds—which meant that they came equipped with some sort of a speaker—and a number of techies had been playing around with music on computers for years. The electronics companies took the next step. They built CD-ROM drives that detected whether a CD contained music or data, applied the correct decoding algorithm, directed data to the computer, and played music over the speakers. That little twist not only helped sell more CD-ROM drives, but also created a demand for enhanced soundboards and speakers. The computer and electronics industries thus worked together to turn desktop computers into high-quality stereo systems. The record companies didn't much mind. After all, the more places that people could play CDs, the more CDs they were likely to buy. Once again, everyone won.

But breakthroughs follow breakthroughs in the wonderful world of technology. The electronics companies next figured out how to make CD-encoding equipment cheap and compact and began selling computer drives that not only *read* CDs encoded by large software companies, but that allowed computer users to *write* their own CDs. The drives quickly became inexpensive and popular, and consumers were empowered to create their own digitally encoded CDs. These recordable CDs plummeted in price quickly to become cheap staple office supplies. Meanwhile, a few engineers interested in packing information more tightly into storage media, like CDs, came up with some clever ways to "compress" large bit strings into smaller ones that could then be "decompressed" back into the larger original; in other words, they added a clever layer to the translation chain that made it easier and cheaper to move digital files from computers to CDs and back. They named the most popular of these compression schemes MP3.

This combination of technologies *did not* make the record companies happy. They had circulated perfect digital copies of their music, confident in two great forms of protection. The IP laws preserved many of the copyright owners' rights to that music—everything that didn't fall under that amorphous category of fair use. Though consumers may have thought of the CDs that they bought as "their own," they were actually in partnership with the owners of the copyrighted content, and each partner retained distinct rights. At least, that was the law. The capital-intensive nature of creating CDs gave the record companies an even stronger form of protection grounded in technology and economics. This new combination of consumer technologies eroded the technical and economic barriers entirely. Consumers had large collections of digitally encoded music and now had the ability to make cheap, perfect copies. The record companies watched their ability to control the circulation of their IP erode slowly, steadily, and surely.

The music-information business had become a digital music-information business, a full-fledged part of the information sector. Companies and executives suddenly faced a problem that had been plaguing software executives at least since a young Bill Gates wrote an open letter from Micro-soft to the hobbyist community: digital products have a life of their own. They simply refuse to stay where their owners put them. Digital products can be copied and moved easily and cheaply. Not surprisingly, people tend to move them around often without worrying too much about infringing someone else's IP rights.

In fact, many people think that IP law doesn't really apply to them unless they plan to turn a profit. Plenty of law-abiding citizens would never develop a "pirate" operation that made cheap copies of their CD collections and sold them on the street. Many of them would even avoid *buying* CDs on the streets because they don't believe in patronizing pirate operations. They wouldn't think twice, though, about making copies for their friends or their families. Where should they draw the line? Copying a CD for your best friend sounds okay, but what about for everyone in your class? What about for the entire school? Should it depend on the size of the school? While most people might recognize that these are tough questions, they would also answer them by drawing an easy line: If I give it away, it's fine. If I sell it, it's a problem. Jessica Litman described this attitude as the way that most people make sense of copyright law, and she's probably right.[13] But she also noted that while this belief may be grounded in common sense and general practice, it's not grounded in IP law. The copyright owners had spread the tools with which to destroy their own business models, and then expressed outrage when electronics and computer firms developed the technology that eroded their protective technical and economic barriers. Their sole recourse lay in IP law. With technology and economics against them, only the law could help them retain control of music distribution.

With that, perhaps the first true war of the information sector began. On one side, technologists reduced the transaction costs inherent in distributing music. On the other, IP owners retained sole legal rights over music distribution. In the middle sat consumers, eager to avail themselves of the new technologies to enhance their own lives, but perplexed by the legal implications. For its first few years, the war took the form of an occasional skirmish, and few outside the IP community paid much attention. But then the technologists struck a devastating blow by using the Internet to move music files around the world. That discovery removed the final transaction cost from the distribution chain, making music distribution a cost-free transaction. The business model that had defined the music-information business for more than a century crumbled. While the record companies still added value to music by finding new acts and by producing the music, their control over distribution had vanished overnight. The record companies had become true victims of the information sector.

The Central Scrutinizer

The music industry has found itself embroiled in a very strange war, pitting huge corporations against their own customers—often kids savvier in the ways of music and electronics than in the nuances of IP law. Technologists are stuck in the middle. As Internet journalist Trevor Merriden noted, "If you line up the five global record companies (Universal, Sony, Bertelsmann, EMI, and Warner Music), you face five massive beasts with huge corporate clout. Set against Napster, effectively you have five Godzillas rounding on Bambi."[14] Corporations hate suing kids; it makes the companies look bad, and they know that they'll never collect much. So instead of suing those who actually infringe their IP rights, the record companies generally chase the corporate middlemen who provide the enabling technology.[15] Some of these technology corporations are little more than Internet startups—often kids masquerading as corporations—but some are big companies. Most of the music battles mirrored the movie studios' contributory infringement claim against Sony's Betamax. Record companies owned the IP rights; technology providers gave individual consumers new alternatives, some of which enabled infringement; the consumers availed themselves of the new opportunities; and the record companies sued the middlemen.

So who were these record companies? Five corporate giants own most of the world's popular music. Though they compete with each other in a truly cutthroat manner, they also recognize that they share a fair number of industry interests. The companies usually coordinate these activities through their trade association (or lobbying group), the Recording Industry Association of America (RIAA). But owning the music doesn't necessarily mean owning all of the rights to that music. Somehow or another, and largely because of the industry's somewhat unusual history, music IP rights have been sliced and diced every which way you could imagine. Broadcast Music Incorporated (BMI), the American Society of Composers, Authors, and Publishers (ASCAP), and SESAC (the name of a group that started out as the Society of European Stage Authors and Composers, but subsequently gave up on being anything other than an acronym) all license music performances—including "performances" of songs played over the radio or as background in a store. They collect royalties using some fairly arcane mechanisms, and then distribute them among the songwriters, *not* the performers. The Harry Fox Agency, a division of the National Music Publishers Association, oversees music publishing rights, known as "mechanical rights," which are, of course, distinct from performance rights.

Sound Byzantine and impenetrable? It *is*. With so many rights and so many people to compensate, it's almost impossible for a newcomer to know where to begin. And virtually everyone interested in Internet music was a newcomer.

Consider the challenge facing Internet media companies that provide streaming media—say a CNN news clip broadcast over the Internet to your desktop computer. If you've ever watched one of those clips appear in your media player, you know that it arrives in two parts: first it "loads," and then it plays. Computer scientists discovered that this two-stage approach is needed any time that a video travels across a network, because network traffic travels in "packets" that arrive in "bursts." When we're reading e-mail, we really don't care if there's a brief delay between sentences. But if we were watching a video, we'd find it pretty annoying. So when the video bits arrive across the Internet, they don't run straight to the media player. They arrive first in the computer's "cache buffer," where they spend a couple of seconds in short-term memory. That way, the buffer fills up in bursts, but feeds the images smoothly to the screen. The buffer gets a little longer when many bursts arrive and a little shorter between bursts, but as long as it's not empty it can continue feeding the screen smoothly without that annoying stop-action effect.

So far so good. But suppose that instead of a CNN news clip, we're streaming a live concert. Here's the question: Are we watching a live performance broadcast as it's being performed, or are we watching a recording captured only seconds before in the cache buffer? Here's a better question: Do we care? Well, we should; different entities own the rights to live performances and recordings. If we don't know which one we're viewing, how can we negotiate an IP license with the owner? And if we don't negotiate a license, aren't we infringing? You see the problem. If ever a dilemma was needed to convince a fourteen-year-old music fan that adults are nuts, this was it.

Between the crazy quilt of IP rights and regulatory hearings and the general legitimate legal questions that are reopened whenever a new technology calls old definitions into question, even an Internet pioneer who wanted to honor the IP laws would have a hard time figuring out what to do—and many of them aren't all that interested in learning. Clearly, infringement would be rampant and lawsuits would follow. The corporate interests representing the music business came together in different alignments on different issues. Together they reached back into Frank Zappa's work from the 1970s to find the idea of the Central Scrutinizer, an official responsible for enforcing laws that have yet to be passed against kids driven to crime by music. RIAA CEO Hillary Rosen because the first real-world central scrutinizer. Her job was to survey the terrain, to see who was infringing their IP rights, and to work to stop them. She monitored the emergence of fan-based distribution networks, filed lawsuits against a number of technology companies, lobbied Congress to change some laws, and generally led the charge to preserve the time-honored business models of the music information business.

While the specific alignment of the players and the rights may have changed from one skirmish to the next, the general battle plan held. Technologists gave consumers new alternatives, economic incentives encouraged them to take them, and the traditional distributors of the music business tried to use IP law to reimpose the transaction costs that were once inherent in copying and distributing music.

The first high-profile battle started in late 1998. Diamond Multimedia Systems, a small tech company based in San Jose, announced that its new Rio PMP300, the first portable MP3 player sold in the United States, would be available in time for Christmas. Now, in the autumn of 1998, the Internet had not yet exploded into the phenomenon it would soon become. Digital music, on the other hand, was already a way of life. Anyone with a decent home computer could convert an entire CD collection into MP3 files stored on a hard drive. Though this situation in and of itself made the record companies a bit queasy, they didn't see much point in fighting it. After all, they had long since made an uneasy peace with the idea that consumers could create "unauthorized" analog cassette copies of their CDs. Equally unauthorized digital MP3 copies sitting on home computers didn't seem to be much more of a threat.

By late 1998, though, a number of Internet companies already had begun to popularize the idea of music downloads. MP3.com made some attempts to honor IP rights, Liquid Audio bent over backwards to avoid infringement, and various other players had already made the scene, but the record companies had yet to decide precisely how to respond to the new technologies. Besides, though the community of fans downloading music seemed to be growing, its size remained manageable. The record companies were cautious and nervous, but neither willing to enter the fray themselves as online music providers nor expend much energy, money, or goodwill fighting those who had filled the gap. The technology didn't seem to be good enough, smooth enough, or reliable enough to leap beyond technogeeks and into the broader realm of "normal" music fans. Then Diamond announced the Rio, and everything changed.

The Rio promised to destabilize the comfortable denial into which the record companies had slipped. The Rio was precisely the technology capable of creating demand among non-techie music fans. It was a tiny portable computer, smaller than a cassette, with a hard disk capable of storing an hour of digital music, and Diamond planned to sell it for $199. People who bought a Rio wouldn't have to sit at their computers to enjoy

MP3 files. They could download an hour's worth of music, clip on the Rio, plug in some headphones, and go jogging. Record companies quickly realized that consumers would find this opportunity attractive— so attractive, in fact, that those consumers would start paying attention to MP3 music files and the Web sites that allowed music downloads. Of course, some of them—and possibly even some of those Web sites— might be less than scrupulous in honoring IP rights. The record companies took a stand on October 8, 1998, when the RIAA sued Diamond to block the Rio's release.[16]

The issues in the case were pretty technical. The RIAA claimed that the Rio violated some provisions of the Audio Home Recording Act of 1992 (AHRA) governing the manufacture and sale of devices capable of making multiple copies of sound recordings. Not to be undone on a technicality, Diamond cited at least two technical reasons that the provision in question didn't apply to the Rio. First, the Rio had no recording capabilities; users would have to record the music elsewhere, convert it into an MP3 file stored on a hard disk, and then move a few bits from the home computer to the Rio. Second, back in 1992, the computer industry had planted a loophole in the AHRA exempting anything that contained software from the relevant definition of "device."

The bottom line, though, is that the technicalities don't matter. The fight wasn't really about the nuances buried in the AHRA. The real question was whether or not the law would let technology create a new opportunity for consumers. Diamond wanted to sell consumers a tool that would let them make MP3 copies of their own CD collections and take them jogging—a practice that everyone conceded was legal. But Diamond knew that it was also selling a tool that would let consumers download pirated MP3 files and take them anywhere—a practice that everyone conceded was illegal. The RIAA objected to the whole deal. It understood that portable MP3 players reduced consumer costs for portable music, and might force its members to adjust their own business models. The information sector was about to take another big bite out of profits, and the record companies hadn't quite figured out how they were going to take it back.

But you can't sue somebody for launching a new consumer good. You must find some law that the product violates, which is why these battles are always so technical. We *know* they're fighting about whether or not consumers should get easy, ready access to MP3 files. But we have to *pretend* that they're fighting about esoteric provisions of an esoteric statute. And so, we've come full circle back to the rift between IP law and IP policy. IP policy should grant rights to promote innovation and to advance human knowledge (and overall welfare). IP law, on the other hand, is what it is. Fights like this one drive the point home. We could have an interesting debate about the ways that readily available MP3 files affect motivation. We might learn something, and we might arrive at a solution consistent with the policies we claim to promote. But that's *not* the way we fight these battles. We fight on the narrow grounds of what IP law *is*. And here, the applicable law was the AHRA.

And so, the RIAA contended that the AHRA prohibited Diamond from launching the Rio, Diamond argued that it didn't—and the judge agreed with Diamond. In the meantime, the RIAA had shot itself in the foot. Not only did the Rio create a demand draw, but the RIAA's lawsuit galvanized the Internet community and focused media attention on a product that it was trying to bury. Even Hillary Rosen, RIAA's CEO and the industry's central scrutinizer, reportedly soon realized that the suit had probably been an error—and that the music industry needed to get its act together quickly.

There's no question that the filing of that lawsuit focused people like a laser on what the record companies were doing, and what people perceived the record companies were doing . . . and that was a terrible mistake on our part in terms of not laying the groundwork earlier for the industry's perceptions of opportunity and interest and enthusiasm. . . . Now, would they have come if we didn't sue? I don't know. Granted, there's some arrogance certainly in the record industry. But there was a lot of arrogance in the technology industry about how the music industry's just going to have to learn the new way.[17]

Regrets or not, when the Rio hit the shelves, the genie was out of the bottle. Consumers, even those who weren't particularly tech savvy, soon discovered the merits of the MP3 format. They soon wanted to convert their CDs to MP3, store them on their hard disks, and play them back. They even made some of these files available on the Internet. The record companies realized that change was coming fast, and they redoubled their efforts on the Secure Digital Music Initiative (SDMI), an uneasy alliance of music, technology, and other businesses working together to ensure that both IP rights and revenue streams could continue no matter how big a bite the information sector took out of their industry—an alliance so uneasy, in fact, that it never really got off the ground. They had no idea what was waiting for them just around the bend, with its huge jaws wide open waiting to swallow them whole.

Turn! Turn! Turn!

To every thing there is a season,
And a time to every purpose under the heaven
A time to be born, and a time to die . . .
A time to kill, and a time to heal . . .
A time to weep, and a time to laugh
A time to mourn, and a time to dance . . .
A time to love, and a time to hate
A time to war, and a time of peace.[18]

What awaited the record companies was their worst nightmare: a kid with an idea. Shawn Fanning wanted music fans to be able to share each other's MP3 files. He wrote a little program called Napster to make his idea a reality, and Napster finished eating the music industry. What had been a time of albums gave way to a time of digital files. And so the record companies declared a time of war.

Fanning was a hacker. He was also a music fan and a frequent visitor to Internet chat rooms. In the autumn of 1998, when the RIAA was busy trying to keep the Rio off the shelves, Fanning was a seventeen-year-old freshman at Northeastern University focused on his personal hacking project. His dream was to combine his MP3 addiction with his chat room experiences. He wanted to write a program that would let him trade MP3 files with strangers around the world as easily as he traded quips with them in a chat room. The impact of his project would be revolutionary, but the project itself wasn't revolutionary at all. All of the pieces were already out there. Fanning didn't invent new technology. He simply assembled existing technologies in a new and clever way. The perfect task for a budding young hacker.

The Web itself began as little more than Tim Berners-Lee's pipe dream. Berners-Lee started with the idea that the researchers connected to the Internet would find it easier to share their files if they adopted a uniform indexing scheme. That idea led him to develop the URL, a simple tag that assigned every file on the Internet a unique address. Several years later, early Web sites like Yahoo! and Alta Vista popularized the idea of a "search engine." When users gave these engines a list of keywords, the engines would systematically roam around the Web looking for sites that contained those words, and then return a list of URLs. Meanwhile, utilities like Microsoft Windows's "search" function let users search for all files of a given type on their own computers.

Fanning put these ideas together to build Napster's core technology. Users could ask Napster to find all MP3 files on the network—possibly with a partial file name—and Napster would return a list of appropriate addresses. Now, of course, there was a bit more to it than that. To begin with, it's important to recall that "the Internet," "the Web," and "the network" aren't synonyms. The World Wide Web is a popular application that runs on the Internet. Most of the computers connected to the Internet, likely the one on your desktop and certainly the one on my desktop, aren't Web servers. When you ask Google to search the Web for a file, Google only looks at Web servers. It doesn't come ferreting around on my desktop to see if I have anything relevant. So how does Google know where to look? Well, it turns out that Web servers hire a guy wearing a digital sandwich board to stand outside their doors yelling: "Yo! Google! Over here! Web server over here!" The self-identified Web server sends Google a few salient keywords and the address of a relevant page, Google combines the information on its own server, and then passes the information on to you. Thus, the Web is really a network of Web servers connected to the Internet, and when you run a Web search, you're only searching those servers.

The Napster network works—or rather, worked—much the same way. You could join the network by downloading the Napster software—which Fanning conveniently placed on the Web. Then, whenever you were in a sharing mood, you could open the Napster application on your computer, turn yourself into a "Napster server," and send a guy wearing a digital sandwich board outside your door to yell: "Yo! Napster! Over here! Napster user over here!" Some other Napster user would ask the Napster application on *her* machine to find her some music. Napster would meet your shouting guy and come poke around in your folder of shareable MP3 files. If you had something that matched her keywords, Napster would give her the file's address. She could then connect directly to your computer and copy the file at the designated address using a direct link across the Internet between two "peer" desktop computers, in a manner that was quickly dubbed *peer-to-peer* or P2P. And best of all, if anyone ever asked Napster about copyright violations, Fanning could simply take inspiration from Shaggy: No matter the circumstances, no matter the evidence, no matter how incredible it may sound, just tell them "It wasn't me."

Napster did contain a handful of other features designed to make it user friendly and powerful, but by and large, it was just a twist on a search engine. But what a twist! While it might not have been a technological breakthrough, it was an extraordinarily clever combination of existing ideas. In the long run, P2P may turn out to be the most significant innovation in the information sector since the Web. It opens a whole new world of file exchanges, and makes yet another layer of communication cheaper and easier. Once again, cheaper, easier communications promise to reduce transaction costs, and reduced transaction costs promise to generate new business models. We can't yet imagine how far it can lead. But in the short run, it set the digital music community on fire and revolutionized the music industry.

Napster was the last missing piece. Digital music had been around for almost two decades, and large hard disks full of compressed MP3 files and CD burners had been around for years. Much to the RIAA's chagrin, portable MP3 players did hit the market. Technology had made it cheap to copy music, the law did nothing to alter that cost reduction, and economics led many people to convert their own CD collections to MP3, to make copies for each of their computers, and to load them onto their Rios. Technology and economics also let people burn CDs to share with their friends and to gain copies of their friends' CD collections. While the law technically prohibited that type of sharing, the record companies couldn't find a way to enforce that law. After all, what were they going to do? Start suing high-school kids?[19] The record companies were visibly unhappy that though they had the legal right to prevent an activity that could be cutting into their profits, they were completely unable to prevent it.

And then, in early 1999, Fanning finished a beta version of Napster, gave it to some friends, and asked them to keep it to themselves. They disregarded his instructions and shared it with other friends. Within days, the Napster network boasted over 3,000 members. That number grew quickly. In October 2000, the network's membership was estimated at 32 million, with about 800,000 logged on at any given time. By February 2001, when Napster met its ultimate—and many believe untimely—demise, membership was estimated at 58 million. By most accounts, Napster was the most rapidly adopted application in the history of software.[20] If nothing else, that suggests that Napster filled a rather glaring and obvious need.

How you characterize that need shows where your sympathies lie. To some, Napster filled the void of people reaching out for like-minded souls with whom to share their music. It was more than just a network of software users; it was a community of music lovers. And the community of benevolent music lovers willing to share their music opened new musical vistas to all. It was suddenly possible to find old songs with nostalgic appeal, to locate hard-to-find collectibles, studio outtakes, and live jam sessions, and to sample new musical styles and artists without having to pay the "admission fee" of a CD's purchase price. For users, the Napster community was for sharing and sampling and reveling in the joy of music. Napster filled a need for community in an age of alienation.

To others, Napster provided digital pirates with a way to circumvent legitimate IP rights. Everyone knew that copying someone else's digital music files without paying royalties constituted theft. Napster thus filled a need for safe rebellion. Anyone could log on to Napster, steal a couple of digital music files, and be pretty confident that they'd get away with it. The perfect crime! And the only ones who'd lose would be some corporate fat cats sitting around a boardroom worried about their stock price. Napster filled a "need" for criminal rebellion in an age of corporatism.

Of course, to those of us savvy in the ways and the wars of the information sector, Napster eliminated a technological barrier to entry into the music distribution business. It removed a critical transaction cost that long had been the basis of the music-information distribution business. It thus destroyed an existing business model and enabled some new ones.

Napster filled a need for music consumers seeking a world without transaction costs.

Well, maybe "destroyed" is a bit harsh. After all, the record companies, BMI, ASCAP, SESAC, Harry Fox, the RIAA, Tower Records, and much of the rest of the established music business is alive and still profitable. Somehow Amazon even sells huge numbers of *official*, *legal* CDs over the Web. The view of Napster as a tool to sample new styles and artists, and to look for nostalgic songs that you might like to hear but would never buy—all of that was true. Many people downloaded songs from Napster and felt motivated to buy the album; I myself bought at least one album under the influence of Napster. While Napster clearly did motivate a certain number of CD sales that probably wouldn't have happened otherwise, plenty of people decided to forego buying CDs that they would have purchased had they not been able to download songs free from Napster.

Though Napster's short-term effect on music sales may have been unclear, its long-term potential is crystalline. In the long run, P2P file swapping will devastate the record companies' traditional business model because in addition to copying and distribution, their models' other critical element is bundling. The "album" is a clever mechanism that forces consumers to buy more music than they want—and to pay for it. I own about 500 CDs. A relative handful of them are polished compilations, where each song leads elegantly into the next to convey an emotional message crafted carefully by a musical artist. The overwhelming majority of them, though, are little more than a dozen-or-so songs by the same artist crammed together onto a single disk. Many even package a song or two that I really like with filler. So here's the irony. I probably wouldn't have been willing to pay $16.98 for the couple of songs I like. But hey, throw in a bunch of other stuff that doesn't really interest me, and you've got a sale. Any good IO economist could tell you that this sort of bundling is common in industry after industry; it's a good way to get consumers to buy what that they otherwise wouldn't have touched. But the prospects for continued album sales in an age of individual music files are grim.

So there you have it: No technological barriers to copying, no technological barriers to distribution, and an imminent end to bundling music into albums. No wonder the RIAA went after Napster! By the end of 1999, less than a year after Fanning's friends circulated his beta version, young Shawn had dropped out of college, started a corporation, moved to California, attracted a huge following, appeared on magazine covers, and gotten himself sued by the major record companies. He'd spend the next fourteen months in court fighting—unsuccessfully—to keep his dream alive. But his dream was the record companies' nightmare, and this time the law supported their case.

Once again, the actual battle hinged on various arcana of IP law. Judge Marilyn Hall Patel's first published ruling in the matter, for example, refused to dismiss the suit against Napster under a safe-harbor provision of the DMCA.[21] But technicalities aside, the real issues were clear. The RIAA and the record companies contended that though Napster didn't circulate music itself—or even allow any music to pass through its own centralized system—it was *still* contributing to copyright infringement. The entire Napster network, they claimed, was set up to make infringement easy. What's more, they somehow felt that Napster's own Web site, which touted its network as the "world's largest MP3 music library" and promised its members "the availability of every song online," was designed to encourage infringement. They also argued that Napster users could hardly hide behind the fair-use doctrine. After all, while the concept of "fair use" may be amorphous (like pornography, something that you know when you see it), the idea that "the entire population of the Internet" constitutes a small circle of friends with whom it's fair to share does strain credulity. Finally, they explained that Napster was making it impossible for them to launch the wonderful, legitimate online music distribution that they had planned, because no one would ever pay to use their legitimate system while Napster made identical pirated copies of their products available free of charge.

These arguments all sounded reasonable, and Napster's legal team knew that it needed help. Napster turned to David Boies, the superstar litigator who represented the government against Microsoft. Napster's basic argument was simple: it wasn't doing anything wrong. Napster was just a search engine, an index, a file directory. That some of its members conceivably might use this directory to infringe the record companies' copyrights could cause the RIAA to chase those members, but what does that have to do with Napster? ("It wasn't me.") Furthermore, Boies argued that copyright is intended as a tool of public policy.

> Copyright is therefore an incentive that we as a society grant so that we may have better access to more original expression. In the end, the copyright laws are for the benefit of the public as a whole, not the individual copyright owners. The balance requires that these rights be limited so that we as a society can share, grow and build upon one another's creativity. But that balance is always at risk in the struggle between copyright absolutists and those who think more limited protections are appropriate.[22]

Boies wanted the court to consider IP policy, to conclude that the P2P systems like Napster served the goals of promoting innovation and creativity, and thus to rule against the RIAA.

That argument—which should be quite compelling—rarely works. The courts tend to look at the text of applicable IP statutes and declare that the law is what it is; policy be damned. And to make matters worse, it's not even clear that Napster would have won the policy debate if the courts had agreed to conduct one. Plenty of people believe that unrestricted P2P wrenches hard-earned rewards from legitimate copyright holders, curbs their incentive to innovate, and threatens to reduce musical creativity. Who knows which camp would have claimed Judge Patel? Setting aside law and policy for the moment, many people have strong moral reactions to unauthorized music downloads. Some see it as theft, plain and simple. Others see it as a benign form of civil disobedience targeted at a corporate system working to stamp out individual creativity and free speech. Had Judge Patel found this case stirring her moral center, it easily could have tilted her view of public policy. And that's precisely why many people believe trial judges *should not* engage in policy debates.

Of course, the policy argument wasn't the only one that Napster forwarded. Boies also tried to convince the courts that there was little difference between Napster and Sony's Betamax—which the Supreme Court had explicitly allowed. But the courts found one. In the judges' opinion, the Betamax had many legitimate uses, starting with personal time shifting. They saw only one use for Napster: encouraging individuals to infringe musical copyrights (though how they missed the obvious popular legal use of swapping uncopyrighted adult pornography remains something of a mystery).

The case never went well for Napster. Early in the proceedings, Napster agreed to shut out any network members known to infringe legitimate copyrights. So a team of lawyers, accompanied by Metallica drummer Lars Ulrich, gave Napster a list of about 300,000 names. Things went downhill from there. Though in the final analysis Napster lost both at trial and on appeal,[23] the specifics of the rulings don't matter much. But the rulings buried the company. Napster ceased operations in February 2001, after a prolonged period of limping along with stripped-down functionality and a reduced membership network.

Now, in all honesty, there was more to the Napster story than that. In fact, there always is. Some egos appear to have gotten in the way at various times. Shawn's uncle John Fanning, for example, has become a common target of opprobrium among erstwhile Napster fans. And in an interesting little denouement, BMG (the Bertelsmann Music Group), one of the five major record labels, broke with the crowd to try to develop a relationship with Napster—essentially to convert the valuable name and the even-more-valuable membership network into one that respected legitimate IP rights—but that deal never quite happened.[24]

More to the point, though, as popular as Napster was, it never had much of a revenue model. While Napster was *great* at making headlines, it's not clear how anyone *ever* expected it to make money. After all, it was little more than a file directory that allowed people to exchange files without paying for them. That left it with a straight advertising model, at best—and that model proved incapable of sustaining most of the many dot-coms that relied upon it. So even under the best of circumstances, Napster may have had a short life expectancy anyway. Its legal troubles may just have buried it sooner, rather than later.

And so, with the Rio on the shelves and Napster off the Internet, the record companies appear to have won one and lost won. But appearances can be deceiving. For while Napster may be dead, P2P music swapping is something of a hydra. Kill one service, two more arise to take its place. The RIAA is now running around the globe chasing Grokster and Aimster and Morpheus and KaZaA. It's discovering the difficulty of proceeding against corporations of one country whose personnel are in a second and whose servers are in a third—each of which interpret their own national IP laws in ways that sometimes differ from those of the

United States. And as KaZaA fans might remind the RIAA, Vanuatu's IP laws are what they are—don't try to confuse them with Vanuatuan IP policy.[25]

In the final analysis, the damage is done and it's long-lasting. Napster, or more precisely P2P, finished a job that started way back when that first insightful composer devised a coded way to "write" music. It converted the music-information business into a permanent resident of the information sector. Technology has removed virtually all transaction costs related to copying and distributing music. Technological advances—mostly outside the information sector—also are reducing the capital costs required to produce original high-quality sound recordings. Garage bands with a bit of computer equipment and a good soundboard can produce their own songs at qualities that were once possible only in professional studios. They can then distribute their recordings as widely as they desire. Economics suggests that someone will devise a lucrative business model that works in this new technological reality. That someone may well be the record companies. They've done it before, and they begin with assets and capabilities that no one else can match. But so far, nothing they've tried has worked. One way or another, though, their traditional business model relies on technological barriers that no longer exist. The law is already straining under the effort of trying to recreate the defunct barriers. It can't hold on too much longer.

That's Entertainment

Entertainment encompasses more than just music. The movie moguls know that they're fated to follow in the record companies' footsteps because in the information sector, there's no real difference between audio and video. Songs and movies are all just bit strings. No matter what the bit string decodes to reveal, users can still create perfect copies at zero cost and then send it zooming around the Internet.

Well, maybe that's a bit of an exaggeration; songs and movies have two significant differences in the information sector. First, movies are longer. There are more bits in a movie than in a song. Movie files are thus harder and more expensive to transmit. Users with modems connected to telephone lines can transmit or download songs in a matter of minutes. Movies could take hours, even days. And if the computer disconnects—for any reason—during the download, the user often must start again from scratch. Even users with broadband connections need patience to download movies. The files are just too big to flow smoothly through our current connections. So size, throughput, and bandwidth make the transaction costs inherent in movie swapping higher than those in song swapping. That buys the movie industry a bit of protection—but only a bit. The technological barrier to movie swapping on the Internet is dropping quickly, and the transaction costs for distribution are likely to soon fall close enough to zero to remove the protection that size affords.

The second difference is a matter of history. While the record companies spent the 1980s and 90s filling our homes with digital content, the movie studios continued to circulate only analog versions of their products. File size was responsible for part of this decision, as well. Movie files are simply too big to fit on a single CD. Had the studios wanted to use CDs, they would have needed to package stacks of them together in ways that forced consumers to essentially "change reels" multiple times during the course of a movie. VHS videocassettes, on the other hand, contained enough tape to capture all but the longest movies—and even those generally fit on two videocassettes. But file size wasn't the studios' only advantage. They had also learned something from their loss to Sony in the Betamax case. And one of the things that they learned was to be wary of new technology. So when innovations like large digital laserdiscs (that is, discs large enough to hold a movie) came around, the studios didn't push consumers to adopt them. Unlike their musical brethren, the studios may have recognized that it's too damn easy to make perfect copies of a bit string. And so, the digitization of movies proceeded at a slower pace than the digitization of music.

But even the wise and cautious studio heads knew that they couldn't hold out forever. They knew that the question wasn't whether they would ever release digital movies to consumers, but rather when, and using what particular technology. When DVDs arrived, they realized that they could stall no longer. They understood that if they continued to refuse to meet pent-up consumer demand for digital movies, some pirate operation would fill the void—and that would be more of a headache than it was worth. There really isn't much of a difference between a CD and a DVD. They both combine advances in chemistry, materials, and optics to encode information as tiny little holes in an otherwise solid disk. The key advance lies in density. DVDs are dense enough to hold a movie on a single, small disk.

The studios finally bit the bullet and developed a popular, digital, consumer good: the DVD movie. But they were more than a bit nervous about it. They understood that DVD technology would follow the same path as CD technology—and likely mature faster because the underlying engineering was already well developed. While electronics companies are still debating some of the standards that they want to include in their products, home computers are already available with DVD burners, and recordable DVDs are available in office-supply stores. It may still be a few years before the dust finally settles on the standards shakeout, but home DVD burners will soon be inexpensive consumer-electronics goods. So the studios did something that the record companies had never bothered to do: they encrypted their digital products before they shipped them. Encryption adds a layer to the translation chain, so that even if I could copy a digital movie bit string, my computer would never understand it without the decryption key that translated a nonsensical bit string into a meaningful one.

The studios chose to protect their valuable content with an encryption scheme called the Content Scramble System (CSS). They licensed the decryption algorithm to companies that manufactured computers running either Windows or Mac software, reasoning that most consumers would then soon own machines containing legitimate decryption algorithms, or in other words authorized playback devices incapable of creating decrypted copies.

Now, if you read through that paragraph quickly, you may have missed a red flag. The studios themselves apparently missed it. The setup allows only Windows and Mac machines to become authorized playback devices. If you, for example, were a Linux user, you couldn't watch movies on your machine. And hackers prefer Linux. The movie studios had announced to a culture dedicated to solving challenging programming problems: "You can't watch our movies until you crack our code!" This ill-advised strategy created a truly perverse situation for the studios. In the vernacular, we call this sort of strategy "not smart." It created a truly perverse situation for the studios. A Windows user could watch a pirated copy of their movies, but a Linux user who actually paid for an authorized, official, studio-released DVD couldn't watch it. Of course, the hackers rose to the challenge and started an open-source project to decrypt CSS. In short order, they had completed DeCSS, circulated it, and made it possible to watch movies on Linux boxes—or, for that matter, on computers running still other platforms.

The hackers' response to the red flag sent the studios into a white rage. They'd spent years avoiding the inevitable distribution of digital content. They'd finally found a situation that they considered workable, but a bunch of hackers quickly showed them just how silly they were. The studios fought back against this technological advance with the only weapon at their disposal—IP law. In a matter of weeks an army of Hollywood lawyers had filed suits seeking to block people from using DeCSS, from circulating DeCSS, and from telling other people where to find DeCSS. The hackers, they reasoned, had made their protective technology disappear, so they would respond by making the hackers' invasive technology disappear. The studios trotted out a number of legal theories to support their goal, but in the clash between law and technology, technology inevitably wins. The best that the law can ever do is make a cheap technology expensive. The record companies learned that lesson with P2P, but it doesn't mean that they—or the movie studios, or the people who oppose stem-cell research or cloning or genetically modified organisms—will ever act upon that lesson. And so, the movie studios followed their musical brethren into war, fighting to halt their industry's inevitable slide into the information sector.

Once again, though the point of the fight was plain, the lawsuit itself focused on some nuanced language buried in an IP statute. In this case, the key law was the anticircumvention provision of the DMCA, the 1998 law that made it illegal to distribute a program that cracks an encryption system. This law—in its most draconian criminal form—landed Dmitry Sklyarov in jail for cracking Adobe's encryption. The studios didn't bother with the law's criminal provisions, but they did ask the courts to find that DeCSS violated the DMCA, and therefore to ban it.

Judge Lewis Kaplan held a lengthy trial and received much useful input. The defendants argued that the fair-use doctrine protected DeCSS, and that the program served an important policy purpose. But Judge Kaplan's ruling was straightforward. He presumed that Congress evaluated the expected affect of anticircumvention on innovation, reached a careful policy decision in line with its Constitutional charge, and wrote a reasonably clear statutory provision banning it. And since, as we all know, IP law is what it is, that provision proved dispositive. Judge Kaplan ruled for the studios and ordered DeCSS blocked.[26] Fifteen months later the Second Circuit Court of Appeals upheld his ruling.[27]

One of the truly offbeat implications of this case—and one that no one was much considering—was what Congress actually did when it passed the anticircumvention provision. That provision was brand new for the DMCA in 1998. The DeCSS case was the first to really look at it. And Judge Kaplan did what he was supposed to do. He presumed that Congress knew what it was doing and meant what it wrote. And it's certainly plausible that when Congress passed this law, it was trying to protect IP like the studios' digital movies and Adobe's eBook reader. But the law that it wrote may be much broader than that. The law as written sounds as though it may allow anyone to create an artificial barrier to entry by placing a technological roadblock in front of a copyrighted product. The technology doesn't have to be good—encryption into the binary equivalent of Pig Latin should work. That's a boon for producers looking to monopolize a particular niche, because it lets them create trivial artificial barriers to competitive entry.

If you're skeptical, consider the Lexmark printers. Much to its chagrin, some of Lexmark's customers prefer to buy replacement toner cartridges from competing suppliers. So Lexmark installed a chip in its toner cartridges that sends a message to the printer verifying that it is, in fact, a Lexmark cartridge. The printer won't work without an authentication message. In other words, Lexmark leveraged its strength in the printer market into the toner cartridge market—shades of Kodak! Static Control Components figured out how to mimic the Lexmark authentication message. So in December 2002, Lexmark sued, claiming that Static Control had circumvented a technological measure in order to access its copyrighted printer software.[28] Chamberlain used the same basic strategy to ensure that consumers who bought its automatic garage doors would also buy its garage-door openers. Skylink cracked the system. Chamberlain sued.[29] Their reasoning was straightforward: I can use technology to protect my copyrighted computer code. If you circumvent my protection technology, you therefore violate the DMCA. Could anyone possibly believe that Congress contemplated creating garage-door-opener monopolists when it passed the DMCA? Not a chance. But in the wonderful world of IP law, it doesn't matter. Policy is irrelevant. Congressional intent is irrelevant. The law is what it is.

The courts are still busy sorting out Lexmark's and Chamberlain's claims. A trial court in Kentucky thought that Lexmark's case looked strong and issued a preliminary injunction prohibiting Static Control Systems from selling its toner cartridges.[30] A trial court in Illinois found Chamberlain's complaint lacking, ruling in favor of Skylink.[31] Now the appeals courts must let us know what they think about these claims.[32] And while it's always hard to know where any given case will come out without knowing the inside details, the two-sentence summaries of Lexmark's and Chamberlain's claims don't sound all that different from the one that the studios used to protect CSS. The information sector, courtesy of the DMCA, may soon swallow a toner cartridge and/or a garage door near you.

And so, we can chalk one up for the movie studios—just like we credited the record companies with a great victory when they shut down Napster. But we can also see a system coming apart at the seams. Technology keeps knocking down transaction costs and economics pushes consumers to do what comes naturally. Increasingly draconian laws may reimpose some of those costs and keep outdated business models in place for a while longer—but at tremendous cost. The DMCA's anticircumvention clause alone already threatens to create *both* another "drug war" chasing criminal IP violators *and* a raft of consumer-goods monopolists using cheap encryption to leverage their monopolies outward. I don't know how much more of this we can afford. We now have laws protecting technologies protecting IP rights that soon could inflict serious damage on the American economy—not to mention on American civil society.

If sounds like I'm blaming the record companies or the movie studios—I'm not. They, like Microsoft, are behaving in a completely rational manner to protect the property rights that Congress gave them and the business models that have been successful for their shareholders. They're doing *exactly* what they should do. Music executives should not be debating American IP policy. That work usually starts in the temples of academe, though the Constitution gave Congress ultimate responsibility. And if Congress can't handle it by itself, it should enlist a bit of assistance from a regulatory agency or the federal judiciary. The "rule of reason" has served us well in antitrust law. Maybe we now need one for IP law as well, because our IP laws seem to be verging on a dangerous lack of reason. The current system just doesn't work in the information sector. And the information sector is growing. Fast. Because while we were considering how it swallowed the music industry, it took a bite out of your printer and your garage door. Let's just hope that we don't end up with a case of national indigestion.

8

Down the Rabbit Hole

What If?

Public infrastructure and private entrepreneurship are the twin pillars of our emerging information economy. Academic scholars have given us the tools to understand what building an infrastructure involves—and to appreciate the impact that infrastructure can have on private ventures. The software and entertainment industries have illustrated the relationship between infrastructure and entrepreneurial innovation—and where that relationship seems to be heading. Those lessons point to the true challenge of living through an epochal transformation. How can we point our emerging information economy in the direction most likely to succeed as history moves from the industrial age to the information age?

The post-bubble Internet showed the importance of retiring the New World view in favor of its wiser New Channel counterpart. New Channel thinking provides half of the groundwork for the information sector's future by helping us see how winners can become winners, how the Internet can help us move closer to a more efficient world of reduced transaction costs, and how life in the information sector can make us all richer one transaction at a time. But that's only half the story. And though New Channel businesses will undoubtedly tell the more visible half of the story, they also will form the less important half. The more significant, though more obscure, half is the infrastructure upon which those New Channel businesses will rest. And perhaps *the* critical element of that infrastructure lies within the realm of IP—where IP law meets IP policy.

We've already seen the record companies use their IP rights to retard digital-music distribution. They argued, persuasively, that IP law granted them the right to prohibit Napster's free-for-all. From a legal perspective that's certainly the right argument, but the policy argument is more intriguing, and more fundamental. The Constitution charged Congress with crafting IP rights that motivate innovation, and it clearly anticipated multiple effects. Wisely crafted IP rights should lead to innovations that *both* enhance human knowledge in the long term and put better products on our shelves in the short term. They should also, however, make many of those new products more expensive than they would be otherwise. In short, the public trades unfettered access to a small innovation pool for restricted access to a larger innovation pool.

But unintended consequences are latent in every bargain. Siva Vaidhyanathan, for example, described an unanticipated situation in the United States that persisted through much of the nineteenth century. Our early copyright laws protected only American authors. But British authors like Lewis Carroll, Charles Dickens, Mary Shelley, and Oscar Wilde, to name but a few, also wrote fine stories in English. Because American copyrights didn't protect their work, American consumers could buy their books without paying them any royalties—making books by British authors less expensive here than books by American authors. At the same time, because British copyrights didn't protect American authors, American authors could hardly earn a living from their books sold abroad. That imbalance may have been great for consumers, but it posed quite a challenge to American authors. And so Mark Twain launched (and eventually won) a crusade to strengthen copyright law—including a reciprocal-rights treaty with England—to make it easier for American authors to make money on their writing.[1]

Now, Vaidhyanathan didn't tell this story with much admiration for Twain. In fact, he saw Twain's crusade as an important step down a perfidious path of ever-increasing IP rights that stifles contemporary expression and threatens creativity. And from a cultural perspective, he may be correct. From an economic perspective, however, the situation that motivated Twain's crusade is simply one example of the unintended consequences of our IP bargains. I'm relatively certain that when our first Congress, freshly independent and still on shaky terms with England, sat around drafting a copyright law, no one suggested rigging it to turn American readers into devotees of English authors. But in retrospect it was a logical consequence of the IP laws that the first Congress passed. A correct interpretation of the IP laws led to an unfortunate policy consequence—and one that eventually led to a major revision of our copyright laws.

We may be at a similar juncture today. When the record companies shut down Napster, they did more than eliminate the Internet's most popular music-swapping site. They also drove P2P development underground—and offshore. And P2P may be the most important information-sector innovation since the Web; broadband-intensive P2P applications have the potential to eliminate the illusory "bandwidth glut" that's often cited as a drag on the telecom sector, if not on the broader economy. But many potential innovators have been scared off because IP law made P2P development unnecessarily expensive. And the loopholes that have kept successor music-swapping sites in business are unlikely to offer developers much solace. Do we really want to force our innovators to set up multijurisdictional offshore corporations? Talk about transaction costs!

The unintended consequences of our IP laws are wending their way throughout our contemporary technology industries. Numerous sectors—pharmaceuticals, microchips, and biotechnology, to name but a few—have encountered discrepancies between the workings of an IP system designed for an industrial economy and the practical necessities of their own postindustrial businesses. Some of these discrepancies mirror the challenge of entertainment industries—traditional forms of protection no longer seem to protect. Others mirror *the lesser* challenge of the software industry—traditional forms of incentives do not seem to motivate. But the greater challenge of software remains unique: only a *sui generis* regime can provide adequate motivation and protection.

These two challenges to software are interrelated. The inability of traditional copyrights and patents to motivate software development—a shortcoming that we encountered in theory in chapter 2, and met in practical terms in both Bill Gates's open letter and the open-source contortion of copyleft in chapters 5 and 6, respectively—made a unique protective regime inevitable.

In many ways, we let Congress off the hook. We never pushed Congress to ask how to best motivate software development and enable software businesses at the lowest cost to the public. Instead, we let Congress, the administrators of the Copyright Office and of the Patent and Trademark Office, and the courts, lard on all known forms of protection. Today, we protect software as an unprecedented combination of patents, copyrights, and trade secrets. And upon closer scrutiny, the situation is even worse. Any program resident on your computer may possess *six* different legal protections: algorithm patents, source-code copyrights, source-code trade secrets, object-code copyrights, shrink-wrap or click-through licenses and a handful of trademarks. Congress has crafted a unique protective regime for software and digital products—a critical component of industrial policy—apparently without ever thinking through either the regime's nature or its consequences to the economy and to society. Such an abdication of analytic responsibility could not help but have far-reaching unintended consequences.

Of course, "unintended" doesn't necessarily mean either "undesirable" or "avoidable." After all, most people recognize that our existing IP laws *do* serve the important public-policy goal of promoting innovation. Though we may detect costs that we'd never expected to bear, we may also detect benefits that we'd never expected to earn. Even if we decide that the IP rights that we've granted are more expensive than anticipated, that hardly means that we'd be better off scrapping the system.

Fortunately, we don't have to make that choice. Though Congress may have abdicated its constitutional role as the guardian of IP policy, we've already met a number of IP reformists who have volunteered to fill the gap back in chapter 2. Some proposed wholesale regime change, going so far as to issue a radical manifesto advocating the development of software-specific IP rights.[2] Others recognized that while such radicalism may be required in the long run, we can take many moderate steps in the short run to alleviate the direst of the unintended consequences. Still others have found clever ways to combine existing IP rights with licenses designed to protect public knowledge. One of the problems with these reformers, though, is that—to put it bluntly—they're academics. They tend to focus on abstract issues beginning to bubble to the fore. Their critiques overflow with plausible extensions of current negative trends. For the most part, they warn of consequences lying just around the bend—consequences that we can avoid only by adopting their preferred reforms today. Many of their discussions are a bit abstract; though they may be right, they're not always helpful.

Their discussions, however, do highlight a key difference between entertainment and software. The entertainment industry's existing business models will have to change; more and more observers are advocating a split of control from compensation. One way or another, in the not too distant future, these "content providers" may be forced to free their products to drift throughout the ether, and be satisfied with some sort of aggregate compensation scheme. Or at least, that's what one currently popular school of thought foresees. But other approaches appear possible in the software industry.

We recognized the challenge of protecting software rights a long time ago. Many people have written about it: Bill Gates and Richard Stallman; congressional advisory committees and the Supreme Court; various IP reformers. Together, they've given us the views from practical software developers, from legislators who write laws and judges who interpret them, and from priests of academe who worry about their broader consequences. They've given us much to think about. But then they gave us a more useful contribution, and one yet to enter the debate fully. They gave us a wonderful historical review of the software markets: the Microsoft trial.

The Microsoft trial, and the various interactions among Microsoft, its competitors, and the government, conveyed a wealth of useful empirical information about a software industry protected by the current IP regime. Somewhat surprisingly, though, we've spent little time digesting these lessons and comparing the empirical evidence with theoretical predictions.[3] So we get to play "what if . . . " Specifically: What if . . . we had different IP laws protecting software? What if . . . Microsoft had started with a different set of rights? How might things have evolved differently? And would we be better off today?

We must create parallel universes and consider the fate of those who dwell within them. And though we could never expect to learn lessons general enough to extend throughout the entire tech sector, the exercise may help to break us out of a dangerous trap—a trap that transcends the boundaries of IP policy and goes to the heart of public policy as a

whole. One of the most dangerous pitfalls for citizens is the conservative assumption that things *must be* as they are. We tend toward this
conservatism even when we believe that things are not as they should
be; better the devil we know than the devil we don't. But in truth, it's a
trap. The devil we know may well be worse than an alternative devil of
our choosing. And so, by exploring these alternative universes of software rights, we may expand our thinking to understand, to address, and
to resolve the many policy debates that we can expect to encounter as
the information sector continues to grow into a full-blown information
economy.

Antitrust Lamentations

IP priests had little say in the Microsoft trial. After all, it was an *antitrust*
trial! Microsoft stood accused of violating the antitrust laws. The victims
were competitors, competitive markets, and consumers—the characters
that animate the antitrust world. The government agency in charge
was the DoJ's *Antitrust* Division and many of the antitrust scholars
running the show would gladly confuse IP law with IP policy. Antitrust
emphatically intertwines law and policy under the rule of reason, the
analytic regime that prohibits many business activities "sometimes,"
depending on the context, the markets, and the competitive environment.
IP law has no comparable rule. And therein lies a perpetual source
of tension between IP and antitrust scholars. Marginalizing, if not
excluding, the IP experts seemed to make sense. And other than Larry
Lessig's brief stint as Judge Jackson's "special master," that's what
happened.

But it turns out that a detour through the temple of IP might have
been in order, after all. For in the government's focus on the perpetra-
tors and their victims, it forgot to consider the weapon. Microsoft owns
little other than IP rights. The administrators of IP had granted Microsoft
the property rights to every product that it used to corrupt the market.
Congress had presumably considered IP policy and issued its results as
the Patent Act and the Copyright Act. But these statutes, for the most
part, ignored the peculiarities of software. Congress left the courts to
grapple with the complexities of products that fit comfortably into *no*

existing IP category. The software industry crafted its own combination of patent, copyright, and trade-secret protection, and in so doing emerged with protection that was likely far stronger than any that Congress had ever imagined. These rights enabled Microsoft to violate the antitrust laws.

Even Microsoft saw these rights as the basis of its power. Microsoft continued to forward its "unfettered liberty" argument years after Judge Jackson first shot it down. The Court of Appeals even felt that:

> Microsoft's primary copyright argument borders upon the frivolous. The company claims an absolute and unfettered right to use its intellectual property as it wishes: "If intellectual property rights have been lawfully acquired," it says, then "their subsequent exercise cannot give rise to antitrust liability." That is no more correct than the proposition that use of one's personal property, such as a baseball bat, cannot give rise to tort liability. As the Federal Circuit succinctly stated: "Intellectual property rights do not confer a privilege to violate the antitrust laws."[4]

Though the relationship between antitrust and IP remains at least somewhat tense, the frivolity of Microsoft's claims seemed clear. Microsoft had strong property rights and behaved as if it had unfettered liberty. A bit over the line? Perhaps. But who's to stop Microsoft from exercising its legally acquired IP rights *before* the antitrust trial is over?

The dilemma runs deeper still. The information sector's key stories unfold where technology, law, and economics intersect. Software technology allowed Microsoft to develop its product line. IP laws defined what Microsoft could and could not do with its products—and what its competitors could and could not do with their own product lines. Economics told Microsoft how to use those products and rights to maximize its profits. Microsoft behaved as expected. When it emerged as a monopolist, Microsoft surveyed the terrain, saw its capabilities, and behaved precisely as a duly empowered, rational monopolist—with perhaps a slightly above average taste for risk—*should* behave. It pushed its actions far into the gray area of antitrust, and paid little heed when it peeked out the other side into the realm of the violator. After all, someone had to catch Microsoft to stop it—and that's never easy. So Microsoft used its IP rights to maintain its platform monopoly, to leverage that monopoly over to the Internet, to deprive consumers of choice, and to narrow the range of software innovation. Microsoft worked very hard to dissuade innovators from developing software that didn't pass through its Windows translation frontier.

The jeremiad of IP thus came to pass. Back in the temple of IP, we heard the anguished cries in abstract terms. The priestly lamentations about the deviation of IP law from IP policy seemed strangely disembodied. After all, who could say that our software was not improving each year, while simultaneously getting cheaper? Who could say that our information sector wasn't thriving? And yet, as the government's case unfolded, it became clear that we could have foreseen—and even predicted—virtually everything that had happened, if only we had focused on the weapon itself. But, as America's foremost defender of weaponry might say: IP rights don't kill markets. Monopolists kill markets. Once again, we chose to ignore the weapon and to focus exclusively upon the shooter.

Now in all honesty, that focus didn't turn out to be so horrible. The government demonstrated how and where Microsoft had hurt competitive markets and—at least by implication, if not explicitly—consumers. The government did a phenomenal job of establishing liability. It proved *both* that Microsoft was a monopolist and that it had violated the antitrust laws. And while the former may seem obvious to anyone not immersed in the technical arcana of antitrust, it remains a subtle and challenging point within the antitrust community itself. And it should certainly be obvious to anyone, inside that community or out, that the latter is always tough to prove. The government's performance on antitrust liability was nothing short of spectacular.

But its oversight cost the government—and us—when it came to the remedy. For with little attention paid to the weapon, seeing how to fix the problem was difficult. Though we debated whether to dismember Microsoft or merely tether it, no serious voice raised the central question: should Microsoft remain armed? This question's absence complicated the end game—and ensured that what many *think* was the end game will not be.

But that's jumping ahead. For the jeremiad of IP leads us back to a central theme of the information sector's formative years. Stories that seem to embody irrationality may in fact indicate little other than misdirection. Much as the bubble may have been powered, in no small part, by the false parallels drawn between the applications barrier to entry of platform software and the Internet barrier to entry of the dot-com world, so too the triumphs and defeats of the government's case against Microsoft may have been powered, in no small part, by the deviation of the IP laws governing platform software from the constitutional pre-scriptions of IP policy.

Manifestos and Buddha Natures

To see how the reformers' prophecies played themselves out in the con-crete context of platform software, we must understand that Microsoft was simply being true to its nature, behaving as a rational monopolist should, seeking to extract every last profit from its property rights, and redistributing maximal resources from consumers to shareholders. By understanding that, we can appreciate the government's case, the invest-ing public's opprobrium for that case, the futility of the apparent end game, and the inevitability of future battles.

Recall the source of the problem. In 1790, the very first Congress rec-ognized that authors and inventors required different incentives. It responded by passing two distinct laws. For more than 160 years, the line between authors and inventors, between copyrights and patents, appeared to be clear. But sometime after Claude Shannon explained that he was going to *write* a chess-playing program rather than *build* a chess-playing machine, the line began to blur. Programmers felt that they deserved protection, and we decided that we wanted to protect them. Somehow, though, we never quite figured out whether they were authors or inventors—or perhaps something fundamentally new. In fact, we never bothered to think about what they were or how we could best motivate them to innovate. And so today, software companies write source code in a high-level programming language that competing pro-grammers can decipher easily. They then compile it into object code com-prehensible only to machines, patent any clever algorithms that they might have captured in their code, copyright both the source code and the object code, hide the source code in a vault where it remains a trade secret, and circulate copies of their copyrighted object code. Software now enjoys a unique combination of protections. But is it the best protective regime possible? Or could we do better with a little explicit thought and an eye toward reform?

Some radical reformers drafted a Manifesto proposing reform, advocating a return to the constitutional bargain. They advised short, broad, deep protection in exchange for full disclosure of the source code. In return for sharing their ideas, implementations, nuances, and API languages with the public at large—including all of their competitors—software developers would get a powerful, albeit brief, monopoly. We added our own little twist—a brief delay between granting the rights and publishing the source code—in order to guarantee commercial opportunities substantial enough to motivate significant innovation.

The Manifesto's creators realized that developers could always opt out of the deal, by simply keeping their source code secret. Developers who chose that route could control their ideas, their implementations, and their APIs, but not the distribution of their object code. Opt-ins and opt-outs would require radically different business models; their choices could even bisect the software industry. But a failure to reform the system, these radicals warned, could lead to disaster. Such was the Manifesto's message.

But temple messages are often opaque, and prophecies often ambiguous. For example, when a monk asked the Zen master Jōshū, "Does a dog have a Buddha nature?" Jōshū replied: "Mu."[5] We may do better by posing our queries to someone other than a Zen master. Does a corporation have a Buddha nature? More specifically, does Microsoft have a Buddha Nature? Those are questions that I can handle without Zen master Jōshū. Microsoft *does* have a Buddha nature. All corporations possess the same Buddha nature. The principle of profit maximization defines the corporate inner essence. Microsoft's behavior was true to its nature. Microsoft tried to use its property rights, in a rational manner, to maximize its profits.

To see the integral nature of those rights in Microsoft's behavior, however, we must take a Zen-like approach. We must continue our journey down the rabbit hole to where the trial was not: the realm of application software. We must then compare Microsoft's behavior to that of Musoft, a mythical platform-software monopolist whose behavior is always true to its nature. Musoft differs from the real-world Microsoft in one important respect. Musoft dwells in Manifestoland, an alternate reality identical to our own, except that the Manifesto's regime protects software IP rights. When we come to understand the relationships between applications and platforms, between prevailing IP rights and the Manifesto's reforms, and between Microsoft and Musoft, we will be enlightened. Only then will we comprehend the Microsoft trial and see the path to a true end game.

Where the Trial Was Not

We now enter the realm of application software to contemplate the impact of the Manifesto's proposed reform. The existing software IP regime is valuable to both platform and application developers, but in subtly different ways. The key difference emerges from a fundamental property of network economics—or at the very least, a property of business plans appropriate in network industries. If your product defines a network, you should always consider pricing it below its full value to maximize its circulation. If you can lock in your customers, you'll find ways to reap significant profits later. If, on the other hand, your product sits on top of a network, you're likely to have to sell it to profit.[6] As a result, we can safely ignore the technical problem of classifying middleware, and simply use "platform" as shorthand for products that define networks and "applications" as shorthand for everything else. Though platform developers may consider many interesting business plans, application developers typically generate their most reliable profit streams via direct sales—a stream that's only possible if they have an IP right protecting their object code.

So we need IP rights to motivate innovation. But they knew *that* when they wrote the Constitution. Give them a copyright, and let's move on. And we could do that. But since we've already seen one of the jeremiad's prophecies come to pass, we should spend a little time thinking about just what software copyrights mean—particularly since something seems wrong. Copyrights last at least ninety-five years, which is effectively forever in the software world. Do we need to offer infinite protection to motivate application developers? And more broadly, could weaker rights motivate just as much software innovation?

Microsoft knocked out DR-DOS by launching Windows, receiving the standard package of IP rights, and leaving Digital Research to play catch-up. What could Digital Research have done? One option, at least in theory, was to clone Windows. But as Gates himself noted, Microsoft held some patents that would have made legal cloning tough; any software that performed the same tasks as Windows would likely have infringed. Digital Research's other option should have been to get DR-DOS to talk to Windows, whether Microsoft wanted them chatting or not. Microsoft obviously agreed that Digital Research had the legal right to do so, because if it could have blocked DR-DOS from the Windows APIs just by stating that using those APIs was not permitted, it would have. Instead Microsoft blocked DR-DOS from chatting with Windows by keeping its source code secret. Microsoft figured out how to use its IP rights to extract stronger protection than anyone had intended to give it. And true its nature, Microsoft used those rights to knock out its primary competitor and to increase its own profits. Its doppelganger Musoft would have been proud.

Speaking of Musoft, though, how did it handle such matters in Manifestoland? Well, when it prepared to launch Mundos—the first graphical interface to DOS—upon an unsuspecting but desirous public, it faced a choice. It could either reveal its Mundos source code, charge for each copy of its object code, and block competing products for a few years, or it could keep its source code secret, make its APIs a moving target, try to ensure that Mundos could sit atop only MU-DOS, and allow the Mundos object code to circulate free of charge.

Suppose first that Musoft had chosen the rights and revealed its source code in exchange for the short-term broad monopoly on offer in Manifestoland. Its chief competitor, DR, would have used its public access to the Mundos source code to bolster its own development efforts. In no time at all, DR would have developed new features and sought IP rights to protect them. That would set up a problem. Musoft couldn't improve Mundos, because DR (and perhaps other companies) would own the rights to the next logical evolutionary steps. But DR couldn't sell *anything* until Mundos' IP rights expired.

Consumers might have been stuck paying a monopoly price for Mundos 1.0 and blocked from buying anything better—at least for a while. But once Musoft's rights expired, the lot of consumers would have improved quickly because DR wasn't the only innovative developer whose work benefited from access to the Mundos source code. The minute the Mundos rights expired, numerous competing second-generation products would have flooded the market, each compatible with Mundos 1.0, and each sporting its own set of protected advanced features. These competing second-generation products would have constrained each others' prices. Third-generation systems, in turn, would have incorporated all desirable second-generation features—and each would be compatible with all second-generation systems. The process would continue from there. Each generation would get better and cheaper—but there could be occasional "dead times" between generations when consumers simply couldn't buy the upgrades they wanted because Manifestoland's broad IP rights blocked them from the market.

But such dead time is far from inevitable. Suppose that rather than blocking each other from the market, Musoft and DR had cross-licensed their rights and marketed Mundos 2.0 together. Consumers would have gained rapid access to the second-generation product, albeit at a monopoly price. Competition would then have moved on to the next set of features—which could also have resulted in cross licensing (or not). The bottom line, though, is that if Musoft had put the Mundos source code in the public domain, it would have had a very hard time knocking DR out of the platform market.

Suppose instead that Musoft kept the Mundos source code secret and simply let its object code circulate freely. That *might* have worked with Mundos because it was technically middleware, but it would prove disastrous with most applications. Musoft quickly would have discovered that it had no way to recoup its development costs—much less to turn a profit. In other words, releasing an application unprotected by IP rights, even those on offer in Manifestoland, would have been inconsistent with Musoft's nature. No, Musoft would have sought and received protection not only for Mundos, but for all applications that it developed in Manifestoland. Unless, that is, Musoft became an open-source advocate. But open-source licenses make little sense in Manifestoland, where *all* recipients of software IP rights open their source code. Open source advocates in Manifestoland can simply set their prices to zero and rely on consulting and customization services as their sole sources of revenue.

Would the Manifesto's edicts be good for consumers of application software? Prices likely would be higher, at least in the early stages. In exchange, consumers would gain some significant benefits, starting with intergenerational compatibility. Because everyone's previous-generation source code for all protected applications is public, all developers would ensure that new products were compatible with all of their competitors' old products. Furthermore, the fury of competing on each and every new feature would probably speed technological development. Intergenerational compatability and rapid product development would serve consumers well. The potential increase in compatibility is particularly significant given the network nature of the software industry. It seems inevitable that all important protected programs in Manifestoland would converge to open standards within their first few generations—a situation that can have significant positive consequences. Open standards lower entry barriers, increase competition, and eventually lead to lower prices.

But winners rarely exist in the absence of losers. If consumers have more choice, better products, and lower prices, and application developers like DR get to stay in business, only Musoft loses. But if Musoft loses by too much, we'd never see Mundos. Musoft, staying true to its nature, would decide that it can't justify the investment necessary to develop a truly innovative new product that might never work—and even worse, that could be finished only a month after a competing new product received IP protection that blocked it from the market. The Manifesto would have undermined the Constitution and failed to promote the progress of science and the useful arts. After all, worse things than monopolists who exploit consumers exist—and potential innovations that die on the vine are among them.

The challenge is finding the right balance. If we've given Microsoft overprotective rights, we must be able to reduce them without reducing overall software innovation. That's the definition of "overprotection." In Manifestoland, we would have to make sure that the limited period of protection before we allowed competing products to enter the market, possibly as well as the lead time between the Mundos commercial launch and the release of its source code, were long enough for Musoft to reap the profits necessary to motivate innovative development efforts. How long is that? I don't know for sure. Jeff Bezos reportedly suggested that three-year software patents should be sufficient. I've heard sillier suggestions—say 95 years. But however long it is, there should be some place in the general vicinity of Manifestoland where revised IP rights lead to *both* happier applications consumers and applications markets that are harder to monopolize and to exploit than are our own.

So much for where the trial was not. As we return to what we did at the trial, rather than watching the story as it unfolds, we'll look beneath the surface to see how our real-world Microsoft was able to achieve things that would have eluded Musoft of Manifestoland.

Through the Looking Glass

If Musoft looked in the mirror and saw the events culminating in Microsoft's trial, it would be jealous. Though Musoft always worked to maximize profits—true to its corporate nature—Microsoft, armed with identical products but stronger IP rights, had been able to foreclose so many competitive threats and become so much more profitable! So Musoft would need to examine the relationship among rights, incentives, and strategies that set its world apart from Microsoft's.

Back in the applications market, our major concern seemed to be that underprotecting applications could deter innovation. There, Musoft launched Mundos 1.0 as middleware and treated it as an application. But here in the platform market, where maximal profits flow to whomever owns the largest network, the situation was a little different. Consider Musoft's calculations as it contemplates launching Mundos 95, a true platform that will define a network. Musoft would like to own that network, but in Manifestoland, Congress doesn't award any IP rights without source-code disclosure. And disclosed source code would turn Mundos into an open standard—no one would own it. So Musoft must consider keeping its source code secret, owning the network, but relinquishing control over object-code distribution—a choice similar to the one that record companies may soon face in a P2P world.

Musoft's choice pits revealing its Mundos 95 source code, charging for each copy of its object code, and blocking competition for a few years, against keeping its source code secret and trying to make money in various aftermarkets. The first option runs right into the network-industry dilemma; the only way that Musoft could earn a decent return on software sales would be to eviscerate the value of its network by charging a high purchase price. The second option appears to be a risky attempt to build a huge Mundos network quickly. If consumers became comfortable enough with Mundos to lock themselves in, Musoft would be in a strong position to profit. Musoft could charge locked-in consumers for service contracts, warranties, support, API access, customization, development tools, and possibly even applications that ran well on Mundos. Manifestoland's consumers would pay less for their platforms, but they'd probably pay more for their applications; after all, many software developers need precisely the services that Musoft would be counting upon to generate profits.

Paradoxically, the business model implicit in secret platform source code looks a lot like an open-source business model. Then again, perhaps that similarity is not all that odd. After all, though source code and object code are different beasts from the perspective of software *developers*, there's not much difference between them to *users*. While open *development* can help a company reduce its costs, open *distribution* just pushes companies toward aftermarket business models and away from direct-sales business models. In that sense, the only real difference between open-source code and unprotected object code is that the original developer controls the customization opportunities in the latter. In other words, a platform developer who opted out of the IP system to keep its source code secret would incur higher development costs but retain greater customization opportunities than an open-source advocate.

Suppose that Musoft, understanding these calculations and tradeoffs, chose to keep its source code secret, effectively inverting the open-source ethos even while adopting its business model. Musoft's calculations return us to the conclusion reached back in the open source bazaar: Service-oriented business models make more sense than product-oriented models in software-infrastructure settings.

In a related vein, for platforms, the dangers of overprotection dwarf any possible fear of underprotection. In our own world, when triple protection combines with a network barrier to entry, extraordinarily powerful rights emerge to protect software and to enable lucrative after-market opportunities. In other words, an infrastructure developer's direct-sales revenues may motivate little additional innovation. Granting the rights that enable those revenues—rights that certainly give their owners powers that we don't want them to have—may not have been necessary. But our decision to grant them should have enabled us to predict virtually everything that followed.

Musoft and Microsoft both must maintain at least four sets of relationships—though given the different rights and choices at their disposal, the nature of those relationships are likely to differ. But one way or another, they must each deal with: the OEMs who build and sell hardware; the ISVs whose software must run on some platform; competing platform developers or would-be entrants into the platform market; and consumers who use their platform networks. Their parallel paths through these relationships reveal the unspoken role that IP rights played in issues raised during Microsoft's trial.

Let's start with the OEMs. Before Microsoft emerged as the platform monopolist, it maintained a symbiotic relationship with OEMs. Most of the OEMs' customers wanted to buy hardware already loaded with a software platform. OEMs wanted to offer their customers as many different platforms as possible. Microsoft's interest, like that of its platform competitors, lay in making its platform available to as many consumers as possible, regardless of their hardware choice. Platform developers and OEMs were in rough power parity. Neither side would have benefited from an exclusive agreement.

But network economics correctly predicted that the platform market would eventually tip to a standard. As it happened, a critical mass of consumers began demanding that OEMs provide them with turnkey systems running Windows. These demands gave Microsoft some serious negotiating power vis-à-vis the OEMs. At trial, the government was able to demonstrate that Microsoft:

charges different OEMs different prices for Windows, depending on the degree to which the individual OEMs comply with Microsoft's wishes. Among the five largest OEMs, Gateway and IBM, which in various ways have resisted Microsoft's efforts to enlist them in its efforts to preserve the applications barrier to entry, pay higher prices than Compaq, Dell, and Hewlett-Packard, which have pursued less contentious relationships with Microsoft.[7]

This type of cost advantage is significant in a market as competitive as the OEM market of the mid-1990s.

Microsoft bestowed favor upon some OEMs and spewed venom upon others. And of all the OEMs, it was IBM that proved to be the greatest target of Microsoft's ire. Why? Remember OS/2? That wonderful graphical interface that would someday displace DOS? The one on which Microsoft had not only partnered with IBM, but invested such great development resources that it even let DR-DOS surpass MS-DOS as the finest DOS on the market? Well, IBM finished the project on its own after Microsoft quit to focus on Windows. OS/2 had the potential to compete with and to surpass Windows, and IBM wanted to offer consumers a choice. IBM was perfectly willing to sell consumers its hardware equipped with Windows. But it also wanted to offer an entirely-IBM system, from its hardware through its OS/2 platform, down to its applications. That choice might have made consumers happy, but it didn't play too well in Redmond.

Microsoft tried to convince IBM to move its business away from products that themselves competed directly with Windows and Office. Microsoft leveraged the fact that [IBM's] PC Company needed to license Windows at a competitive price and on a timely basis, and the fact that the company needed Microsoft's support in many more subtle ways. When IBM refused to abate the promotion of those of its own products that competed with Windows and Office, Microsoft punished the IBM PC Company with higher prices, a late license for Windows 95, and the withholding of technical and marketing support.[8]

Microsoft used its position as the platform monopolist to secure the OEM channel. Consumers were unable to buy any competing platform preloaded onto a PC.

Over in Manifestoland, Musoft couldn't control distribution. Manifestoland OEMs purchased a single copy of Mundos 95 and distributed it freely with their hardware. That worked fine for Musoft, who'd already decided to sacrifice short-term revenues to focus on network growth. But it did leave Musoft with little of Microsoft's asymmetric strength during negotiations covering the various "more subtle ways" that OEMs need platform developers.

Microsoft and Musoft both understood that their relationships with ISVs were trickier than their OEM relationships. Because the technical skills necessary to develop platforms and applications are quite similar, some ISV products that *complement* their platforms actually *compete* with their applications. These complicated relationships, in which potential competitors are also potential customers, force every platform developer (and every firm who controls the core product of a network industry, for that matter) to face the tension between *access* and *control*. Platform developers must find the appropriate balance between maintaining tight control, thereby forcing ISVs to work on competing platforms, and granting those independents access to the API and development tools they might need. Most commercially viable long-term strategies lie between the extremes of total access and total control.

Microsoft chose this middle ground, licensed its APIs but not its source code, and thereby defeated Apple. Musoft had no such luxury. Manifestoland's constraints forced Musoft to pursue an access-oriented strategy as the price of secrecy. This choice, however, also posed a quandary in thinking about alliances with ISVs. How could Musoft share the Mundos APIs safely without protective IP rights? Corporations who share their trade secrets with potential competitors don't rely on IP rights for protection. The laws of trade secrets, licenses, contracts, and business torts are both more powerful and more appropriate tools to protect these relationships. Also access to an API, particularly during the prerelease stage, provides an ISV with a tremendous market advantage. An ISV who shares the API with a competitor is squandering that advantage. Because the relationships between platform developers and ISVs aren't contingent on IP rights, Musoft's relationships with ISVs shouldn't have to differ much from Microsoft's.

Which leaves us with one burning question concerning the relationship between a platform monopolist and ISVs: *What did Microsoft actually do?* Microsoft may, on occasion, give its own developers a tiny lead time on API changes hoping to gain a leg up in the relevant applications market, and it varies its APIs often enough to dissuade cloning, but by and large, Microsoft's strategy leans strongly towards access. Microsoft *wants* ISVs to write programs that run on Windows. The last thing that Microsoft wants to see is a huge increase in Linux or Mac applications. As a result, Microsoft works hard to ensure that developers get what they need to develop new Windows applications—for with each new application, the applications barrier to entry grows stronger, the

Windows network becomes more valuable, and Microsoft's monopoly becomes more secure.

There are, however, two exceptions worth noting. The first deals with Microsoft's Office suite. For a while, competing application developers produced popular, powerful office programs, including some that ran on Windows; Lotus 1-2-3 and WordPerfect come immediately to mind. These programs retained strong market positions and large shares—at times, even larger than those of Microsoft's own Excel and Word—well into the Windows era. And yet, Microsoft was able to reduce both to relatively small niche players. Much of this came from Microsoft's ability to exert negotiating strength with OEMs—applying leverage that, as we noted, grew from the nature of its IP rights and would not have been available to Musoft. After all, many consumers purchase new hardware configured not only with a platform, but also with an office suite. But leveraging OEMs only could accomplish part of the goal. Microsoft likely also applied some of the same moving-target-API strategies to these competitors that it had with DR-DOS. But though such actions were likely, we can't know with any degree of certainty precisely what Microsoft did in these markets. These stories didn't unfold during the trial because applications were where the trial was not; we have less data about Microsoft's behavior in applications markets than we might like.

The second exception is even more important—for it leads us into the relationships among direct platform competitors. The developers of powerful middleware applications threaten to dethrone platform monopolists through one of the two paths that network economics left open to them. They can develop new products that are so far superior to Windows that consumers would be willing to incur the switching costs; or they can develop new products that expand the market by so much that the new consumers using their products generate a network larger than the Windows network.

How can these circumstances arise? Computer science tells us that in platform software, these conditions arise only during transitions between successive generations. These periods represent the all-important junctures when the translation frontier evolves upward by integrating enough new middleware (or applications) to alter its entire look and feel, and thus to invite a whole new group of human users who'd never bothered to learn the specialized language of the old translation frontier into the wonderful world of computing. When that migration occurs, the winners of the middleware competition easily could gain ownership of the next-generation platform. We've already seen that migration happen once, when MS-DOS swallowed the Windows middleware application to become a true platform. At trial, Judge Jackson ruled that Microsoft had violated the antitrust laws by squelching nascent threats from IBM, Intel, Apple, and RealNetworks.[9] But by far the most significant threat had come from the combination of Netscape's Navigator and Sun's Java—a direct middleware threat.

Now Musoft never learned to squelch these threats; they still exist in the competitive markets of Manifestoland. Through the looking glass, Musoft watched Microsoft's exploits in the fabled browser wars.

The Mosaic Code

Microsoft consolidated its dominance of the PC desktop before the days of the Internet. But even as Microsoft worked feverishly to integrate Windows into DOS, a team of students at the University of Illinois busily developed a graphical Web browser, Mosaic. And somewhere around the time that Microsoft announced Windows 95's imminent release, much of the Mosaic team moved west to commercialize the graphical browser idea as Netscape Communications.

We saw the influence that the Netscape IPO had on the Internet's emergence from a sleepy research project to a global information infrastructure and how all those initial hopes were dashed somewhere between Bill Gates's Pearl Harbor Day speech in 1995 and AOL's acquisition of Netscape in 1998 (chapter 4). The browser wars tell the story of what happened in between, of how Sun Microsystems was dragged into the mess, and of how, above all, Microsoft stayed true to its nature and squelched this most dangerous of all middleware threats.

All middleware threatens platform owners because middleware is inherently ephemeral. The natural process of software evolution will eventually migrate selected middleware into the platform to define a next-generation translation frontier. But middleware has yet another feature that scares platform owners. Middleware can translate platform

APIs into a foreign language. What's more, if the middleware developer decides to learn several different platform APIs, she can turn her middleware into a universal translator. If an ISV learns the middleware's APIs, and the middleware knows how to speak to multiple platforms, the middleware's potential market will necessarily be larger than those of any of the platforms. Rational application developers will learn the middleware's APIs—and the middleware will define the largest, most valuable network.

Netscape's Navigator was a Web browser that ran on top of any platform—Windows, Mac, Unix, or other. Sun's Java was a programming language that allowed application developers to write programs that ran on top of Navigator. Together, they provided a comfortable, flexible, programming environment in which ISVs could develop new applications without learning the Windows APIs. The threat to Microsoft was obvious.

Microsoft met the challenge with some intense strategic thinking. The first stage was tried-and-true. Microsoft threatened OEMs who offered consumers access to the new exciting middleware. But OEMs were only one of Navigator's distribution channels. So Microsoft expanded its strong-arm tactics to ISPs, Web developers, and virtually anyone else in the software or computing industries. Strong-arming alone helped Microsoft foreclose most of Navigator's obvious and attractive distribution channels. None of this was possible in Manifestoland.

Microsoft knew that stage one was only temporary. After all, if consumers really wanted the new middleware, they'd find it somewhere; Microsoft couldn't keep Navigator off the market entirely. What more could Microsoft do with the wondrous IP rights granted by *our* Congress but denied to the citizens of Manifestoland? Microsoft could introduce incompatibilities to prevent the middleware from running on its platform, but that easily could backfire. Anything that confuses middleware developers is also likely to confuse ISVs—precisely the souls and minds that Microsoft was fighting to keep. Furthermore, consumers may chase truly exciting middleware all the way to a competing platform; exciting new technology is precisely the sort of disruption that induces consumers to eat their switching costs. If consumers all migrate to competing platforms running the middleware, Microsoft would risk not only losing its monopoly, but also the bulk of its customers. That's how a market leader slides into oblivion.

Microsoft would have to do something bolder with the short time it gained by blocking distribution channels. Microsoft needed to develop a competing product. But its product had to perform the same tasks as Navigator, while running only—or at the very least, most efficiently—on Windows. And then Microsoft had to go one step further, for the threat to Windows would remain as long as platform-independent middleware persisted. Microsoft would have to drive Netscape from the market. Microsoft had to drive its smaller competitor's profits so low that Netscape couldn't develop a sustainable business model. And that, Microsoft knew how to do. If Microsoft drove its own price down to zero, Netscape would have to either match it or forego most of its sales. Either way, in this game of mutually assured destruction, the richer party always wins.

But what if, somehow, Navigator was better than Microsoft's competing Internet Explorer? What if it were so much better that people were willing to pay a premium for it—a large enough premium for Netscape to stay in business. Well, then Microsoft would have to override the gospel of software engineering and forego modular, evolutionary design. Microsoft would have to elevate marketing strategy over the imperatives of sound product design. In violation of all the basic tenets of software development, Microsoft could launch this complex new function as an integrated part of its platform.

Any consumer who purchased Windows—which would be almost everybody—would already possess Navigator's basic functionality. Few would be willing to search out the few odd distribution points to get even a superior realization of these same functions, sold at a price capable of sustaining a small, standalone company with high product-development costs. Internet Explorer didn't even have to be *good* when Microsoft launched it. It only had to be passable. At trial, the government established that Microsoft employed all of these leveraging strategies to destroy Navigator and Java, two of the most exciting and innovative software products of the 1990s.

Meanwhile, back in Manifestoland, poor Musoft couldn't even foreclose a distribution channel. It actually had to compete *on the merits of its products*. But Musoft wasn't the only software company in Manifestoland forced to make a choice. Its upstart middleware competitor Netscope also had to decide whether it wanted IP rights or trade secret protection. As a small firm with a single product, Netscope chose to protect its only revenue source—product sales. Netscope revealed its source code to the public in exchange for a brief browser monopoly. When it took that deal, Musoft was stuck. Musoft couldn't launch a browser without violating Netscope's IP rights. Netscope, rather than Musoft, gained the time window in which to entrench its technology. And once Netscope's source code became both public and popular, *all* platform developers, including Musoft, would ensure that their platforms worked well with Netscope's middleware browser.

The story of Musoft's development in Manifestoland demonstrates how Microsoft, doing nothing but being true to its nature and using the rights that congressional IP policy gave it, maintained its monopoly position at the expense of consumer welfare. It shows that the wrong IP rights in the wrong hands can truly be dangerous. And yet, neither the DoJ, Judge Jackson, nor anyone else spent much time talking about Microsoft's IP arsenal. Microsoft had devised a tactically brilliant strategy designed to maximize its profits. And it was able to enact this strategy in large part because of the IP rights that Congress had authorized—allegedly to motivate innovation.

These rights have led to an unfortunate public strategy. We've effectively decided to offer software developers a powerful combination of patent, copyright, and trade-secret protection, to instruct those developers not to misuse those rights by violating the antitrust laws, to watch them behave like rational corporations, and then to conduct massive, expensive, politically charged, time-consuming trials. Is such a strategy necessary? Or might a Musoft, given only the weaker rights of Manifestoland, have equaled—or even surpassed—Microsoft's levels of innovation? If so, the Manifesto's IP bargain would probably have given us a software industry—and a broad information sector—even more vibrant than the one that we have today, and we the consumers could all be enjoying even greater levels of entertainment and productivity at a fraction of the cost.

We the People

OEMs and other distributors. Application developers and ISVs. Potential competitors. That leaves only one critical set of relationships to consider: the platform monopolists' relationships with *us*. Musoft and Microsoft both sell their products to the public. They must each spend part of their time worrying about their relationships with consumers. And if we're to believe the government and the courts, Microsoft's various attempts to leverage its monopoly from the desktop to the Internet harmed consumers. How do we feel about that? And would we feel any differently if we could glimpse the alternative scenario in Manifestoland?

Our considerations as consumers are more or less the flip side of the corporate drive toward profit maximization. As software consumers, we're the end users who pay for platforms developed and priced under the IP laws. Our platform developers price their products as a relatively small component of a total system that combines hardware, a platform, applications, training, support, and service. Over in Manifestoland, platforms are free because Musoft opted out of the IP system—but consumers do pay more for training, support, service, warranty contracts, and at least some applications.

The indirect impact of the different IP regimes here and in Manifestoland is likely to be more profound than a bit of a pricing differential. It's likely to alter the entire structure of relationships throughout the industry—and thus the very nature of the industry. Musoft's inability to restrict distribution channels would lead to a radically different power balance between Musoft and OEMs than between Microsoft and OEMs. As a result, Musoft would be unable to extract many monopolistic terms and conditions from other vendors in the supply chain. As we've already seen, the likely outcomes of this industry restructuring would include an increase in consumer choice, an increase in competition, a change in the rate at which a de facto standard is adopted, a reduction in incentives to platform development, and a consequent possible reduction in platform innovation—quite likely a net win for consumers.

Were we to try some sort of Manifesto-like reform and decide that while it cleared up some existing problems, it created others, that hardly would be either shocking or disastrous. Reform doesn't have to be all or nothing. If reform points us in a good direction but still needs a bit of tweaking, by all means, let's tweak it. It would be naive to believe that our first broad-brush pass at a reform as complex as software IP rights could be correct in all of its specifics. If we ever attempt radical reform, we have to recognize our first try as the *start* of a new process amenable to corrective tinkering, *not* as the endpoint in our reform efforts. The Manifesto's proposal would uproot our value calculations from their current locale and land them in a radically different place. We'd undoubtedly need a few incremental steps to move from that new place to a societal optimum. Foreseeable potential disasters, say a possible reduction in platform innovation, suggest areas in which we should monitor empirical evidence and consider moderate patches.

These issues are particularly thorny because society's relationship with platform developers focused on network economics is rather complex, and it's hard to separate the value that the developer places on direct revenues from those that it places on long-term control. The Manifesto's proposal, if adopted, might clear up many of the existing antitrust problems without deterring innovation or retarding progress. On the other hand, it might simply shift the tension from anticompetitive behavior to the inadequacy of IP rights, thereby necessitating a round of tinkering following a radical reform. It's also possible that political transition costs will render any radical reform untenable. Many people believe that regulated industries tend to "capture" the agencies that regulate them, often to the point that regulation stops serving the public. If we chose to implement IP reform by creating numerous agencies, each with industry-specific responsibilities, we might fall into that same trap. But again, that's something to watch for when we make our implementation decisions—and we're nowhere near that yet.

We the people are not a particularly radical bunch. If we wanted to establish a more perfect information sector and establish justice, we'd turn first to the voices of moderation. Fundamental reform in this country *never* happens before we hit a crisis. We'd never try something radical—like redoing our IP system from scratch—to avoid a looming crisis. We've consistently demonstrated our aversion to radical reform with health care, with energy, with taxation, with security, and with privacy rights. We certainly won't start radical reform with IP. Manifestos may be fun to talk about in academia, but out here in the real world they look more than a little risible. Fortunately, though, the humor dissipates if we look at central messages rather than at specifics. The essence of the Manifesto's proposal lies in the idea that *no one* should have IP protection for something that they're not willing to share with the rest of us. Now, that's hardly a radical claim. It's simply a return to the Constitution's desire to promote both progress and knowledge; secrecy may promote progress, but it's singularly ill-equipped to advance scientific knowledge

How would that observation play with the more moderate reform voices—and what might it be able to tell us about dealing with Microsoft? Some opponents of the deal that Microsoft cut with the DoJ floated "compulsory licensing" at Judge Kollar-Kotelly's Tunney Act hearing. Under a compulsory licensing regime, Microsoft would have to put its products on the market, announce their price, and let anyone and everyone willing to pay the price take the product. While that might not seem to be much of a concession, compelling Microsoft to offer such licenses to its APIs would curtail its ability to strong-arm OEMs. This solution—like a similar compulsory licensing scheme gaining popularity among observers of digital entertainment—splits distribution rights from compensation. Everyone would continue to pay Microsoft for Windows, but Microsoft would lose its ability to control distribution, to bestow favors, and to punish competitors. Now, that's not a bad idea. It represents a step toward changing Microsoft's incentives and abilities, and it's strikingly similar to one of the more promising reforms proposed to restructure the music industry. But it does present problems. While it's certainly less complicated than a structural remedy, it requires the courts to do more than a bit of monitoring. So while a compulsory license may be a good idea, we probably could do better.

Misuse remedies, whether of the well-accepted patent variety or the more avant-garde copyright variety, tell a rights holder who misused its property rights by harming a related market to fix that market—and not to bother suing anyone for infringement until the market has been fixed.

Could the government apply a misuse remedy to Microsoft? After all, Microsoft would undoubtedly complain—with some justification—that it was simply using the IP rights that the government gave it. It seems unfair to take away IP rights, *property*, just because the owner misused them. Behavioral remedies tell monopolists how to use their property more responsibly, which is why behavioral remedies are generally preferable. But behavioral modification can't fix markets that have suffered irreparable damage. Those markets need more draconian remedies, and misuse remedies fit the bill. And the government *can* impose them. Microsoft cited its "unfettered liberty" to use its IP rights as it saw fit numerous times. But the Supreme Court said way back in 1917 that a monopolist's liberty to use its IP rights is *not* unfettered, and can constitute misuse.[10] What's more, the Supreme Court also has explained that a monopolist who misuses patents to violate the antitrust laws risks losing those patents, even if it never defended its anticompetitive actions as the legitimate exercise of its property rights.[11] There's no reason to treat misused copyrights any differently. Microsoft has misused the entire portfolio of IP rights protecting Windows, and thereby put all of those rights at risk.

Misuse remedies may fix the software market—if not now, then someday, during one of those future Microsoft trials lurking just around the corner. A misuse remedy applied to Windows' entire IP portfolio would accomplish a few things. First, Microsoft would find itself holding a valuable trade secret of platform source code shorn of IP rights, which is exactly what Musoft had over in Manifestoland. And we've already seen that Manifestoland's IP rights create a better situation for everyone but Musoft. Second, had the courts imposed a misuse remedy in 2001, Windows XP never would have integrated middleware like a media player and an instant messenger. After all, had they remained independent modular applications dangling off the edge of the translation frontier, Microsoft would have retained its IP rights. If Microsoft chose to integrate them into the platform, it would have lost those rights. WMP would thus remain an application, and it would compete *on its merits*, win or lose.

But misuse remedies are not without potential downsides. When applied only after the fact to abused software, they can wreak havoc on the translation frontier's natural evolution. The same forces that motivate Microsoft to avoid integrating functionality into Windows prematurely also could motivate it to avoid integrating mature functions into the platform. We could actually miss an appropriate evolutionary stage in the platform's development. But eventually, things would probably correct themselves, Microsoft would regain its IP rights over some future platform, and the technology would get back to where it should have been. The question then is whether the risk of incurring this potential problem is worth the cost of imposing the misuse remedy. It seems to me that it is.

From a more pragmatic perspective, though, misuse remedies pose another problem. Much of the government's support—and many of its witnesses—came from tech companies, most of whom have pretty substantial IP portfolios. Part of the sociology of litigation is that many lawyers feel that today's new case is exactly like the story on the front page of today's newspaper. The Microsoft trial led to an increase in tying claims and maintenance of monopoly claims—not a problem if the claims are legitimate, but a thorn in the side of defendants dealing with nuisance claims when they aren't. If the court imposed a misuse remedy on Microsoft, it would hit the front pages, make it to the Supreme Court, and lead to a rash of misuse suits against anyone and everyone in the tech sector. So the companies urging the government to curb Microsoft's power might have been more than a bit squeamish about pushing a misuse remedy into the public view.[12]

So there you have it. The radical Manifesto let us glimpse a world in which software companies would have to choose between IP rights and trade secret protection—but reminded us that to get there, we'd have to redo our IP system. The more moderate voice of misuse remedies suggested that we might be able to restrict that choice to rights holders who misused their IP. In other words, if a future court once again decides that Microsoft has leveraged its monopoly from one generation of the translation frontier to the next, it can call upon the priests of IP to bless its misuse remedy. And that might be the best way to restore competition and to protect consumers.

Then again, the open-source movement contributed its own ideas. We still don't know just how radical a restructuring open-source software could impose on the information sector. As we've seen, a large part of the answer may lie in government action. Governments who adopt open-source infrastructures increase the probability of a positive impact. The proliferation of software patents or court rulings that invalidate key open-source license terms decrease its likelihood of having any impact. But in the final analysis, open source is only part of the story. Because while it may restructure software, it's not clear what impact it will have across the rest of the information sector. And as the record companies and movie studios could tell you, we seem to run into new problems each time the information sector extends its reach across another industry.

The record companies and movie studios also could tell you that those problems seem to be pushing us toward splitting compensation from control. This split's power is that it continues to reward *production*, but refuses to reward obsolete approaches to *distribution*. It promises to direct innovation toward harnessing new technologies rather than toward reimposing transaction costs that technology can eliminate. Though entertainment-industry incumbents may lament the loss of tried-and-true business models, they nevertheless hear this critical message of the information age. This message is well worth remembering whenever we contemplate IP reform—and whenever the information sector swallows yet another industry and threatens to disenfranchise its incumbent, powerful distributors. IP laws that push innovators to harness technology will serve us well; those that push innovators to deter technology serve us ill.

One way or another, the transition from an industrial age to an information age will force us reconsider the relationships among IP policy, IP law, innovation, competition, scientific knowledge, and consumer welfare. Have we harmed ourselves? If we gave Microsoft the weapons with which to violate the antitrust laws—in the form of needlessly strong IP rights—we were complicit in our own anguish. And if we were, it certainly doesn't let Microsoft off the hook, but it does tell us how to avoid getting hurt again. If we want corporations to innovate and to maximize profits without disturbing the market's natural competitive forces, perhaps we should give them the tools they need to innovate and to maximize profits—but deprive them of the weapons most useful in disturbing markets. That would be a great form of consumer protection, and not too shabby for shareholders, either—at least for the shareholders of innovative companies other than the monopolist. The bottom line, though, is that if we don't want monopolists to destroy competitive markets or to harm consumers, we must disarm them.

Our trip down the rabbit hole has thus taught us a new way to think about lubricating the economy. Distributors in the information sector will invariably try to use IP law to preserve existing transaction costs. At times, we may agree to preserve those costs. But we don't have to accept their arguments carte blanche. We always should consider alternative proposals, all within the appropriate constitutional framework for IP policy: grant only those rights necessary to promote the progress of science and useful arts.

9

Sand in the Vaseline

Wind of Change

The public infrastructure of the information age could arise through a series of informed decisions. It could also arise haphazardly, through our inattention. But either way, it will develop within a context set by our education, labor, security, defense, and economic policies. Its critical defining feature, though, will remain IP policy.

Our private sector entrepreneurs will adjust and accommodate themselves to whatever public infrastructure we develop. These twin economic pillars then will work together to determine the future. Our prospects for success in the information age will rest upon the combination of public infrastructure and private entrepreneurship. And our approaches to both will rest upon the lessons that we take away from the first, bubble-driven stage of our information economy.

During the bubble, the tech sector's innovation and entrepreneurship blew a wind of change across the economy, a change whose ripples are working their way throughout our broader social and political worlds. Microsoft, Intel, Cisco, and AOL emerged from nowhere to join the ranks of the world's most important (and for a while, its most valuable) companies; a cottage industry of dot-coms emerged to emulate them. We learned—slowly and painfully—that their initial flashiness was unsustainable. We came to appreciate the misdirection that led us to believe first that we could leave Microsoft's rights, abilities, and motives intact yet still hope to change its behavior, and second that entrepreneurs could recreate those rights, abilities, and motives easily throughout the New World of the Internet. We invested substantial public resources to restrain

Microsoft's drive to stifle innovation that it couldn't direct through Windows, and substantial private resources chasing the inevitable monopolists who would become the next Microsoft. And though we did gain some measure of restraint over Microsoft's behavior, and we did uncover a few Internet gems, the returns on our investments continue to disappoint. For the most part, we invested in a very expensive education.

We learned some lessons long known in various academic disciplines, but rarely combined—and never before tested in such intricately inter-woven real-world patterns. We learned of network economics and of evo-lutionary software. We learned of antitrust and IP. But mostly, we learned the lesson that Coase had preached decades ago: reductions in transac-tion costs lubricate the economy. They help us move money, informa-tion, and goods to where they're most valuable—and most useful. That was the key lesson of the Internet's youth. We thought that it would make us all rich as investors. We learned instead that it would enrich us pri-marily as consumers.

Armed with that knowledge, we saw information-sector innovators realize that this lubricated world enabled new modes of production and of distribution. Hackers exchanged information freely to form a global bazaar culture. An invisible hand from Helsinki emerged from that chaotic bazaar to develop a robust, powerful product at a mere fraction of the cost of any reasonable competitor. Meanwhile, the pioneers of digital music developed an equally chaotic, yet even more efficient, dis-tribution model. With but a few tweaks to existing technology, they built a global network of peers capable of enriching each other in a virtually cost-free environment. Those experiences led to our next set of lessons. If consumers win, someone must lose. A lubricated world is hardly a perfect world. And though transaction costs always slow us down, many of them exist for valid reasons—reasons that provide us with margins of safety and security, and that serve a number of important policy objectives.

Some transaction costs exist for technological reasons alone. When technology improves, we remove the transaction costs and benefit as con-sumers. The interstate highway system, for example, was a 1950s lubricant that made it easier and cheaper to move goods around the country. Consumers gained, as prices fell and variety rose—all thanks to technological improvements. The government's investment of our tax dollars in that particular bit of infrastructure has paid dividends many times over. Few of us even bother to consider what life might be like without adequate roads. Others are not quite so lucky.

People who actually live and work in countries with rotten infrastructure have to cope with the consequences every day. These are as profound as they are malign. So to investigate how bad roads make life harder, [the article's author] hitched a ride on a beer truck in Cameroon, a pleasant, peaceful and humid country in the corner of the Gulf of Guinea.... The plan was to carry 1,600 crates of Guinness and other drinks from the factory in Douala where they were brewed to Bertoua, a small town in Cameroon's south-eastern rainforest. As the crow flies, this is less than 500km (313 miles)—about as far as from New York to Pittsburgh, or London to Edinburgh. According to a rather optimistic schedule, it should have taken 20 hours, including an overnight rest. It took four days. When the truck arrived, it was carrying only two-thirds of its original load....[1]

The ultimate lesson is that "there is no substitute for building and maintaining better infrastructure. In some areas, such as telecoms, private firms will do the work if allowed to.... The private sector does not, however, spontaneously provide roads, because the beneficiaries cannot easily be charged."[2] Sometimes collective action is the only way to cut transaction costs. Government investment in such circumstances is critical. The private sector only can take over after the infrastructure is in place. Entrepreneurship unleashed into the wild will falter; entrepreneurship unleashed into a supportive environment will soar. One of the greatest lessons that the information sector has already taught us is that minds freed from thinking about infrastructure will innovate, advance, and improve society. The removal of technological transaction costs always will make us richer.

Other transaction costs exist to serve public policy. These costs are artificial, imposed as a matter of law. Our securities laws, for example, limit the ways that corporations can raise capital to pursue innovative projects. Though these laws undoubtedly delay, deter, and increase the costs of launching many valuable ventures, they also delay and deter huge amounts of fraud. Yet another painful lesson of our years as tech investors was that we might need more—not less—of such grit in our financial system. The information sector taught us that lesson, too.

The truly perplexing transaction costs exist for reasons of *both* law and technology. The wide and varied world of e-commerce reveals the vestiges of many such combinations—markets in which our new technologies have reduced information costs, yet laws and policies force them to remain in place. Every major automobile manufacturer, for example, offers customized cars on the Web. You can do everything at their sites except buy a car. The site will direct you to a local dealer because state laws prohibit the direct sale of automobiles from manufacturers to drivers. These are old laws, put on the books to protect local auto dealers, often among the wealthiest and most influential business leaders in fragile local economies. Legislatures likely passed these laws when direct sales seemed important to neither automobile companies nor consumers. Certain transaction costs were inherent in the distribution of automobiles, and a network of franchised dealers seemed to be a reasonable distribution model. But technology has improved, and direct sales today could almost certainly remove many costs—leading to appreciably lower prices for consumers and increased sales for producers. Yet the laws remain in place, a vestige of another era.

Do we want such transaction costs to remain? Or do we want to reform the laws that impose them? After all, these laws harm consumers and producers. Then again, we didn't pass these particular laws to help either consumers or producers. They served other interests, namely local businesses. Sound public policy balances the concerns of different interest groups to enhance overall societal welfare. Some policies serve consumers, some producers, some distributors, some local businesses, etc. Nothing is inherently wrong in striking a balance among interest groups—as long as we do it intelligently and intentionally. The ban on direct auto sales may have been a good deal when we adopted it. Consumers and producers lost little; local businesses gained stability. But technology may have changed the equation. If consumers and producers are now sacrificing more than local businesses are gaining, it's a bad deal. We'd be much better off finding a different way to help local businesses—or more importantly, to help the people who rely on those businesses for their welfare and their livelihood.

Transitions always impose pain. Transition management may be the toughest challenge that the information sector poses as it eats more and more industries; it's easier to lubricate some parts of our economy than others. The information sector long ago ate our financial system. We can move money around the world with the click of a mouse. We can move information outlining our tastes and desires as quickly and as easily. We can shift our investments from tech to autos to pharmaceuticals to retail and back to tech. We can ship packages nationwide overnight, and throughout the developed world almost as quickly. We've built an efficient, well-lubricated economy. Except for one little item. We still don't know how to move people efficiently. We are sand in the Vaseline.[3] Moving workers or jobs from tech to autos to pharmaceuticals to retail and back to tech is just not possible—at least not at anything like the speed that we'd need to keep up with the rapid drift of finances and resources. We must develop ways to lubricate our networks of human capital as efficiently as we've lubricated our networks of financial capital.

Therein lies the key to successful transition management. Our skill at meeting this challenge will determine how well we navigate the transition to an information economy—and even further to an information society. We must develop a "human capital infrastructure" that maximizes every person's potential, that keeps every person engaged in lifelong learning, that helps every person make the most productive use of his or her skills, and that relocates people comfortably to facilitate that productive use. Our current thinking about education addresses the needs of a liberal democratic republic with an industrial economy. In earlier ages, most people were illiterate; they trained as apprentices, often in family businesses. Concepts of universal literacy and of widespread elementary and secondary education arose only with the growth of liberalism and industrialization. We must rethink our approach for the information age. We must transcend the notion of public investment in educating *children* to begin investing fully in educating *citizens*. Education, training, and labor mobility are the lifeblood of the information age. We need to cut transaction costs in these areas as surely as we do in all of the others. Our transition will be complete only when we have devised appropriate models and invested enough to develop a full-blown human-capital infrastructure. And that's no task for the squeamish.

Gilded Cages

Our first few tales of the information sector were little more than heralds of things to come. We are in the early stages of a full-blown transition to the information age. The challenges facing our software and music industries will be but the first of many. They'll only become tougher as the information sector takes bigger and bigger bites out of the traditional economy. Proprietary software vendors try to combine leverage and IP rights to slow the spread of open-source software—reintroducing transaction costs eliminated by a lower-cost development model. The entertainment industry uses IP rights, and legislation designed to safeguard those rights, to slow the spread of more efficient means of distribution. In both instances, the incumbents claim that the transaction costs exist to serve an important public policy. In the absence of adequate IP rights protecting software and recorded music, they claim, we would have less software and less music, and what we'd get would be of lower quality. They may be right. After all, that was the reason that we granted them those rights to begin with.

Then again, they may be wrong. After all, the transaction costs that enabled their business models always combined technological and legal barriers. The costs that consumers bore in granting the legal rights were only the costs that the laws added over the technology. But as technological barriers plummeted, the laws that grew to replace them became more and more expensive. Incumbents intent upon preserving their revenue streams in light of these reduced barriers clamor for increasingly intrusive laws imposing increasingly expensive transaction costs. Legislators often accede to their pleas without analyzing the costs they impose. There's no way for us to know whether we're still getting a good deal—or whether we're overpaying by a considerable amount—without reconsidering the inherent costs and benefits.

But as in any policy debate, winners—or at least some particularly vocal winners who have fared well with reduced technological barriers—would like to take all. Some Napster backers, for example, insist that record companies have *no* legitimate rights, despite Congress's decision to protect their IP. That can't be right. Even in the absence of distribution, the record companies add tremendous value to their products—at a bare minimum in the areas of scouting, selecting, producing, and branding musical acts. We need to motivate innovation in these arenas, as well. We may still need some legal transaction costs, even in an era of plummeting technological barriers. Finding the right balance, though, will take some work. And it will undoubtedly lie somewhere between insisting that profit streams remain untouched by technology and insisting that once-important policy goals have become irrelevant.

The software and entertainment businesses may prove to be among the industries best suited to weather this transition. Their leading corporations are wealthy, diverse, and geographically dispersed. Their workers are better educated than average, technologically adept, and already comfortable in the information sector. Their management has navigated changes to both technology and business models before. They have high public profiles. Government pays attention to them. Above all, they know that their existing business models are living on borrowed time. And so they adapt.

Traditional software companies are reconciling themselves to open-source development, and some, like IBM and Sun, have become ardent supporters. Growing segments of the music industry are coming to recognize—grudgingly—that their future may lie in relinquishing their distribution rights and retaining only their rights to compensation and attribution. They're exploring new "digital rights management" (DRM) technologies, and seeking viable ways to develop subscription-based services. When Microsoft's integration of WMP into Windows XP included DRM technologies keyed to its own proprietary format, WMA (rather than to the MP3 open standard), some of the record labels approved. When Apple launched a subscription-based streaming music service for Macintosh and iPod users, the record labels approved. When Roxio raised Napster from the dead and incorporated a revenue model, the record labels approved. It may be a while before we can get a fair reading of long-term fan reaction to any of these developments—or the others that are certain to follow. But an increasing amount of smart money seems to believe that music may soon become a utility; music fans may soon receive a monthly bill in exchange for the right to hear whatever they want whenever they want it. We may yet see that much-vaunted, long predicted, celestial jukebox.[4]

The revolution in information-sector business models may run even deeper. Many recent media mergers[5] were designed to marry conduit to content, essentially betting that in the near future, content no longer will be king, and royalties will flow primarily to those capable of delivery. Many software companies, including Microsoft, Oracle, and other open-source opponents, foresee a similar future for themselves under the "application systems provider" (ASP) model. ASPs are service providers, not software sales forces. ASPs offer their customers access to software residing on their own servers via high-speed connections. Customers pay monthly subscription fees for the service. Software, like music, may soon join electricity, gas, water, and telephony as ubiquitous monthly utility bills.[6]

The notion of music as a utility would mark a radical departure for the record companies. While many hurdles still remain, this utility model promises to employ legal rights that work *with* technology, not against it. It appears to be a business model well suited to the music industry of the future. But it takes a certain amount of courage for the record companies even to contemplate it. After all, it's hard to tell whether their profits will grow or shrink once the transition is complete. As a result, if we want them to adopt it—or to adopt some alternative model that modifies IP rights so that they reinforce technology and motivate innovation—we may want to think about ways to ease the transition, not to mention to compensate the existing rights holders for the rights that they'll have to relinquish.

But that's just part of transition management. The true key lies in recognizing that it's in the enlightened self-interest of a transition's putative winners to compensate its putative losers. Our economy becomes "more efficient" when it grows. But even though society as a whole wins when the economic pie gets bigger, not all of society's members win. Those poised to lose will understandably fight to prevent generally beneficial changes. If the pie is truly bigger, though, no one should have to lose. In an ideal transition, the economic pie will grow, society as a whole will gain, some members of society will win overtly, and *no one* will lose— possibly because the overt winners will compensate putative losers.[7] But not all forms of compensation are equally appropriate. Programs that help people adjust to the future are much better than those that help them cling to the past. Investments in education, training, employment counseling, and relocation assistance are critical.

The past few generations have witnessed a number of painful transitions; we've handled some more smoothly than others. The United States began as an agrarian nation, and the family farm still plays a uniquely important role in American mythology and in the American psyche. It does not, however, play an important role in the American economy. Family farms stopped being economically viable in the developed world decades ago. Small farms tend to do fine in good years. But as soon as weather conditions either curtail production (driving volumes down) or lead to an unusually bountiful harvest (driving prices down) they teeter on the verge of insolvency. Large corporate agribusinesses diversify their farming across so many different crops in so many different parts of the world that they can always sustain themselves. Family farms can support only a few crops in a single weather zone. Were it not for government subsidies, family farms in the developed world would have become a memory long ago. The Europeans, though far worse in this respect than the United States, have at least begun to discuss the problem. In the summer of 2003, the EU floated a proposal to replace production subsidies with income subsidies—in other words, to support its farmers without damaging the market. Perhaps someday, they will go the entire way towards paying their farmers—and their farmers' children—to retrain and relocate, so that the problem of the inefficient European family farm recedes into history, where it belongs. In the meantime, though the proposal was noble, action seems unlikely to follow.[8]

All of us in the developed world must ask ourselves: Are we really helping these family farmers? Are these direct subsidies a good form of transitional assistance? It may be true that our subsidies help middle-aged and elderly farmers live out the life that they know and love—and keep the myth alive. That's all for the good. But what of their children? Is it fair to trap today's children in that same life, destined to remain reliant on government subsidies? Wouldn't we be better off helping them adjust to the modern age? Shouldn't we emphasize education and skills that will help them contribute to the future? Shouldn't we help them relocate to wherever the greatest opportunities exist? Programs like these would help the children of today's farmers have better futures; instead, we just trap them on the farm.

To make matters worse, our "helping" subsidies also create two other problems. We're giving large parts of our farm subsidies to wealthy agribusinesses that neither need it nor deserve it, and we're making things harder for people who *can* run economically viable small farms—primarily in the developing world. And lest you think that agricultural subsidies have little to do with the information sector, bear in mind that our global economic network connects all sectors. In the Uruguay Round of trade negotiations leading to the founding of the World Trade Organization (WTO), the developed and developing worlds struck a deal. The developing world would respect IP rights and "trade in services," and the developed world would reduce its agricultural subsidies. But only half of the deal bore fruit—and it wasn't the agricultural half. Much of the developing world is now obliged to enforce the rights that allow our information industries to extend their global reach, yet we accepted few reciprocal obligations.

Subsidies supporting vestigial forms of agriculture serve as a poignant example of a transition that we should have managed better. Instead, we fell into a trap that only can be attributed to our best intentions and our sense of justice. It seems unfair that technological advances run amok should upend anyone who means well, works hard, and relies on long-standing expectations. Often, we express our sympathy by trying to lock their expectations in place. Such sympathetic lock-in is a trap.[9] *Every* transition produces people whose plans are dashed and whose incomes collapse despite hard work and exceptional skill. While it's not fair, and it offends our sense of justice, the most obvious fix—legislating their incomes in place—inevitably leads down a path towards even greater injustice. It locks us all in and impedes our growth.

Already we can see the battle lines forming over the next set of transition issues. Though we as workers may be sand in the Vaseline, unable to reorient our skill or to relocate quickly enough to keep up with the flows of other resources, our jobs are becoming increasingly mobile. By late 2003, people began to notice that even service-sector jobs, once considered safe from offshore outsourcing, were losing that immunity.[10] Our information-sector entrepreneurs not only were learning how to turn production industries into service industries, they were learning how to increase their efficiency by relocating those service industries.

As always, advocates of two extreme positions scream loudest about this newly noticed phenomenon. One pole insists that the trend is healthy, and that the economy will eventually create more new jobs than it loses. This argument is correct, but it ignores the significant pain of transition. The other pole features shrill protectionist rhetoric, promising to lock workers into their present dead-end jobs. Such policies would serve as a short-term palliative while recreating the unfortunate consequences of our farm policy. They would trap American workers in dead-end jobs while deterring or delaying the developing world's liberalization. As the years go by, these protectionist policies would require us to work ever harder to keep ourselves ever poorer—as restrictions on free trade always do.

Neither approach can solve the underlying problem. Our remarkable infrastructure investments over the past few decades have taught us how to move finances, physical objects, information, and increasingly jobs, much more quickly than we can reallocate workers and skills. Those who would do nothing are content to wait for workers and skills to catch up on their own. Those who favor barriers would slow the reallocation of all resources to the speed of labor. The intelligent solution is to find infrastructure investments that improve our labor mobility. Investments in retraining and relocation, tying unemployment benefits to skill acquisition, encouraging immigration, and helping employers and employees find each other, are all likely to be critical. And though these investments may be expensive up front and may generate tax burdens and/or deficits that some would prefer not to bear, they are critical to maintaining our world leadership. The nation that best invests in this next great infrastructure development will dominate the twenty-first century—and the rest of the information age.

We need to navigate our ongoing transition to the information age wisely. But transitions raise tough questions that we'd prefer to avoid. Sound transition management requires investments that we might prefer not to make. We've gotten used to the way things are, and it often seems cheaper in the short run to prop them in place. We recognize people's interests in the status quo, and gild their cages to trap them into environments and business models that will never again succeed. We do it with farming. We do it with steel. We do it with textiles and sugar and mohair and who knows what else. If some have their way, we'll be doing it soon with music, with movies, with software—maybe even with garage-door openers. And it won't stop there. We must avoid this trap as the information sector continues swallowing broad swaths of the economy. Our spending on education, training, employment, and relocation must increase. Our labor markets must become as lubricated as our financial markets. Because when they do, we'll all become richer.

And yet, we're already falling into the same old trap. We noticed IP rights eroding and advocated technological solutions to promote encryption and data security. Then we noticed that crackers could circumvent such technology, so we passed an anticircumvention provision. Then we realized that people might be willing to figure civil penalties into the cost of doing business, so we criminalized circumvention. All to help companies protect antiquated business models that limit the benefits that we can reap from technological advancement. People on the inside clamor for stronger protection. Every time technology reduces a transaction cost, they want more gilding. And every time that we accede, they retreat even further into an unsustainable business model—and we lose part of our ability to explore and to innovate. Yet, while some of the current players in those industries probably wouldn't make the transition successfully if we uncaged them, it's not at all clear that the industries as a whole wouldn't soar in the clear skies of the information sector.

Falling into the trap of favoring lock-in over growth in easy. Incumbent distributors are established entities, often boasting strong political connections, seeking to protect identifiable interests. Lock-in serves them well. Growth, and in particular network growth, is nebulous, and its benefits are diffuse. Growth serves the broad public interest in ways that are typically hard to predict. The voices clamoring for lock-in are invariably vocal and powerful; those favoring growth are invariably diffuse and at times inaudible. And so, we adopt policies that sacrifice growth in favor of lock-in. Every now and then, we should ask ourselves who we're really helping—and at what cost.

The Thing with Feathers

The key to a successful transition lies in continued innovation. And innovative technological advancement thrives on hope. When hopes soar, imagination accepts few boundaries, what was once unimaginable becomes suddenly mundane, and technology advances in leaps and bounds. Those advances allow us to assume responsibility for more of the world's poor, to help make the poor richer, to make it easier for the poor to become the rich, and to encourage the rich to make themselves much richer. Everyone wins. In periods of hope, we manage to expand *both* opportunity and incentive. No better prescription exists for enhancing societal welfare as we undergo our transition to an information economy.

Every technological transformation has expanded opportunities and incentives and improved the overall human condition. Refrigeration, indoor plumbing, heating, air conditioning, medicine, food safety, and many other modern "necessities" began as luxurious hallmarks of wealth. They worked their way throughout society, reaching more and more people every year and every generation. At times, we even felt that these one-time luxuries had become so important that we accepted societal responsibility to make them universal. "Trickle down" theories are inevitable for long-term technology, if not for short-term economics. Recent scientific advances in the medical, agricultural, and information sciences may still cluster among the wealthiest societies' wealthiest members. But they'll eventually work their way downstream. The only question is at what speed. That's the true beauty of network economics. There's more than enough to go around. Expand opportunities and raise the floor. Expand incentives and raise the ceiling. They are emphatically *not* contradictory goals—at least not in the long-term. The broader our concept of societal responsibility, the higher we raise the floor, and the fewer constraints we put on the ceiling, the richer we *all* will become.

But these advances can flourish only in an environment of hope. Some work will be necessary to restore that hope, and the information sector is a fine place to look for guidance. As it broadens its reach, we must wonder how it will reshape society, beginning with industry and commerce, where its impact has been most pronounced. Though we know that the information sector reduces transaction costs, we've only seen those reductions in a few high-profile places. We need to consider what happens as increasing numbers of industries avail themselves of this new infrastructure channel. We must revisit the Internet to understand the New Channel paradigm. Because as New Channel thinking works its way throughout the economy, transaction costs will fall, we'll become a bit richer one transaction at a time, and we'll realize that there is plenty of cause for hope. The information sector can help us raise the floor, raise the ceiling, and let the luxuries of the ceiling become the necessities of the floor. And if we're lucky, they'll even trickle down on Internet time.

The key message of New Channel thinking is that *the Internet changes the economics of information*. Information that once was hard to find and expensive to collect became so cheap that it created the contemporary problem of information overload. The timeless challenge of collecting desirable information morphed almost overnight into the chore of discarding useless information. In the Internet-enabled world, collection is often (though not always) trivial, but finding a coherent story amidst a flood of data is trickier. Filtering has replaced collection as the key activity of information professionals.

By reducing information costs, the Internet provides a new way for firms to communicate with each other, with their customers, and with potential new customers—in short, a new channel important to commerce. Any other benefits of the Internet derive from this single enabling mechanism. Because information costs are a form of transaction costs, the Internet moves us closer to a transaction cost–free world. But though such a world might benefit consumers, it's not friendly to everyone. As distributors of both music and software could attest, reduced information costs can have their downsides. In fact, while this cost reduction introduces many new business opportunities, it also reduces consumer commitment and loyalty. If you discover how to use the Internet to deliver a product or a service more efficiently, consumers will insist that you give them the bulk of your savings in the form of lower prices. And they'll bail in droves if one of your competitors mimics your innovation and gives them a greater share of *his* savings. While it's easy to see how reduced information costs can help an Internet company *attract* customers, it's harder to see how this newly attractive entrant will *retain* them. A truly viable New Channel business plan must explain both to be worthy of investment. Such business plans are likely to be relatively rare.

As a result, we're unlikely to see a rapid, rampant restructuring of the industrial terrain. We are likely, however, to see intellectual ferment among normally staid managers in mature industries. Because the Internet changes the economics of information, they'll be forced to reassess a number of transaction types that once appeared unprofitable. For some, the lack of profitability may have arisen from the expense of collecting and/or disseminating information—in other words, a cost imposed by the limitations of information technology. In those instances, the Internet is likely to generate cost-saving efficiencies that render these transactions both viable and profitable. This change, in turn, will have a ripple effect on all other mechanisms that companies have long used to transact the business in question. Relative efficiencies, price/quality trade-offs, turnaround times, and the degree of customization may all come into play. Some existing channels may disappear, some may reduce their prices, some may integrate the Internet to form hybrid "brick-and-click" channels, and some may remain unchanged. Branding and first-mover advantage will be no more important than they have been in the physical world, Internet "spaces" will vary from those with few to those with many competitors, and network effects may be present but are unlikely to be widespread.

Changes in the economics of information change the relative merits of various types of transactions. Different industries will feel this effect in different ways.[11] In any industry, some companies may choose to rely exclusively on the Internet, others may ignore it, and still others will fall somewhere between these extremes. Each level of Internet usage will allow competing companies to offer a distinct level of service under a different cost structure. Consumers will then be free to choose among them. And that, in a nutshell, is the New Channel paradigm.

To apply this paradigm, we must realign the questions that we ask about the Internet. Bob Litan and Alice Rivlin got us started by chairing a two-day conference in September 2000 featuring early New Channel thinkers. Now, they probably didn't *know* that they were New

Channel thinkers; the significance of the paradigm shift may not yet have been clear. But whether or not they realized that their analyses were a radical departure from virtually everything that preceded them, they laid out many foundational questions of New Channel analysis:

• Is the [Inter]net just a new way to communicate—an alternative to phone or fax or airmail—and thus not likely to have a fundamental impact on the functioning of the economy?

• What does it mean for the importance of the Internet that investors were willing to pour billions into Internet companies with dubious earnings in the late 1990s only to find many of them virtually worthless by the end of 2000?

• Will the Internet prove to be a major economic phenomenon, significantly increasing productivity and enhancing the prosperity of average wage earners?

• Will the net alter the structure of industries and the size of companies, while enriching the variety of products and services available to consumers and their ease in obtaining them?[12]

Litan and Rivlin's study addressed the Internet's impact on the economy as a whole. But the key to that impact lies in understanding the behavior of people and companies that combine to generate that overall effect. Litan and Rivlin broke their questions open and asked each of eight contributing teams to address a distinct sector of the economy: manufacturing, automobiles, financial services, trucking, retail, health care, government, and higher education. By their estimate, these sectors collectively account for about seventy percent of U.S. GDP (gross domestic product, which was then around $10 trillion). Each team attempted to project annual savings from the new, more efficient business models that the Internet enabled. Litan and Rivlin concluded that it was highly realistic to expect the Internet to generate well-defined annual savings exceeding 0.25 percent of GDP (about $2.5 billion). More interesting than their numeric calculations, though, were their general conclusions—because they give us some insights into the types of questions to ask as we contemplate Internet business plans and investment opportunities.

• The *potential* of the Internet to enhance productivity growth over the next few years is real.

• Much of the impact of the Internet may not be felt in e-commerce per se, but in lower costs for quite mundane transactions that involve information flows—ordering, invoicing, filing claims, and making payments—across a wide range of existing "old economy" sectors, including health care and government.

• The Internet produces considerable scope for management efficiencies in product development, supply chain management, and a variety of other aspects of business performance.

• The Internet will enhance competition, both increasing efficiency and reducing profit margins throughout the economy, but the profit squeeze itself should not be counted as a productivity enhancement.

• The Internet is improving consumer convenience, increasing choices, and leading to other benefits that may not be readily measured, or if they are, may show up as productivity gains in industries or sectors other than those in which the savings may be initially generated.[13]

In other words, they only were able to measure some of the Internet's benefits. Of course, we already knew that; the benefits of infrastructure rarely show up anywhere measurable. They just change everything. If you run a business, you probably get monthly bills for electricity and telephones. These bills show up on your financial statements as costs. And they're *pure* costs. Your financial statement probably doesn't identify any specific benefits or revenues with electricity or telephones. So from a straight balance-sheet perspective, you'd be better off if you cut out costly frills like electricity or telephones. You'd be out of business, but at least your balance sheet would be clean.

The key message is that balance-sheet analyses don't apply to critical infrastructure. Yet even with that general caveat in place, Litan and Rivlin's teams still were able to find significant savings. The Internet may not generate a New World of inevitable monopolists, but it should generate enough savings and enough winners to reignite our hope in the future. Those winners are well worth looking for, and New Channel analysis will help us find them. And when we do, we're likely to find—as Litan and Rivlin did—that "[our] conclusions rest on a far firmer foundation than . . . the many (now defunct) dot.com firms that so populated the business landscape and garnered so much attention from the media only a short time ago."[14]

We're also likely to find ourselves back where we started, by noting that if you want to start a profitable company, you'd better be able to answer three questions: What's your product? What makes your product special? How are you going to use that "special quality" to generate profits? The first time we hit these questions, Tom Friedman heralded Lyle Bowlin as the David who would slay Goliath Amazon. Back when we thought of the Internet as a New World, it was just a cute story. Now that we see the Internet as a New Channel, we're going to have to come up with answers. Due diligence is back in style.

Of perhaps even greater importance than due diligence, however, is honest reflection. If we want the future to be better than the past, we must understand why the past unfolded as it did. The Internet investment bubble is an interesting story, but without a focus on the future it's just that: a story. It's easy to dismiss it as irrationality, exuberance, mania, alchemy, or simply a Ponzi scheme. All of those things may be true, but they're also incomplete. I'd hate to dismiss two years that changed the world as a case of America getting excited, greedy, and ultimately silly. I prefer to believe that it contained some important lessons about this still-new and intriguing medium known as the Internet.

The bubble *built* the Internet. We held a lottery using Web sites as tickets. While a few lucky winners became billionaires, we as a society emerged with a functioning commercial information infrastructure. We may have endured a roller coaster ride to get it, but in the long run we accomplished something long considered impossible: we developed infrastructure with minimal governmental input. In all fairness, of course, without the government, we would have had nothing upon which to build. R&D investments in twenty-plus years of the ARPANET provided the framework for the commercial Internet. Ascribing the Internet to "pure" capital markets and entrepreneurship would be highly disingenuous. It is fair to say, though, that the government provided both a practical and a legal framework within which investors and entrepreneurs could interact. The private sector then built around it a full-fledged medium for communication and commerce. Would that we could find a comparable formula for improving our other infrastructures.

Perhaps the most important lessons of the bubble, though, are those that take the greatest effort to extract. Thanks to the nationwide (or global) quest for Internet gold, we've been able to accumulate voluminous empirical data about the Internet. Every Internet venture launched during the bubble had a business model based on little more than a hunch. While entrepreneurs and venture capitalists (VCs) prided themselves on their ability to predict likely successes and failures, they turned out not to be very good at it after all. Their poor performance is hardly surprising. They made all of their decisions in an experiential vacuum. At best, they reasoned by weak analogy to other technologies that bore some cosmetic similarity to the Internet. The Internet community's famed laissez faire attitude was a matter of practical necessity. *None of them knew what they were doing because they had no reliable data on which to base their decisions.*

The bubble changed all that. We've been privy to the inner workings of more Internet approaches to more sectors of commerce than we possibly could have imagined. We now know *a lot* about what works, what doesn't—and if we're willing to think about it, why. We've gained significant insights into the nature of positive feedback, the need for commitment, the challenge of maintaining customer loyalty, the value of branding, the ease of entry, and above all the importance of viable business plans outlining credible paths to profitability. The amount that we now know about e-commerce—a phenomenon *still* less than ten years old—is truly remarkable. Now we must apply that knowledge.

The New Channel paradigm provides the framework for that application. And perhaps the single most important key to appreciating the New Channel view of the world lies in remembering that incumbents don't like losing their customers. As soon as they see a new entrant—Internet-based or otherwise—beginning to make inroads into their markets, they're likely to come out fighting. This reaction always has occurred in competitive markets, and it always will. It's simply the nature of the beast—and the essence of competition. That competition, in turn, will necessarily rest upon the infrastructure that we build for it.

Phoenix Rising

The infrastructure of the information economy rests in IP law, filtered through our broader policy decisions and public investments. But the primary importance of public infrastructure lies in the opportunities that it creates and in the ways that private parties avail themselves of those opportunities. Economic development in the information age may rest upon public infrastructure, but private entrepreneurship will determine its course. And private entrepreneurship will need to harness New Channel thinking.

The New Channel paradigm defines industries by the goods and/or services that vendors provide to customers, by the geographic reach of those vendors, and at times by the demographics of the customer base. In other words, it changes nothing.[15] Only New World advocates thought that they could define an industry around its preferred mode of communication. New Channel inquiries into the viability of an Internet business plan must identify the relevant industry and then consider the Internet's likely impact on the transactions that govern that industry. Which information costs will it reduce, and how great an impact will these reduced costs have on the overall transaction? Those Internet-specific questions are where we begin evaluating whether a pure play has a prayer. Because the vast majority of cases will generate negative answers, we'll have to continue our analyses using the tools that people usually use when evaluating business plans in the industry in question. That can be tough work—and it serves as a subtle reminder that most new businesses fail.

But pure plays will continue to arise, and some even will succeed. They may not be as plentiful as we once expected, and they'll certainly need a better business plan than: "trust me, I'm online," but they will develop and thrive. People need information, and under the right circumstances they're willing to pay for it. How can we identify such opportunities? We can begin with the casual observation that the Internet is much more likely to *revolutionize* information industries than physical industries—and with the less obvious split between *single-use information goods* and *reusable information goods*.

In the single-use side of the information sector, news providers, sites answering frequently asked questions (FAQ sites), and "infomediaries" providing detailed information about a narrow topic, all have become popular—if not always lucrative. The basic challenge in running such a site is convincing users to pay for the information—or finding some other way to convert your popular site into a source of revenues. Because few if any entry barriers appear to protect such sites, some infomediaries or FAQs try to generate revenues by varying their fees according to "freshness," in an Internet-based application of "versioning."[16] It's not clear, however, that this sort of approach will prove workable—at least as a general rule. In fact, good general ways to drive standalone FAQs or info-mediaries to reliable profits may not exist. As a result, while it's easy to believe someone who claims that his radical, new Web site will become popular, it's best to remain a bit skeptical when he insists that popularity will make it lucrative. Even true devotees are unlikely to pay much to use it, and few or no barriers to competitive entry exist. The best bet for the future of infomediaries or FAQs seems to rest with groups not interested in running them for a profit: "educators," including universities, governments, advocacy groups, nonprofits, etc.; and companies seeking to "attract attention" to their real businesses. In either case, direct revenues from the site are unlikely to be the provider's primary goal. That challenge makes them a dubious choice for pure plays.

Advertising revenues—set, at least in part, by the amount of traffic driven through a site—remain central to many Internet business models,[17] though it's hard to see a revenue model based on banner ads working for more than a small number of very popular sites. But not all advertising models are equal. In *one-way advertising*, a seller broadcasts a message that he hopes a consumer will see. Media companies charge the seller to carry his message.[18] Web sites must compete for these advertising dollars with every other channel commanding the occasional and partial attention of those eyeballs, including newspapers, television, radio, and billboards. *Two-way advertising* is less common—though particularly well suited to interactive media like the Internet. Two-way ads emerge in markets in which both buyers and sellers are prone to advertise. Examples include matchmaking, employment, barter, and collectibles, where either or both of the "seller" and the "buyer" may advertise; in some, transactional symmetry even blurs the line between the two. The unique feature of two-way advertising is that it requires matching. Anyone who enters into such a transaction has a set of filtering criteria necessary to find an appropriate match. Few people approach a matchmaking system seeking a randomly selected mate. Companies don't assign random jobs to employees. Barter services work because people gain goods or services that they want. Collectors collect specific items, not just "things." The keys to successful two-way advertising are matching and filtering—algorithmic tasks at which computers can provide a clear benefit. Such sites can be profitable; the employment site Monster.com, for example, began to show profits in 2001.[19]

Heavy reliance on advertising revenues is likely to work only in select places. But another category of single-use information goods, *rights and permissions*, appears almost ideal for e-commerce. A ticket is little more than a very simple contract backed up by both a collection of default legal rules and specific rules enumerated on the ticket. Tickets may be the ideal item for Internet distribution—particularly when they provide entry into a commoditized, well-understood, or easily describable event, such as a specific flight, a game between two named sports teams, or a concert by a known band.

The role of the Internet in simple ticket sales is a straightforward convergence of technological and legal interests—with a commission structure providing a well-defined business plan: A ticket sale is an exchange of rights—a purely informational transaction. Internet transactions, by reducing the cost of information exchange, reduce the costs of ticket sales. Internet ticket sales should thus help consumers pay smaller service charges, help service providers sell more tickets, and still leave enough of a commission for the agent. While the shift to the Internet has undoubtedly put many traditional travel agencies—particularly small ones—out of business, their lobby is neither particularly large nor particularly well funded, and therefore unlikely to be able to reimpose too many of the reduced information costs. The general weakness of traditional intermediaries[20] makes tickets an ideal product for e-commerce, though Ticketmaster's continuing stranglehold on various categories of ticket sales demonstrates once again how monopolists can exploit consumers.

Less well-understood sales provide yet another potential venue for pure plays. *Hybrid infomediary/ticket* sites may be able to sell both the information needed to understand complex products and the products themselves.[21] But entrepreneurs launching such sites must exercise constant vigilance. Their business models must ultimately lie in their ability to charge enough to cover their data acquisition and coordination costs— plus a profit. As always, price differentials create possibilities for both free-ridership and arbitrage; users may obtain information from the infomediary and then take their purchases to a discounter. Furthermore, from a legal perspective, sites providing dated or inaccurate information may discover unanticipated areas of liability. Such sites show a good deal of promise, but a good business plan still must explain how to lock in consumers—as well as to demonstrate attention to more standard considerations like product quality, personnel, managerial acumen, and timing.

Beyond the land of "infomediaries," ticket vendors, dating services, and hybrids, though, lies an entire realm of reusable information products that we've been buying for ages—long before we came to think of them as information products. In traditional off-line business models, vendors of reusable information goods charge customers either for every use (e.g., by selling admission to a movie) or for every copy (e.g., by selling music CDs). The ease of producing and redistributing multiple copies of digital goods has strained those models. That complication makes reusable information goods among the most interesting battlegrounds not only of the Internet, but of the entire tech sector—far beyond what we've seen in the worlds of software and music.

The era of the print encyclopedia, for example, is over; just ask the folks at Britannica.com.[22] Publishers of reference books have had to redo *both* their products and their business models to enter the information sector. They've developed full hypertext versions of their works to include links that make it easy to surf their own little corners of the Web. In many ways, our formerly linear encyclopedias are coming to resemble the complex exegetic structure that Jonathan Rosen found in the Talmud. Conversion to the information sector imposed real costs on reference publishers—even as it caused the prices of their products to plummet. Meanwhile, the rest of the book-publishing industry has encountered its own set of technological challengers. Books on tape came first. Electronic books (or e-books) have followed.[23] As the technology for delivering them improves, publishers will have to adapt. New business models will have to follow.

Advertising long has been the primary source of revenue for newspaper and magazine publishers. To a large extent, the same is true with Internet periodicals. But Internet and print publications lend themselves to different variants of competition. Playboy and Penthouse, for example, long have been the two most popular gentlemen's magazines, in part because they cater to a broad audience. The explosion of online pornography catering to narrow fetishes has made major inroads into the popularity of their flagship products; Penthouse has reportedly been on the verge of terminating its paper version since at least 2001, and Playboy's print sales are far below their peak. In other words, while the key to success in the relatively high fixed-cost world of magazine publishing appears to have been broad appeal, the Internet's lower fixed costs tend to favor narrow specialization.[24] Once again, new business models that avail themselves of reduced information costs are likely to chase the tried-and-true.

The publishers of archival periodicals like the *New York Times* faced their own set of challenges when they entered the information sector. They discovered early on that sales to database publishers could generate additional revenues. But their freelance writers also discovered a potential new revenue source. When a newspaper buys an article from a freelancer, what it actually buys are the rights to publish that article in its newspaper. Under general principles of copyright law, it also purchases the auxiliary right to include that same article in some specific sorts of anthologies, such as a special "best stories of the year" issue. With the advent of commercial databases like Lexis/Nexis, however, the newspapers began selling the rights to republish these articles in a different format—as parts of an archival database. The Supreme Court ruled that the freelance authors hadn't relinquished their rights to this sort of republication—and that the publications had thus infringed the authors' copyrights.[25]

This ruling exemplifies an important aspect of our transition to an information economy. The length of modern copyrights suggests that a new valuable technology always could be just around the corner. If no one's thinking about these developments when they sign contracts, who gets the windfall revenues? The courts have reminded us that this question has no general answer. Copyrights are what copyright law says they are, and contracts say what they say. If a question arises as to who retains a right, we look to the statute and to the contract—never, mind you, to a policy objective. And if one party or the other feels ripped off for having "relinquished" rights that it never contemplated, that's just too damn bad. While it may affect the transition to the information sector, it's unlikely to have major consequences on the success or failure of various business models going forward. Yet again, IP rights dictate the transition's shape.

The entire category of reusable information goods is thus a veritable legal minefield replete with potentially lucrative business opportunities and few proven business models to exploit them. Many of the valuable and desirable goods that Internet vendors can sell easily are reusable information goods, but the legal challenges surrounding this transition are likely to be fierce. In fact, any attempted entry is almost certain to raise a legal issue, because distributing reusable information goods is so easy and so cheap that consumers may balk at the thought of paying for them—and even more at the thought of letting some "owner" control their flow.

It's an arena in which law, economics, and technology eye each other warily, each poised to jump as the other two develop new ways of either invading its turf or constraining its reach. Technology sets information goods free. Law tends to constrain them. Economics hovers around the edges insisting that there must be some way to convert desirable goods into profitable ventures. This tension highlights the relationship between the two economic pillars of the information age: public infrastructure and private investment. It demonstrates quite clearly how our allocation of IP rights will constrain business planning—and thereby determine which plans will succeed and which will fail.

IP rights will play a lesser—though hardly insignificant—role in delimiting the Internet's impact on the electronic sales of physical goods. There, industry-specific analyses will dominate future business models. Nevertheless, the empirical data of the bubble already have taught us some powerful general lessons. First, buyers who know what to expect upon delivery are likely to be particularly amenable to Internet purchases. Items that are essentially commodities or branded may be easier Internet sales than those that are experiential, tactile, or sensual. Second, collectibles will continue to sell well on the Web despite the general rule that consumers like to know what they're getting. Though collectibles do tend to be one of a kind, the Internet has reduced the search cost—an important information cost—inherent in collecting. Third, fulfillment will pose a perpetual challenge. Perishable goods (like groceries) that require timely delivery and careful handling will continue to challenge Internet vendors. Fourth, the Internet provides an easy mechanism for taking customizable orders. In the past, the expense inherent in determining the preferences of a specific customer has generally restricted customization to a relatively small number of expensive goods, such as homes or automobiles. Fifth, Internet vendors are well poised to customize *prices* as well as *products*. Customized pricing derived from low-cost information about consumers' individual tastes, preferences, and budgets promises to help make goods more widely available while simultaneously increasing corporate profits. Nevertheless, it has some drawbacks. Various types of "price discrimination" are illegal,[26] and even the legal types can hurt a vendor's reputation.[27]

In short, the future of commercial development on the Internet is likely to look a lot like the history of commercial development before the Internet. Entrepreneurs will need to struggle to succeed, incumbents will need to fight to stay ahead, investors will need to exercise due diligence in selecting their investments, and the government will need to experiment gingerly to determine the appropriate amount of guidance and regulation needed to foster development on different parts of the Internet. But savvy Internet entrepreneurs will understand how a reduced information cost can restructure an industry—and then make it happen.

We need both economic pillars of the information age to succeed. If we invest in developing a suitable public-information infrastructure, and if our private information entrepreneurs stay grounded in New Channel thinking, we can look forward to a bright future. And all that we'll have to worry about are those pesky distributors who decide to fight back rather than to let their profit streams evaporate as we drift closer to a world sans transaction costs. That—and our still tentative levels of hope and trust.

Don't Stop Thinking about Tomorrow

The interconnections among hope, trust, tech, and our modern economy show up all over the place. From the perspective of investors, most tech companies are growth companies. Even those few that *could* be value companies try not to be. In January 2003, for example, Microsoft announced that it would soon pay its first dividend. Its stock immediately plummeted. Microsoft's executives went out of their way to reassure investors that they weren't shifting to a value strategy—that they remained focused on growth. Value stocks tend to follow stable, steady business plans in mature industries and earn reliable returns year after year. They typically share some of those returns with their owners by paying dividends. Growth stocks, on the other hand, encourage investment by promising huge returns in the future. In other words, growth investors focus on the long term; they assume that significant profits will arrive eventually; they apply a low discount rate to value those future profits at something close to their face value; and they trust management to invest wisely and to develop profitable products. In the 1990s, investors believed that rapid infrastructure buildup would lead quickly to marketable, popular, profitable products. They trusted tech companies, believed in tech products, developed hope in a tech-driven future, invested heavily, and powered growth.

But investors were only part of the picture. Over in the business world, the late 1990s were also an interesting time. Y2K (a fear factor) and the Internet (a hope factor) forced companies to assess their IT abilities and needs. They learned about new tech and telecom capabilities that would increase their productivity and cut their costs. Businesses were excited. They invested in technological upgrades, often buying cutting-edge capabilities that they could justify only by projecting long-term payoffs. They also invested to get on the Internet, often without a meaningful plan for their Web presence. In other words, businesses bought into the same basic formula as investors. They focused on the long term; they assumed that their technology investments would generate significant profits; they applied a low discount rate to value those profits at something close to their face value; and they trusted tech companies to continue developing productivity-enhancing products. That too helped power the tech sector's growth.

Consumers followed a similar pattern. The Internet, new wireless phones, PDAs, MP3 players, and assorted other gadgets excited consumers. New devices quickly became "must have" equipment, and consumers favored high-end gadgets that promised to incorporate the next wave of exciting new functions and capabilities. Consumers, too, focused on the long term, projected significant product innovations, convinced themselves that the innovations would arrive quickly, and trusted tech companies to develop great products.

That was the world of the late 1990s. A world of widespread—some might say irrationally exuberant—hope and trust that tech would power wave after wave of growth. And then the trust and the hope began to erode. That epidemic erosion began with holiday shoppers disappointed by fulfillment problems, dimming consumer hope. Then the flow of tech products slowed. Consumers realized that they wouldn't lose much by deferring their purchases, and consumer hopes dimmed further. Tech clients stopped paying their bills. Businesses holding unpaid bills noticed that the flow of new products had slowed, and ceased investing in new equipment. Business hope dimmed. But the epidemic exploded into a full-fledged plague only when it hit investors—who had trusted the most, hoped the most, and felt the most betrayed. When tech investments declined, investor hope dimmed. When non-tech investments declined, investor hope dimmed further. When investors learned that accounting conventions allow corporations to game their earnings, investor hope dimmed yet further and investor trust began to erode. Finally, when the press revealed a few high-profile accounting frauds, investor hope and investor trust both evaporated.

The coup de grâce hit us all in one fell swoop on 9/11. Hope, trust, and growth fell far from the forefront of our minds. Our focus shifted to the short term. We worried about security; we kept our investments close to home; we projected meager profits into the future and applied steep discount rates to undervalue cash not yet in hand; we watched companies cut costs and lay off their workers. We found ourselves trying hard to remember the last time we actually "had" to have a new tech product and trying hard to imagine that broadband would someday finish rolling itself out. But above all, *we lost our trust in corporate America*. We're unlikely to see a serious, sustained turnaround until we've recovered our hope in the future and our trust in the innovators and entrepreneurs who will bring us there.

Nurturing that hope is a job for the government. The tech sector—and the American economy—can thrive only if our economic policies allow it to thrive. Those economic policies, in turn, must embrace the pillars of market liberalism: broad opportunities, free choices, and ample incentives. They also must recognize that a sophisticated information economy requires an expanded definition of infrastructure—and savvy investment in infrastructure is among the key jobs of government in a free, liberal economy.

Government "investment" can take several different forms. Sometimes, the government invests by using its own people and resources. Sometimes it oversees the performance of contractors. Sometimes it regulates the behavior of private actors. And sometimes it enforces liability on private actors. Different mixes are right for different settings at different times.[28] But one way or another, the government must apply its best efforts to ensure that our infrastructure defines a solid platform for growth. Appropriate approaches to IP and competition law are critical parts of that information infrastructure, but they are hardly sufficient.

"Infrastructure," like "investment," can assume many forms. Roads, highways, the electricity grid, the telephone system, TV, radio, and the Internet define the infrastructure underpinning our physical and information sectors, not to mention occupying most of our free time. The market cops who police oligopolists and monopolists, the real cops who police the streets, the soldiers who police the world, and the emergency workers who help clean up after their rare failures define the infrastructure underpinning our security. Legal systems that enforce property rights, contracts, and liabilities define the infrastructure underpinning our economy and our social fabric. Education systems that prepare our workers for the information economy, employment systems that help match workers to jobs, and welfare systems that support people while they're retraining or reorienting their skills, define the human infrastructure necessary to navigate the information age. The network that we call the free world defines the global infrastructure of a prosperous future. The government needs to develop, to maintain, and to improve all of these infrastructures.

The government also must ensure that our tax system generates enough revenue to support all of those infrastructure investments, without dampening incentives, restricting opportunities, or distorting behavior. The government thus has a challenging—and critical—role to play in transition planning. It must ensure that we have an infrastructure upon which growth is possible, an expansive pool of people with the skills necessary to innovate and to take entrepreneurial risks, and a market in which they can compete unencumbered by either public or private monopolies. Within that free market, some of those entrepreneurs will succeed, some will fail, and society will emerge as the big winner.

The best way to restore our faith in corporate America—so that once again we can invest with confidence and be excited about business and technology—is to wed ourselves to global market liberalism. Ideas like free trade, low-to-moderate tax rates, minimal distortions in the tax code, tough enforcement of antitrust and securities laws, collaborative industry/government/university research, IP rights that promote more innovation than they deter, political and economic liberalization abroad, an effective education system, retraining and relocation assistance, and unemployment-to-retraining and welfare-to-work programs all provide our best prospects for success.

But liberal markets also have a dark side; they tend toward bazaar-like chaos. The growth bubbling up from below can be phenomenal, both in network and in nonnetwork industries, but it's also difficult to direct. Market liberalism tends to favor the process over a preselected outcome. And market processes are notoriously hard to control. Misperceptions can lead to misdirected investment, to irrational exuberance, to bubbles, and to terrifying losses. The bubble was a speculative gloss that eventually blew off an impressive record of growth. Real productivity growth and the excitement that it engendered drove the 1990s' economic boom—as well as our roller-coaster ride through the information sector.

Retrenchment after the last part of our ride has motivated something of a backlash against market liberalism, and driven many to seek safety in stable, reliable incumbents. Today's information-sector investors and observers, like their government, are more sympathetic to Microsoft and the record companies than were their recent predecessors. In the broader worlds of technology and communications, incumbent media outlets and the Baby Bells have fared much better than their late start-up competitors. We have fallen prey to a tech sector governed more by lock-in than by growth. And therein lies a classic danger, for we run the risk of allowing a few powerful incumbents to plan the information sector's future—even as we aver that we would never accept such an outcome. Friedrich Hayek, who won the 1974 Nobel Prize in economics for his resounding defense of liberal economic policies, foresaw this danger with his characteristic prescience.

Few central planners are content to say that central planning is desirable. Most of them affirm that we can no longer choose but are compelled by circumstances beyond our control to substitute planning for competition. The myth is deliberately cultivated that we are embarking on the new course not out of free will but because competition is spontaneously eliminated by technological changes which we neither can reverse nor should wish to prevent. This argument . . . is devoid of foundation. The tendency toward *monopoly and planning* is not the result of any "objective facts" beyond our control but the product of opinions fostered and propagated . . . until they have come to dominate all our policy.[29] . . .

There is yet another theory which connects the growth of monopolies with technological progress. . . . It contends that . . . it will be impossible to make use of many of the new technological possibilities unless protection against competition is granted, i.e., a monopoly is conferred. This type of argument is not necessarily fraudulent. . . . No doubt in many cases it is used merely as a form of special pleading by interested parties. Even more often it is probably based on a confusion between technical excellence from a narrow engineering point of view and desirability from the point of view of society as a whole.

There remains, however, a group of instances where the argument has some force. . . . [It] must be admitted that it is possible that, by compulsory standardization or the prohibition of variety beyond a certain degree, abundance might be increased in some fields more than sufficiently to compensate for the restriction of the choice of the consumer. *It is even conceivable that a new invention may be made some day whose adoption would seem unquestionably beneficial but which could be used only if many or all people were made to avail themselves of it at the same time.* . . .

It is true that in such situations we may have to sacrifice a possible immediate gain as the price of our freedom—but we avoid, on the other hand, the necessity of making future developments dependent upon the knowledge which particular people now possess. By sacrificing such possible present advantages, we preserve an important stimulus to further progress. Though in the short run the price we have to pay for variety and freedom of choice may sometimes be high, in the long run even material progress will depend on this very variety, because we can never predict from which of the many forms in which a good or service can be provided something better may develop. . . . [T]he argument for freedom is precisely that we ought to leave room for the unforeseeable free growth. It applies, therefore, no less when, on the basis of our present knowledge, compulsion would seem to bring only advantages, and although in a particular instance it may actually do no harm.[30]

Milton and Rose Friedman, who like Hayek, are typically associated with critiques of *government* planning, similarly recognized that the true danger of planning is inherent in the structure of a monopoly market rather than in the identity of the planner. "The great danger to the consumer is monopoly—whether private or governmental. . . . Alternative sources of supply protect the consumer far more effectively than all the Ralph Naders of the world."[31] Consumers locked in to monopoly suppliers are unprotected. They remain subject to the monopolist's whims and tastes. Innovation and technological development cease being the result of a competitive marketplace and become instead the diktat of the incumbent planner.

With each passing day, powerful incumbents lock us ever more deeply into their proprietary standards, and ensure that all future innovation will pass through the narrow channels that they already control. We find fewer choices and fewer exciting innovations. We lose the job growth powered by entrepreneurial start-ups. We rely increasingly on paternalistic incumbents, and hope that they prove to be good parents. We seem able to do little but to fight for second-best fixes, like antitrust enforcement or procurement legislation. The underlying problem—our potentially anachronistic IP system—appears to remain sacrosanct.

We've already seen this problem permeate the information sector. We're likely to see it recur throughout the broad world of technology. Companies pushing new innovations frequently find a powerful incumbent in their way, not as a direct competitor, but rather as the "controller" of an industry or a market, acting as a de facto central planner. The entrants ask the government to prevent the incumbent from leveraging its strength, either by tough enforcement actions or by changing the governing laws and regulations; the incumbent objects. The government's choice will dictate who will succeed and who will fail.

So there it is in a nutshell. We must rebuild our sense of security and our feeling of trust if we ever want to return to long-run network growth. Those are tasks for the government. But even after we start thinking about the long term and trusting the corporations best poised to build it, we'll *still* need to see an exciting enough future to jump into it happily. That's the tech sector's job. When we regain our hope in the future, technology will continue making us all richer (government permitting). Until we do, until we learn to trust again, to look to the future, and to hope for a better tomorrow, we're not likely to go anywhere fast. That's how the information sector relates to the tech sector, to the broader American economy, and in turn to the world: it promotes hope in a better future.

Of Hope, Growth, and Hard-Won Wisdom

The lessons of the information sector's glorious debut continue to unfold. Today, too many people seem content to focus on the greed, the silliness, the hype, the promotion of hope over reason, and the conflicts of interest that we learned about only after the fact. They seem to be happy shaking their heads sadly and saying either "I told you so," or "I should have known better," as the case may be. And they seem to want to "blame" the whole debacle on our lesser nature. But they forget....

The information sector's debut was the dominant economic story of the late 1990s, and the late 1990s were a wondrous time in America—as in much of the developed world. We were happy, and excited, and successful. And we were all looking forward to an even more wonderful future. The many people who now deride the New Economy forget what it was really about: unbounded opportunity, growth without limits, steady improvement, motivating creativity, rewarding success, and above all having enough of everything to go around. Tech companies hired based on merit, led the way in promoting domestic-partner benefits, and recognized talented immigrants as people coming over to help make us even richer—not to take our jobs. The gestalt of those years pushed the concepts of tolerance, equal opportunity, talent, merit, motivation, and reward further than they'd ever gone before.[32] The workplaces of the New Economy were casual and comfortable because the happiness of the workers mattered *and because the owners assumed that it would enhance their wealth*! In the late nineteenth century, the folks who owned coalmines insisted that they would go broke if they had to pay their miners a living wage. In the late twentieth century, the folks who owned tech companies insisted that they would go broke unless they could award partial payment in stock options. I sense forward movement in there somewhere.

America in the late 1990s got a rare glimpse of peace, prosperity, and hope—revisionist naysayers notwithstanding. To those who complain that we elevated hope over reason, I must ask: *What's wrong with a little hope?* The world would be a better place if there were more of it around. When our hope collapsed, we learned that our excitement over the bubble may have led us to pay too little attention to events unfolding elsewhere. That reality came crashing down upon us to tragic effect. But our memories of the bubble, coupled with the lessons we have learned since its collapse, can give us valuable insights into the subtle relationship between the values of liberalism and the lessons of network growth. We now can appreciate why genuine network growth, constant innovation, and social advancement only can occur within a liberal framework.

Freedom, individual rights and responsibilities, equal opportunity, and personal choice are all network goods. The larger our free-world network, the more valuable the membership. Expansions of the network expand opportunities, bring new potential innovators into the picture, fuel the network's further growth, and make us all richer. The miraculous growth of the1990s came as Eastern Europeans and Latin Americans became freer, and as the International Monetary Fund (IMF), the World Bank, the WTO, NATO, and the European Union helped nurture their membership—an expansion of the liberal network abroad. It came as a generation of minority Americans entered leadership positions, the substantial return on our investment in a great society—an expansion of the liberal network at home. We fostered it with sound domestic economic policies that promoted innovation, entrepreneurship, and small-business growth, rather than policies designed to help the successful businesses of previous eras lock in their profits—and their customers. Domestic and international forces converged to make us all richer through the magic of network economics. Though we may not have identified the networks we were building, we succeeded in harnessing the ultimate gospel of network effects. The much-maligned New Economy attitude played an important role in that construction.

In today's information sector, technologists make information ever cheaper. Consumers and savvy producers benefit, and distributors become increasingly unhappy. The record companies try to shut down P2P development to maintain control over music distribution. Microsoft attempts to shut down middleware threats and open-source development to keep all information flowing through its own tollgates. Various other industries apply different laws or follow in the footsteps of these giants; auto dealers use state laws to keep transaction costs in place, and garage-door manufacturers introduce needless encryption to establish a monopoly. All try to reintroduce transaction costs to bolster their own bottom lines.

Though we already can see the battle lines of the future forming, our more basic challenge is to see these battles for what they are—and to remember where our broader interests lie. On one side, we must never allow entrenched interests to restrain the innovation that powers technological development. On the other, we must recall that many transaction costs exist to support important policy goals. We must not wipe them away simply because we can. Wherever we eliminate laws that serve worthy goals but that have become unjustifiably costly, we must devise alternate ways to meet those goals. Technology may change our calculations, but it shouldn't alter our underlying values.

The information sector stands poised to influence more and more of our industries, and larger and larger parts of our lives. In every new industry that it encounters, numerous people—some weak, some strong—will stand to lose as most of us gain. The forces of growth benefiting all will inevitably come into conflict with the forces of lock-in favoring a few. We as a society will have to choose between two strategies for coping with the conflict.

One strategic approach is to fight each battle as it arises, confident that we'll win in some industries, lose in others. Where society as a whole wins, network growth will take over, and the industry will blossom as innovation enriches consumers and savvy producers. The losers may suffer horribly, but at least their demise will be swift. Where society as a whole loses, the industry will languish, as the victorious incumbents will continue to force all innovation through the narrow channels that they control. These locked-in "winners" will work their way into a slow, painful death spiral from which there can be no escape, though inevitably they'll try to inflict greater pain on the rest of us with each downward twist.

A better strategic alternative would be to plan our transition wisely by investing in the infrastructure needed to grow our networks. We can work with the people trying to adjust to new lives in the information sector. We can compensate companies whose rights technology tramples, and invest enough to retrain and to relocate workers whose jobs become obsolete. We can deliberate and debate the most effective ways to ensure that our economic, technology, and industrial policies evolve coherently to promote both opportunity and incentive—the key ingredients to robust long-term growth.

This second route promises to return us to an era of hope and growth, an era when the information sector will once again make us all richer, happier, and better—if only we choose to let it. The choice is ours. The future of more than just the information sector hangs in the balance.

Epilogue

Beyond Enlightenment, a Dialectic

Books rarely move at Internet speed. This one is no exception. In early 2001, while sifting sadly through the rubble of my carefully-crafted portfolio of tech stocks, I felt a visceral need to understand where I had gone wrong. My gut told me that I had misapplied some of the very techniques that I employ as a professional. It said that the lessons of software development, antitrust analysis, intellectual property, and network economics *had* to lie along the path to enlightenment, and that the contrast between Microsoft's successes and the dot-coms' failures would reveal that path. I embarked upon my quest.

It took me to many different places. The information sector, the broader economy, and the world at large all refused to sit still. New data became available, new issues rose to the fore, old topics faded from centrality to obscurity. Open source flitted into view. The more I pondered it, the more I saw it as part of the same story. The P2P furor provided yet another part of the emerging whole. The various drafts of this book followed the ebbs and flows of current events, as America's attention—and mine—turned from the digital economy to taxes, terror, war, and elections. And though I believe that the information economy plays a central, if sometimes subtle, role in all of these tales, I tried to focus the book on the information sector's inner workings. The closing chapter began to plumb its relationship to broader societal concerns; this epilogue continues that work.

By early 2005, the Internet investment bubble will feel like ancient history, a dim relic of a halcyon era. Little public interest remains in the specifics of either its meteoric rise or its tortured unwind. Its centrality to this book faded with each successive draft. Though it remains a critical data source and a cautionary tale, it has lost much of its ability to engage. And yet, a glimmer of this once-consuming phenomenon remains mired deep in the public psyche—witness Google's recent IPO. With humor and hubris harkening back to the heady days of the bubble, Google's prospectus promised to do "good things," and not to "be evil." As its first corporate "good thing," Google eschewed the classic scheme for allocating IPO shares among large investors in favor of a "Dutch auction"[1] that allegedly provided greater opportunities for small investors. The auction unfolded amidst considerable interest, press scrutiny, SEC inquiries, and general uncertainty. Google halted the auction early, accepted a disappointing opening valuation—and then saw its shares rise considerably when listed trading began. Was the Google IPO a seminal event in the tech resurrection or a microcosmic reprise of the bubble? As I write these words, the question remains open. By the time you read them, we all may be wiser.

As the dot-coms fade into memory, Microsoft manages to stay in the news—and not just because of its appeal pending in Europe challenging DG Comp. In fact, the biggest Microsoft story of summer 2004 was its decision to *help* consumers—at least those consumers fortunate enough to also be Microsoft shareholders. Microsoft announced plans to return $75 billion to its shareholders over a four-year period, the single largest corporate cash disbursement in history, and a notable strategic change for a company that has long prided itself on its ability to invest its cash surplus more wisely than could its investors. *The Economist*, typically something of a Microsoft critic, couldn't help but be impressed, citing "many signs that the company is seeking to change its image—from evil predator . . . to upstanding corporate citizen."[2] Perhaps. But behavior modification is tougher than an image upgrade, and we've given Microsoft no reason to change its behavior—an inexcusable failure of public policy. Even assuming that Microsoft now possesses the noblest of intentions, it has no rational reason to avoid leveraging its dominance into software markets adjacent to Windows, or to stop trying to block innovations incompatible with Windows. To do so would serve its shareholders ill—cash dividends notwithstanding. Nevertheless, these dividends do indicate a significant strategic shift, and as Microsoft has helped to teach us, all things are possible in the information sector.

As to Microsoft's open-source bête noires, government adoption seems to be gaining speed. In June 2004, the city of Munich, Germany, announced plans to permanently migrate more than fourteen thousand desktops to a Linux platform, Sun's OpenOffice, and the Mozilla browser—reportedly history's largest migration from proprietary to open-source software.[3] Various other municipal, provincial, and national governments are moving toward open source—though few announcements attract as much attention or as much intense lobbying as did Congressman Villanueva's bill. Despite the attention, and perhaps because of the lobbying, that bill never became Peruvian law.[4] Meanwhile, in March 2003, SCO (formerly Santa Cruz Operation) sued IBM for infringing property rights that it claimed lay buried within Linux, and threatened to broaden its suit to challenge individual Linux users. In something of an understatement, *Fortune* explained that Linux, "the free operating system—backed by IBM, HP, and others—is breaking Microsoft's monopoly. But a lawsuit by SCO, which claims to own parts of the code, could wreck the party."[5] Indeed it could. If SCO can prove its claim, it may be able to shut down Linux development, at least for a while, and scare off many individual and institutional users contemplating open-source adoption, likely for a good while longer. And yet, even as the fate of the open-source business model hangs in the balance of the SCO suit, its promise as a general development model is spreading; some think that it might even revolutionize medical research.[6]

This growing curiosity about open-source development stems from the new opportunities in product development, production, and distribution that the new economics of information creates. Though it remains unclear precisely *how* we will develop, produce, and distribute information-age products, it is becoming increasingly clear that many industrial-age models are nearing the end of their useful lives. Their demise will bring revolutionary change to numerous industries. And open-source development holds enough promise to warrant closer scrutiny among those anticipating the revolution.

In one industry already in midrevolution, central scrutinizer Carey Sherman builds upon Hillary Rosen's fine work. He's sued numerous kids driven to crime by digital music, at times even extracting their meager life savings as compensation for their illicit downloads.[7] Meanwhile, the DMCA wends its way through the economy, granting content owners access to confidential information about accused file-swappers and holding increasing numbers of technologists liable for illicit circumvention. The summer of 2004, though, saw some surprisingly positive developments. The Ninth Circuit found some serious limitations on vicarious liability for technologists who enable infringement.[8] The Federal Circuit announced that DMCA liability could exist only if there was a reasonable relationship between the circumvention and a right that the copyright laws protect, and then applied that rule to save your garage door from the information sector's insatiable appetite.[9] The Sixth Circuit followed suit, and announced that that you can *probably* use your printer with impunity—but sent the matter back for a trial, just to be sure.[10] So go ahead. Drive home, use your garage, run upstairs, and print the online promotional materials for this book, all with a clean conscience. You can still feel morally superior to kids downloading music. But don't get too smug. After all, the jury's still out on your toner cartridge.

The jury is also still out on the DMCA. Most previous critiques of the law have focused on its ability to stifle expression, creativity, and the distribution of works unprotected by copyright—all important topics for debate.[11] Such criticisms, limited as they are to concepts like cultural expression, free speech, privacy rights, and civil liberties, typically play better within the temple walls than on the more utilitarian streets of Main and Wall. It is hard to imagine anything more utilitarian, though, than the profound economic harm latent in laws, like the DMCA, that elevate existing business models above technological development.

When Congress restricts public uses of innovative new technologies to help businesses lock in obsolete business models, it risks distorting the entire economy. Such distortions rarely appear overnight; they often gestate for decades. Between the 1950s and the 1980s, we "decided" that rather than devising the best ways to motivate innovation in the new, functional, textual product called software, we would extend existing bodies of law to cover it—albeit uncomfortably—and granted software developers an unprecedented combination of patent, copyright, and trade-secret protection. Only in the 1990s did we come to appreciate how a dominant software developer could abuse these property rights to distort software markets. We were left trying to fix this fundamental mistake in our assignment of property rights using the blunt, slow, tools of antitrust—and then looking elsewhere for other second-best, after-the-fact patches. We should have been able to do better then, and we should be able to do better now. Though the DMCA's most pernicious effects on the economy are likely still larval, we can already see some signs of infestation. This six-year-old law has retarded P2P, and consequently the demand draw for broadband rollout; the United States now lags much of the developed world in broadband access. The court's recent preservation of your right to open your garage using a competing-brand clicker notwithstanding, numerous manufacturers of consumer products would undoubtedly like to use the DMCA to leverage themselves into aftermarket monopolists. Future courts will evaluate their claims on a case-by-case basis. Some are likely to succeed—leading to DMCA distortions rippling throughout the broad economy.

If we remain unwilling to reconsider the fundamental nature of IP rights as we transition to a fully information-based economy, we are likely to see growing conflicts between the legal rights that we grant to IP owners and consumers' basic right to use the products that they buy. Technology simply will make it too easy for members of the public to infringe legal rights; if the law won't accommodate technology, it will have to fight it. That clash between technology and law will distort the economy and damage us all. This looming battle remains the single greatest threat to the information sector's promise to enrich us all as consumers. And current trends are disheartening. Whenever technology makes it harder for copyright owners to control distribution, Congress grants them stronger protection by prohibiting activities that once were legal. After the DMCA banned circumvention, technology continued to improve—and copyright owners continued to complain. The Senate recently passed an "inducement to infringe copyrights" bill designed to ban music-swapping sites.[12] In other contemplated legislation, a panel of the House Judiciary Committee voted for the "Family Movie Act," which, in the words of the *Washington Post*, would "let parents strip smut from movies."[13] Precisely how an editing device can enable smut-stripping without simultaneously enabling a full range of editing capabilities remains something of a mystery. What's not a mystery, though, is why the Inducement to Infringe Copyrights bill is more likely to become law than is the Family Movie Act: only the former strengthens existing rights and entrenched interests.

The challenge, as always, lies in getting public policy right. Though Microsoft and the record companies may have damaged our economic and technological interests, they *are not* villains. These companies are doing *exactly what they are supposed to do*. They're using the legal rights that *we gave them* to maximize shareholder value. If we don't like the way that our corporate citizens are behaving, we must rethink their motivation. As long as we make it possible for them to lock in their consumers and to leverage their areas of dominance outward, they will do so—at least until we tell them that they have hit the boundaries of antitrust law. Anything else would be irrational, delinquent, and irresponsible to their shareholders.

Stated simply, if we can't get public policy right, we can't fairly blame our largest corporations for following the policies we have rather than those that we espouse. And we have delegated the task of setting public policy to Congress. Congress must remember that though laws and regulations can alter the economic calculi driving the information sector, technological developments will always dominate those calculi. Sensible regulation can change only behavior at the margin. Laws designed to combat technology will have to become increasingly draconian as the technology improves. Sound policies must therefore recognize that digital technologies change the economics of development and distribution. Good laws and regulations that serve public policy will promote innovative and efficient business models. Bad laws and regulations will lock in existing, and increasingly obsolete, business models. It's hardly too late for us to get it right—though the longer we follow the wrong path, the harder corrective action will become. That simple message encapsulates the enlightenment that I sought when I first embarked upon my quest.

But one quest leads to another. Though the information sector's key *internal* stories unfolded more or less as I expected while *Digital Phoenix* worked its way from idea to manuscript to book, I failed to anticipate the speed with which our young information sector would begin to transform our broader economic, political, and social environments. In my quest to comprehend the bubble, I came to see that the global transition to the information age will be fully as profound as was the transition to the industrial age—and that transitional battles will arrive at Internet speed, giving us nary a chance to catch our collective breaths. The public's sudden recognition that our industrial-age approaches to education, training, and reemployment were becoming obsolete is a case in point; I had anticipated the issue, but not the speed with which it would become front-page news. Understanding the relationships among the information sector, its general lessons, and the broader events that have unfolded since the bubble collapsed sets the stage for the next quest.

As any good economic determinist might say, the means of production will determine the organization of society. We've already seen how technology creates new opportunities, commercial laws promote some opportunities and deter others, and economics motivates new business models. That's when the transition leaps beyond the economic realm, because the remainder of our social structures will adapt to the economics. The sorts and locations of jobs available will dictate whether we work for large or small concerns, whether we live in rural, suburban, or urban communities, what we choose to study, and which skills will prove most lucrative. We will form new associations, affiliations, and alliances, rethink long-accepted "truths," and revise every element of every social organization. Leaders of traditional organizations undergoing rapid change and possible dissolution will react with the same hostility that we've come to expect from disintermediated middlemen. The transitional battle of the information age will play itself out in every corner of our lives. Information technology will eliminate transaction costs and empower individuals. Savvy innovators will develop new techniques to improve life by working with the new technologies. And threatened incumbents, sensing the imminent loss of their stranglehold on the channels of information flow—the ultimate source of their power—will fight to retard progress.

When I started writing this book in 2001, most people recognized that we were heading into a full-blown global information economy. In the economic sphere, individual empowerment leads to capitalism. The book's key prescription for the information economy is a legal environment that spreads opportunities broadly while policing rational cheating. My policy proposals—from those detailed for antitrust and IP to those outlined for broader societal concerns—all stem from a fundamental belief that an environment in which all people are truly free to make informed choices among a wide array of options will enhance social welfare, make us all rich as consumers, and maximize our prospects for a glorious future. Tough enforcement of the antitrust laws in the software realm will make it harder for monopolists to leverage their way from markets whose dominance they earned into those that are still competitive. Severing distribution rights from compensation will keep innovators motivated to craft new digital products without retarding new distribution technologies. And tailoring protective rights on digital products to reward innovators quickly inside a narrow window of exclusivity will lead to the rapid, efficient, dissemination of high quality products into the marketplace. Meanwhile, a reformed education system that trains citizens at all stages of life in information-age skills, and that then matches them with jobs requiring those skills, will create a true "opportunity economy." The elimination of international trade barriers will open those opportunities across the globe, thereby maximizing innovative fervor and the consequent likely return on our infrastructure investment. The information economy spreads information and opportunities while enabling competition among innovative ideas. Policies formulated in this vein will make us all rich as consumers. All of this was foreseeable in mid-2001.

As I conclude this book in early 2005, it has become increasingly clear that we also may be heading toward a full-blown global-information polity—in ways that may not have been evident three or four years ago. In the political sphere, individual empowerment leads to constitutional liberal democracy. The legal environment appropriate for this information polity will spread opportunities broadly while policing rational cheating. An environment in which all people are truly free to make informed political choices will maximize our prospects for accountable (if not enlightened) leadership—that's liberal democracy. Rules preventing incumbent majorities from cheating their way into permanent dominance will preserve that liberal democracy—that's constitutionalism. The politics of the information age will help us grow the network of empowered individuals that we call the "free world," and we will all benefit from that growth.

At least, *almost* all of us will benefit.

And therein, as always, lies the problem. Because much as disintermediated businesses will fight to restrain empowered individual consumers, disintermediated authoritarians will fight to restrain empowered individual citizens. But unlike discontented competitors whose attempts to divert technology to extend their dominance nevertheless acknowledge prevailing social norms, threatened authoritarians rarely exhibit either morality or decency. And make no mistake about it, we *do* threaten them. We threaten to empower "their" people with information and choice. We boldly assert that *all* people possess inherent rights and dignity and freedom of choice. In large parts of the world, these assertions remain subversive. The authoritarians who long have controlled information and choice will lose their dominance as our liberal ethos spreads. The growth of our free-world network necessarily imperils the very existence of their controlled networks. And they know it. They will stop at nothing to retain their members.

Though such authoritarian incumbents are entrenched from Zimbabwe to Burma and from North Korea to Belarus, they remain centered in the Middle East. For decades, we in the free world have allowed totalitarians and terrorists to claim all Arabs and Muslims as "their own." For decades, we have watched silently as Saddam, the Assads, Arafat, the House of Saud, the Iranian Ayatollahs, and their ilk stripped "their" people of individual rights, freedom of choice, and basic human dignity. For decades, we have cynically accepted the intolerable, regarding even such atrocities as Syria's occupation of Lebanon, serial genocide in the Sudan, the widespread refusal to resettle Arab refugees, the systematic oppression of Christians, Jews, Kurds, and women, and even legalized slavery, as matters internal to "their people." We have endorsed these incumbents' refusal to empower "their" people—tacitly at some times, overtly at others—often perversely thanking them for curbing the extremism of "the street."

That decades-long approach cannot persist in the information age. Though constitutional liberal democracy is well suited to a networked world, it is *not* the only societal model capable of harnessing network effects; the loosely-linked terror network also avails itself of information-age advances. People already suffering from a lack of empowerment and individual dignity are easy prey for information-age terror networks. Terror leaders will wean some away from incumbent totalitarians, kill those that they can't convert, and generally make it difficult for us to recruit "their people" into our free-world network. Our past—and in many cases ongoing—support of incumbent authoritarians similarly committed to preventing the empowerment of "their people" leaves us with little credibility to counter the terror networks' membership drives. "Those people" whom we long ago abandoned to totalitarian kinsmen now have become both the front-line victims and the hapless cannon fodder of the information age's networked terrorists.

Totalitarians and terrorists differ only in their methods, never in their goals. Both seek to maximize their monopolies of "the truth" by limiting human dignity, access to information, and freedom of choice. Totalitarians consolidate absolute control over small networks before leveraging their way outward; terrorists define and control network specifications, open their membership to all who adopt those specs, and attempt to crush incompatible ideas as they arise. In other words, much as totalitarians perverted industrial-age technology to control society,[14] so terrorists pervert information-age advances to control behavior. But both seek the same goal—an elimination of all choices other than their own monopolized "truth." In the past, we have trusted selected totalitarians to restrain terrorists—a morally reprehensible strategy that nevertheless did seem to work. The superior suitability of the terrorist model to an age of networks and information, however, suggests that such deals with the devil are unlikely to work much longer. And we are up against a formidable network with straightforward specs: a contempt for liberalism, a total devaluation of human life, a commitment to anti-Semitic, anti-Christian, and anti-American verbiage, and a devotional belief in the superiority of an aberrant strand of Islam. The Islamofascist terror network has become so popular that even former Marxist-Lenninist notables have adopted its specs as the best way to continue their antiliberal, anti-Western jihad. And it threatens incumbent totalitarians throughout the Arab and Islamic worlds.

But the terrorists' ability to harness the lessons of network theory will do more than threaten totalitarians. It will bring them into inevitable and constant conflict with our liberal free-world network, and our own recent advances in the Islamic world. Whereas it at least was possible to coexist with totalitarians who limited their atrocities to "their own people," our free-world network simply cannot coexist for long with a terror network. The "market" will tip toward one or the other; the loser will crumble into insignificance. And the terror network cannot truly crumble until we convert "their people" to members of "our" network. One way or another, the information age *will* empower all individuals to make at least some choices. Those for whom the only viable alternatives are totalitarians and terrorists will choose to follow one or the other—increasingly the terrorists, for no reason other than the superior suitability of their model to a networked world. If we want to promote a third choice, we must create new opportunities. *We* must defeat both totalitarians and terrorists to enable "their people" to join the free-world network. And *we* need to pierce the venomous opprobrium of the incumbents to make liberalism relevant and attractive to "their people." Those tasks promise to be difficult, but they are entirely necessary. A global information polity that does not move toward constitutional liberal democracy will necessarily devolve into either anarchic terror or totalitarian control.

Though it receives little press, we actually entered the information age with a promising start. In the 1990s, we did try to change the rules. With peace and prosperity seemingly breaking out everywhere, we attempted (with varying degrees of success) to empower individual Arabs and Muslims, from Kuwaitis and Palestinians to Bosnians, Kosovars, Somalis, Kurds, and Indonesians. The United States took the lead in offering them full membership in our free-world network. Shimon Peres, then Israel's Foreign Minister, spoke hopefully of a New Middle East, "a regional community of nations, with a common market and elected centralized bodies, modeled on the European Community."[15] But Peres's vision threatened to disintermediate too many incumbents—and like most visions of the 90s, paid insufficient heed to the nascent terror network, growing silently alongside our own. His nation fell into a trap that paralleled that of the dot-coms—though with much bloodier results. Israel had dared to dream that economic development and the new opportunities that it creates would lead its neighbors to want peace. The promise of progress seduced Israel, a key contributor to the information economy, as it did much of the free world. But what we see as promise, others see as threat. The terrorists and totalitarians who currently control information and choice throughout the Muslim Middle East spurned our numerous overtures to empower "their" people, first in Jerusalem in September 2000, a year later in New York and Washington, and around the globe in the three years since. These incumbents understood that they could never maintain their monopolies of "truth" and power in a peaceful world rich in individual opportunities. And true to their nature, these incumbents elevated their own interests above those of "their people." "Their people," uncertain whether we stand for stable incumbents, for true empowerment, or for narrow, self-serving interests, understandably seethe in rage at both those of us who had invited them to join the free world and those who declined our invitation in their names.

The battle for the global information polity surely will be the bloodiest of our transition to the information age. And though we may need guns and tanks and bombs to clear out the incumbent detritus preventing true information-age empowerment, we cannot win this battle with military might alone. To win, we must convert newly empowered people into full members of our free-world network—and we can do that only if we remember that their rights, needs, and interests remain important to *us*.[16] After all, they are prospective members of our network, and *we* will become safer, richer, and stronger when they join.

The information economy is both our best weapon and our most vulnerable target. Terror is a tactic that increases transaction costs; safety and security measures are necessary grit in an economy that we would prefer to lubricate. And the masters of the terror networks begin with a significant advantage; it is simply easier to destroy than it is to build. But network magic remains on our side—if we use it wisely. The more successfully we grow the information economy, the more we will be able to share with our new members, and the more appealing full membership in the free-world network will become. A robust information sector is the key to many battles of the transition. Not only will it improve our lives directly, it also will increase our resources for spreading opportunities broadly. A robust information economy will let us grow the free world and destroy the competing unfree networks. That is, a robust information economy will enable these marvels if the threatened incumbents don't kill us and destroy our handiwork first. And therein lies the key to understanding the transitional political war of the information age: We seek to build and to empower; they seek to destroy and to control.

The digital economy that dominated the 1990s and the currently dominant tales of terror and war are not the same story—and this book did justice only to the former. But they are interconnected. They both grow from the ways in which information empowers individuals and drives disintermediated incumbents to fight that empowerment. It is hardly coincidental that the information age's first great story involved its potential to enrich us all through empowerment and growth, while its second great story involves its potential to impoverish us all through restraint and destruction. Our next great imperative is to devise a strategy that will help us return the first story to dominance while quashing the second story's challenge. We must terminate both terrorist movements and totalitarian states to facilitate robust economic growth. Robust economic growth, in turn, will facilitate our victory over totalitarians and terrorists. The emergence of a global information polity, respectful of human dignity and individual rights, and grounded in constitutional democratic liberalism, rests in no small part upon the health of the information economy. These two stories are thus the thesis and antithesis of our current global transition. They will reach synthesis only when we move the planet and all of its peoples into an information age of empowered individuals.

The patterns taking shape as we transition to an information economy will recur as each aspect of society transitions to the information age. Our primary challengers throughout this transition will be powerful incumbents poised to lose as the vast majority of us win. If we meet these challenges wisely, we can make the world a better place, where free, informed people will form opinions, exercise choices, bear responsibility for poor choices, benefit from good choices, and learn how to make better choices.

Such being the reasons which make it imperative that human beings should be free to form opinions and to express their opinions without reserve; and such the baneful consequences to the intellectual, and through that to the moral nature of man, unless this liberty is either conceded or asserted in spite of prohibition ... he who lets the world, or his own portion of it, choose his plan of life for him has no need of any other faculty than the ape-like one of imitation. He who chooses his plan for himself employs all his faculties. He must use observation to see, reasoning and judgment to foresee, activity to gather materials for decision, discrimination to decide, and when he has decided, firmness and self-control to hold to his deliberate position.[17]

John Stuart Mill penned those words in the midst of Europe's transition to a fully industrial age. If we successfully adapt Mill's thoughts to guide us through our current transition, the information economy will soar once more, rising like a digital phoenix from the ashes of the once-proud Internet bubble to make the information age the glorious era that it has the potential to become. If we fail, the outcome may be catastrophic. The choice *is* ours. And the future of more than just the information sector *does* hang in the balance.

Notes

Chapter 1

1. For a while, at least. When the bubble burst, Time Warner learned that it had sold itself into one of the worst mergers in history. The merged company soon dropped AOL from its name, to become Time Warner once again—though now with a new AOL division.

2. Robert Shiller, *Irrational Exuberance*, Princeton University Press, 2000.

3. John Cassidy, *Dot.con*, Harper Collins, 2002.

4. I coined the terms "New World" and "New Channel" to describe the paradigm shift in "From Investor Fantasy to Regulatory Nightmare: Bad Network Economics and the Internet's Inevitable Monopolists," *Harvard Journal of Law and Technology*, 16(1): 159–228, Fall 2002.

5. *Id.*

6. Thomas Friedman, "Amazon.you," *New York Times*, February 26, 1999, Op Ed page, available at http://www.nytimes.com/library/opinion/friedman/022699frie.html, viewed April 22, 2003.

7. *Id.* (Emphasis in original).

8. Thomas Friedman, "KillingGoliath.com," *New York Times*, March 3, 1999, Op Ed page, available at http://www.nytimes.com/library/opinion/friedman/030999frie.html, viewed April 22, 2003.

9. *Id.* (Capitalization in original).

10. Scott Rosenberg, "Amazon vs. the Ants," Salon, March 10, 1999, available at http://www.salon.com/21st/rose/1999/03/10straight.html, viewed April 22, 2003.

11. *Id.*

12. Thomas Friedman, "Saga of an Online Pioneer," *New York Times*, March 3, 2000, Op Ed page, available at http://www.nytimes.com/library/opinion/friedman/030300frie.html, viewed April 22, 2003.

13. *Id.*

14. Scott Rosenberg, "Death of a David.com," Salon, March 3, 2000, available at http://www.salon.com/tech/log/2000/03/03/friedman/, viewed April 22, 2003.

15. *See*, Hernando de Soto, *The Mystery of Capital*, Basic Books, 2000.

16. Purists may decry our efforts as vast oversimplifications that omit the myriad preconditions, exceptions, and caveats needed to ensure technical completeness. To them, I have but one answer: *mea culpa!* Anyone who ever invested in an Internet stock, read an article about the Microsoft trial, engaged in e-commerce, was bound by a shrink-wrap or click-through license when installing a piece of software, or got frozen out of Napster, deserves to understand how the information sector works.

Chapter 2

1. U.S. CONST. Art. I § 8.

2. *Eldred v. Ashcroft* 123 S. Ct. 769 (2003).

3. Lessig described his personal take on the largely unsuccessful journey that he, eldred, and myriad well-wishes took through the courts in *Free Culture*, ch. 13 (Penguin Press, 2004).

4. In practice, most commercial software companies safeguard their software with *quadruple* protection, by adding terms of sale in a click-through or shrink-wrapped license above and beyond those already guaranteed by patent, copyright, and trade-secret law. These licenses remain the subject of academic and practical controversy.

5. For this and related reasons, I joined the growing chorus suggesting that the current IP regime protecting software is inconsistent with the Constitution's policy goals. *See* "Promoting Innovation in the Software Industry: A First Principles Approach to Intellectual Property Reform," *Boston University Journal of Science and Technology Law*, 8: 75–156, 2002.

6. Lawrence Lessig, *The Future of Ideas*, Random House, 2001.

7. Lawrence Lessig, *Code and Other Laws of Cyberspace*, Basic Books, 1999.

8. Jessica Litman, *Digital Copyright*, Prometheus Books, 2001, pp. 11–14.

9. For two slants on this story, see http://www.eff.org/IP/DMCA/US_v_Elcomsoft/us_v_elcomsoft_faq.html and http://www.adobe.com/aboutadobe/pressroom/pressreleases/200108/elcomsoftqa.html.

10. For example, the Berman P2P Bill, a law proposed but not passed in 2002, would have exempted copyright owners from *all* civil and criminal penalties for any damages that they may have imposed on infringers in the course of trying to detect and correct the infringement of their copyrights by P2P users. For the text of the bill, *see* http://www.house.gov/berman/p2p.pdf. For a strongly libertarian analysis and objection to its provisions, *see* http://www.eff.org/IP/P2P/20020802_eff_berman_p2p_bill.php. Both sites were viewed August 20, 2003.

11. *See e.g.,* Andrew Orlowski, "Elcomsoft not guilty—DoJ retreats from Moscow," the Register, http://www.theregister.co.uk/content/55/28612.html, viewed August 20, 2003. Jury verdicts are notoriously hard to read, and unlike judges who decide opinions, juries are never required to explain their resasoning. In this case, it seems likely that sympathy for the defendants, Adobe's lost interest in the case, and general outrage about criminal copyright laws all played at least some role in the verdict—along with the standard technical argument about the nuances of IP law.

12. Siva Vaidhyanathan, *Copyrights and Copywrongs*, NYU Press, 2001.

13. Paul Goldstein, *Copyright's Highway*, Stanford University Press, 2003 at 141.

14. For an excellent discussion of the history of software IP rights, *see* Robert P. Merges, Peter S. Menell, Mark A. Lemley, and Thomas M. Jorde, *Intellectual Property in the New Technological Age*, Aspen Law & Business, 1997, ch. 7.

15. Congress established the National Commission on New Technological Uses of Copyrighted Works (CONTU) in 1974. Congress followed CONTU's recommendations in 1980 by extending copyright protection explicitly to cover software, notwithstanding the principle that "any idea, procedure, process, system, method of operation, concept, principle, or discovery" cannot be copyrighted. For a good general discussion of the CONTU report—and Commissioner Hersey's spirited dissent—*see Id.* at 860–862.

16. *See Diamond v. Diehr*, 450 U.S. 175 (1981).

17. *See In re Alappat*, 33 F.3d 1526 (Fed. Cir. 1994) (en banc).

18. *See State Street Bank & Trust Co. v. Signature Financial Group, Inc.*, 149 F.3d 1368 (Fed. Cir. 1998).

19. *See Amazon.com, Inc. v. Barnesandnoble.com, Inc.*, 73 F.Supp.2d 1228 (W.D. Washington, 1999).

20. *See Amazon.com, Inc. v. Barnesandnoble.com, Inc.*, 239 F.3d 1343 (Fed. Cir. 2001).

21. See Abramson, *supra* n. 5.

22. Pamela Samuelson, Randall Davis, Mitchell D. Kapor, and J. H. Reichman, *A Manifesto Concerning the Legal Protection of Computer Programs*, 94 Col. L. Rev. 2308, 2315 (1994) [*hereinafter*, Manifesto].

23. National Academy of Sciences, The Digital Dilemma, (2000) [*hereinafter*, Digital Dilemma].

24. Perhaps I should speak only for myself and defer to those who *do* already know exactly what the right answers are. But—in what may be my own peculiar form of arrogance—I prefer analysis to deference.

25. Julie E. Cohen and Mark A. Lemley, *Patent Scope and Innovation in the Software Industry*, 89 Cal. L. Rev. (2001).

26. *Motion Picture Patents Co. v. Universal Film Manufacturing Co.*, 243 U.S. 502 (1917). For the sake of technical accuracy, the products at issue in this suit weren't quite projectors and movies. The patent actually covered only part of the projector's feeding mechanism, and the license restricted its use to certain categories of film. For the sake of illustrative storytelling, however, this distinction is insignificant; the point and the effect remain unchanged by my woefully nonlegalistic literary license.

27. Also known as *The Clansman* and *In the Clutches of the Ku Klux Klan.* (1915). Directed by D. W. Griffith. At the time of the film's release, both the NAACP and W. E. B. Du Bois condemned it as likely to inflame racial tensions. Some historians site the massive race riots that swept across the country in the next few years as proof that they were correct. Nevertheless—or perhaps in part because of its horrible impact—the film has assumed a unique place in American artistic and cultural history.

28. Brett Frischmann and Daniel Moylan, *The Evolving Common Law Doctrine of Copyright Misuse: A Unified Theory and Its Application to Software*, 15 Berkeley Tech. L.J. 865 (Fall 2000).

29. *See Lasercomb v. Reynolds*, 911 F.2d 970 (4th Cir. 1990) (CAD/CAM software); *Practice Management Information Corp. v. American Medical Association*, 121 F.3d 516, (9th Cir. 1997) (a coding system for medical procedures); *Alcatel, Inc. v. DGI Technologies Inc.*, 166 F.3d 772 (5th Cir. 1999) (diagnostic equipment).

30. *See* http://www.gnu.org/licenses/gpl.html. The *GPL Frequently Asked Questions* are particularly helpful.

31. The best known of these licenses is probably the BSD license, originally developed for the Berkeley Software Distribution but subsequently adopted by many open-source developers. The BSD license allows anyone to copy and to use the source code; the only condition is that the new users must attribute the code's original creators.

32. The Patent Bar is not a typical "bar." Membership in the Patent Bar qualifies people to work as patent examiners and to prepare patent applications. No formal legal training is required to take the Patent Bar, but a solid technical background is considered important. *See* http://www.uspto.gov/web/offices/dcom/olia/oed/grb15oct03.pdf, viewed April 23, 2003.

33. Cass Sunstein, *Republic.com,* Princeton University Press, 2002.

34. Cohen, J. "A Right to Read Anonymously: A Closer Look at 'Copyright Management' in Cyberspace." *Connecticut Law Rev. 28,* no. 4 (Summer 1996): 981–1039.

35. "The enumeration in the Constitution, of certain rights, shall not be construed to deny or disparage others retained by the people." U.S. CONST. Amend. 9. *See also* U.S. CONST. Amends. 3, 4, 5, 14; *Griswold v. Conn.*, 381 U.S. 479 (1965).

Chapter 3

1. Curiously enough, Coase didn't coin the Coase theorem; George Stigler extracted it from some of Coase's work. What's more, Coase tended to view the theorem as a sideline, a useful idea that he introduced to help motivate economists to study transaction costs. *See*, R. H. Coase, *The Firm, the Market, and the Law*, University of Chicago Press, 1988.

2. The Supreme Court discussed the legality of much oligopolist behavior in *Brooke Group v. Brown & Williamson Tobacco*, 509 U.S. 209 (1993).

3. At least under U.S. law. European Union law differs in some of its specifics, though not in any relevant manner.

4. George Stigler provided the classic discussion of this distinction among natural and artificial barriers in his groundbreaking IO work in the 1960s. *See* George J. Stigler, *The Organization of Industry*, at 70 (Irwin, 1968).

5. M. Mitchell Waldrop, *Complexity: The Emerging Science at the Edge of Order and Chaos*, Simon & Schuster, 1992.

6. W. Brian Arthur, "Positive Feedbacks in the Economy," *Scientific American*, 262, 92–99, February 1990.

7. *Id.*

8. Waldrop, *supra* n. 5 at 39–40.

9. *Id.* at 35.

10. Arthur, *supra* n. 6 (emphasis added).

11. *Id.*

12. J. Rohlfs, "A Theory of Interdepndent Demand for a Communications Service," *Bell Journal of Economics and Management Science* 5(1): 16–37 (Spring 1974).

13. Paul A. David, "Clio and the Economics of QWERTY," *American Economic Review*, 75:332–337 (1985).

14. Michael L. Katz and Carl Shapiro, "Systems Competition and Network Effects," *Journal of Economic Perspectives* 8(2): 93–115 (1984); Michael L. Katz and Carl Shapiro, "Network Externalities, Competition, and Compatibility." *American Economic Review* 75(3): 424–440 (1985).

15. Liebowitz, S. J. and S. E. Margolis, "The Fable of the Keys," *Journal of Law and Economics* 33: 1–26 (1990).

16. Matthew 25:29 (King James translation).

17. Rohlfs recently tried to disentangle the confusion. *See* J. H. Rohlfs, *Bandwagon Effects in High-Technology Industries*, MIT Press, 2001. I presented a more detailed explanation of the relationship between these two "sins" and the Internet investment bubble in "From Investor Fantasy to Regulatory Nightmare: Bad Network Economics and the Internet's Inevitable Monopolists," *Harvard Journal of Law and Technology*, 16(1): 159–228 (Fall 2002).

18. Generally credited to Bob Metcalfe, the inventor of the Ethernet and the founder of 3Com.

19. Robert H. Bork, *The Antitrust Paradox*, Basic Books, 1978.

20. See *Eastman Kodak Co. v. Image Technical Services, Inc.* 504 U.S. 451, 1992.

21. See *Eastman Kodak*, 504 U.S. 451, 1992 (Scalia, J., dissenting).

22. Not surprisingly, the advent of a new theory generated a fair amount of excitement within the antitrust community. A sizable collection of articles discuss the Kodak case and its broader implications. See e.g., Steven Salop, "Kodak as Post-Chicago Law and Economics," *Charles River Assoc. Persp.* (1993); Carl Shapiro, *Aftermarkets and Consumer Welfare: Making Sense of Kodak*, 63 Antitrust L.J. 483 (1995); Benjamin Klein, *Market Power in Antitrust: Economic Analysis after Kodak* 3 Sup. Ct. Econ. Rev. 43 (1995); Steven C. Salop, *The First Principles Approach to Antitrust, Kodak, and Antitrust at the Millennium* 68 Antitrust L.J. 187 (2000); and Bruce D. Abramson, *Analyzing Antitrust Analysis: The Roles of Fact and Economic Theory in Summary Judgment Adjudication*, Antitrust L.J. 303 (2001).

23. Carl Shapiro and Hal R. Varian, *Information Rules*, Harvard Business School Press, 1999.

24. Shapiro, as a former Deputy Assistant Attorney General for Economics in DOJ's Antitrust Division, was well positioned to offer such a warning.

25. Clayton Christensen developed this theory in depth. See Clayton Christensen, *The Innovators Dilemma* (Harvard Business School Press, 1997).

26. *Hush-a-Phone Corp. v. United States*, 238 F.2d 266 (U.S. App. D.C., 1956).

27. Geoffrey A. Moore, Paul Johnson, and Tom Kippola, *The Gorilla Game*, revised edition, Harper Business, 1999; earlier version published 1998. The "Gorilla Game" outlined a strategy of investing broadly across a new technology, reasoning that when one or two of its early players emerged as winners, gains from those winners would dwarf losses from the others. Players who took the time to read the book would have discovered that its definition of "technology" explicitly excluded the Internet. Nevertheless, the hype surrounding *The Gorilla Game* could easily have misled investors; the book jacket covering the 1999 revised edition even announced: "New! Finding the Internet Gorilla."

28. George Gilder, *Telecosm: How Infinite Bandwidth will Revolutionize Our World*, Free Press, 2000. Gilder proposed that the "telecosmic" revolution made bandwidth free, and sought companies whose technologies and marketing strategies seemed best positioned to take advantage of it. Gilder first publicized many of his ideas through his proprietary newsletter. See www.gildertech.com. After several of Gilder's long-time picks began to appreciate rapidly, his acclaim spread into the investment community at large, where his devotees' tendency to snap up stocks immediately upon his recommendation generated a price spike that even publications like the *Washington Post* and *Business Week* came to recognize as "the Gilder effect." See e.g., Howard Kurz, "Letterman Does a Number

on The N.Y. Times," *Washington Post*, September 4, 2000 at C1; David Shook, "What Disclosure Could Do for George Gilder," *Business Week Online*, May 24, 2000. Gilder had little if anything to say about Internet firms; he emphasized infrastructure. Telecosmic firms would *build* the Internet and collect the tolls as data flowed across it. He found this technology both exciting and promising. Pure plays attempting to commercialize content never garnered much of his interest. What his followers did with his theories, though, is another story entirely.

29. Christensen, *supra* n. 25. Clayton Christensen, a professor at Harvard Business School, studied a number of large (and once successful) companies that had been overtaken by upstart competitors—along with the upstarts. His analysis built on Joseph Schumpeter's notion of "creative destruction;" he noticed that low-end start-ups often managed to surpass their larger, established rivals even though the incumbents had adopted sound business practices and reasonable strategic plans. He posited that their downfall was an almost inevitable consequence of the ways in which the entrants' new technologies rendered the incumbents' existing products and brands obsolete. Internet investors were intrigued. They saw the Internet as the ultimate disruptive technology—and were all too eager to apply Christensen's theories to prove that brick-and-mortar firms couldn't possibly transition to the New World. But that was their analysis; Christensen himself had little or nothing to say about Internet pure plays.

30. Stanley M. Besen and Joseph Farrell, *Choosing How to Compete: Strategies and Tactics in Standardization*, 8 Journal of Economic Perspectives 117.

31. Michael A. Cusumano and David B. Yoffie, *Competing on Internet Time*, The Free Press, 1998 at 4.

32. John del Vecchio and Mike Trigg, "What the Next Microsoft Will Look Like," December 4, 2000, available at http://www.fool.com/news/2000/msft001205.htm. Viewed November 5, 2001. The Motley Fool was and is a popular investment site. Other sources generalized the theory even further. Hostpulse.com, a glossary of Web-hosting terms, defined increasing returns as simply "[t]he idea that the more dominant a company becomes, the bigger its future advantage over competitors will be. http://www.hostpulse.com/app/tquo/default.asp?quo=ht2&stitle=150. Viewed November 5, 2001.

33. Skeptics were hard to find at the time and even harder to track after the bubble deflated. But a few were out there—if you knew where to look for them. Aussie David Walker was among the best:

The Internet stock boom, huge though it now is, rests on one Big Theory: that in certain circumstances the Internet provides entrepreneurs with what economists call increasing returns to scale. Get in early and get big, in other words, and the Internet will provide you with huge returns after, say, five years. The Big Internet Stock Theory is neither profound nor well developed. . . . Yet Internet investors seem determined to ignore all these rules: . . . Increasing return remains relatively rare, even on the Internet—but investors act as if it happens on every

Web site. . . . On the Internet, just about every stock reaps rewards for "learning" well before they make any profit—in other words, before it's clear that their learning is actually worth anything. . . . Investors seem determined to pretend that expansion costs every Internet business nothing at all. . . . In their very brief history, Internet brands have shown themselves more volatile than most—HotBot, the cool search engine of 1998, has faded in the face of Google—yet investors assume the Internet brands of 1999 are here forever. . . . Investors in today's Internet stock boom no longer feel the need to believe even the rather flaky economics of the Big Internet Stock Theory. Rather than investing in a theory, they're simply investing in a word—Internet. They're not so much Wired as Weird. . . . Venture capitalists flood the markets with new contenders for the Internet user's dollar. And the competition between all these well-funded sites is making sure that none of them reach profit. Rather than increasing returns, today's Internet stock boom is instead creating increasing losses.

"Internet Business Investors Now Ignore Even the Simplest Rules," written February 1, 2000; text cited from modifications as of February 21, 2000, available at http://www.shorewalker.com/commerce/commerce72.html, viewed November 5, 2001.

34. *See,* del Vecchio and Trigg, *supra* n. 82:

Attempts to find the next Microsoft have reached legendary proportions, resembling such storied endeavors as the plight of the Mayflower and Armstrong's journey to the moon. Rather than lead investors to believe that such a company exists, however, we've chosen to identify three key factors—controlling the value chain, dominant market share, and a tectonic shift in computing—that helped Microsoft achieve world domination. A company able to garner even one or two of the aforementioned metrics could be well on its way to creating significant shareholder wealth.

For a description of a conference for firms believing that they might be the next Microsoft, *see* "Is the Next Microsoft Out There?" July 2, 1998, available at http://www.cnn.com/TECH/computing/9807/02/startups.idg/, viewed November 5, 2001.

35. *See,* Gregory J. Werden, *Network Effects and Conditions of Entry: Lessons from the* Microsoft *Case,* at 69 Antitrust Law Journal 87: 88–89 (2001) (citations omitted):

The potentially decisive impact of network effects is illustrated by the *Microsoft* case, in which network effects have been much commented upon. . . . The district court based its finding that Microsoft unlawfully maintained a monopoly on what it termed the "applications barrier to entry," which it described as arising from a "positive network effect." . . . *Microsoft* presents a fascinating case study, although its most important lesson may be that assessing conditions of entry in the presence of network effects is likely to be a complex and highly fact-intensive process. The mere presence of network effects does not imply anything important about conditions of entry.

Chapter 4

1. H. A. Simon, *The Sciences of the Artificial*, second ed., 1982, The MIT Press.

2. *Id.* at 131–132. Simon maintained most of this discussion in his second revision, but he dropped his optimism about academic computer science. Instead, he pointed with pride to a unique interdisciplinary Design Research Center at Carnegie Mellon. H. A. Simon, *The Sciences of the Artificial*, third ed., The MIT Press, 1996, at 114.

3. And highlighting the difference between the French "informatique" and the English "computer science."

4. Simon's distinction between "natural" and "artificial" sciences leaves some topics typically categorized as "social" sciences in the natural column, where they rarely appear inside modern academia.

5. I retain a personal attachment to this challenge because one of my first research tasks in graduate school was to survey the history of computer chess, and many of the lessons that I learned from that survey worked their way into my dissertation. This just means that many people did interesting work on computer chess long before I showed up. In fact, much of the work on computer chess began before I was born. *See* B. Abramson, "Control Strategies for Two-Player Games," ACM Computing Surveys 21(2), June 1989; B. Abramson, *The Expected-Outcome Model of Two-Player Games*, Pitman Publishing, 1991.

6. C. E. Shannon, "Programming a Computer for Playing Chess," *Philosophical Magazine*, 41: 256–275, 1950.

7. J. Von Neumann and O. Morgenstern, *Theory of Games and Economic Behavior*. Princeton University Press, 1944.

8. M. M. Botvinnik, *Computers in Chess: Solving Inexact Search Problems* (A. Brown, transl.) Springer-Verlag, 1984.

9. *See*, Hans J. Berliner and Carl Ebeling, "The SUPREM Architecture: A New Intelligent Paradigm," *Artificial Intelligence* 28(1): 3–8 (1986); Hans J. Berliner, "New Hitech Computer Chess Success," *AI Magazine* 9(2): 133 (1988).

10. *See* http://www.research.ibm.com/deepblue/.

11. "A Proposal for the Dartmouth Summer Research Project on Artificial Intelligence, Aug. 31, 1955," available at http://www-formal.stanford.edu/jmc/history/dartmouth/dartmouth.html, viewed November 2, 2002.

12. *Id.*

13. *See* John McCarthy and P. J. Hayes, "Some Philosophical Problems from the Standpoint of Artificial Intelligence," in D. Michie, ed., *Machine Intelligence 4*, American Elsevier, New York, 1969.

14. *See* Peter Jackson, *Introduction to Expert Systems*, Addison Wesley, 1990 (second ed.). For a description of how some of these systems were able to recommend decisions in uncertain, complex environments, *see* Keung-Chi Ng and Bruce Abramson, "Uncertainty Management in Expert Systems," *IEEE Expert*, April 1990, 29–48.

15. The final blow to the rejection of probability theoretic reasoning came in the late 1980s, when several statisticians, decision analysts, and computer scientists all converged to similar results at about the same time. They demonstrated both the practicality and the utility of representing uncertain information as networks of probabilities. See Peter Cheeseman, "An Inquiry into Computer Understanding," *Computational Intelligence* 4(1): 58–66, 129–142, 1988; Ronald A. Howard and James E. Matheson, eds., *The Principles and Applications of Decision Analysis*, Strategic Decisions Group, 1989; Stephan L. Lauritzen and David J. Spiegelhalter, "Local Computations with Probabilities on Graphical Structures and their Applications to Expert Systems," *J. Royal Statistical Society B*, 50(2): 157–224, 1988; Judea Pearl, *Probabilistic Reasoning in Intelligent Systems*, Morgan Kaufmann, 1988.

16. Izhar Matzkevich and I presented a survey of these systems in "Decision Analytic Networks in Artificial Intelligence," *Management Science* 41(1): 1–22, 1995.

17. The concepts underlying neural networks originated in Norbert Weiner's classic work *Cybernetics* (The MIT Press, 1948). They remained the subject of various (mostly theoretical) studies for the next two decades, until *Perceptrons*, by Marvin Minsky and Seymour Papert (The MIT Press, 1972) demonstrated an entire class of problems to which these concepts were inapplicable. That discovery, coming on the heels of McCarthy and Hayes's general warning against numeric reasoning, shunted the attention and funding of the research community in other directions. Interest began to pick up again in the early 1980s, with John Hopfield's "Neural Networks and Physical Systems with Emergent Collective Computational Properties" (in *Proceedings of the National Academy of Sciences of the USA*, 79: 2554–2588, 1982). The real excitement, though, began when Danny Hillis published his doctoral thesis, *The Connection Machine* (The MIT Press, 1989) and founded Thinking Machines, Inc., a supercomputer company.

18. Frederick P. Brooks, Jr., *The Mythical Man-Month*, anniversary ed., Addison Wesley, 1995 (first ed., 1975).

19. *Id.* at ch. 19.

20. The new application may, in turn, contain its own APIs to allow still more programs to run upon it. Programs whose communication with hardware must pass through a preexisting platform, but that nevertheless expose APIs to other programs, qualify as "middleware"; true applications communicate only with users, while middleware can behave like an application when dealing with users or a platform when dealing with other applications.

21. *See e.g.*, http://www.zakon.org/robert/internet/timeline/ and http://www.internetindicators.com/. Both sites viewed January 23, 2002.

22. Tim Berners-Lee, *Weaving the Web*, Harper Business, 1999.

23. Jonathan Rosen, *The Talmud and the Internet*, Picador, 2001.

24. *See e.g.*, http://www.breslov.com/talmud/talmud.htm.

25. Gopher, for example, was a popular, early text-based Internet browser originally developed at the University of Minnesota as a campus-wide document-retrieval system—an application of obvious value to researchers, but of limited broad appeal. While Gopher had its fans, it also encountered some problems. The academic bent of most Internet users had made them accustomed to free access. When the university exercised the right to charge for Gopher's use, a near boycott ensued. *See,* Chris Sherman, *A Pre-Web Search Engine, Gopher Turns Ten.* Searchday, available at http://searchenginewatch.com/searchday/article.php/ 2159211 (viewed March 29, 2004).

26. And the subject of Michael Lewis's entertaining *The New New Thing: A Silicon Valley Story,* W. W. Norton & Co., 1999.

27. When Netscape formally announced that it was filing for an IPO June 23, 1995, its underwriter (Morgan Stanley) initially estimated a price of $12 to $14 a share. The IPO took place August 9, 1995—only sixteen months after the founding of the company, which had never turned a profit—with 5 million $28 shares. On the first day of trading, the stock opened at $71, traded as high as $74.75, and closed at $58.25. The stock exhibited extreme volatility, selling as high as $174 per share in early December 1995 before losing more than half its value over the next few months. For a review of Netscape's early trading history as summarized for a business school case study, *see* http://www.stern.nyu.edu/ ~tucci/netscape/finbkgd.htm, viewed January 23, 2002.

28. Michael A. Cusumano and David B. Yoffie, *Competing on Internet Time,* The Free Press, 1998.

29. *See* http://www.corp.aol.com/whoweare/history.html.

30. *See* "Napster. The Players Speak Out. Lars Ulrich," *The American Prospect On-Line,* available at http://www.prospect.org/controversy/napster/ulrich-l.html, viewed August 20, 2003.

31. *See* "Napster. The Players Speak Out. John Perry Barlow," *The American Prospect On-Line,* available at http://www.prospect.org/controversy/napster/ barlow-j.html, viewed August 20, 2003.

32. *See* http://www.eff.org.

33. Fed Chairman Alan Greenspan coined the term "irrational exuberance" in December 1996. *See* "Remarks by Chairman Alan Greenspan at the Annual Dinner and Francis Boyer Lecture of The American Enterprise Institute for Public Policy Research," Washington, D.C., December 5, 1996, available at http://www.federalreserve.gov/boarddocs/speeches/1996/19961205.htm, viewed October 31, 2001. By early 2000, even Greenspan appeared willing to forgive at least some of the irrationality and the exuberance:

What should be indisputable is that a number of new technologies that evolved largely from the cumulative innovations of the past half century have now begun to bring about awesome changes in the way goods and services are produced and, especially, in the way they are distributed to final users. . . . The exceptional stock price volatility of most of the newer firms and, in the view of some, their outsized valuations, are indicative of the difficulties of divining from the many, the particular few of the newer technologies and operational models that will prevail in the decades ahead.

"Remarks by Chairman Alan Greenspan, Technology and the Economy," before the Economic Club of New York, January 13, 2000, available at http://www .federalreserve.gov/boarddocs/speeches/2000/200001132.htm, viewed October 31, 2001. Professor Robert Shiller later adopted Greenspan's phrase as the title of his book, *Irrational Exuberance*, Princeton University Press, March 2000.

34. Dan Goodin and Hane Lee, "Pixelon's Golden-Tongued Salesman Busted," *The Industry Standard*, April 13, 2000, http://www.thestandard.com/article/ 0,1902,14113,00.html:

Michael Fenne made a name for himself back in October when as head of Pixelon he orchestrated the most outrageous promotional event ever seen in the Internet Economy. To celebrate the streaming media company's launch last fall, Fenne paid $12 million to stage a star-studded party in Las Vegas. This week, he was back in the news when Virginia authorities jailed him without bail, ending a four-year manhunt for one of the state's most-wanted fugitives. David Kim Stanley, who under the name Michael Fenne persuaded investors to hand over at least $20 million to fund Pixelon, turned himself in Wednesday. In 1989, he pleaded guilty in Virginia to 24 counts of defrauding victims, many of them elderly parishioners at his father's church. He also pleaded guilty to 31 similar charges in Tennessee. . . . Representatives from Pixelon's investor, a Chicago brokerage called Advanced Equities, were not available by press time to comment on the revelation that it had handed $20 million to a convicted felon.

See also, Joanna Glasner, "Perilous Fall of Pixelon," *Wired News*, May 16, 2000. Available at http://www.wired.com/news/exec/0,1370,36243,00.html. Both sites viewed February 2, 2003.

35. *See, Ebay, Inc. v. Bidder's Edge, Inc.*, 100 F.Supp.2d 1058, (N.D.CA., 2000).

36. *See* e.g., Katrina Brooker, "The Nightmare before Christmas," *Business 2.0*, January 2000; Paul Elias, "Is Jeff Bezos Father Christmas," *Red Herring*, August 11, 2000; "Seven Internet Retailers Settle FTC Charges over Shipping Delays during 1999 Holiday Season," Federal Trade Commission press release, July 26, 2000, available at http://www.ftc.gov/opa/2000/07/toolate.htm, viewed October 31, 2001.

37. This high-profile problem with fulfillment led many observers to reconsider e-commerce. They noted that in addition to potential problems with delivery deadlines, online retailers were at a serious disadvantage vis-à-vis their brick-and-mortar competitors when it came to returns and exchanges. For a detailed demonstration of the broad drop of Internet equity prices from their earlier highs, *see* "The Internet Wasteland," in Anthony B. Perkins and Michael C. Perkins, *The Internet Bubble*, revised (Harper Business, 2001) at 289. Investors began to grasp that there was no such thing as "an Internet company," and in particular that it was meaningless to think of a company as "an e-tailer." Petstore.com and Pets.com, two sites devoted to the sale of pet food and pet supplies, were among

the most anticipated Internet IPOs of 1999. Pets.com acquired Petstore.com in June 2000 and ceased retail operations before the year was out. In groceries, Webvan, once a highly visible and valuable pure play, acquired its once equally valuable rival, Homegrocer.com in early 2001. Four months later the merged firm went out of business. Albertsons, Wegman's, and Tesco, on the other hand, introduced Internet presences to augment their supermarket chains, demonstrating the viability of brick-and-click grocers.

38. Parties operating on "Internet time" rarely paid much attention to their contracting practices. Most Internet firms signed contracts drafted so poorly that litigation was inevitable. Nevertheless, few of these cases made it beyond procedural issues, as many of the parties ran out of the money to pursue their claims— or came to realize that the adverse party's finances made them effectively judgment-proof. *See e.g. Iballs, Inc. v. Wildbrain.com, Inc.*, 2001 U.S. Dist. LEXIS 13394, (S.D.N.Y. 2001) (Iballs sought to recover for unpaid services and expenses incurred in launching an Internet advertising campaign on Wild Brain's behalf); *About.com, Inc. v. Aptimus, Inc.*, 2001 U.S. Dist. LEXIS 6102, (S.D.N.Y. 2001) (Parties disagreed about the relationship among two potentially contradictory agreements); *900 Support, Inc. v. Microportal.com, Inc.*, 2001 U.S. Dist. LEXIS 8603 (D. Oregon 2001) (Plaintiff continued service to defendant, despite defendant's failure to pay, because of representations by the defendant that its officers' other corporations would make the payments); *Paramount Brokers, Inc. v. Digital River, Inc.* 126 F.Supp.2d 939 (D. Maryland 2000) (Plaintiff contended that defendant's "letter of interest" constituted a binding exclusive agreement.).

39. Zefer Corp., a large, popular Internet-consulting and Web-development firm is a case in point. Zefer originally had planned to raise $50 million in its May 2000 IPO, then decided to reschedule for September 2000, but the IPO never happened. Zefer closed its doors and sold off its assets about a year after it gave up on going public. *See*, "It's Official: Zefer Calls Off IPO," September 19, 2000, available at http://www.internetnews.com/IAR/article/0,,2051_463951,00.html; David Apanovich, "Zefer Cuts 15 Percent of Workforce," February 2, 2001, available at http://www.internetnews.com/IAR/article/0,,2001_577571,00.html; David Aponovich, "Zefer Closes Boston HQ," September 6, 2001, available at http://www.internetnews.com/IAR/article/0,,12_879431,00.html. All sites viewed October 31, 2001.

40. *See* Perkins and Perkins, *supra* n. 37 at 207–209.

Chapter 5

1. *See* Ken Auletta, *World War 3.0*, Random House, 2001, pp. 145–146.

2. Bill Gates, General Partner, Micro-Soft, "An Open Letter to Hobbyists," February 3, 1976, first published in MITS Computer Notes, and now widely available on the Web. *See e.g.*, http://www.bluemud.org/article/23189. *See also*, "Key Events in Microsoft History," http://www.microsoft.com/msft/download/keyevents.doc. Both sites viewed August 20, 2003.

3. Carl Shapiro and Hal R. Varian, *Information Rules*, Harvard Business School Press, 1999.

4. I discussed this idea in what was almost certainly too much detail in "Analyzing Antitrust Analysis: The Roles of Fact and Economic Theory in Summary Judgment Adjudication," *Antitrust L.J.* 303 (2001).

5. It also reaps huge profits from these two products. For the first quarter of its 2003 fiscal year (ending September 30, 2003), Microsoft reported that its division responsible for these two products earned about $4.88 billion in profits. Those earnings represented margins of about 86% for Windows and about 78% for Office. All other divisions lost money. *See* Microsoft Corporation's form 10-Q for the period ending September 30, 2002. *See also* Joe Wilcox, "Office, Windows Cover Microsoft Losses," CNET News.com, November 19, 2002, available at http://zdnet.com.com/2102-1104-966219.html, viewed August 20, 2003.

6. It's hard to underestimate the importance of the Gates Foundation's work to help find cures for diseases that impact primarily the poor and, of more immediate concern, to distribute preventative and palliative medication and promote heath education among the world's poor. In many ways, Gates has stepped into a role callously abdicated by the world's governments. And yet, an unfortunate cloud hangs over this work. In the words of *New York Times* columnist Nicholas Kristof, who had the privilege of accompanying the Gateses on one of their trips to Africa, "Mr. Gates's achievements in public health are undermined by cynicism that all this is just a promotion for Microsoft. And frankly, the world needs AIDS and malaria vaccines more than it needs a new version of Windows. So Mr. Gates should think about moving full time to his foundation to concentrate on what he does best—fighting malaria and AIDS, and, yes, holding research consultations with Botswana prostitutes." Nicholas Kristof, "Fighting the Fevers," *New York Times* op-ed page, September 24, 2003.

7. Stan J. Liebowitz and Stephen E. Margolis, *Winners, Losers, and Microsoft*, revised ed. The Independent Institute, 2001.

8. *Id.* at 135–136.

9. *See, Caldera v. Microsoft*, 72 F.Supp.2d 1295, 1298 (D.Utah, 1999).

10. *See* Andrew Schulman, "The Caldera v. Microsoft Dossier," available at http://www.oreillynet.com/pub/a/network/2000/02/07/schulman.html, viewed November 10, 2002.

11. *Caldera*, 72 F.Supp.2d 1295 n.1, citing Stan Miastkowski, "A Cure for What Ails DOS," *BYTE*, Aug. 1990, at 107.

12. *Id.*, citing Bill Machrone, "7th Annual Awards for Technical Excellence," *PC Magazine*, Jan. 15, 1991, at 100.

13. Schulman, *supra* n. 10.

14. *Id.*

15. *Id.*

16. This test, known alternatively as the *Altai* test or as the abstraction-filtration-comparison test, was first articulated in *Computer Associates International v. Altai, Inc.*, 982 F.2d 693 (2d Cir. 1992). In under a decade, it gained broad acceptance, not only in U.S. courts, but also in Canada, the United Kingdom, and France. *See* Robert P. Merges, Peter S. Menell, Mark A. Lemley, and Thomas M. Jorde, *Intellectual Property in the New Technological Age, Aspen Law & Business*, 1997, at 889.

17. *See Apple Computer, Inc. v. Microsoft Corp.*, 35 F.3d 1435 (9th Cir. 1994).

18. *The Economist*, "Giving the Invisible Hand a Helping Hand," November 9, 2002, p. 14.

19. Michael A. Cusumano and David B. Yoffie, *Computing on Internet Time*, The Free Press, 1998.

20. David Bank, *Breaking Windows*, Free Press, 2001.

21. Dmitry Mehlhorn and I expanded on this idea in "The Fettered Liberty to Integrate: Legal Implications of Software Engineering," *Boston University Journal of Science and Technology Law*, 2004.

22. Bank, *supra* n. 21 at 96.

23. "Sun," Wired News Report, Feb. 1, 1999. http://www.wired.com/news/business/0,1367,17645,00.html. Viewed November 14, 2002.

24. "Scott Says . . . 'Kick Butt and Have Fun' A candid interview with Scott McNealy, Sun's CEO, Interviewed by Maureen Taylor, May 16, 1996." http://www.sun.com/960601/cover/#toc8, viewed November 14, 2002.

25. *United States v. Microsoft*, 980 F.Supp. 537, 543 (D.D.C. 1997).

26. See Bank, *supra* n. 21 at 121.

27. *Id.* at 122.

28. Joel Brinkley and Steven Lohr, *U.S. v. Microsoft*, McGraw-Hill, 2001.

29. Auletta, *supra* n. 1.

30. *United States v. Microsoft Corp.*, 65 F.Supp.2d 1 (D.D.C. 1999) [hereinafter MS-facts] at ¶ 67.

31. *Id.* at ¶ 68.

32. *Id.* at ¶ 77.

33. *Id.* at ¶ 133.

34. Even the nation's top IO economists split on this issue. *See e.g.*, David S. Evans, Franklin M. Fisher, Daniel L. Rubinfeld, and Richard L. Schmalensee, *Did Microsoft Harm Consumers? Two Opposing Views*, AEI-Brookings Joint Center for Regulatory Studies, 2000.

35. Many of the structural vs. behavioral debates among antitrust priests were fairly technical. For a relatively accessible debate, *see* R. C. Romaine and S. C. Salop, "Slap Their Wrists? Tie Their Hands? Slice Them into Pieces? Alternative Remedies for Monopolization in the Microsoft Case.," *Antitrust Magazine*

Summer 1999 (advocating a structural remedy); J. E. Lopatka and W. H. Page, "A (Cautionary) Note on Remedies in the Microsoft Case," *Antitrust Magazine*, Summer 1999 (advocating a behavioral approach).

36. *See, United States v. Microsoft Corp.*, 253 f.3d 34 (D.C. Cir. 2001) [hereinafter MS-appeal] at 190–196.

37. http://www.microsoft.com/net/basics/whatis.asp.

38. *New York vs. Microsoft*, 224 F.Supp.2d 76 (D.D.C. 2002), quoting Niccolo Machiavelli, *The Prince*, ch. 18 (1514).

39. *See*, United States *v.* United Shoe Machinery Co., 247 U.S. 32 (1918); United States *v.* United Shoe Machinery Corp., 110 F. Supp. 295 (D. Mass., 1953); United States *v.* United Shoe Machinery Corp. 391 U.S. 244 (1968).

40. John Burgess, "EU, Microsoft Cannot Agree on Settlement," *The Washington Post*, March 19, 2004, A1.

41. *Id.*

42. By way of full and fair disclosure, I worked as a consultant to parties involved in the European Commission proceedings against Microsoft. Some of the positions that I advocated made their way into the Commission's findings.

Chapter 6

1. *The New Hacker's Dictionary*, third edition, complied by Eric S. Raymond, MIT Press, 1996.

2. For example, as *Business Week's* cover story on March 3, 2003.

3. *See* http://www.cs.helsinki.fi/linux/whatis.html.

4. *See* http://www.gnu.org/philosophy/free-sw.html, viewed April 27, 2003.

5. Richard Stallman, "The GNU Operating System and the Free Software Movement," in *Open Sources*, Chris DiBona, Sam Ockman, and Mark Stone, eds., O'Reilly & Assoc., 1999.

6. Bill Gates, General Partner, Micro-soft, "An Open Letter to Hobbyists," February 3, 1976, first published in MITS Computer Notes, and now widely availabe on the Web. *See e.g.*, http://www.bluemud.org/article/23189.

7. Richard Stallman, "The GNU Operating System and the Free Software Movement," in DiBona, Ockman, and Stone, eds., *supra* n. 5.

8. Simson L. Garfinkel, "Is Stallman Stalled?" *Wired* issue 1.01, March/April 1993, available at http://www.wired.com/wired/archive/1.01/stallman.html.

9. Michael Tiemann, "Future of Cygnus Solutions, An Entrepreneur's Account," in DiBona, Ockman, and Stone, eds., *supra* n. 5.

10. *See* Eric Raymond's home page, http://tuxedo.org/~esr/.

11. *The New Hacker's Dictionary*, *supra* n. 1.

12. Raymond's essays on hackerdom and open-source are collected in Eric S. Raymond, *The Cathedral and the Bazaar*, O'Reilly & Associates, 1999. They are also available through Raymond's home page, http://tuxedo.org/~esr/.

13. *The New Hacker's Dictionary*, *supra* n. 1.

14. *See* http://www.netcraft.com/survey/, viewed November 25, 2002.

15. "The Cathedral and the Bazaar," in Raymond, *supra* n. 12 at 21–22.

16. http://www.opensource.org/docs/definition_plain.php, viewed November 28, 2002.

17. Frederick P. Brooks, Jr., *The Mythical Man-Month*, anniversary ed., Addison Wesley, 1995 (first ed., 1975).

18. M. Mitchell Waldrop, in *Complexity: The Emerging Science at the Edge of Order and Chaos*, (Simon & Schuster, 1992) told the stories of the scientists who studied these emergent properties in various fields.

19. *See* Martin Fink, *The Business and Economics of Linux and Open Source*, Hewlett Packard Company, 2003, chapter 1.

20. *See* Eric Raymond, "Homesteading the Noosphere," in Raymond, *supra* n. 12.

21. *The New Hacker's Dictionary*, *supra* n. 1.

22. Jim Hamerly, Tom Paquin, and Susan Walton, "Freeing the Source," in DiBona et. al., eds., *supra* n. 5 at 197.

23. The unique challenges posed by opening a software project already subject to the sorts of contractual obligations common in the world of proprietary software also led Netscape to develop a new variant of the open-source licensing scheme, the Mozilla Public License (MPL).

24. Michael A. Cusumano and David B. Yoffie, *Competing on Internet Time*, The Free Press, 1998, at 139.

25. *See* http://www.sun.com/software/star/openoffice/, viewed November 28, 2002.

26. *See* http://www.synthesist.net/writing/onleavingms.html, viewed April 27, 2003.

27. A complete discussion of the concerns underlying software-selection decisions is beyond the scope of this book.

28. WTO compliance is hardly China's only concern. The Chinese government has come to realize the potential value of IP rights as a driver of innovation—precisely the policy concern reflected in the U.S. Constitution. For a discussion of the history of IP rights in China, recent government moves toward improving both its IP regime and the enforcement of IP rights, and the specific case of software piracy, *see* Mark A. Groombridge, "The Political Economy of Intellectual Property Rights Protection in the People's Republic of China," in Clarissa Long, ed., *Intellectual Property Rights in Emerging Markets*, AEI Press, 2000.

29. Letter reproduced in translation at http://pimientolinux.com/peru2ms/ alt_ms_to_villanueva.html, viewed November 28, 2002. I corrected a few spelling and grammar errors in the translation.

30. Letter reproduced in translation at http://www.theregister.co.uk/content/4/ 25157.html, viewed November 28, 2002. I corrected a few spelling and grammar errors in the translation.

31. In fact, Congressman Villanueva was involved with the Free Software movement in Peru for several years prior to drafting his bill, and he credited various open-source organizations in both Peru and Argentina with supporting and enabling his efforts. *See* Richard Vernon and Don Marti, "An Interview with Dr. Edgar Villanueva," *Linux Journal*, May 24, 2002. Available at http://www.linuxjournal.com/article.php?sid=6099, viewed July 28, 2004.

Chapter 7

1. Copyright law protects the property rights of lyricists, much as it does of all authors. Authors, myself included, who wish to quote more than a few lines of lyrics from well-known songs to enhance their own presentations, must secure the permission of the copyright owner or risk being sued for infringement. This requirement immediately imposes a potentially significant transaction cost on authors wishing to quote song lyrics, thereby deterring the practice. This deterrence has an immediate negative effect on artists who *would like* to see their work quoted widely, but does make it possible for other artists, typically those who are already famous, to extract additional royalties from their work. Earlier drafts of this chapter excerpted quotes from several songs by several artists. The Grateful Dead and Tori Amos thoughtfully granted me permission to quote their work in mine, without imposing any conditions. To the extent that a citation in *Digital Phoenix* provides any promotional value, I encourage all readers to buy any and all Grateful Dead and Tori Amos albums. Other artists and the corporate owners of their copyrights were less forthcoming, as is their right. Proffered conditions included initial fees ranging into the hundreds of dollars, grants to allow citation in only a fixed number of copies of this book, and the right to ferret through my accounting. These are all conditions that the copyright law allows copyright owners to request. Because I both respect their right to request these terms and consider these terms to be outrageous, I have chosen to omit all quotations from their songs. These omissions do not affect this book's substance, but they do impoverish its presentation—at least in a minor way. The broad societal effect of this phenomenon, however, is far from minor. For a good discussion of the ways that a "permissions culture" stymies cultural development, *see* Larry Lessig, *Free Culture*, (Penguin Press, 2004).

2. Though I suppose that folks in the financial services industry could also lay claim to the title of "first to be swallowed."

3. The Grateful Dead, *The Music Never Stopped*. Words by John Barlow. Copyright Ice Nine Publishing Company. Used with permission.

4. *See* Jessica Litman, *Digital Copyright*, Prometheus Books, 2001, for a succinct review of this history.

5. *Eldred v. Ashcroft* 123 S. Ct. 769 (2003).

6. *Eldred v. Ashcroft* 123 S. Ct. 769 (2003) (Stevens, J. dissenting).

7. *Sony v. Universal Studios*, 464 U.S. 417 (1984).

8. For an excellent discussion of the fair use doctrine, *see* Robert P. Merges, Peter S. Menell, Mark A. Lemley, and Thomas M. Jorde, *Intellectual Property in the New Technological Age*, Aspen Law & Business, 1997, at 458–506.

9. The Grateful Dead, *Dire Wolf*. Words by Robert Hunter. Copyright Ice Nine Publishing Company. Used with permission.

10. *See* Bruce Haring, *Beyond the Charts*, OTC Press, 2000, for a good review of the critical wave of events leading up to the advent of Napster. Haring provides a terse, readable discussion of the way that the digital revolution crept up to take over the world of music. Unfortunately, he finished his book just a bit too early. It covers events only through 1998—and thus misses the Napster story entirely.

11. *Id.* at 44, citing RIAA President Hillary Rosen.

12. Tori Amos, *Crucify*. Words by Tori Amos. Copyright Sword and Stone Publishing, Inc. Quoted with permission.

13. Litman, *supra* n. 4.

14. Trevor Merriden, *Irresistible Forces*, Capstone, 2001 at 33.

15. Frustration and desperation can still prevail. In September 2003, the record companies launched a wave of lawsuits against known KaZaA users, mostly kids who downloaded music. Though parents lined up immediately to begin to settle for a few thousand dollars, the record companies know that they will never recoup their legal fees. The strategy is a scare tactic—though they may have to apply it relentlessly to have a long-term effect.

16. *RIAA v. Diamond Multimedia Systems, Inc.*, 29 F.Supp.2d 624, (C.D.Ca., 1998).

17. Haring, *supra* n. 10 at 125.

18. Ecclesiastes 3:1–8. Adapted and set to music by Pete Seeger. Recorded by various artists.

19. In fact, that's exactly what they started doing—though not for another four years under the auspices of Carey Sherman, Hillary Rosen's successor as Central Scrutinizer.

20. Merriden, *supra* n. 15 at 8 and 15.

21. *A&M Records v. Napster*, 2000 U.S. Dist. LEXIS 6243, (N.D.Ca. 2000).

22. Merriden, *supra* n. 15 at 55–56 quoting attorney David Boies.

23. *A&M Records v. Napster*, 239 F.3d 1004 (9th Cir. 2001).

24. In late 2003, Roxio resuscitated the Napster brand name with a new service selling online music.

25. For a readable explanation of the music industries' *legal* arguments, *see* Ian C. Ballon and Robert R. Begland, "Ninth Circuit *Grokster* Case Challenges the Applicability of Traditional Copyright Principles to Digital Media and the Internet," *Intellectual Property Today*, 11(2): 32–36, February 2004. Ballon and Begland are attorneys who represent various trade associations and unions whose members own copyrights. The article is an adaptation of their amicus brief filed in the appeal of the *Grokster* case. Though, as expected, it makes primarily legal arguments, it nevertheless closes with a plea to policy considerations: "Unless reversed, the district court's radical reformulation of the standards for third party copyright liability will serve to embolden and empower potential infringers and dramatically increase the costs of infringement to copyright owners and to the American economy."

26. *Universal City Studios v. Remierdes*, 111 F.Supp.2d 294 (S.D.N.Y. 2000).

27. *Universal City Studios v. Corley*, 273 F.3d 429 (2nd Cir. 2001).

28. *Lexmark International v. Static Control Components*, No. 02-571-K5F (E.D. Ky. Dec. 30, 2002).

29. *Chamberlain Group v. Skylink Technologies*, Civ. No. 02-C-6376 (N.D. Ill. filed Sept. 6, 2002).

30. *Lexmark Int'l, Inc. v. Static Control Components*, 253 F.Supp.2d 943 (E.D. Ky. 2003).

31. Chamberlain Group, Inc. v. Skylink Techs., Inc., 292 F.Supp.2d 1040 (N.D. Ill., 2003).

32. The appeals court decided both cases while this book was going to press. See the Epilogue for the stunning outcomes.

Chapter 8

1. Siva Vaidhyanathan, *Copyrights and Copywrongs*, NYU Press, 2001.

2. We already have unique rules applying to the protection of semiconductors and pharmaceuticals. The current debate centers on how many modified protective regimes we might need, what the best ways to effect those modifications might be, and whether or not existing laws are already flexible enough to accommodate industry-specific nuances without major legislative action. For one good discussion set in the context of patent law and policy, *see* Dan L. Burk and Mark A. Lemley, "Policy Levers in Patent Law," *Virginia Law Review*, 89: 1575–1696, (2003). By and large, Burk and Lemley contend that existing patent laws are flexible enough to accommodate different needs in different industries, and that widespread *sui generis* regimes are unnecessary.

3. I presented my first detailed attempt at such an analysis in "Promoting Innovation in the Software Industry: A First Principles Approach to Intellectual Prop-

erty Reform," *Boston University Journal of Science and Technology Law*, 8: 75–156, (2002).

4. MS-appeal, *citing* Appellant's Opening Brief at 105 and *In re Indep. Serv. Orgs. Antitrust Litig.*, 203 F.3d 1322,1325 (Fed. Cir. 2000).

5. *See* Douglas R. Hofstadter, *Gödel, Escher, Bach: An Eternal Golden Braid* (Basic Books, 1979) for an in-depth discussion of the relationship between this classic example of Zen philosophy and scientific inquiries at the cutting edge of many different fields.

6. Even many open-source advocates recognize this distinction—though often grudgingly. The case for open source is strongest in infrastructure settings; the more esoteric the application, the weaker the case for opening the source. *See* "The Magic Cauldron," in Raymond, *supra* n. 12.

7. Ms-facts at ¶ 64.

8. *Id.* at ¶ 116.

9. *Id.* at ¶ 133.

10. *Motion Picture Patents Co. v. Universal Film Manufacturing Co.*, 243 U.S. 502 (1917).

11. *United States v. Glaxo Group, Ltd.*, 410 U.S. 52, 53 (1973).

12. Then again, I might be wrong. Christian Nadan, an Associate General Counsel for Sun, recently published an article about open-source licenses that spent a great deal of time discussing copyright misuse. *See* Christian H. Nadan, "Open Source Licensing: Virus or Virtue?" *Texas Intellectual Property Law Journal* 10:349–378 (2002).

Chapter 9

1. "The Road to Hell is Unpaved," *The Economist*, December 19, 2002.

2. *Id.*

3. *See* Talking Heads, *Sand in the Vaseline (Popular Favorites, 1976–1992)*, 1992.

4. *See e.g.*, John Borland, "E-Music: Where's the 'Celestial Jukebox'?" *ZDNET*, January 9, 1991. Available at http://zdnet.com.com/2100-11-527065.html, viewed October 25, 2004.

5. For example, AOL/Time Warner, Newscorp/DirectTV, and Comcast's February 2004 bid for Disney (eventually dropped).

6. DRM, media consolidation, ASP models, content/conduit marriages, and the convergence of computing, entertainment, and communications are all detailed and intriguing topics that could lend themselves to entire chapters. They are all likely to play important roles in the coming stage of the information sector's development. For present purposes, though, their primary significance is that they help demonstrate the drift of both software and entertainment from industries based on product development and sales to industries based on service and

delivery. As we have seen elsewhere, these trends are likely not only to continue, but to accelerate.

7. In standard economic terms, such a transition is known as a move towards Pareto optimality.

8. See "Cap It All," The Economist, June 26, 2003. Ongoing negotiations to free global agriculture return to the headlines every few weeks, sometimes to announce encouraging progress and sometimes to announce dashed hopes. By the time you read this book, the WTO's members may have agreed upon a meaningful plan that actually turns agricultural markets into free markets. If that occurs, count me among the surprised. The pleasantly surprised, but the surprised nonetheless. More likely scenarios include both no agreement at all and a variety of half-measures that delay or deter real reform while enabling the world's diplomats to claim victory at conquering one of the world's most challenging points of international economic contention.

9. Friedrich Hayek warned us of this trap almost sixty years ago, but we keep falling into it anyway. See Friedrich A. Hayek, The Road to Serfdom, fiftieth anniversary ed., University of Chicago Press, 1994, p. 136 (first published 1944).

10. See e.g., "The New Jobs Migration," The Economist, February 21, 2004, p. 11. In this article, The Economist did more than simply notice the new mobility of the service sector; it made it the cover story.

11. I presented a brief taxonomy of industries likely to undergo significant changes during their transition to the information economy in "From Investor Fantasy to Regulatory Nightmare: Bad Network Economics and the Internet's Inevitable Monopolists," Harvard Journal of Law and Technology, 16(1): 159–228, (Fall 2002).

12. The Economic Payoff from the Internet Revolution, Robert E. Litan and Alice M. Rivlin, eds., Brookings Institution Press, 2001, at 1–2. See also Robert E. Litan and Alice M. Rivlin, Beyond the Dot.coms, Brookings Institution Press, 2001; BRIE-IGCC E-conomy Project Task Force on the Internet. Tracking a Transformation: E-Commerce and the Terms of Competition in Industries, Brookings Institution Press, 2001.

13. Litan and Rivlin, eds., supra n. 12 at 19.

14. Id. at 26.

15. Exceptions to this general rule are rare. In 1997, the FTC blocked Staples's attempt to acquire Office Depot. Staples and Office Depot insisted that they were but two of many competitors who sold office supplies. The FTC insisted that they were two of only three competitors who sold office supplies in superstores, and that their merger would lead to a monopoly in many cities. The judge eventually accepted the government's claim that prices in office supply superstores aren't constrained by local stationers or catalog sales—but only because the government presented hard empirical data to back up its strangely counterintuitive claim. See FTC v. Staples, 970 F.Supp. at 1066 (D.D.C, 1997). The FTC identified a potential Internet-only market as late as 2001, when Monster.com tried

to acquire HotJobs, and CareerBuilder tried to acquire Headhunter.net. These firms, all big players in the online employment-ad business, believed that they competed with everyone else who sold classified ads. The preponderance of New World documents still circulating drove the FTC to wonder whether the market might really be limited to a small number of high-profile Internet firms. The FTC never reached a conclusion because it had spent so much time deliberating that Yahoo! made HotJobs a better offer. Monster decided to drop the fight. *See,* Bruce Abramson, "From Investor Fantasy to Regulatory Nightmare: Bad Network Economics and the Internet's Inevitable Monopolists," *Harvard Journal of Law and Technology*, 16(1): 159–228, Fall 2002.

16. *See* Carl Shapiro and Hal R. Varian, *Information Rules*, Harvard Business School Press, 1999, at ch. 3 for a detailed discussion of versioning and the ways that network owners can use it to increase their profits. The basic strategy is for vendors to develop multiple versions of their product, to charge top dollar for the truly powerful version, and to make a weaker version available either free of charge or at a very low price. Internet versioning has appeared most prominently on financial sites offering free stock quotes delayed by twenty minutes throughout the trading day, but charging for up-to-the-minute quotes.

17. Adwords, the basis of Google's primary business model as it headed into its planned 2004 IPO, places ads relevant to a user's search terms near the results of the search. Adwords reportedly was generating more that $250,000 in monthly revenues within two years of its introduction. One customer estimated that his company received $1.70 in business for every $1 spent on Adwords. *See* Fred Vogelsten, "Can Google Grow Up?" *Fortune*, December 8, 2003, 102–112.

18. The development of appropriate metrics for setting rates for advertising on the Internet remains an open question. *See* Maryann Jones Thompson, "The Measure of Web Success," *The Industry Standard*, Feb. 22, 1999, available at http://www.thestandard.com/article/display/0,1151,3501,00.html, viewed January 25, 2002.

19. *See e.g.*, "Face Value: A Monster Success," *The Economist*, March 27, 2004.

20. Though the travel and tourist lobbies are rarely considered behemoths among U.S. interest groups, tourist industries and even tourist *ministries* carry a great deal of political clout in other parts of the world.

21. Not all ticket purchases are straightforward. The general extension from simple *travel* tickets to complicated *tourism* "tickets" suggests an area in which the infomediary model may prove lucrative. For example, e-cruise—an apparent casualty of the dot-com bust—was conceived as an essentially infomediary model serving the cruise industry and its potential customers. *See* http://www.e-cruise.com, viewed August 20, 2003. More recently, the New Channel Maxbanx attempted to coordinate vacation rentals on the Outer Banks of North Carolina. *See* http://www.maxbanx.com, viewed August 20, 2003. Both represent tourism niches in which dispersed incomplete data can frustrate consumers seeking reliable information about the availability and the variety of suitable offerings.

22. *See* http://www.britannica.com.

23. E-books also posed a different quandary to publishers. Authors typically sell certain rights to publishers in order to have their work published. Prior to the electronic age, most publishers contracted to obtain the rights to publish "in book form." With the advent of both the Internet and handheld devices in the late 1990s, several prominent authors sold their e-book rights to new e-book publishers. Traditional publishers contended that e-books were books, and that they (not the authors) owned these rights. The court disagreed. *See Random House, Inc. v. Rosetta Books*, 150 F.Supp.2d 613 (S.D.N.Y. 2001).

24. The fragmentation of the porn industry illustrates the balkanization of readership that Cass Sunstein decried in *Republic.com*, Princeton University Press, 2002. The emergence of this profitable industry catering toward fetishists also highlights the danger of government regulation of Internet content. In 1996, Congress passed the Communications Decency Act (CDA), allegedly to protect children from online pornography. A nearly unanimous Supreme Court recognized that the CDA was simply censorship by a fancier name, and threw out most of its provisions. *See Reno v. ACLU*, 521 U.S. 844 (1997). The Court did, however, allow Congress to require adult sites to insist that all visitors prove that they are adults—say, by presenting a valid credit-card number. As a result, porn sites are now among the only places on the Web in which you have to check your credit card at the door. This practice enables impulse buying—a benefit of particular value to vendors of downloadable pictures. The net result of this attempted government censorship was thus to enhance the business prospects of online pornographers.

25. *See New York Times Co., Inc., v. Tasini*, 533 U.S. 483 (2001).

26. The Robinson-Patman Act, a populist holdover typically mischaracterized as an antitrust law, prohibits price discrimination in the sale of goods—subject to a very lengthy set of exceptions.

27. Paul Krugman, "What Price Fairness?" *New York Times*, October 4, 2000, for example, was far from complimentary about Amazon's experiment with "dynamic pricing," despite acknowledging that the practice was both economically sound and likely to become widespread as the technology for gauging a consumer's willingness to pay improved.

28. The shift in economic policies between the Clinton and Bush administrations is a case in point. President Bush entered office as a marvelous boom period was sliding into recession. By early 2001, few doubted that the United States needed a stimulative tax cut. The debates centered on which taxes we should cut, and by how much. Similarly, few doubted that the American economy remained structurally sound, and that it would eventually recover. Analyses that tie the Bush tax cuts of 2001 and 2003 to the *fact* of the subsequent recovery therefore miss the point. The question worth exploring is the relationship between the specifics of the Bush tax packages and the timing and character of the subsequent recovery. A broader exploration might consider the relationship among the selection of supply-side cuts over true tax reform (i.e., reducing distortions,

complexity, and rates), the various regulatory postures favoring sizable incumbents over small entrants, the weakening of the dollar, the resurgence of protectionism, and the long period of sluggish job growth—all consistent with favoring incumbent lock-in over entrepreneurial growth.

29. Hayek, *supra* n. 9, p. 49 (emphasis added).

30. *Id.*, pp. 56–58 (emphasis added).

31. Milton Friedman and Rose Friedman, *Free to Choose*, Harvest Books, 1990, p. 226.

32. With the possible exceptions of the military, sports, and parts of the entertainment industry.

Epilogue

1. In a classic Dutch auction, a seller offers a fixed number (say X) of identical items for sale, and agrees to accept bids throughout a fixed period. At the end of the allowed time, the seller sets the price for all of the items at the highest level at which all items will sell (i.e., the Xth highest bid), and assigns the items to all bidders who exceeded or met that price. Dutch auction IPOs are a bit more complicated, but follow this basic outline.

2. "Giving $75 Billion Back, with Plenty to Spare," *The Economist*, July 23, 2004.

3. Jo Best, "Munich to Stick with Open Source," C|NET.com, June 17, 2004, available at http://news.com.com/Munich+to+stick+with+open+source/2100-7344_3-5237356.html, viewed July 27, 2004.

4. *See* http://odfi.org/archives/2003_05.html#4, viewed July 27, 2004.

5. *See* Roger Parloff, "Gunning for Linux," *Fortune*, May 5, 2004.

6. *See* "An Open-Source Shot in the Arm?" *The Economist*, June 10, 2004.

7. Lawrence Lessig described some of the early battles in *Free Culture*, Penguin Press, 2004.

8. *MGM Studios, Inc. v. Grokster Ltd.*, 380 F.3d 1154 (9th Cir. 2004).

9. *Chamberlain Group, Inc. v. Skylink Techs., Inc.*, 381 F.3d 1178 (Fed. Cir. 2004). By way of full and fair disclosure, I was a law clerk to the Hon. Arthur Gajarsa of the United States Court of Appeals for the Federal Circuit when that court heard and decided this matter.

10. *Lexmark Int'l, Inc. v. Static Control Components, Inc.*, 387 F.3d 522 (6th Cir. 2004).

11. Discussions of the DMCA abound. The works of Lessig and Litman cited throughout this book are excellent examples of this genre. A simple Google search, however, will reveal numerous scholarly articles and even more numerous blog entries on the topic.

12. *See* http://thomas.loc.gov/cgi-bin/query, viewed July 28, 2004.

13. *See e.g.*, Ted Bridis, "Lawmakers Approve Bill to Let Parents Strip Smut from Movies," *washingtonpost.com*, July 21, 2004, available at http://www .washingtonpost.com/wp-dyn/articles/A2877-2004Jul21.html, viewed July 28, 2004.

14. *See* Hannah Arendt, *The Origins of Totalitarianism*, Harcourt, Inc., 1951.

15. Shimon Peres, *The New Middle East*, Henry Holt, 1993, p. 62.

16. Israel's Supreme Court, sitting squarely at the front lines of this war yet retaining its ability to speak deliberatively, best articulated the key to our success:

"This authority [to maintain security] must be properly balanced against the rights, needs, and interests of the local population. The law of war usually creates a delicate balance between two poles: military necessity on one hand and humanitarian considerations on the other." H.C. 2056/04, *Beit Sourik Village Council v. The Government of Israel* (2004).

17. John Stuart Mill, *On Liberty*, Penguin Books, 1974, pp. 119–121 (first published 1859).

Index